Teaching Legal Research

Legal research is a fundamental skill for all law students and attorneys. Regardless of practice area or work venue, knowledge of the sources and processes of legal research underpins the legal professional's work. Academic law librarians, as research experts, are uniquely qualified to teach legal research. Whether participating in the mandatory, first-year law school curriculum or offering advanced or specialized legal research instruction, law librarians have the up-to-date knowledge, the broad view of the field, and the expertise to provide the best legal research instruction possible.

This collection offers both theoretical and practical guidance on legal research education from the perspectives of the law librarian. Containing well-reasoned, analytical articles on the topic, the volume explains and supports the law librarian's role in legal research instruction. The contributors to this book, all experts in teaching legal research, challenge academic law librarians to seize their instructional role in the legal academy.

This book is based on a special issue of *Legal Reference Services Quarterly.*

Barbara Bintliff, Nicholas Rosenbaum Professor of Law at the University of Colorado Boulder and former president of the American Association of Law Libraries, has been a leader in legal education for several decades and has written extensively and consulted on law school curricula and pedagogy.

Duncan Alford, Associate Dean and Director of the Law Library at the University of South Carolina School of Law, has held various positions in law libraries along the East Coast, has taught legal research in several law schools, and has published articles on law librarianship and international banking law.

Teaching Legal Research

Edited by Barbara Bintliff and Duncan Alford

Routledge
Taylor & Francis Group
LONDON AND NEW YORK

First published 2011
by Routledge
2 Park Square, Milton Park, Abingdon, Oxon, OX14 4RN

Simultaneously published in the USA and Canada
by Routledge
711 Third Avenue, New York, NY 10017

Routledge is an imprint of the Taylor & Francis Group, an informa business

First issued in paperback 2011

This book is a reproduction of *Legal Reference Services Quarterly*, vol. 28, issue 1-4. The Publisher requests to those authors who may be citing this book to state, also, the bibliographical details of the special issue on which the book was based.

Typeset in Garamond by Value Chain, India

British Library Cataloguing in Publication Data
A catalogue record for this book is available from the British Library

ISBN13: 978-0-415-58087-8 (hbk)
ISBN13: 978-0-415-50897-1 (pbk)

Contents

ABSTRACTS

Commentaries on Hicks' 'Teaching Legal Bibliography': With an Addendum by Robert Berring
MICHAEL CHIORAZZI and SHAUN ESPOSITO

In an attempt to write a history of legal research in law schools, Chiorazzi and Esposito found that very little has been written to chronicle the history of this important function of academic law libraries; but they did rediscover a gem written by Frederick Hicks, the godfather of law librarians, almost 100 years ago. Much of that which he speaks is still relevant. The authors decided that there was no better way to begin a discussion of the history of legal research instruction than the text of Hicks' article. The authors have reprinted the entire Hicks article and have added their own comments throughout. And, of course, they knew no discussion of Hicks would be complete without the comments of Bob Berring on one of his personal hero's work. No law librarian has followed more closely in the intellectual footprints of Hicks than Professor Berring.

Thinking Like a Research Expert: Schemata for Teaching Complex Problem-Solving Skills
PAUL D. CALLISTER

The difference between expert and novice problem solvers is that experts have organized their thinking into schemata or mental constructs to both see and solve problems. This article demonstrates why schemata are important, arguing that they need to be made explicit in the classroom. It illustrates the use of schemata to understand and categorize complex research problems, map the terrain of legal research resources, match appropriate resources to types of problems, and work through the legal research process. The article concludes by calling upon librarians and research instructors to produce additional schemata and develop a common hierarchical taxonomy of skills, a "Bloom's Taxonomy," which would define legal research problem-solving skills more precisely and set benchmarks for assessment.

Teaching Advanced Legal Research: Philosophy and Context
ROBERT C. BERRING and KATHLEEN VANDEN HEUVEL

Is there a philosophy that grounds the teaching of advanced legal research (ALR)? Can a coherent identity be found? The authors draw upon the experience of twenty-five years of teaching ALR to large numbers of students to puzzle this question out. Are we teaching a mechanical skill? Are we offering a course in jurisprudence? Are we simply forcing the students to teach themselves? Has the information revolution changed the whole enterprise? Basing the discussion on the context of legal information, the students, and the law, the authors try to find an answer to these fundamental questions.

A Motivational Perspective on First-Year Legal Research Instruction
KRIS GILLILAND

This article examines some recent pedagogical concepts and trends, such as signature pedagogy and student-centered learning, and their application to legal research instruction. Law librarians and other legal research instructors have long utilized a core instructional model known as the bibliographic method. But, given a rapidly changing information environment and today's born digital students, we must question whether its traditional teacher-centered approach can still motivate students and provide them with the authentic experience necessary for effective learning.

Best Practices: What First-Year Law Students Should Learn in a Legal Research Class
NANCY P. JOHNSON

Legal research instructors seldom have adequate class time to teach students the print and online sources needed to complete a research task successfully. However, there are core principles that first-year students should learn in a legal research class. The author discusses best practices in teaching the legal research process, along with the important research sources, including judicial opinions and reporters, digests and finding cases, statutes, administrative publications, citators for updating research, and secondary sources.

On Teaching Advanced Legal Research
CHRISTOPHER A. KNOTT

This article addresses the issues faced by instructors of courses in advanced legal research. Everyone teaching in this area must have a strategy for organizing the subject matter, drafting problems and assignments, constructing a syllabus, and planning and delivering a course designed to meet its stated goals. Most importantly, the instructor must give serious thought to the desired outcomes at which he or she aims. In this article, Professor Knott has categorized outcome targets into three levels: competency, fluency, and mastery. The instructor's decisions about desired outcomes will have implications for all aspects of course design and delivery. The article identifies and discusses these issues and provides a framework instructors can use when designing their own courses. Attached as appendices are specific examples of many of the kinds of materials discussed in the article, all drawn from material prepared for use in the author's advanced legal research classes.

The Skills They Need: International and Foreign Legal Research
MARY RUMSEY

Law schools should offer classes in international and foreign legal research (IFLR) because the increasing globalization of law practice requires new skills of lawyers. Moreover, internationalized law school programs and curricula, including human rights clinics, exchange programs, and transnational law courses, require complementary research skills. Currently, few schools offer a standalone IFLR class. This article describes an ideal IFLR class, which would cover public and private international law, foreign law, and selected topics, and provide students with basic IFLR skills. The author notes that librarians are best suited to teach such a class because of their extensive knowledge of IFLR resources and usage.

State-Specific Legal Research Instruction: Curricular Stepchild or Core Competency?
VICTORIA K. TROTTA and BETH DiFELICE

The authors argue that proficiency in state-specific legal research is a competency all law students should attain in law school, for the primary reason that many (if not most) students begin practice in the state where they attend law school, a reality of even those who attend so-called national law schools. Ten state-specific legal research courses currently offered are discussed by the authors, who also present a model syllabus for a one, two, and three unit state-specific legal research course.

Tubs, Buckets, and a Variety of Lumber: Developing a Strategic Approach to Legal Research
ALLEN MOYE

Today's instructors of legal research face a number of challenges. With an increasing variety of formats and access points for obtaining information, the landscape of legal research material is fluid and evolving. Teaching students the value of some of the more traditional methods of research in a technology-saturated world focused on instant gratification requires some creativity and innovation. Using simple references and metaphors from everyday life, the author focuses on creative ways of helping students to develop a practical strategy for approaching any legal research problem.

Legal Research Assessment
SIMON CANICK

Legal research instructors seek to provide their students with a working knowledge of important research tools, strategies with which to develop a rational research plan, and the skill to conduct research efficiently, among other things. A well-conceived legal research class may utilize short-answer assignments, quizzes, and scavenger hunt exercises as a means to establish a baseline of knowledge with critical sources; a series of research problems, with grading based upon students' ability to describe a coherent and logical progression; and a pathfinder or process-oriented final exam, all depending on the instructor's goals. Ultimately, the variety of available assessment tools suggests room for creativity and the existence of many appropriate alternatives. As long as instructors use a multifaceted approach, selecting assessment tools to suit course objectives, students will be engaged in the process and will become stronger, more confident legal researchers.

"Like Sands Through the Hourglass. . .": How to Develop a Good Legal Research Problem
SUSAN T. PHILLIPS

Attorneys have a duty to conduct adequate legal research. Law schools have an obligation to educate students in the standard research techniques. To learn research, students must actually perform research using research problems. Therefore, professors must design appropriate problems for students to learn research skills. The first part of this article discusses the fundamentals of developing a research problem. The second part provides examples of research problems with an explanation of their development.

Teaching Legal Research Online
SUSAN HERRICK and SARA KELLEY BURRIESCI

Online instruction has great potential for accommodating the learning styles and preferences of Millennial law students, as well as for the effective teaching of legal research in the digital age. While integrating instructional technology into a face-to-face classroom legal research course is highly desirable and relatively easy, designing and teaching a purely distance or hybrid distance course provides some unique challenges as well as some distinct benefits for both instructors and students. This article will first evaluate individual instructional technologies independently of each other, since any of them could be used to supplement traditional face-to-face research instruction, whether formal or informal. Consideration will then be given to special problems of teaching a graded legal research course entirely or predominantly online. Legal research instruction presents some opportunities for experimentation and innovation with online learning techniques that may serve students better, accommodate the librarian's technology skills and abilities and her time constraints, and inspire others at our law schools to follow suit.

Who Gets to Be the Expert?: Legal Research Skills Certification in Legal Education
RICHARD LEITER

This article considers the question of whether there is a need for law schools to offer certification for specialization in legal research skills and discusses various approaches to legal research skills certification. The author argues that it is unnecessary to offer legal research certification as it is presupposed that a basic legal education should include instruction in how to find and read the law. Anything less is a failed legal education.

Testing for Research Competency on the Bar Exam: The Next Steps
STEVEN M. BARKAN, SUSAN M. CASE, MICHAEL KANE and ERICA MOESER

All new lawyers should be competent in the fundamental skills of legal research, which suggests that legal research competency should be covered on the bar exam. The authors discuss the essential attributes of a bar exam and the methods that might be used to test for legal research competency.

They recommend a multiple-choice testing method, but argue that before legal research competency can be tested on the bar exam, determinations need to be made about the definition of competency and the subject matter to be tested.

Great Expectations: New Associates' Research Skills from Law School to Law Firm
JILL L. K. BROOKS

This article is a perspective on what research skills new associates in legal practice need. Knowledge of print and electronic resources and cost-effective search strategies are the main focus of the article. A checklist of research skills is included along with recommendations on what law schools and law firm librarians can do to assist law students and new attorneys in learning these skills.

The Development of the Skills Curriculum in Law Schools: Lessons for Directors of Academic Law Libraries
DUNCAN ALFORD

Recent challenges to the status and tenure of law library directors has questioned their role law as teachers and scholars. This article analyzes the development of the legal research, clinical, and legal writing curriculum in U.S. law schools and identifies strategies that law librarians could choose to employ to bolster their status as the preeminent teachers of legal research in the academy.

Notes on Contributors

Duncan Alford is Associate Dean and Director of the Library and Associate Professor of Law at the University of South Carolina School of Law. Professor Alford received his J.D. from the School of Law of the University of North Carolina at Chapel Hill, a B.A. from the University of Virginia, and a M.L.I.S. from the University of South Carolina College of Library and Information Science. Prior to joining the faculty at USC, Professor Alford served on the inaugural faculty of the Charlotte School of Law, at Georgetown University Law Library, Princeton University, and at the Columbia University Law Library, and was an attorney in private practice for 10 years.

Steven M. Barkan is Professor of Law and Director of Library and Information Services at the University of Wisconsin Law School in Madison, Wisconsin. Barkan earned his undergraduate degree from the University of Wisconsin-Madison, his M.L.S. from the University of Michigan, and his J.D. degree from Cleveland State University.

Robert C. Berring is the Walter Perry Johnson Professor of Law at University of California, Berkeley Law School, Boalt Hall. He was Dean of the School of Library and Information Studies at Berkeley and served as Interim Dean of the University of California, Berkeley Law School. He is a Past-President of the American Association of Law Libraries. He worked in the law libraries of the University of Illinois, the University of Texas, and the University of Washington. His undergraduate degree is from Harvard and his J.D. and M.L.S. were earned at the University of California, Berkeley.

Barbara Bintliff is the Nicholas Rosenbaum Professor of Law and Director of the William A. Wise Law Library, University of Colorado at Boulder. She previously worked at the University of Denver Westminster Law Library, and in the private sector. In 2001-2002, she served as President of the American Association of Law Libraries. Professor Bintliff holds an undergraduate degree from Central Washington University, and J.D. and M.L.L. degrees from the University of Washington.

Jill L. K. Brooks is the Director of Library Services at Robinson, Bradshaw & Hinson, P.A. in Charlotte, NC. Her undergraduate degree is from Appalachian State University and her M.L.I.S. is from the University of North Carolina at Greensboro.

Sara Kelley Burriesci is an Electronic Resources and Services Librarian at Georgetown University Law Library, Washington, D.C. Her undergraduate degree is from the College of William and Mary, her M.L.S. is from the University of Washington, and her J.D. was earned at the University of South Carolina. She previously worked at the Microsoft Corporation and the University of Maryland Law Library.

Paul D. Callister is Director of the Leon E. Bloch Law Library and an Associate Professor of Law at the University of Missouri-Kansas City School of Law. Professor Callister received his B.A. from Brigham Young University, his J.D. from Cornell Law School, and his M.S. in Library and Information Science from the University of Illinois at Urbana-Champaign. He practiced law in Southern California for nine years.

Simon Canick is the Associate Dean of Information Resources and Associate Professor of Law at the William Mitchell College of Law in St. Paul, Minnesota. Professor Canick received a B.A. from Hamilton College, a J.D. from Boston University School of Law and an M.L.I.S. from the University of Washington School of Library and Information Science. Prior to joining the faculty at William Mitchell, he worked at the University of Connecticut School of Law and the Columbia University Law School.

Susan M. Case is the Director of Testing at the National Conference of Bar Examiners. Her B.A. is from the University of Connecticut, her M.S. is from West Chester University of Pennsylvania, and her Ph.D., in measurement and evaluation, was earned at the University of Pennsylvania. She spent 25 years on the staff of the National Board of Medical Examiners before coming to NCBE.

Michael Chiorazzi is the Associate Dean for Information Services at the James E. Rogers College of Law, Cracchiolo Law Library, University of Arizona. Professor Chiorazzi received his B.A. from the University of Miami, his J.D. from Gonzaga University School of Law, and his M.L.L. from the University of Washington. He previously held positions at the Duke University and Boston College law libraries. Professor Chiorazzi also has a joint appointment in The School of Information Resource and Library Science at the University of Arizona.

Beth DiFelice is the Assistant Director and Head of Public Services at the Ross-Blakley Law Library, Sandra Day O'Connor College of Law at Arizona State University. She previously worked at the University of Nebraska. She has J.D. and M.L.L. degrees from the University of Washington, and an undergraduate degree from Centenary College of Louisiana.

Shaun Esposito is the Head of Public Services and Adjunct Assistant Professor of Legal Research at James E. Rogers College of Law, Cracchiolo Law Library, University of Arizona. Prior to becoming a law librarian, he worked at the Florida State University College of Law, as an attorney in public defender and legal services offices, and as the law clerk for a Kentucky Supreme Court justice. He has a J.D. from the University of Louisville's Brandeis School of Law and a M.S.L.S. from the Florida State University.

Kris Gilliland is Associate Professor of Law and Director of the Library at the University of Mississippi School of Law. Her undergraduate degree is from Vanderbilt University, her J.D. is from the University of Alabama, and she earned a M.L.Lib. at the University of Washington. Prior to her arrival at the University of Mississippi in 2000, she served at the Georgetown University Law Center, and at the Columbia University Law Library.

Susan Herrick is a Research Librarian at the University of Maryland School of Law. She received a B.A. from the College of Wooster, a M.S.L.S. from Case Western Reserve University, and a J.D. from the University of Maryland.

Nancy P. Johnson is the Law Librarian/Professor of Law at the Georgia State University College of Law Library. She formerly held positions at the University of Illinois and the University of Chicago. She received a B.A. in History from Marycrest College, a M.L.S. from the University of Illinois, and a J.D. from Georgia State University.

Michael Kane is the Director of Research at the National Conference of Bar Examiners. Previously, he served as a professor in the School of Education at the University of Wisconsin, and worked at ACT (American College Testing) and at the National League for Nursing. He earned a Ph.D. from Stanford University.

Christopher A. Knott is the Associate Dean for Academic Affairs, Associate Professor of Law and Director of the Donald L. Garbrecht Law Library at the University of Maine School of Law. Before coming to Maine, he worked in the law libraries of the Georgetown University Law Center, and the Columbia Law School. Knott earned a B.A. at the University of Iowa, a J.D. at the University of Michigan, and a M.L.I.S. at Indiana University.

Richard Leiter is Professor of Law and Director at the University of Nebraska College of Law, Schmid Law Library. Prior to that he worked at Howard University School of Law, Regent University School of Law and the University of Texas School of Law, and in the private sector. Leiter earned a B.A. from the University of California, Santa Cruz, a J.D. from Southwestern University, and a M.L.I.S. from the University of Texas at Austin.

Erica Moeser is the President of the National Conference of Bar Examiners. She received a B.A. and M.S. from Tulane University and a J.D. from the University of Wisconsin. Ms. Moeser served as the Chair of the American Bar Association's Section of Legal Education and Admissions to the Bar.

Allen Moye is Director of the Library and Associate Professor of Law at DePaul University's College of Law, Chicago, Illinois. Moye received a B.A. from Howard University, a J.D. from the University of Richmond, and a M.L.S. from the Catholic University of America.

Susan T. Phillips is Professor of Law at Texas Wesleyan University School of Law, where she previously served as Associate Dean and Director of the Law Library. She was educated at the University of Dallas, earning a B.A. degree, and the Catholic University of America where she earned J.D. and M.S.L.S. degrees. Phillips previously served at Pepperdine University School of Law Library.

Mary Rumsey is the Foreign, Comparative & International Law Librarian at the University of Minnesota Law Library. She earned a B.A. from the University of Wisconsin, a J.D. from the University of Chicago, and a M.L.I.S. from Dominican University. She previously worked at William Mitchell College of Law, and practiced law.

Victoria K. Trotta is the Associate Dean for Information Technology and the Ross-Blakley Law Library, Sandra Day O'Connor College of Law, Arizona State University. She holds a B.A. from Occidental College, a M.L.S. from the University of California, Los Angeles, and a J.D. from the University of Southern California. She previously worked at the University of Southern California Law Library.

Kathleen Vanden Heuvel is Associate Dean and Lecturer at the University of California, Berkeley Law School, Boalt Hall, where she also serves as Director of the Law Library. She earned a B.A., J.D., and M.L.I.S. from the University of California, Berkeley.

Introduction

Legal Research: MacCrate's "Fundamental Lawyering Skill" Missing in Action

BARBARA BINTLIFF

Nicholas Rosenbaum Professor of Law, and Director, William A. Wise Law Library, University of Colorado at Boulder, Boulder, Colorado, USA

> "It can hardly be doubted that the ability to do legal research is one of the skills that any competent legal practitioner must possess."[1]

The American Bar Association's 1992 MacCrate Report[2] was the catalyst for major changes in American legal education. With its identification of "fundamental lawyering skills," MacCrate provided detailed guidance and structure for law schools to assess and as needed, enhance their curriculum to prepare students for the practice of law.

Some of the biggest changes brought about by the MacCrate Report were in legal writing instruction and clinical offerings, the programs through which most fundamental lawyering skills are taught. The MacCrate Report helped catalyze then-existing trends to professionalize legal writing instruction and increase clinical offerings (both live-client and simulated). In addition, mock trial and moot court competitions increased, providing additional outlets for the application of client skills and multiple writing opportunities; as often as not, clinical or writing faculty supervised these competitions. Law schools reallocated resources and invested significant funds in improving their offerings in these areas. For the most part, these programs taught the fundamental lawyering skills identified in the MacCrate Report; legal education and law graduates are the better for it.

However, little attention has been paid to one fundamental lawyering skill—legal research. The large majority of U.S. law schools have assigned research instruction responsibilities to their legal writing faculty.[3] Unfortunately, this model all but guarantees that research instruction will be underemphasized. Teaching writing and teaching research require different knowledge bases and approaches, not unlike other seemingly similar fields, such as securities law and corporate taxation or labor law and employment discrimination. Writing faculty are, by and large, writing and communications experts and not research experts. Many legal writing programs acknowledge this by bringing law librarians, who *are* research experts, into the classroom for legal research instruction; a few schools even offer separate research classes, usually taught by librarians.[4] Frequently, the research instruction takes place while the writing faculty are grading papers with the consequence of further underemphasizing research because "real faculty" are not teaching it.

Who can blame the writing faculty for paying less attention to research? Legal writing is time and labor intensive. It requires significant acculturation of students into a new system of communication and instruction in multiple writing genres and styles. This is a tremendous challenge for both new law students and writing faculty, and few can claim credibly that too much time is spent on writing instruction currently. In addition, the demands of the doctrinal faculty to bring new law students' writing skills up to the level required by a professional school places intense pressure on the writing faculty. Legal writing faculty members respond to this pressure by emphasizing writing in their classes, and as a result, research instruction receives less attention.

An illustration of the lack of emphasis on legal research is found in the 2008 Annual Survey of the Association of Legal Writing Directors/Legal Writing Institute (ALWD/LWI), which shows that of 20 questions related to the curriculum, only two questions (numbers 18 and 19) elicit information on the research component of the legal writing class. One question asks who in the law school teaches the legal research component of the class, and the other, which asks for the content of assignments, includes options of several types of research assignments.[5] Requests for information about advanced legal research classes is buried in two or three questions that are part of the "Upper Level Writing Courses" section of the survey. This lack of survey coverage exists despite the fact that as noted above, so many law schools combine legal research instruction into their writing program curricula.[6]

The lack of focus on legal research instruction is ironic, given the timing of the MacCrate Report. The early 1990s saw an explosion in the sources and formats of legal information resources and featured the widespread availability of Westlaw and Lexis to law students and faculty at a relatively modest cost. By the mid-1990s, the Internet became commonly used as an information dissemination platform, especially after the development of the World Wide Web and after electronic commercial and not-for-profit sites made legal research resources available to almost anyone with a computer. Primary sources from all levels of government were increasingly accessible electronically, and more secondary sources that analyzed and explained the law were produced in print and online each year.[7] Furthermore, within the academy, tremendous emphasis was placed on interdisciplinary legal studies, requiring faculty and students to access the world of non-legal information.[8] Navigating the new information environment required knowledge of available sources; constant attention to changes in content, format, and currentness; and evaluation of credibility and authoritativeness. No longer was legal research a matter of finding a few cases and a relevant statute. And yet, just as legal research was becoming increasingly complicated, less and less attention was paid to research instruction by law schools.

There are many possible reasons for this neglect of legal research instruction. For example, law faculties have become more and more focused on "academic" pursuits to justify their place and their salaries among Ph.D. faculty in the academy. Theoretical and doctrinal classes are perceived as being more intellectual than "professional" or "skills" classes. Many law faculty members prefer the analytical to the applied (and would be practicing law if it was the other way around). Law teachers are, more and more, removed from their own practice experiences (if any)[9], which probably included significant research work. Further, law librarians, through responsive services tailored to faculty needs, have so successfully insulated law faculty from the realities of today's research environment that the faculty are not making their curricular decisions based on actual knowledge of how research has changed since their years in law school and how it is currently conducted in law firms. For at least the last fifteen years, academic law libraries have emphasized "faculty services," dedicating personnel to providing expert research services to faculty on demand and assisting and supervising faculty research assistants to enable them to do the same. Many law faculty members no longer know how to perform the research themselves and have lost sight of the importance of being able to research in both legal education and the daily practice of law. The end result is that law schools have decreased their emphasis on legal research instruction, neglecting this critical component of legal education.[10]

The MacCrate Report notes that legal research is "far more than a mechanical examination of texts; the formulation and implementation of a research design are analyzed as processes, which require a number of complex conceptual skills."[11] The literature in this compilation shows the truth of this statement. Individual articles in this collection discuss course content; pedagogy; and assessment methods and tools for a variety of legal research offerings. The intellectual structure of research tools is explored, and the impact of structure on research results and learning is analyzed. The primary role and extensive experience of law librarians in legal research instruction are highlighted.

The compilation begins with a commentary by Mike Chiorazzi and Shaun Esposito on Frederick Charles Hicks' classic article, *The Teaching of Legal Bibliography*. The authors set the stage for the following articles by placing the law librarian at the heart of legal research instruction. Today's dean of legal research instruction, Robert Berring, adds his thoughts in an addendum.

Three pieces discussing the theory and philosophy of legal research pedagogy follow. Paul Callister pushes our understanding of research pedagogy in *Thinking Like a Research Expert: Schemata for Teaching Complex Problem-Solving Skills*. As is his wont, Callister presents several schemata—mental constructs—that are useful in understanding and categorizing complex legal research problems, and he calls on legal research instructors to develop a common hierarchical taxonomy to define legal research problem-solving skills. Robert Berring and Kathleen Vanden Heuvel discuss the philosophy that grounds their teaching of advanced legal research. *Teaching Advanced Legal Research: Philosophy and Content* draws on their twenty-five years of experience in teaching advanced legal research to try to answer fundamental questions on the meaning of the course. *A Motivational Perspective on First-Year Legal Research Instruction* by Kris Gilliland examines recent pedagogical developments and trends, including the "signature pedagogy" discussed in the Carnegie Report[12] and questions whether the existing pedagogy of legal research instruction is adequate.

The next articles address pedagogical practices and offer guidance on developing a variety of legal research classes. Nancy Johnson, long recognized as a national expert in legal research instruction, offers *Best Practices: What First-Year Students Should Learn in a Legal Research Class*. She discusses the core principles that first-year law students must learn, offering guidance in how the major resources can be taught. *On Teaching Advanced Legal Research* by Christopher Knott identifies and discusses important components of teaching an advanced legal research class, including choosing the subject matter, constructing a syllabus, drafting problems and assignments, and delivering content to meet course goals. His categorization of levels of research abilities—competency, fluency, and mastery—provide a framework for designing an advanced research class. Mary Rumsey's *The Skills They Need: International and Foreign Legal Research* and Tory Trotta and Beth DiFelice's *State-Specific Legal Research Instruction: Curricular Stepchild or Core Competency?* is a forward-looking description of legal research courses that should be available at every law school. The article outlines a curriculum and coverage of their subjects. *Tubs, Buckets, and a Variety of Lumber: Developing a Strategic Approach to Legal Research* by Allen Moye focuses on creative ways to help students organize their research problems and develop effective strategies for addressing the problems.

These authors especially, address the argument that legal research must be taught in the context of a legal writing or doctrinal class. As these authors, all highly experienced legal research faculty, have demonstrated, legal research can be taught as effectively in a stand-alone course as in the context of a larger discussion. Good research instructors provide research context in their classes as illustrated by these articles.

Beginning with Moye's article described above, Part Two of the compilation covers assessment and instructional techniques next.[13] Assessment and instructional techniques are covered next. Simon Canick evaluates a variety of legal research assessment techniques, including short-answer questions, quizzes, scavenger hunts, extensive research problems, exams, and pathfinders, in *Legal Research Assessment*. He recommends instructors use a multifaceted approach to legal research assessment, selecting tools to fit course objectives. Susan Phillips, well known for her work in designing legal research exercises, offers expert advice in *'Like Sands through the Hourglass ... ': How to Develop a Good Legal Research Problem*. Her discussion of the choices faced in problem development will provide guidance to both experienced and novice research teachers. *Teaching Legal Research Online* by Sara Kelley Burriesci and Susan Herrick brings us into the world of online legal research instruction. They assess individual instructional technologies and consider special problems of teaching an online legal research course.

The compilation continues with coverage of legal research certification and bar exam testing. Richard Leiter, in *Who Gets to be the Expert? Legal Research Skills Certification in Legal Education*, considers whether there is need for a certificate program in legal research. His conclusion is that certification is unnecessary; legal research instruction is basic to legal education and should be a skill all students learn. A quartet of authors—Steven Barkan, Susan Case, Michael Kane, and Erica Moeser—suggest adding legal research competency to the multistate practice exam in *Testing for Research Competency on the Bar Exam: The Next Steps*. Case, Kane, and Moeser are all with the National Conference of Bar Examiners. They recommend defining research competencies and the subject matter to be tested as a preliminary step in developing a research test.

Great Expectations: New Associates' Research Skills from Law School to Law Firm by Jill Brooks looks at legal research skills from a law firm librarian's perspective. She provides a checklist of research skills that all new associates should know and recommends steps librarians should take to assist law students and new attorneys in learning the skills. Duncan Alford concludes the compilation with *The Development of the Skills Curriculum in Law Schools: Lessons for Directors of Academic Law Libraries*. He analyzes the development of the legal research, legal writing, and clinical curricula and the corresponding effect on those who teach the respective skills classes. His conclusions highlight some of the reasons legal research instruction has been underemphasized in legal education.

This compilation of articles delivers a challenge to the American Bar Association (ABA) and all law schools to re-examine their programs providing and evaluating legal research instruction. Instruction in every other "fundamental lawyering skill" identified in the MacCrate Report has been, in the main, implemented in a distinct program with specialized faculty. Legal research instruction, however, generally has been incorporated into the legal writing program—not taught by the librarians, the research experts in the law school. Legal research instruction remains the unimplemented fundamental lawyering skill. The consequences of this omission are well documented with research abilities of law clerks and new associates being noted as deficient or lacking in study after study.[14] Law librarians see this lack of research instruction daily; this first-of-a-kind compilation responds to the problem and offers advice on how to tackle it from a variety of avenues.

If the ABA Section on Legal Education and its Accreditation Committee thinks legal research is important—and there is every reason to believe they do given accreditation Standard 302(a)(1) that "[a] law school shall require that each student receive *substantial* instruction in ... legal research ... "[15] —then legal research should be given much more attention than it has received in accreditation decisions, including during site visits and in written materials submitted as part of the law school's accreditation process. The lack of enforcement of Standard 302(a)(1) perpetuates the inattention paid to this fundamental skill by law schools across the country and undermines the entire accreditation system's purpose to serve the public interest.[16] Legal research is indispensable to the competent practice of law. It is no longer a skill that can be taught as time, interest, and expertise allow, but rather it must be incorporated fully into the curriculum of every law school as a fundamental part of every student's legal education. To do less is to shortchange our students and to fail in our educational mission.

NOTES

1. ABA, Section of Legal Education and Admissions to the Bar, *Legal Education and Professional Development: An Educational Continuum: Report of the Task Force on Law Schools and the Profession: Narrowing the Gap, Statement of Fundamental Lawyering Skills and Professional Values* (1992) [hereinafter the MacCrate Report or MacCrate].

2. *Id.* at 163.

3. Of 181 schools reporting on the 2008 survey, 151 responded that legal research instruction was integrated with legal writing instruction. *ALWD/LWI, 2008 Survey Results*, responses to questions 10 and 18, available at http://www.alwd.org/surveys/survey_results/2008_Survey_Results.pdf.

4. See, as an example, Nancy Johnson, *Best Practices: What First-Year Law Students Should Learn in a Legal Research Class*, 28 Leg. Ref. Servs. Q. 78 (2009) (describing the legal research class taught at Georgia State University Law School).

5. *ALWD/LWI 2008 Survey Results 1*, available at http://www.alwd.org/surveys/survey_results/2008_Survey_Results.pdf.

6. The extent to which research instruction has been subsumed into legal writing is shown by this definition from ALWD/LWI 2008 Survey: "LRW means legal research and writing, sometimes simply referred to as legal writing." *Id.* (emphasis in original).

7. In 1988, 1,343 legal titles were published. *The Bowker Annual of Library and Book Trade Information Almanac* (Filomena Simora ed., 36th ed., R. R. Bowker 1991). By 2004, this number had grown to 3,316 print legal titles; 4,733 print legal titles were published in 2006. *Library and Book Trade Almanac: The Bowker Annual* (Dave Bogart ed., 53rd ed., Information Today, Inc. 1241 2008).

8. *See e.g.* Graham C. Lilly, *Law Schools without Lawyers? Winds of Change in Legal Education*, 81 Va. L. Rev. 1241 (1995); Harry T. Edwards, *The Growing Disjunction between Legal Education and the Legal Profession*, 91 Mich. L. Rev. 34 (1992).

9. *See e.g.* Bethany Rubin Henderson, *Asking the Lost Question: What is the Purpose of Law School?* 53 J. Leg. Educ. 48, 76 (2003).

10. At the risk of sounding like a complainer, I note that often there is a status hierarchy within law schools that can influence the perception of the importance of a subject, including which classes are approved (or not) by the voting faculty. The statuses, analogized to Hindu castes, are, in order,

"tenured and tenure track faculty, deans, clinical faculty, law library directors, legal writing directors and faculty, and adjunct faculty. The untouchables, who are barely mentioned when we talk about what our institutions teach students, are of course the professional staff of law schools." Kent Syverud, *The Caste System and Best Practices in Legal Education*, 1 J. ALWD 12, 13 (2002). Law librarians may be faculty but often are professional staff; this could well influence the perceived importance of legal research, librarians' subject expertise.

11. MacCrate, *supra* n. 1, at 163.

12. William M. Sullivan et al., *Educating Lawyers: Preparation for the Profession of Law* (John Wiley & Sons, Inc. 2007).

13. Part Two of this compilation will be published in the next issue of the *Legal Reference Services Quarterly*.

14. *See e.g.* Robin K. Mills, *Legal Research Instruction in Law Schools, The State of the Art or, Why Law School Students Do Not Know How to Find the Law*, 70 L. Lib. J. 343 (1977); Joan Howland & Nancy Lewis, *The Effectiveness of Law School Legal Research Training Programs*, 40 J. Legal Educ. 381 (1990); Thomson West, *Research Skills for Lawyers and Law Students*, White Paper (2007), available at http://west.thomson.com/pdf/librarian/Legal_Research_white_paper.pdf.

15. ABA, Section on Legal Education and Admissions to the Bar, *Standards for Approval of Law Schools,* available at http://www.abanet.org/legaled/standards/20082009StandardsWebContent/Chapter%203.pdf (emphasis added) [hereinafter *Standards for Approval of Law Schools*]. The Association of American Law Schools, a membership organization to which most ABA-accredited law schools belong, includes a similar requirement in its regulations: "... member schools shall offer instruction that provides students with an opportunity to develop the skills of legal research ..." Association of American Law Schools, *Executive Committee Regulations*, ECR 6–7.9(b), available at http://www.aals.org/about_handbook_regulations.php#6.

16. *Preamble, 2008–2009 Standards for Approval of Law School*, available at http://www.abanet.org/legaled/standards/20082009StandardsWebContent/Preamble.pdf.

Commentaries on Hicks' 'Teaching Legal Bibliography': With an Addendum by Robert Berring

MICHAEL CHIORAZZI and SHAUN ESPOSITO
Cracchiolo Law Library, James E. Rogers College of Law, Tucson, Arizona, USA

In an attempt to write a history of legal research in law schools, Chiorazzi and Esposito found that very little has been written to chronicle the history of this important function of academic law libraries; but they did rediscover a gem written by Frederick Hicks, the godfather of law librarians, almost 100 years ago. Much of that which he speaks is still relevant. The authors decided that there was no better way to begin a discussion of the history of legal research instruction than the text of Hicks' article. The authors have reprinted the entire Hicks article and have added their own comments throughout. And, of course, they knew no discussion of Hicks would be complete without the comments of Bob Berring on one of his personal hero's work. No law librarian has followed more closely in the intellectual footprints of Hicks than Professor Berring.

The teaching of legal research by law librarians in American law schools has almost become a given.[1] Over the last several years, the Association of Legal Writing Directors (ALWD) has surveyed law schools to see who teaches legal research. In its most recent (2007) survey of 149 responding programs, at 45 schools, the law librarians taught legal research, at 61 schools, it was jointly taught by law librarians and legal writing faculty, and at 79 law schools, legal research was taught by legal writing faculty. This does not, however, tell the full story. For instance, at how many of those schools is advanced legal research taught by librarians? Is it part of the required curriculum? How often do librarians go to subject-specific courses to teach a segment on legal research? Are voluntary, non-credit legal research classes taught, etc? It is not just a question of who teaches, but how, why, and when.

A glance at the ALWD surveys shows that while the numbers of each of the three groups has gone up and down slightly in the past eight years, it is a mixed landscape. The professional law librarianship literature is full of examples of those schools that do teach legal research and the need for librarians to be involved in the first year as well as in an upper-level offering of some sort. But not surprisingly, there is no real literature from those law librarians who believe we should not be teaching legal research in the first year or perhaps not at all.

The fact is we don't have a complete picture of the how, why, when, and by whom the teaching of legal research in American law schools takes place. Who is doing it? Who decides who teaches it? When should we be teaching it? How many schools believe they are doing an effective job of teaching it? How is legal research integrated into the curriculum? How would you change the teaching of legal research in your institution if you had the power to do so? How much oversight is there from the legal writing programs or curriculum committees? We all come to the table with preconceived notions on how, why, and by whom legal research has been taught. It is easy to believe that librarians have been teaching legal research for years and should continue to do so. But should it be the same as it ever was? Perhaps when it comes to legal research instruction we need to ask the Yirka question, "What are we doing now that we shouldn't be doing?"[2]

Much of what the profession does know is based on anecdote and our own personal histories. We talk to each other at meetings and conferences. We e-mail or phone colleagues at peer schools to see what they are doing. We operate more on zeitgeist, intuition, and our own senses of what is appropriate for our schools rather than strictly looking at what other law schools are doing.

And this is as it should be. Librarians have long adjusted their work to meeting the needs of their institutions. We receive our direction from our institutions' missions and strategic plans. Ideally, we look not just to meet needs but to anticipate them and to fill voids where they exist. As computer technology became more a part of our professional lives and the lives of our schools, we continued to embrace it and expand our services to meet the growing needs that this ongoing technological revolution continues to create and expand. If there is a secret to the success of our profession, it is just that: we sought to meet, anticipate, exceed, and perhaps even create needs. Are we teaching legal research because no one else wants to do it? Is it a skill beneath our faculty's scholarly perceptions of their educational roles in the institution? Or is it just because we are the most qualified?

This essay will not attempt to answer the questions posed above; instead we will rely on the articles in this issue to do that. We will narrowly focus on one approach to better understanding the teaching of legal research in law schools—its history—and perhaps put it in a framework to better understand why we are where we are today. To do this, we will use a somewhat unusual device: we will reprint, in full, an article by Fredrick Hicks, which was first published in 1918, and use it as a vehicle to discuss the history of teaching legal research in American law schools.[3]

Why focus on Hicks? Simply, he is the best known and most influential law librarian of his time and perhaps all time. He still has much to teach us. More than any other law librarian, Hicks moved law librarianship from a technical craft to a true profession. In his classic 1918 article, *The Teaching of Legal Bibliography*, Frederick Hicks sets out a brief history of the teaching of legal bibliography in American law schools.[4] After reading this article early in our research and reading it again as we sought to put pen to paper, we realized that this article serves as a perfect outline to our topic. The issues presented still exist in modern American law schools. Granted, the research picture has become much more complicated than Hicks could have ever imagined, but that is more a problem of scale—the core issues are fundamentally the same. If you are reading Hicks for the first time, you may be amazed. You might even agree with us that he articulates some universal truths of law librarianship. Hicks was more correct than he could have ever imagined! We will mention the evolution of the teaching of legal research in law schools since the time of Hicks, but we will focus on the period of 1970s to the present. Why the 1970s? We think the easy answer is that there are several contributing factors that resulted in a tipping point (or is it the perfect storm?) that led to academic law librarians being asked to teach legal research: the number of law schools and law students dramatically increased (fed in part by the Vietnam War and the Civil Rights, Environmental, and Women's Movements); skills training like clinics, moot courts, trial practice courses, and client counseling began to appear in the curriculum; more law graduates with library degrees made for a ready market of skilled librarians; and, perhaps most importantly for the subject before us, Lexis and Westlaw entered our world and forever changed it. While it is an oft-overused phrase, the 1970s presented us with a paradigm shift. There was simply much more to learn how to use—and law school faculties had no interest in teaching legal research during a time when a whole world of interesting legal topics—both new and developing—were availing themselves for study.

For the sake of clarity, we will use a different typeface when we comment on Hicks' work. Whether or not you find our commentary useful, we believe you will find Frederick Hicks' article fascinating.

In Dick Danner's seminal article, *Redefining the Profession*,[5] he quotes Sidney Pierce who questioned the "lack of the theoretical underpinnings in librarianship [comparing it] to sociology, a discipline in which graduate students take a basic course requiring them to read the classic works of the field. The course was often called 'Dead Germans,' and for Pierce, 'Dead Germans' is what sociology students have in common: 'A common body of theory shaping the intellectual traditions of the field.'"[6] Pierce thought that there was not a sufficient body of classic works in librarianship. Dick Danner's point is clear: he finds law librarianship also lacking in a classic literature. This is our attempt to introduce the reader to perhaps the greatest of law librarianship's "dead Germans"—Frederick C. Hicks.[7]

HICKS' 'THE TEACHING OF LEGAL BIBLIOGRAPHY'

> In the history of legal education, the study of the legal bibliography and the use of law books is more ancient than formal teaching of the subject. Since the days when precedent was first firmly seated on the throne of English law, lawyers have bowed down to it, and wise men have admonished the tyro to seek knowledge in the books wherein are set down a multitude of isolated instances of authoritative rulings of the courts. Less homage has been paid to those commands of governments which appear in the form of statutes; altho [sic] their superiority over all but a few of the classical treatises is invariably pointed out. A long line of writers beginning with Fulbeck in 1599, and including Coke, Doderidge, Sir Matthew Hale, Phillips and Roger North, have told the student how, when, where, by what method, and in what books to seek knowledge. Much that they have said may, however, be summed up in the advice of my Lord Coke to "seek the fountains." But in his day those fountains were few in number and easily recognized. It was at least a reasonable proposal to send the student to a group of books which with diligence might be read thru [sic] in a life-time. The identical books referred to were also those which would be relied on in practise [sic]. It was humanly possible to become as familiar with them as with a well-thumbed textbook. The study of legal bibliography as such did not need to be separated from the study of the law; for unconsciously every apprentice made his own study and found his own habitual avenue of approach to the fountains.
>
> Precedent still is enthroned, and *petere fontes* is still good advice, but the fountains have been submerged in an ocean of books. Chart and compass are needed to guide one over the trackless waters to the well-springs now more or less obscured. In phrases now almost stereotyped, modern writers complain of the great increase in the number of law books, especially reports. It was the difficulty of providing a sufficient number of copies of these reports to enable students to read the precedents in their original form that led to the compilation of "case-books." While these selections of cases reprinted to serve as the basis of instruction enabled the so-called case method to reach its present place of preeminence in legal education, they do not lead the student to an intimacy with the vast literature with which on graduation he is presumed to be familiar. Even with the case method, it is entirely possible for the honor graduate to be completely at a loss when called upon to find the evidence of the simplest legal truths if it is not contained in the identical books which he has studied. He may be ignorant of the fact that, vast as

> is the literature which fills our law libraries, it is more minutely indexed than any other literature of like proportions. The needs of the practitioner have been met by the enterprise of the indexer, the compiler, and the publisher; but the student struggling to master the contents of the few books may pass by the guide posts to the many. He must return to them sooner or later in order to reach the right road, and this he does either at the expense of himself, his employer, or his clients. Lawyers in active practise [sic], even of long standing, either admit that they do not know easily how to extract information from their books, or bewail the fact that they did not learn it earlier in their careers. Law teachers also have said repeatedly in print and from the platform that a knowledge of legal bibliography is an essential part of the education of a lawyer. It is an obvious corollary of King George the Third's reputed remark that lawyers do not know so much more law than other people, but they know better where to find it. And yet the history of the teaching of this subject in law schools is not two decades old. Indeed, the schools as such can not lay claim to the credit of having recognized the need and acted on it promptly. The initiative came from without, and the idea that the subject is one for which a place should be made in the curriculum is not yet generally accepted. Of the 117 law schools in the United States, less than half have provided such instruction, and the science of teaching the subject is still in its infancy. Before pointing out in detail some of the unsolved questions involved in formal teaching of legal bibliography, it may, therefore, be helpful to review the history of its entrance into our schools. By this method something may be learned from the logic of events.

First, what is there not to love about Hicks' prose? In the current law student vernacular, it is "totally old school." It is peppered with Latin quotes and English spelling and only imagines a professional world of men practicing law. He bows to the English common law and appears every bit the Anglophile. His was a world of convention and tradition, but it was also a world in the midst of the devastation of World War I. This article was written when the fate of Europe was still uncertain—yet the lessons and costs were already readily apparent. The lessons of the War to End All Wars needed to be heeded, and only through the rule of law could the future of the world be secure.

In 1918, the world of legal education for Hicks consisted of 117 American law schools, whereas today, we have just over 200 American Bar Association-accredited schools. Legal research teaching is still in its infancy. He states that the study of legal bibliography is less than two decades old and not taught in most schools. And, same as it ever was, an honors graduate of a law school could enter practice painfully ignorant of how to do legal research.

Yet it is also helpful to remember that law schools in Hicks' time were not as sophisticated as in ours. The Socratic method was dominant. He states, "Law teachers also have said repeatedly in print and from the platform that a knowledge of legal bibliography is an essential part of the education of a lawyer." This was the era of "the sage on the stage" in legal education. There was little room for skills training, practice-oriented classes, clinics, practicum, moot court competitions, independent study options, and study abroad. One of the few educational opportunities outside the classroom in Hicks' time—the law review—was a very different creature from its current incarnation: the work of the staff focused on editing and writing brief case notes and comments.[8] These notes were rarely longer than two or three pages and merely described the holding in the case and its implications to the existing case law. There was no sophisticated analysis.

To strain Hicks' metaphor, the "ocean of books" to which he alludes is now a tsunami of legal information with a proliferation of print materials he could not have imagined, not to mention Lexis, Westlaw, Loislaw, and other online services. As late as 20 years ago, who could have predicted the Internet? Even with consolidation of major publishers, there is no decrease in the production of legal information in all formats.[9]

A perspective on the legal information world of Hicks versus the present: At the time Hicks wrote, there were only some 250 volumes of the United States Reports and 275 volumes of the Federal Reporter (which at the time, included both court of appeals and district court decisions). Administrative law was all but nonexistent. The Stock Market Crash and the New Deal were years away. International law barely existed. Comparative legal research meant looking almost exclusively at Commonwealth materials and then primarily British.

The casebook as a teaching tool was one inevitable outcome of this explosion of materials—an innovation in Hicks' time. One cannot help but wonder if the casebook can continue to be the dominant course material in the modern law school, despite the strong financial interests of the publishing houses and law professors, when more up-to-date and easily amended e-texts are easily created and available for free or more reasonable purchase.[10]

Law libraries in Hicks' time were mere shadows of the current academic law library and they varied greatly in size and quality. It would not be until a decade after Hicks' article that any standards existed for law libraries. "In 1927, the American Association of Law Schools established a minimum [standard] of 7,500 volumes and a minimum expenditure on collections of $1,000 [for academic law libraries]."[11] Today's collection sizes and expenditures dwarf those of Hicks' time.

Obviously, the teaching of legal research was a much simpler task. Here is one simple example: the teaching of citation verification. For decades, the only way to do this was to use Shepard's Citations. While it was a somewhat daunting task at first to learn how to Shepardize with its strange numbers and cryptic abbreviations, it was in fact a fairly easy task to master. It was the only game in town. Every lawyer in America knew how to Shepardize. Then the legal information world changed. In the late 1990s, Dan Dabney, currently Senior Director, Thomson Global Services, along with the technical staff at West Publishing, created a competitor to Shepard's Citations: KeyCite. This complicated the task of learning citation verification and legal research. No longer was Shepard's the final word, but now there was another source to examine—and compare. So, not only were there two systems to learn rather than one, but one must additionally be able to compare and contrast the two services. In other words, it now takes the modern law student more than twice the time it once took to master this one legal research skill. We can multiply this experience again and again as new products enter the market and few disappear.[12]

THE WORK OF THE PUBLISHING HOUSES

> Whether we attribute the action of the publishers to well-considered commercialism or to some higher motive, the credit of arousing interest in law books as a study must be given to them. They were the pioneers in a work, begun with enterprise and foresight, at considerable expense, and still carried on with intelligent persistence. Moreover, they have taught not only several thousands of students, but by example and precept, a number of instructors. Two publishing houses, the West Publishing Company, and the Lawyers Cooperative Publishing Company, are today employing representatives to visit law schools and when permitted, to deliver lectures on the use of law books. The former was the first in the field and has the longer record of service.
>
> The active work of the West Publishing Company in this connection was entrusted to three men who jointly are responsible for initiating and developing the plans. They are Alfred F. Mason, C. Willard Smith, and Roger W. Cooley. The first step was the publication in October 1902 of the first number of the *American Law School Review*, a periodical by means of which a direct appeal could be made to the law schools of the country. In the third and fourth numbers appeared articles on Instruction in Finding Cases and on The Use of Law Books. Then in the Winter of 1904 was announced a Case Finding Contest offering $200 in prizes to those students who submitted correct lists of citations showing where ten cases, of which the facts only were given, are to be found in the law reports. The names of the winners and the correct answers were printed in the Spring number, 1904. Other contests known as Brief-making Contests were held in 1905 and 1906, a winning brief being published in the Spring number, 1907. It is significant that in the initial contest, most of the prizes went to students of Northwestern University, that school being then almost alone in teaching the use of law books, whereas in the later contests, the winners ranged all the way from Stanford to Columbia and from St. Paul to Pittsburgh. It was evident that law teachers and students were thinking about the advantages of systematic instruction in the use of books and that the argument had been driven home that a brief cannot be written until the authorities have been collected and

digested. Advantage was taken of these facts by the publication in 1906 of the first edition of *Brief Making and the Use of Law Books*, edited by Professor Nathan Abbott, then Dean of the Leland Stanford University Law School; and by visits to a number of law schools for the purpose of arranging for lectures to be given by a representative of the company. In preparation for the lectures, Mr. Cooley and Mr. Smith, field agents of the sales department, applied themselves to devising some easy means of finding cases with the result that the "descriptive word" method was formulated. During the winter of 1906–1907, Mr. Cooley visited Wisconsin, Minnesota, Northwestern, Michigan, and Chicago Universities, and the Detroit Law School, lecturing and conferring with students and instructors. The experiment was so successful that Mr. Mason began an active campaign to interest practically all the law schools of the country, and in the fall and winter of 1907–1908, Mr. Cooley lectured at twenty law schools. From 1906–1911, the work grew until in 1911 when Mr. Cooley retired from the company to become Professor of Law at the University of North Dakota, he was regularly visiting thirty schools, devoting seven months of each year to the trips. In all, he had lectured at thirty-seven different schools.

In the meantime, in 1909, a second edition of *Brief Making*, edited by Mr. Cooley, had been published; and a new project had been started. This was the establishment early in 1910 of a Practitioners' Correspondence Course in Brief Making for the benefit of young lawyers and law students not attending law schools. The basis of the course was the second edition of *Brief Making*, but in the preparation of the lesson sheets and quizzes, the whole subject was gone over anew by Mr. Cooley. The cost of tuition was $10. Nearly 300 students enrolled, and actual work was begun; but as its successful continuance would involve a large expenditure of money, the course was soon abandoned. A desirable result of the attempt was, however, the publication of the third edition of *Brief Making*,which was issued in 1914.

Mr. Cooley's successor as traveling lecturer was Mr. Raleigh A. Daly of the Chicago Bar, who has since 1911 widened the field of operation so that in the winter of 1915–1916, he visited seventy-one schools and lectured at fifty-six. During the academic year 1916–1917, his schedule called for visits to seventy-five schools, with lectures at sixty. Since 1913, the company has promoted the establishment of local courses as a part of the regular curriculum. At that time, the number of men properly qualified to teach the subject was limited. The problem, therefore, was to recruit a group of men willing to apply themselves to a new subject not yet formally recognized by law schools. This end was sought by two means. In the summer of 1913, the company invited twelve law schools in the South to send representatives to its offices in St. Paul for the purpose of receiving special instruction in the use of its publications. The schools which sent representatives were: Tulane University, the University of Texas, the University of Florida, John B. Stetson University of South Carolina, University of Oklahoma, University of Kentucky, University of Tennessee, Atlanta Law School, University of Mississippi, and the

> University of Denver. The conference resulted in the establishment of courses in most of these schools. The other means employed was the reverse of that just mentioned. A representative was sent to spend several months in the law schools of the Southern states to assist in qualifying local instructors for the work. This enterprise was entrusted to Mr. Charles L. Ames who introduced experimental courses, many of which became permanent.
>
> The other large publishing house, which is now arousing interest in the use of law books, is the Lawyers Cooperative Publishing Company. It has only recently entered this particular field but now has a special representative, Mr. F. S. Schoonover, who devotes his energies to work with the law schools. During the last winter, he has visited almost all schools east of the Rocky Mountains, lecturing in seventy of them.

For the academic law librarian, this section immediately calls to mind the presence of the Lexis and Westlaw reps in our schools. The law schools of Hicks' era relied on the book sellers to assist them in teaching legal research. As commercial enterprises, the book publishers used standard marketing devices, prizes and the offer of "free" use of the company's staff, to assist the schools and libraries.

In the following section, Hicks identifies two problems that every academic law library in the country faces who avails themselves to the "It's free!" siren song of the vendors: who should do the teaching of legal research, the vendors or the librarians; and was this offer of assistance in teaching a "well-considered commercialism" or was the willingness of vendors to teach law students how to do research guided by "some higher motive?" It is hard to know if Hicks was being facetious or somewhat naive, but no one believes that anything the legal publishers—and especially Westlaw and LexisNexis—do is based on anything but the profit motive. They not only come to our schools to train students, faculty, and librarians, but they now have helpful "Web developers" who write to tell us how we might better highlight their services to students on our Web pages and *helpfully* provide us with that content. To their credit, the vendors push the marketing envelope on occasion but always retreat when confronted with blatant attempts at marketing. They know they have the undivided attention of the future market, so they can go easy.

Any discussion of the place of vendors in the legal research curriculum begs the question of, what we are paying for when we subscribe to Lexis and Westlaw? Is it the endless giveaways, pens, plastic cups, and "frequent flyer" promotions? Is it for the student representatives? Our own view is that—despite their eagerness to help fellow students—these student representatives spend a lot of time writing e-mails and surfing the Internet. Truth be told, we are guilty of not paying sufficient attention to their work, so who can blame them? (The authors hereby resolve to pay more attention to the work of our Lexis and Westlaw student representatives in the upcoming year!)

It goes without saying, however, that much more has also changed since the times of Hicks. Academic law libraries are now multimillion dollar operations. Whereas it was unusual to find even one lawyer librarian in the library in 1918, now all academic law libraries have several.[13] Academic law libraries' missions have also changed significantly. Support of faculty research is as important and in many cases more important than supporting law student research. Part of this trend can be explained by the fact that with more of an emphasis on teaching, librarians are heading off the reference questions at the pass. Law students come into the library more educated. And there are now several other places to ask reference questions, be it the Lexis and Westlaw hotlines, Ask Jeeves, Google, or the many free legal databases available to those who search the Web. And given the likelihood that the student in need of reference help is at a computer as the need arrives, the idea of even walking a few steps to the law library seems unnecessary.

In addition, there is little doubt that law schools are becoming less professional schools and more academic institutions. There is a much greater emphasis on scholarship, creating institutes, and think tanks and interdisciplinary studies. A current term in vogue is trans-disciplinary study; interdisciplinary doesn't quite capture the modern legal scholar.[14] This also forces us to examine the amount of time we spend teaching law students versus meeting the research needs of our faculty. Lacking the staff to properly do both, what do we choose?

Finally, it occurs to the authors that there may be many law librarians reading this article who do not know the history of the great legal publishers of the past, like Lawyers Cooperative Publishing, Bancroft Whitney, Little Brown, perhaps even Matthew Bender. How does the modern law librarianship student learn of the history of legal bibliography? We write under the assumption that our readers know the difference between legal bibliography instruction and legal research instruction, but we may in fact define the term legal bibliography quite differently. Has any one of the current generation of law librarians read *Men and Books Famous in the Law*?[15] This classic, also written by Hicks, was once required reading of all law librarians. Now sadly, it is forgotten.

THE WORK OF THE SCHOOLS

> The number of law schools giving definite instruction in this subject by resident teachers is gradually increasing. During the last year, information concerning the courses in twenty-nine schools has been compiled by a committee of the American Association of Law Libraries. In a few of these, lectures are still given by representatives of the publishing houses in addition to those provided by the schools. Aside from the mere fact that the schools are taking up the work, the most significant point noticeable is that methods have not been standardized and that each school is solving its own problem on the basis of local expediency. The time

> when the courses are given, and the method, means, form, and status of the instruction show no uniformity. Instruction under the auspices of the schools is intrinsically more useful than that given by publishing houses. The latter frankly admit that their primary object is to call attention to their own publications. Their lectures lack a scientific basis and are limited in scope. The permanent local instructor on the contrary has the opportunity of presenting his subject in an unprejudiced way, comparing and evaluating the publications of different houses. The courses can be longer, with opportunity for discussion and practise [sic], and attention can be paid to the needs of the individual student.
>
> Assuming, therefore, that eventually legal bibliography will be taught in a formal way in all recognized law schools, it may be worthwhile to state some of the questions which men now working independently might discuss for their mutual advantage. These questions roughly group themselves in two overlapping divisions, viz., Administration and Problems of Teaching.

Today, no real standardization of legal research instruction exists. In addition to the ongoing teaching legal bibliography versus teaching legal research process dichotomy discussed below, other variations persist. With regard to teaching legal research in the first year of law school, a long-standing split still occurs between those teaching research separately and those teaching as part of an integrated legal research and writing program. While law librarians have reviewed the change from separate to integrated courses,[16] legal writing instructors have generated much of the literature on this topic.[17] The increasing dominance of online legal research has led to a split between schools, some insisting that librarians rather than vendors teach classes on online research[18], and increasingly, a move to integrating online and print research instruction for simultaneous coverage.[19] As noted recently by perhaps the most prolific writer of legal research texts, the only certainty is that legal research instruction methods will continue to change and evolve.[20]

ADMINISTRATIVE PROBLEMS

> The moment that the decision is made to elevate the subject into a formal part of the curriculum, the Dean of a law school is confronted with the problem of finding a place for it in the curriculum. In a three-year course, eight months of the year, with twenty-four required subjects and ten others either given in alternate years or as electives, with moot courts clamoring for fuller recognition and new courses proposed, where can a place be found for so humble a subject as legal bibliography? And then, before this question can be answered come the definite queries. In what year shall it be given? Shall it be given in a continuous course or in two parts? Shall it be taught as a separate subject or in connection with

> another? How many hours shall be devoted to it? Shall it be required or elective, and in either case, shall credit be given?
>
> On all of these points the testimony of students and recent graduates should have some weight. In many schools where such a course is offered as an elective without credit, students voluntarily add it to their regular work, because the knowledge gained can be put to immediate use and has a definite marketable value in law offices where clerkships are sought. They express the opinion that the instruction should be given in any case, whether at the expense of more hours' work, or as a substitute for one or more of the special courses for which credit is now given. As to the year when the instruction should be offered, there is a difference of opinion, depending on the scope of the particular course with which they are familiar. All agree that certain phases of the subject ought to be presented in the first year or as soon as the student is expected to get beyond the covers of his casebooks. Others feel that there are two distinct portions of the subject and that the more advanced part should be given in the second or third year, when it could be joined to instruction in brief making or court practise [sic]. In nineteen of the twenty-nine schools of which the writer has a record, the course is offered to first-year men only; in four, to second-year men only; in four, to third-year men, and in two, to the whole school. Students seem to be quite indifferent to the question [of] whether credit should be received but in general agreement that the course should be required. This is on the ground that the new student may overlook a subject for which no credit is given and which has no prominent place in the schedule, thus omiting [sic] something which will be of use to him in his preparatory study and in his early practise [sic]. They say also that unless it is required, the tendency is to make no place for it in the schedule, thus causing conflicts and preventing many students from taking the course. They are willing to give as many hours to the course as the instructor will offer, and in schools where the work is optional, some students take it a second time in order to tighten their grasp upon it. In our law schools, the practise [sic] varies so much as to the number of hours offered that little can be learned from the figures. The range is from three to thirty-six hours, the largest number offering fifteen hours. In twenty-one schools the course is required and credit given.
>
> These are a few of the problems that confront the administrator. Obviously they cannot be solved in a particular school without reference to other questions. Fundamental among these are, what shall be taught, who shall teach it, and what methods shall be used?

Things have not changed much since Hicks wrote this. Hicks recognized that if research was "a subject for which no credit is given and which has no prominent place in the schedule," it would be overlooked by students.

Any discussion about the credit hours and status afforded legal research (and writing) courses commonly turns to a mention of too few credit hours leading to students dismissing the importance of the course.[21] Many schools have attempted to remedy the deficiency of first-year legal research instruction with upper level classes in research, particularly with advanced legal research courses.[22] Even among schools offering advanced legal research instruction, there is a wide variety of models and methods employed.[23]

That is not to say that other models of legal research instruction have not been proposed in recent years. The University of Southern California School of Law experimented with bringing law students to school before the first-year regular classes began to give them a rudimentary understanding of legal research. While it had its successes, it was ultimately scrapped for teaching too much too soon.[24] At our institution, the decision was made to teach legal research in the second semester of the first year in the hope that a semester of law school would provide a context that would make the learning of research skills easier. Students would have already had a semester reading cases and at least a rudimentary understanding of legal analysis. This delay has helped provide that context, but it is still too soon in the life of a law student for them to have the necessary background to fully understand the various legal research sources and when to appropriately use them. In addition, the delay of producing a significant writing sample causes significant law student consternation as they begin to look for summer jobs after their first year of law school. One cannot help but wonder what law students did during the summers of their first and second years of law school during the time of Hicks?

In partial response to the dilemma of preparing students for their first summer of clerking, we began teaching an Intermediate Legal Research course, which we nicknamed "boot camp" because it is a one-week, 40 hour-long research class that offers a significant amount of individual attention and hands-on research. It begins the week immediately after spring semester exams conclude and is intended to prepare students for their first summer legal job. While well received, it is still probably too soon in the life of a law student to properly instruct them in the subtleties of legal research in areas of complex litigation and administrative law. So we continue to rely on teaching Advanced Legal Research, a graded, three-credit course.

These are merely examples to prove the point that we as a profession have continually tinkered with the legal research curriculum, but almost always under substantial constraints from our institutions. Legal research has always been relegated to second-class status in the curriculum and no report, be it the MacCrate Report or the Carnegie Report, appears to have the influence to change the inertia that is law school curriculum reform.

PROBLEMS OF TEACHING

> There are at least three divisions of the subject which we have spoken of as legal bibliography. They are, first, legal bibliography proper, which deals with the repositories of the law; second, methods of finding this

> law, which is an art to be acquired; and third, brief making, which has to do with the orderly presentation of arguments based on authorities and in conformity with the rules of the court to which they are addrest [sic]. Legal bibliography proper is not merely a description of books. It is also a study of the record of the jural life of a people. This record shows the evolution of law and the civilization back of it. Its very language, diction, and style are products of contemporary literary taste; while the evolution of printing, binding, and bookmaking can be traced in the history of law books. Decisions never become obsolete merely from the passage of time. On the contrary, many of them gather weight with age; and therefore, the study of the history of law books is not merely fanciful or recondite. The modern lawyer can not rely on modern books alone. In fact, a knowledge of the history of the great classes of law books is necessary in order to select the authorities on which to rely. Legal bibliography proper should, therefore, be presented as a historical subject by means of which a background is given to the modern picture. In days when business methods are making it difficult for the law to maintain its position as a profession, no better means of instilling respect for the law into the minds of students can be found than by teaching the history, authority, and usefulness of its vast literature. For these reasons, it seems advisable to teach this part of the subject in the first year of the law course.

We think it fair to say that few, if any, modern teachers of legal research would approve of this method. In fact, it can be argued that this belief is at the core of the Wren & Wren debate with Bob Berring. In a 1988 article, "the Wrens attacked traditional methods of teaching legal research, which they described as 'bibliographically oriented,' containing too much unnecessary information about law books without grounding students in the proper context of the legal research process."[25] The Berring response emphasized teaching of bibliographic tools in the context of an advanced legal research course.[26] The next year, the Wrens replied to the Berring article, claiming that it mischaracterized their original article and that "has only reinforced our conviction that process-oriented legal research instruction provides a far more appropriate focus than bibliographically oriented instruction."[27] In a final shot in the volley of articles, Berring wrote that "the heart of the matter is that we have a serious set of disagreements with the Wrens about how to best teach legal research."[28]

> The second part of the subject is the one which makes the most direct practical appeal to the student. As soon as a case or statute is cited to him in class, he finds himself face to face with an elaborate system of reference, which is new to him. Only the exceptional student masters this unaided in time to be of service to him in his early researches. [sic—yes, that tortured sentence is what Hicks wrote!] And even he acquires it in an unsystematic way and without certain knowledge of the reference

> books, which will help him in case of doubt. It is a mistake to speak of any of the processes of finding the law as mechanical processes, for one has not truly found the law until one understands it, and this requires a knowledge of substantive law which comes only with the passage of time and much experience. Nevertheless, there is a species of manual training in the use of law books and libraries, which should be learned before or coincidently, with the substance of law itself. This has been defined as the art of finding known cases and statutes and includes the use of catalogs, the arrangement of libraries, the interpretation of citations, their translation from one form to another, the location of cases when only their titles are known, the tracing of the legislative and judicial history of statutes, and the judicial history of cases. Every practical consideration demands that an opportunity to acquire such knowledge be given the student at the beginning of his course. He has less need of finding unknown cases and statutes until a later period. He has neither the occasion, the time, nor the technical equipment to find the whole law applicable to a state of facts until after the intensive study of the fundamental doctrines in many departments of the law. His introduction to the digest and subject-index may, therefore, better be deferred to the end of the first year, and the careful study of them to the second or third years.

Once again, Hicks makes a seeming recommendation for advanced legal research.[29] We think he would also approve of our institution's decision to offer Intermediate Legal Research (boot camp) at the very end of the first year.

> Brief making is the attempt to put into practise [sic] all of the knowledge of substantive law, of legal bibliography proper, of legal research and its mechanical processes, of analysis, of logic, and finally of constructive argument which the lawyer possesses. The brief is the supreme result of the application of all the legal faculties. Obviously such a subject can not be taught in its entirety as one topic. The instructor must assume such a previous knowledge as will enable the student to analyze his case, determine the principles which probably apply, search out the opposite statutory and case law, and locate it in authoritative repositories. He can then take up the problem of the orderly and logical presentation of this material, giving form to the argument in accordance with legal rules, and with the support of authorities properly cited. Such a course necessarily cannot be given advantageously until the third year.
>
> It would be possible for much of the material above mentioned to be taught in connection with other subjects, and in some schools the only instruction given is in courses designated as Elementary Law, Introduction to Law, Study of Cases, Practise [sic] Court Work, and the like. In other schools reliance is had on the initiative of professors to teach the bibliography of their own subjects, and incidentally to give the student

> both a respect for books and a practical knowledge of how to use them. This means that only a fragmentary exposition is made leaving the student largely to his own resources, with the usual result that he falls in the midst of many stools. Undoubtedly the course can best be given separately but with the cordial cooperation of the whole corps of teachers.

Obviously, our protests to the contrary, the first-year curriculum has undergone some significant changes since the times of Hicks. The legal realist Soia Mentschikoff was one of the early proponents of the need for an overarching view of the law in the first year, often called legal methods, both as a professor of law at the University of Chicago and dean at the University of Miami School of Law.[30] Legal responsibility and ethics have been added to many first-year curricula. Still, the more things change, the more they stay the same. The first year is not radically different from the times of Hicks. The case method still dominates, as does the Socratic method. Classes are still relatively large for graduate education.

> This leads to the question of the qualifications and status of the instructor. Should the course be given by the law librarian or partly by him and partly by another instructor? Evidently this subject has more direct connection with the work of the librarian than any other in the curriculum. Long before it was thought of as a formal subject, he was already teaching it to individual students, and if alive to his opportunities, he will always continue to do so. It is a subject requiring an intimate and extensive knowledge of legal literature, which is the special province of the librarian. Moreover, he must as a matter of course know his books, not only in their contemporary development but in their historical origins. He must have this knowledge in order to be an efficient librarian. But he must also be trained in the law and have had some experience as a practitioner. Conversely, an established professor of law who essays to teach legal bibliography must have the training of a librarian. And in either case the man selected must have ability and willingness to teach by methods both arduous and monotonous. He must be able to draw inspiration from changing groups of students rather than from rapid development of this subject from year to year. As a matter of fact, it makes little difference in the formal part of the instruction whether the teacher be librarian or professor, so long as he be properly qualified. The subject, however, is the only one in the whole curriculum which can be taught by the librarian without drawing his interest away from the library. Moreover, he ought to become a better librarian from the necessity of systematic revision of his knowledge in preparation for the annual course of instruction. His library is the laboratory for the course, and his office or even the library itself the logical place for holding classes. He is more accessible to the student than the professor usually is and can, therefore, carry on individual instruction supplementing the regular course.

Nothing would strike more fear into the heart of today's legal research teacher than the thought of a requirement for the "ability and willingness to teach by methods both arduous and monotonous." Much of the literature on legal research instruction and legal education in general deals with methods of keeping instruction interesting for the students, particularly with the use of new technology. Today, teachers use a variety of technology from Computer-Assisted Legal Instruction (CALI) exercises to Microsoft PowerPoint to podcasts to keep students interested. They emphasize active learning and take into account the various learning styles of today's adults.[31]

> The solution of practically all of the questions which have always been raised depends on the methods which are used in teaching. These now vary with the aptitude, time, and predilections of the teacher. While the case method of teaching substantive law has been almost universally adopted, the method of teaching legal bibliography has yet to be standardized. In some schools only lectures are given, in others lectures with demonstrations by the instructor. To the latter method are sometimes added problems to be solved and presented in written form. A fourth method is to give preliminary lectures to the whole class followed by practise [sic] work given to small sections of the class. Instructors who have tried several methods usually fall back on a combination of them all. Recurring to the three phases of the subject above outlined, it is evident that legal bibliography proper, the origin, history, and description of the repositories of the law, [are] susceptible of presentation in the form of lectures, with exhibition of notable examples of great books, outlines of legal literature, and required reading in works descriptive of law books. How to find the law is a problem best solved by trying to do it. But this attempt must be under proper guidance. Each student needs personal attention, and this he cannot get in large classes. A certain amount of exposition is required at each stage of development of the subject which can be given to large groups, but the actual driving home of points so that the student feels their force must be done in seminars of from twelve to fifteen students. Each student must be given individual problems and must be carefully checked up by the instructor. This method while most helpful to the student throws a large burden on the teacher. The preparation of the problems is tedious and taxing and actual class work for each problem is multiplied by the number of sections. For instance, in one school, in order to give each student one hour a week, it was necessary for the librarian to hold nine seminars a week. He became in fact, a hard-working drillmaster, but was amply repaid by the results of his labor. All that has been said about methods of teaching how to find the law seems to the writer to apply with equal force to brief making. The instructor needs to serve in the critical capacity of both opposing counsel and judge in order that the student may have a proper incentive to prepare a brief that will stand such tests as are applied in actual practise [sic].

Perhaps more so in the preceding few sentences than anywhere else in his article, Hicks lays out succinctly the similarities and differences between legal research instruction in his day and what occurs today. Few research instructors today would spend much time lecturing on "legal bibliography proper, the origin, history, and description of the repositories of the law. . ." Instead today's legal research instruction focuses on what Hicks calls "how to find the law." Just as in Hicks' day, this requires instruction in smaller groups with librarian instructors providing hands-on guidance. While many of today's instructors might have hoped that technology would relieve them of some of this "how to" instruction time, resources, such as CALI legal research lessons, at most augment and reinforce what is learned in small group instruction; CALI lessons cannot replace personal guidance from a legal research instructor.

> The purpose of this article has not been to state conclusions but to raise questions for discussion by men now teaching legal bibliography. If any categorical statements have been made they are merely expressions of personal conviction at the present stage of the writer's experience. The authoritative word on present problems of the teacher of legal bibliography has not yet been spoken, and it can spring only from the combined thought of men who have common interests and problems. Legal bibliography is not the most important subject to be treated in law schools, but it is one worthy of serious attention, and it presents pedagogical difficulties as well as those of substance. If overcome in a scientific way, the results may be of service to those who are attempting to teach the bibliography of other subjects than law.

Throughout the years since Hicks penned this conclusion, legal research teachers have continued to struggle with the best way to impart a knowledge of legal research to law students. From separate legal bibliography classes to integrated research and writing classes to advanced legal research and other more novel ways of teaching research,[32] as mentioned previously, the evolutionary struggle continues. A review of Hicks' seminal article on teaching and the many articles that have discussed legal research instruction since then are perhaps best illustrated by the famous French proverb, "*plus ça change, plus c'est la même chose*."[33]

ADDENDUM: THOUGHTS ON 'TEACHING LEGAL RESEARCH'

Robert C. Berring, Walter Perry Johnson Professor of Law, School of Law, University of California, Berkeley

What atreat to be given the chance to comment on Professor Hicks' seminal article, *Teaching Legal Bibliography*. Professor Hicks is my culture hero as a law librarian and as a teacher of legal research. As Mike and Shaun point out in their annotations to the article, Hicks anticipated many of the problems that we still battle with 90 years later. Was he that prescient or has the field, for all of the technological advancement and industry consolidation that surrounds it, changed at a glacial pace? This is a tougher call than it should be.

Hicks was a scholar, a teacher, and a librarian. His understanding of the process of legal research ran deep. He lamented the passing of a time when mastering legal materials meant reading every possible volume. In that halcyon era, the erudite lawyer read every available volume and internalized it. His brain organized and synthesized it. Hicks saw this era end and saw the rise of indexes, digest, and citators. How different are we today, lamenting the end of the printed book, the Key Number system and paper volumes of Shepard's? Professor Hicks should guide us; we should move on.

Even as he recognized the changes in legal information and the consequent need for systematic research training, he perceived the larger issues. Hicks saw that one cannot separate the teaching of legal research from the understanding of legal information. The student cannot master the use of research tools without understanding the tools themselves. Legal research skills do not exist in the abstract—they must be mastered by employing them. The Hicks approach, pejoratively called the "bibliographic approach" in the memorable article by Christopher and Jill Robinson Wren that Mike and Shaun discuss, is a misnomer. Hicks does not envision instruction that is grounded in examining the sources of legal authority as sets of books with only a bibliographic identity. He paints a picture of where the work came from, where it fits in the universe of authority, and how it is put together. This is the motivating theme behind his classic work, *Men and Books of the Law*. This inestimable volume, which is still in print, chooses a handful of classic legal works and writes the story of the book, the author, and why it is important. The reader sees the book in context, and the book takes on three dimensions. I still ask my research assistants to read it.

As Hicks talks of the great minds that produced legal literature and the hard-working lecturers from West and Lawyers' Cooperative Publishing Company who, in the days of train travel, crisscrossed the country carrying the gospel of legal research to law schools, he both humanizes and contextualizes the research process. This is the reason that I tell the story of John West, Frank Shepard, Jim Adler, and others when I teach Advanced Legal Research. If the students see where the information came from and why it is relied upon, it sticks. If a student understands how a judicial opinion or a statute is created, that student can deal with it in any format. But instruction cannot stop there. One also stresses the process, which is why we require open-ended research exercises when we teach Advanced Legal Research. We want context for the tools too. If the biographical approach does not catch the students' attention, perhaps explaining where the legal information fits in the world of legal theory might. Hicks' thoughts on the "jural" place of the books is spot on. It is humbling to think that I still follow the path laid out by Hicks so long ago.

For the rest, we can only marvel at how little has changed. Legal research courses still get little respect. Vendors of legal information play a much bigger role in the lives of law students than legal research instructors. Like the weather, everyone complains about legal research skills but almost no faculty is willing to do anything that involves devoting resources to it or conferring status upon those who teach it. It is surprising to see that the Lexis and Westlaw promotions to win iPods and trips to Hawaii had antecedents in the West Company brief writing contest. The biggest change may be Professor Hicks' confident and exclusive use of the masculine personal pronoun throughout.

One special point is worth pausing over. Hicks speaks of librarians going far beyond the job description to teach legal research. This is a dilemma that the profession still faces. With the increased role of legal writing at many law schools, librarians are offered the chance to offer courses of their own initiative with no reward other than what Hicks characterizes as the feeling of a job well done. The number of law librarians who do in fact teach courses and offer lectures for no reward and often for little recognition heartens and surprises me. But a vital program cannot be sustained in that environment. To change that calls for a change in the culture of law school. Such a change may soon come, but neither the MacCrate Report nor the current work of the Carnegie Foundation is making much headway at top tier schools. Harvard Law School's much ballyhooed retooling of its first-year program actually de-emphasized research training. But we can hope.

In the end, I am glad that the work of Professor Hicks is there. It reminds one that early on, the problems were identified. It is just that we have not solved them.

NOTES

1. *Association of Legal Writing Directors Legal Writing Institute Surveys:* 1999-2007, available at http://www.alwd.org/surveys/2004-2007.html.

2. Carl A. Yirka, *The Yirka Question & the Yirka Answer: What Should Law Libraries Stop Doing in Order to Address Higher Priority Initiatives?* AALL Spectrum 28 (July 2008).

3. There are several good articles that go into some detail about the history of legal research instruction. *See* Hicks, *infra* n. 4; Robin K. Mills, *Legal Research Instruction in the Law Schools, The State of the Art or, Why Law School Graduates Do Not Know How to Find the Law*, 70 L. Lib. J. 343 (1977); Thomas A. Woxland, *Why Can't Johnny Research? Or It All Started With Christopher Columbus Langdell*, 81 L. Lib. J. 451 (1989); Joyce Manna Janto & Lucinda D. Harrison-Cox, *Teaching Legal Research: Past and Present*, 84 L. Lib. J. 281 (1992).

4. Frederick C. Hicks, *The Teaching of Legal Bibliography*, 11 L. Lib. J. 1 (1918).

5. Richard Danner, *Redefining the Profession*, 90 L. Lib. J. 315 (1998).

6. *Id.* at 327–329.

7. For a biography of Hicks, we recommend, William R. Roalfe, *Frederick C. Hicks: Scholar-Librarian: Biography*, 50 L. Lib. J. 88 (May 1957).

8. By contrast "[n]ow, law reviews contain more than just lead articles and student case notes, but also contain essays, book reviews, and substantial student articles called 'comments.' Law review members not only write shorter case summaries or case notes, but also author comments that are similar

in style and content to non-student lead articles." Michael J. Closen & Robert J. Dzielak, *The History and Influence of the Law Review Institution*, 30 Akron L. Rev. 15, 17 (1996) (citations omitted).

9. For an analysis of how this information explosion affects legal information users, see Robert Berring, *Chaos, Cyberspace, and Tradition: Legal Information Transmogrified*, 12 Berkeley Tech. L.J. 189 (1997); and Claire M. Germain, *Legal Information Management in a Global and Digital Age: Revolution and Tradition*, 35 Intl. J. Leg. Info. 134 (2007).

10. For a recent criticism of the casebook method of instruction, see Benjamin H. Barton, *A Tale of Two Case Methods*, 75 Tenn. L. Rev. 233 (2008).

11. Laura N. Gasaway, *Academic Law Library Statistics, 1876–1922*, 84 L. Lib. J. 573, 576 (1992).

12. For a wonderful history of the citator, see Laura C. Dabney, *Citators: Past, Present and Future*, 27 Leg. Ref. Servs. Q. 165 (2008).

13. Statistics for the latest year available, 2007, show that of academic law libraries responding to the annual salary survey, 46.7% of academic law librarians have both the M.L.S. and J.D. degrees. *See Respondent Background, 2007 Annual Salary Survey*, available at http://www.aallnet.org/members/pub_salary07/background.pdf

14. For a recent and thorough review of the changes in legal scholarship, see Marin Roger Scordato, *Reflections on the Nature of Legal Scholarship in the Post-Realist Era*, 48 Santa Clara L. Rev. 353 (2008).

15. Frederick C. Hicks, *Men and Books Famous in the Law* (Lawyers Coop. Publg., 1921) (also available in the Making of Modern Law database).

16. *See* Anita L. Morse, *Research, Writing, and Advocacy in the Law School Curriculum*, 75 L. Lib. J. 232 (1982) (provides a good review of the change from legal bibliographic instruction to combined research and writing programs); *see also*, Nancy P. Johnson, *Best Practices: What First-Year Law Students Should Learn in a Legal Research Class*, 28 Leg. Ref. Servs. Q. 78 (2009) for an example of research classes still taught separately from legal writing.

17. *See* Helene S. Shapo, *Commentary: The Frontiers of Legal Writing: Challenges for Teaching Research*, 78 L. Lib. J. 719 (1986) (discussing the decline of separate legal research/bibliography instruction and the rise of an integrated program); Jill J. Ramsfield, *Legal Writing in the Twenty-First Century: The First Image: A Survey of Legal Research and Writing Programs*, 1 Leg. Writing 123 (1991) (summarizing surveys about the number of schools adopting integrated programs); Jill J. Ramsfield, *Legal Writing in the Twenty-First Century: A Sharper Image*, 2 Leg. Writing 1 (1996) (updating the data in the previous article).

18. For the most recent article on this topic with summaries of earlier articles, see Shaun G. Nevers, *Candy, Points, and Highlighters: Why Librarians, Not Vendors, Should Teach CALR to First-Year Students*, 99 L. Lib. J. 757 (2007).

19. For a law librarian's argument for teaching online research with or before print research, see Theodore A. Potter, *A New Twist on an Old Plot: Legal Research is a Strategy, Not a Format*, 92 L. Lib. J. 287 (2000); for a similar view by a legal writing professor, see Carrie W. Teitcher, *Rebooting the Approach to Teaching Research: Embracing the Computer Age*, 99 L. Lib. J. 555 (2007).

20. Roy M. Mersky, *Legal Research versus Legal Writing within the Law School Curriculum*, 99 L. Lib. J. 395 (2007).

21. *See* Lydia M.V. Brandt, *The MacCrate Report and the Teaching of Legal Research: A Justified Scenario for Educational Malpractice*, 2 Tex. Wes. L. Rev. 123 (1995–1996) (pointing out the "gross disparity between the recognition given legal research in the MacCrate Report and the message sent to law schools," and quoting extensively from Woxland, *supra* n. 3) and Mersky, *supra* n. 20 at 396 ("Legal writing instructors have often been treated like poor relatives of the law school. But as bad as that position and status may have been within the law school community, the teaching of legal research, eclipsed by legal writing, was for some time relegated to an even lesser position."); *see also*, Duncan Alford, *The Development of the Skills Curriculum in Law Schools: Lessons for Directors of Academic Law Libraries*, 28 Leg. Ref. Servs. Q. (in press).

22. Ann Hemmens, *Advanced Legal Research Courses: A Survey of ABA-Accredited Law Schools*, 94 L. Lib. J. 209 (2002); for a recent survey of advanced legal research programs, see Victoria K. Trotta & Beth DiFelice, *State-Specific Legal Research Instruction: Curricular Stepchild or Core Competency?* 28 Leg. Ref. Servs. Q. 151 (2009).

23. Hemmens, *supra* n. 22. *See also*, Matthew C. Cordon, *Beyond Mere Competency: Advanced Legal Research in a Practice-Oriented Curriculum*, 55 Baylor L. Rev. 1 (2003); Peter C. Schanck, *Mandatory Advanced Legal Research: A Viable Program for Law Schools?* 92 L. Lib. J. 295 (2000); Charles J. Ten Brink, *A Jurisprudential Approach to Teaching Legal Research*, 39 New Eng. L. Rev. 307 (2005) (describing the

integration of the theoretical and the practical in an advanced legal research course); Trotta & DeFelice supra n. 22 (discussing an advanced legal research class centered on state law research); and *Mary Rumsey, The Skills They Need: International and Foreign Legal Research,* 28 Leg. Ref. Servs. Q. 131 (2009 discussing specialized advanced legal research courses in foreign, comparative, and international law research).

24. Conversation with Albert Brecht, 16 Sept. 2008.

25. Paul Douglas Callister, *Beyond Training: Law Librarianship's Quest for the Pedagogy of Legal Research Education,* 95 L. Lib. J. 7, 12 (2003) (summarizing Christopher G. Wren & Jill Robinson Wren *The Teaching of Legal Research*, 80 L. Lib. J. 7 (1988)) (the Callister article provides the most recent and in-depth analysis of the debate as well as suggestions for moving to a new model of teaching legal research).

26. Robert C. Berring & Kathleen Vanden Heuvel, *Legal Research: Should Students Learn It or Wing It?* 81 L. Lib. J. 431 (1989).

27. Christopher G. Wren & Jill Robinson Wren, *Reviving Legal Research: A Reply to Berring and Vanden Heuvel*, 82 L. Lib. J. 463 (1990).

28. Robert C. Berring & Kathleen Vanden Heuvel, *Legal Research: A Final Response*, 82 L. Lib. J 495 (1990); for his perspective on the bibliographic/process debate, tempered by the passage of years, see Robert C. Berring, *Twenty Years On: The Debate Over Legal Research Instruction*, 17 Persps. Teaching Leg. Research & Writing 1 (Fall 2008).

29. See discussion, *supra* n. 22–23 for a discussion of advanced legal research offerings.

30. For a history of the development of Dean Mentschikoff's teaching methods, see John T. Gaubatz, *Of Moots, Legal Process, and Learning to Learn the Law*, 37 U. Miami L. Rev. 473 (1983).

31. *See* James B. Levy, *The Cobbler Wears No Shoes: A Lesson for Research Instruction*, 51 J. Leg. Educ. 39 (2001); Pearl Goldman, *Legal Education and Technology II: An Annotated Bibliography*, 100 L. Lib. J. 415 (2008) (providing a comprehensive review of articles about the use of technology in legal research instruction and legal education in general).

32. Some of the approaches involve an accelerated course of instruction either preceding the first semester (*see* Albert Brecht, *Accelerated Legal Research at U.S.C. Law Center*, 75 L. Lib. J. 167 (1982)) or following the first year as an intensive "boot camp" experience designed to prepare students for clerking.

33. Attributed to "an epigram by Jean-Baptiste Alphonse Karr in the January 1849 issue of his journal Les Guêpes ("The Wasps")." Wikipedia, available at http://en.wiktionary.org/wiki/plus_%C3%A7a_change,_plus_c%27est_la_m%C3%AAme_chose see also, Oxford English Dictionary, http://dictionary.oed.com/cgi/entry/50182078.

Thinking Like a Research Expert: Schemata for Teaching Complex Problem-Solving Skills

PAUL D. CALLISTER

Leon E. Bloch Law Library, University of Missouri–Kansas City School of Law, Kansas City, Missouri, USA

The difference between expert and novice problem solvers is that experts have organized their thinking into schemata or mental constructs to both see and solve problems. This article demonstrates why schemata are important, arguing that they need to be made explicit in the classroom. It illustrates the use of schemata to understand and categorize complex research problems, map the terrain of legal research resources, match appropriate resources to types of problems, and work through the legal research process. The article concludes by calling upon librarians and research instructors to produce additional schemata and develop a common hierarchical taxonomy of skills, a "Bloom's Taxonomy," which would define legal research problem-solving skills more precisely and set benchmarks for assessment.

"We do not first see, and then define. We define first, and then see."
—Walter Lippman[1]

One critical difference between experts and novices as they approach problems is that, "[E]xperts notice features and meaningful patterns of information that are not noticed by novices."[2] Experts see what novices do not, both in the problem and in the resources available. The knowledge of experts is also highly organized and easily retrievable for application.[3] Schemata are the key to expert problem solving. Schemata are "organized representations of things or events that guide a person's thoughts and actions."[4]

For law students to acquire complex problem-solving skills, they must build schemata sufficient to the task. This paper illustrates the relationship of schemata to problem solving and presents a complex problem with a succession of schemata necessary for its resolution.

PROBLEM-SOLVING SCHEMATA

To illustrate how schemata help solve problems, consider the task of finding Ursa Major, a constellation in the night sky, demonstrated in Figure 1.

The problem for law librarians as instructors of legal research is that we forget what it is like not to know the schemata—what it is like not to be able to see Ursa Major as the Big Dipper. There is no going back. The challenge is to find what is implicit in expert legal research that needs to be made explicit. To this end, the definition of schemata, such as the outline of the Big Dipper (see Figure 2), is essential to making the invisible visible to our students. As noted above, "We do not first see, and then define. We define first, and then see."[5]

FIGURE 1 The task of finding Ursa Major in the night sky becomes easier once we know that Ursa Major is the "Big Dipper."

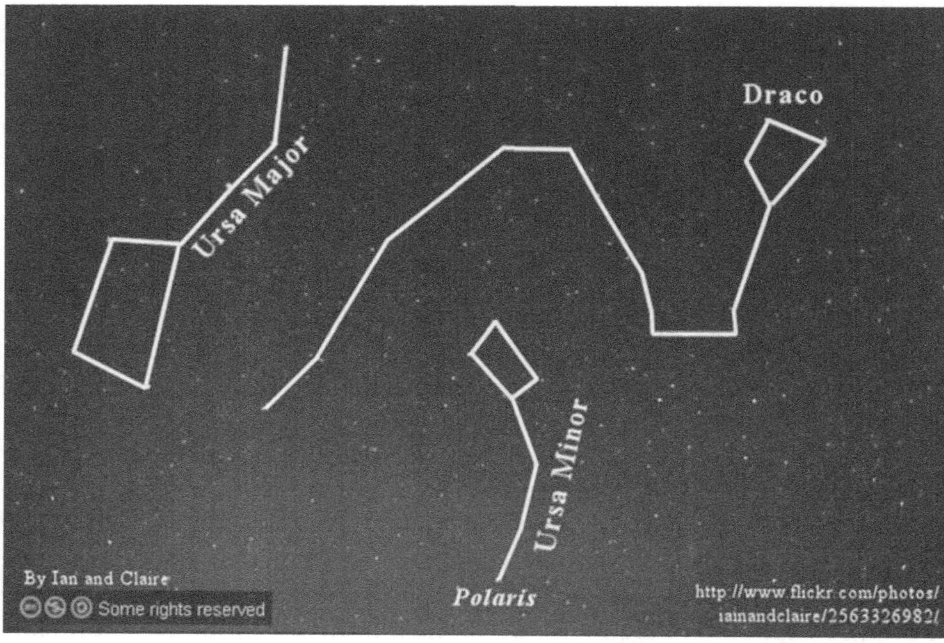

FIGURE 2 The same is true of Draco, Ursa Minor, and other constellations. We cannot navigate the night sky without these schemata.

A COMPLEX PROBLEM

To illustrate the importance of schemata, consider a complex problem as presented in Figure 3—the kind that makes students respond with a "deer in the headlights" expression and that leads to a lot of "wheel spinning."

Although carefully stated using terms of art, this is a challenging problem, similar to what I sometimes dealt with in practice. Hypothetically, the problem has been stated by a senior attorney who knows a lot about pension plans, so the researcher has the advantage of technical vocabulary being used "from the get go." Also the senior attorney has a fairly clear idea of what she wants; if the associate will just pay attention, a number of important clues present themselves.

SCHEMATA FOR SEEING THE PROBLEM

Apollo 13 and 'Working the Problem'[6]

"Houston, we have a problem" harbingered one of the most important rescues of the last century—the near-fatal disaster aboard Apollo 13. In the

Your firm has been asked to advise O.J. Simpson over whether his creditors can seize assets in his profit-sharing plan. During his football career, O.J. set up a profit-sharing plan, sponsored by a corporation, for his commercial endorsements. The plan is funded with over four million dollars. O.J. is the sole shareholder of the corporation and only participant in the plan. A senior partner informs you that the federal statute, ERISA, generally protects profit-sharing plans from the reach of creditors. However, since O.J. was the sole shareholder of his corporation, the plan is not deemed to have any employees, and consequently it does not fall under ERISA's exemption provisions.

You have been asked to find out if, after 1990, any California court has applied exemptions under California state law to protect a profit-sharing or other retirement plans like O.J.'s from the reach of creditors. Even though O.J. prefers not to file for bankruptcy, you are instructed to search the Federal Bankruptcy and Ninth-Circuit courts, since sometimes exemptions under California law are applied (and interpreted by federal courts) in bankruptcy. See 11 U.S.C. § 522(b).

FIGURE 3 Find the key terms.

movie Apollo 13, NASA flight director Gene Krantz must bring order to the scientists and engineers in the Houston Flight Center who are reacting to a flood of negative information about Apollo 13.[7] As portrayed by Ed Harris, Gene Krantz demands that his staff "work the problem" and avoid simply guessing.

The Apollo 13 crisis parallels the initial reaction of new attorneys and law clerks when presented with legal research problems. Reacting to panic, the researcher trips over herself in an effort to foresee an immediate solution. The important lesson to draw from Apollo 13 is to work the problem, not the solution. To do that, the researcher must first find out everything there is to know about the problem. After this initial step, she can match the problem to appropriate strategies and resources for an expedient solution.

Back to Middle School English—Who, What, Where, When, Why, and How

"Working the problem" is something like learning to conduct a good reference interview or completing a writing assignment in middle school. A heuristic model, such as a checklist, can be helpful, but the most important task is to think through the problem and learn as much about it as possible. Medical doctors are taught to do this; vital signs are called out as a patient is wheeled into an emergency room. Law students must also be taught this skill.

Table 1 breaks down the analytic elements of a typical research problem a new attorney may encounter as part of client interview or as part

TABLE 1 "Working the Problem" Schema

What you need to know	Sample questions
	Who?
Parties	Who are we representing (i.e., which side of the issue are we on–buyer or seller, plaintiff or defendant, etc.)? What legal entities are involved (any trusts, corporations, partnerships, etc.)?
	What?
Descriptive Words of Facts or Terms of Art	Besides the term "profit-sharing plan," are there other terms I should be using, like "pension" or "retirement"? I'm not sure if I understand the difference or if it matters. How else might a "sole shareholder" be described in the literature?
Descriptive Words of Legal Issues	Do you think that the best subject heading to describe the problem is "exemptions from creditors"?
Specific Sources to be Used	For my research on retirement plans and exemptions from creditors, is there any specific treatise or looseleaf service I should consult in addition to CCH's Pension Plan Guide?
	Where?
Applicable Jurisdictions	Do you want me to research federal bankruptcy law as well as California debtor-creditor law? Do you want me to confine my federal research to California? Are you interested in any other states? Are there any choice-of-law issues?
	When?
Time Periods	What time periods do you want me to research? Are the last two years sufficient? Does the time period (day, night, season, etc.) of any of the events in the case matter?
Time Deadlines/Priority	Do you want a quick answer or exhaustive research? If I complete this by Tuesday morning, is that OK?
	Why?
Objective	What are we trying to accomplish with this memo, brief, motion, contract, etc.? How do we want this to come out?
	How?
Precision/Recall[8]	Do you want all of the relevant journal articles or just the best article on the topic? Do you want all of the cases dealing with retirement plans in debtor-creditor law or just two or three cases that bear the closest relationship to the issue?
Billable Time/Costs	How long should this take me? Are billable hours limited? May I use Lexis and/or Westlaw? Which parts of the research, if any, would you do online? Do you want me to try and use free sources for my research? Has anyone ever done similar research on the topic that I should know about?
Presentations of Results and Reporting Back	How do you want me to present my results? Do you just want printouts marked with highlighter or a full memo? Should I check back with my initial results before proceeding any further?

of an assignment from a supervising attorney. For librarians, this may be recognizable as a reference interview, adapted for use in a law firm setting.

Considering the O.J. Simpson hypothetical in Figure 3, the task is to extract the terms that will lead to an understanding of the issue and ultimately the answer and relevant authority on the issue.

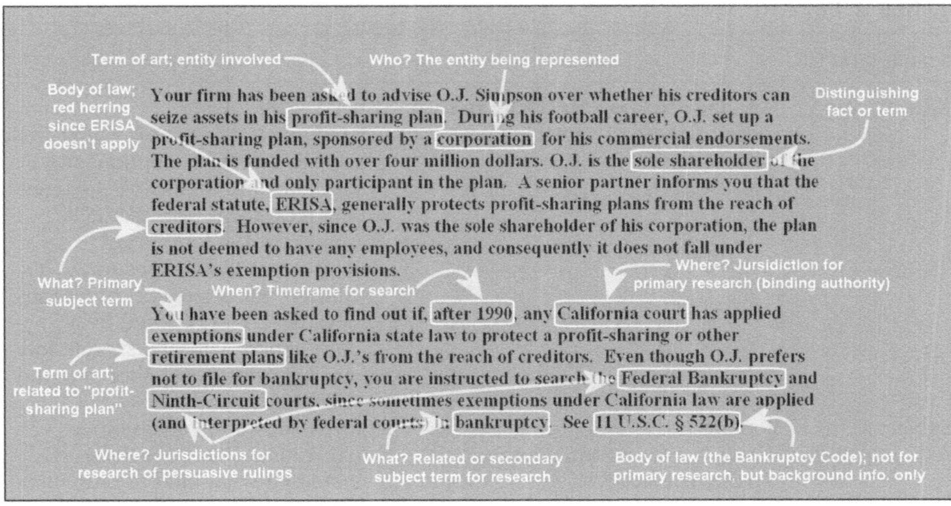

FIGURE 4 Illustration of key terms.

In the problem, as illustrated in Figure 4, the general subject area is the intersection of qualified retirement plans (or "profit-sharing plans") and debtor-creditor law. A possible start would be to use some index to either look up "creditor" under "profit-sharing plans" or inversely, "profit sharing" under "creditor." The issue involves the subject of "exemptions," which is generally a subtopic of debtor-creditor law. The narrow issue is the application of exceptions to "single person plans," which is a term of art used by practitioners, but often not found in indexes. If no such entry exists or a search for items using such terms bears no fruit, then I would search using combinations of "sole," "single," and "only" with "shareholder" and "stockholder." Finally, the research should only concern cases after 1990 in California state courts and in the Ninth Circuit (but limited to California cases).

What Kind of Problem Is It?

In library school, I had a marvelous teacher who gave me a schema for looking at types of problems related to government documents. While I immediately realized that the table could be readily adapted for legal research, the greater revelation was that while not all problems were alike, they could be grouped into types with certain types of problems requiring specific, yet different, strategies and resources for resolution. For instance, one of my first research problems in practice was, "What is the average age of retirement for female obstetricians/gynecologists in the Los Angeles area?" I was totally unnerved by the problem because it was of a type I had never encountered. Fundamentally, statistical problems require different strategies

TABLE 2 Problem Typing

Search type	Used for	Example
Known Item	You already know the citation, case name, name of an act, or have a very specific fact pattern to research.	I need *Roe v. Wade*. I need any California or Ninth Circuit case involving exemptions from creditors and the debtor's interest in a retirement plan that falls outside of the Employee Retirement Income Security Act's (ERISA) anti-alienation provisions, because it is sponsored by a corporation with one shareholder and no employees other than the shareholder.
Subject	You are not looking for a specific item but for information on a particular subject.	I am looking for something explaining ERISA generally, including what kind of retirement plans it covers. I need to understand exemptions from creditors in California.
Institutional	You know what you are looking for will be found at a particular institution, agency, or organization, or you want to find out what agency administers a particular program or enforces a particular law.	I need Department of Justice Rulings and Opinion Letters on when the merger of two large medical groups falls within the safe harbor provisions for antitrust issues. I need any Department of Labor rulings regarding the anti-alienation provisions of ERISA.
Statistical	You need statistical information from a government or other trustworthy source.	I need to know the percentage of children living below the poverty level in Los Angeles.
Special Techniques	You are searching for materials that require special interpretive or interdisciplinary skills.	I need legislative history and current legislation and regulatory action; budget, patent, census, and historical materials; government documents; international and foreign law; tax forms and IRS materials; scientific and technical reports; public records; or competitive business intelligence. I need the legislative history of the ERISA anti-alienation provisions.
News	You are searching for news stories.	I need accounts of the lawsuit in France by a humanitarian group against Yahoo!
Reference	You need basic background or definitional information.	I need to know the etymology of "escrow." I don't even know what "ERISA" is.

and resources to solve than do questions about the rule against perpetuities in North Dakota.

Table 2 was developed by my former Government Documents instructor from library school; I have modified it for legal research.[9]

Returning to the O.J. Simpson problem in Figure 3, even after having "worked" the problem with a "who, what, why, where, when, how" analysis (see Table 1), the researcher is not ready to start until she has figured out what kind of problem or problems she has on her hands. However, before suggesting problem types and matching them to resources, we need to map the terrain of resources.

SCHEMATA FOR UNDERSTANDING RESOURCES—CONCEPTUALLY MAPPING THE TERRAIN OF LEGAL RESOURCES

Like problem types, legal resources fall into different classes that can be organized in different ways. Two of the most common ways of arranging them are based on the distinction between primary and secondary and by chronology, subject, and citation.

Mapping Primary and Secondary Resources

Hopefully, students learn the distinction between primary and secondary resources during their first year. Because of the heavy focus during the first year on official or "flagship" primary resources (like the United States Code and United States Code Annotated), what is often more difficult to grasp is the appropriate use of combined primary and secondary resources. Table 3 illustrates a schema to help students arrange or map resources in relation to primary and secondary authority and their respective uses.

As a practicing attorney for nine years in the areas of tax, retirement plans, transactional law, and estate planning, combined resources of primary and secondary materials, such as the CCH Standard Federal Tax Reporter, dominated my research. The ability to jump between the Internal Revenue Service (IRS) code, regulations, commentary, and annotations was essential to understanding the law and efficiently researching complex problems. I suspect that for many attorneys, regardless of their area of expertise, secondary and combined resources dominate their research. Most questions are of a subject type, and so secondary and combined resources become more important than the use of the primary materials, which are often emphasized in firstyear legal research and writing.

The Wren Matrix

In 1986, Christopher G. Wren and Jill Robinson Wren introduced a matrix showing how all three branches of government had reporters or codes that were published in both chronological and topical formats.[11] Table 4 illustrates the Wrens' schema, but adding a new column for arrangements based upon citation.

TABLE 3 Primary and Secondary Authority

Type of resource	General examples	Binding upon	Used for
Primary	Constitutions	All branches of government.	Known item and institutional searches where you need binding authority.
	Codes and Session Laws (Statutes at Large)	Except as found unconstitutional, all branches of government.	
	Court Decision Reporters, Case Digests and *Words and Phrases* (1940-)[10]	Binding upon lower courts of the same jurisdiction and other branches of government.	
	Codified Regulations or Administrative Codes and Administrative Registers or Regulations	Legislative regulations (i.e., when Congress has delegated legislative rulemaking to an agency) may be binding upon the issuing agency and the general public. Interpretive regulations (i.e., issued to provide guidance of an agency's position on an issue or to clear up ambiguity) may hold an agency and the public bound to a particular interpretation of legislation to the extent courts do not disagree.	
	Administrative Agency Opinions and Rulings	Generally binding upon the agency. Sometimes, may only be binding upon the agency with respect to the parties in question.	
Secondary	Encyclopedias (e.g., *American Jurisprudence* (2d ed. 1961-)) Treatises and Hornbooks (e.g. Ronald D. Rotunda & John E. Nowak, *Treatise on Constitutional Law: Substance and Procedure* (4th ed. 2007) and David G. Owen, *Products Liability Law* (2d ed. 2008)) Law Reviews (e.g., articles reviewing particular areas of the law, such as Meredith L. Taylor, *North Carolina's Recognition of Tort Liability for the Intentional Infliction of Emotional Distress During Marriage,* 32 Wake Forest L. Rev. 1261(1997)) Professional & Bar Journals (e.g., Paul D. Callister, *Charitable Remainder Trusts: An Overview*, 51 TAX LAWYER 549 (1998)) Form Books (e.g., Jacob Rabkin and Mark H. Johnson, Current Legal Forms, with Tax Analysis (1948-))	Not binding.	Subject, statistical and special experience searches where you need to understand the issues and background of an area of law or problem. Also use to confirm your interpretation of a primary source.
Combined	Looseleafs (e.g., CCH Standard Federal Tax Reporter (1913-)) News Services (e.g., BNA, U.S. Law Week (1933-)) American Law Reports (6th ed. 2006)	Only primary sources have any binding authority.	Use when ease is important. Looseleafs combine statutes, regulations, commentary, and case law annotations in a topical arrangement with a good table of contents and indexing system.

TABLE 4 Arrangement of Primary Sources

		How the law is published (Arrangements)		
Institution	Kind of law	Chronologically	Topically	By citation
Legislature	Statutory Law	Session Laws	Statutory Codes	Shepard's, KeyCite, Annotated Codes
Courts	Case Law	Case Reports	Case Digests (summaries of primary authority)	Shepard's, KeyCite ALR
Agencies and Executive Branch	Administrative Law	Administrative Registers or Regulations	Administrative Codes	Shepard's, KeyCite, Annotated Codes

Going beyond the Wren's schema, I have added a column suggesting that the law is also organized by citations. Shepard's, KeyCite, code annotations, and American Law Reports (ALR) organize the law into "streams of precedent"[12] for cases and place codes within the context of their interpretation by courts and other statutes or regulatory materials. They allow researchers to see the law, not as a single case or statute, but as it evolves through time and interacts with other law around it. A former colleague of mine, Peter Hook, once suggested that the table could also be expanded to add a column for the "making" of the law: legislative history documents, briefs, tables of authority,[13] hearing transcripts, motions, and pleadings, regulatory rulemaking and agency decisions, executive orders, etc. Conspicuously missing from the arrangement is a row for constitutions and corresponding documents. Furthermore, international treaties and conventions might also be added as a row to the table. The point is to start with a simple schema and add on new resources and explain where they would fit. For example, the Digest of Decisions of the Federal Labor Relations Authority comes from the administrative branch and is topically arranged; it would find its place in the box with administrative codes.[14]

Intermediation Versus Disintermediation—The Final Dimension of Legal Research

Having divided the universe of resources into primary versus secondary and chronological versus topical arrangements, it is time to introduce the distinction that has profoundly impacted legal research—print versus electronic—and promptly denounce it as an inadequate distinction for failing to address the more important phenomenon of disintermediation and the collapse of hierarchical authority. A better way to describe the dichotomy is between human-intermediated indexes and disintermediated computer algorithms, such as free-text searching (whether incorporating Boolean terms and connectors or relevancy-ranked natural language algorithms).[15] Google and

Yahoo! illustrate this distinction. Google's natural language search mechanism works through a computer algorithm producing relevancy-ranked search results. In contrast, Yahoo! (which stands for "Yet Another Hierarchical Officious Oracle")[16] finds information based upon a hierarchical taxonomy classifying links intermediated by human beings. Web site operators submit links to Yahoo! Directory with category suggestions, and Yahoo! editors review the submission before linking the suggested site into the Yahoo! hierarchy.[17] Other current Web examples of intermediated systems are Wikipedia[18] and Delicious[19] where users vet and submit entries. In some ways, these systems might be described as user mediated, rather than expert intermediated (although the relative expertise of the content contributors of such systems is open to debate).[20]

The critical distinction for students to understand is between intermediation and disintermediation. In most instances, that distinction aligns with whether the service includes a controlled vocabulary index designed by human beings or whether access is provided via computer search algorithms of full text. Pedagogically, grounding the instruction in the difference between print and electronic promotes an underdeveloped schema for understanding the terrain of resources and hampers modeling how to match resources to problem types.

SCHEMATA FOR MATCHING PROBLEMS TO RESOURCES

Mapping Octants for Known Item and Subject Searches

In Figure 5 below, the terrain of research resources has been divided into octants. First, quadrants are formed by axes of primary versus secondary authority and chronological versus subject arrangement. Next, octants are formed by dividing the quadrants with the addition of a third axis—human-mediated controlled vocabulary indexes versus disintermediated computer algorithms. Most resources can be placed into this schema. The shaded areas illustrate the starting points for "known item" and "subject" searches, as previously defined in above. I have also posted an interactive schema that gives examples of resources in each of the research octants on the Web.[21]

To illustrate the schema's use, consider the O.J. Simpson problem. The researcher has been asked to find any cases in California courts or in the Ninth Circuit that have applied state law exemptions to prevent creditors from reaching the assets held in profit-sharing plans that do not fall under the anti-alienation protections of the Employee Retirement Income Security Act (ERISA; because they have single shareholder owners and technically no employees). These facts and issues are very narrow and particular. While the researcher does not know if such a case exists, this research question is a "known item" problem because a case with such a pattern of facts and issues may actually exist and therefore can be located and "known." If not,

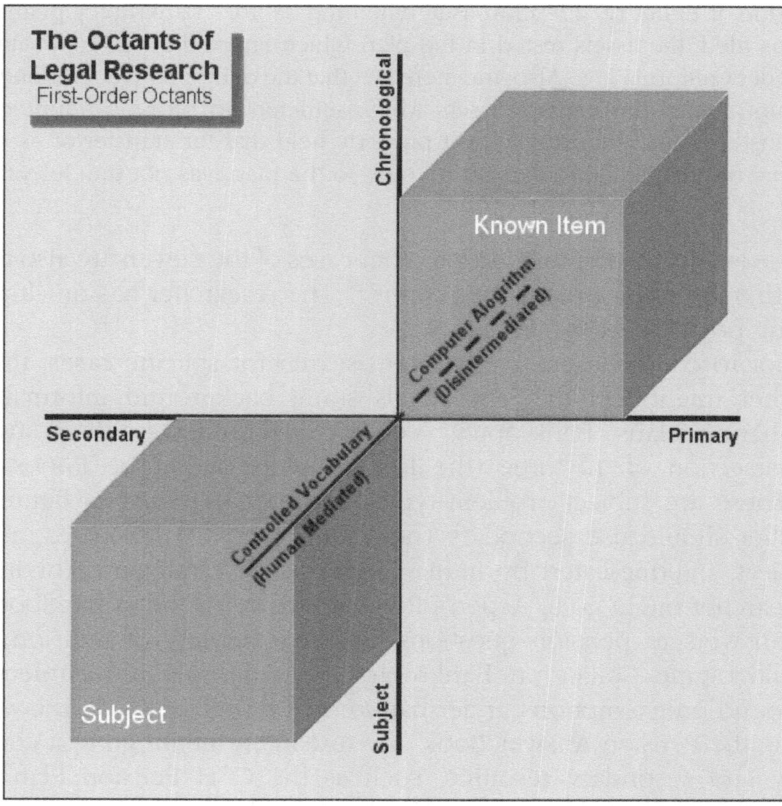

FIGURE 5 Legal research octants.

the researcher will have to broaden his or her search, including looking for an analogous situation, or move on to a subject search.

Per the octant schema in Figure 5, the researcher should probably start by searching the CA Federal & State Cases, Combined on Lexis (or similar database on Westlaw),[22] which is a primary, chronological, and algorithmic resource. A detailed terms-and-connectors search can be structured using the key terms identified in Figure 4 above:

((Creditor or Debtor)/p Exemption) & ("Profit-Sharing Plan" or "Retirement Plan") & ((Sole or Single or Only)/2 (Shareholder or Stockholder)) & (Date > 12/31/1990)

In this instance, the Lexis search retrieves eleven cases. Lexis' overview for the first case, *In re* Stern, reads:

> The appellate court found that the district court properly determined that the plan was not ERISA qualified at the time of the bankruptcy filing and thus, the plan's assets were not exempt from the bankruptcy estate by

> virtue of ERISA qualification. But, when the debtor's bankruptcy petition was filed, the assets rested in the plan which enjoyed an exempt status under California law. Also, the mere fact that the debtor converted nonexempt assets into exempt assets was insufficient to prove a fraudulent transfer. Thus, the district court properly held that the transfer of assets from the individual retirement account to the plan was not fraudulent.[23]

This case is directly on point. Seven other cases of the eleven are also relevant and within the appropriate jurisdictions.[24] The researcher has quickly found a starting point for further research.

Prior to conducting a known item search for specific cases, the same researcher might feel that she needs some background information on profit-sharing plans, bankruptcy,[25] debtor-creditor law, and, if available, the intersection of all three (the last of which might be impossible to find). These are subject problem types, and, per the chart in figure 5, the researcher should use secondary (non-"authoritative") resources, arranged by subject, intermediated by human indexers or catalogers. For instance, the researcher might go to Aspen's Pension Answer Book (a handbook with quick answers to pension questions and an overview of pension law),[26] the multivolume Collier on Bankruptcy, or California Jurisprudence (for background on exemptions under bankruptcy or debtor-creditor law). After perusing the Pension Answer Book, the researcher might go to a combined primary and secondary resource, such as the CCH Pension Plan Guide, accessing pertinent subjects by the index ("Bankruptcy ... exemptions ... failure to establish an ERISA plan)."[27]

Because the goal is to learn to use intermediated resources, instructors should not be concerned whether the students use these secondary, subject resources online or in print, provided that the online databases include usable indexes and tables of contents (that can be "drilled down").

In the above example, orienting the research toward a "subject" problem type does not retrieve resources that have dealt with the specificity required to answer the questions about retirement plans not falling under ERISA, but which still might be exempt from the reach of creditors; however, it does produce some important background for understanding the overall problem. In contrast, a known item search retrieved cases exactly on point. Consequently, understanding methodologies appropriate for each of the problem types is critical to the solution of this complex problem.

What about resources in the other six octants? There are resources that can be placed into each of these quadrants. They have their uses, as will be discussed below, but not in the initial stages of research with the only exception being for statutory law. Most of the time, the code (a topical arrangement of the law) is cited, rather than the chronological arrangement. Consequently, many known item problems referring to a statute may require searching the code, rather than the Statutes at Large or state session laws.

On the other hand, sometimes what is presented in the problem is the name of an act, such as ERISA, or a recently enacted bill. Answering this type of problem typically requires access through a "Popular Name" table for statutes (available in print and on Lexis and Westlaw), or on the Web through a free-text search of Thomas (using the name of a recently enacted bill).[28] Indeed, when codified, the text of many acts is separated and scattered throughout the code, and it is often easiest to read a statute in its chronological form in the Statutes at Large or state session laws.

In sum, the octants schema is really designed to help researchers separate those resources that should be used first from those that will be used later in the research cycle.

The Research Cycle

The uses of other octants in Figure 5 become more apparent in consideration of the larger research cycle.

Find the Most Relevant Documents

In Figure 6, the researcher starts at the top of the schema with "Finding the Most Relevant Documents" and then proceeds through each of the steps

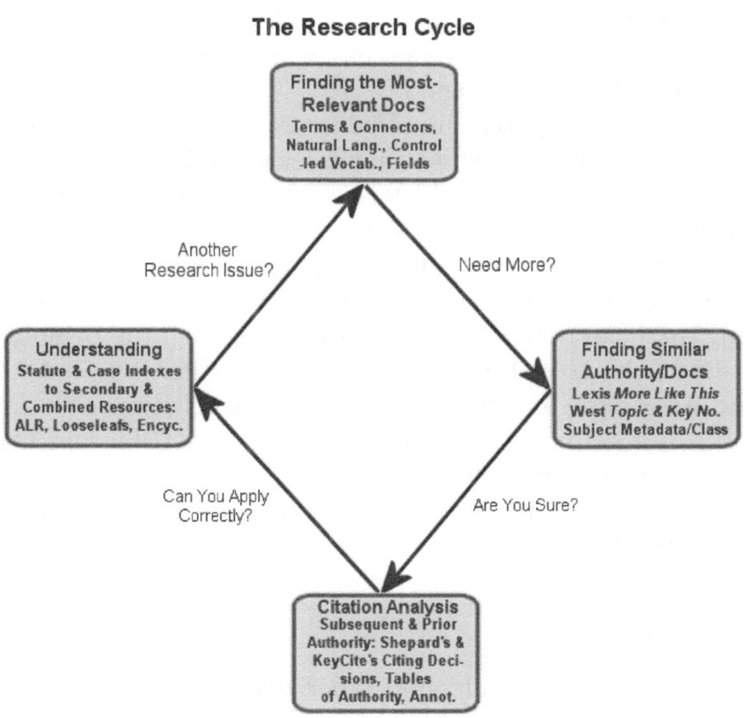

FIGURE 6 The research cycle.

until returning to the beginning, perhaps starting again with a new research issue. The first step in any research project, after "working the problem" and determining its type, is not to find everything on point—a common mistake among the uninitiated—but to find the most relevant document (or documents) on point. By moving quickly and rejecting items, even if tangentially related but not directly on point, the researcher can then go on to finding everything else she needs.

To illustrate "Finding the Most Relevant Document" in the O.J. Simpson problem, I used a "known item" methodology and constructed a term-and-connector search, limited by a date field, to attempt to find the most relevant cases on point in the Lexis CA Federal & State Cases, Combined.[29] Eight of my eleven cases were on point and within the relevant California and Federal jurisdictions. If I look at Lexis' Headnote 2 for *In re* Cheng,[30] the fifth case on point, it discusses the application of a specific statute, California Code of Civil Procedure § 704.115, which exempts assets of a profit-sharing plan from the reach of creditors in bankruptcy.[31]

Finding Similar Authority

Next I proceed to the step of the cycle of "Finding Similar Authority"—in this instance, other similar cases. I follow the hyperlink reading "More Like This" on the top navigation bar.[32] As seen in Figure 7, I use the "core terms" suggested by Lexis' natural language index and run my search in California Federal and State Cases, Combined.

The search retrieves one hundred cases because a relevancy ranked algorithm is used, but the most relevant cases should be on top, and indeed, the first case after *In re* Chang, which is its own best match, is *In re* Witwer.[33] In this decision, the Bankruptcy Court exempts profit-sharing assets from creditors under the same statute, California Code Civil Procedure § 704.115.

In Westlaw, finding similar cases can be done by searching for similar cases using the head note, Topic and Key Numbers at the beginning of the decision. By clicking on Key Number 163k49 k (Pension and Retirement Funds and Accounts), and then by using the search interface in Figure 8, I then can run a search in State and Federal Cases, California and find all similar cases as classified by West editors.[34]

Having found similar cases, it is now time to do citation analysis to check the status of the case law.

Citation Analysis

Citation analysis will also help find other relevant cases. With respect to Lexis and Westlaw, it is important to consider not only subsequent cases and history which may cast doubt on whether the original case is still good law,

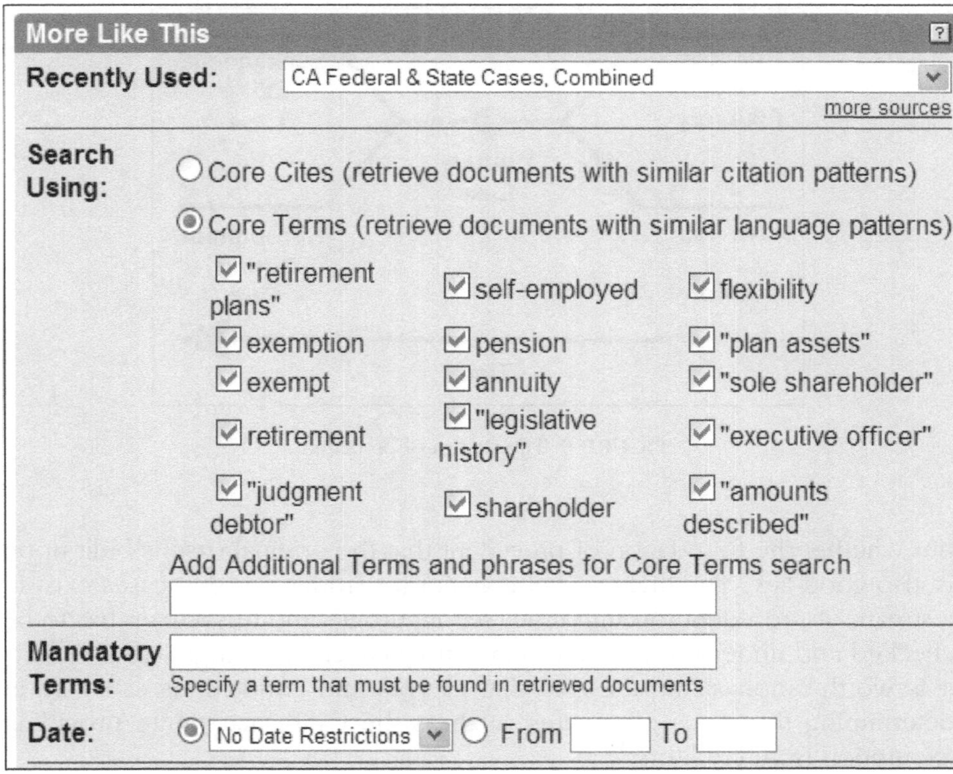

FIGURE 7 Lexis "More Like This" search.

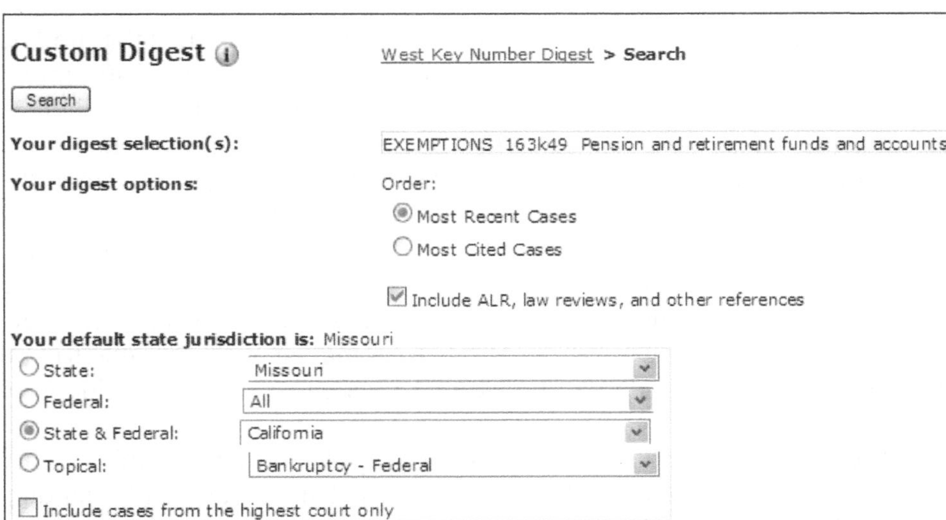

FIGURE 8 West key number search for similar cases.

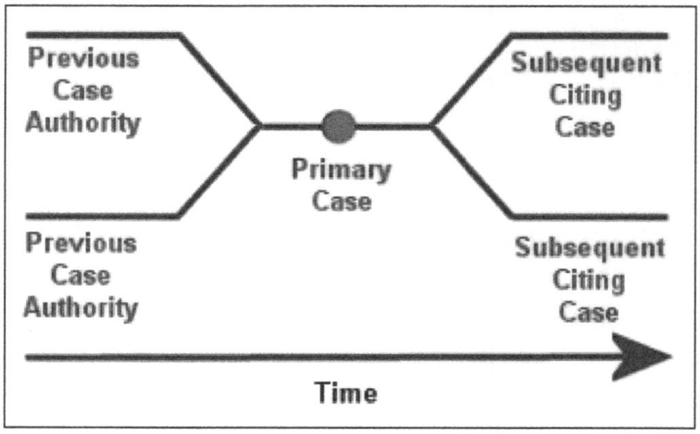

FIGURE 9 The stream of precedent.

but whether the foundation of precedent that the original case is built upon is also good law. The higher level concept for students is that cases exist in a stream of precedent through time (see Figure 9), and this stream has to be checked and understood, rather than simply checking a single case. Finally, it is worth emphasizing the role that citators and annotations can play in determining the status of statutes, such as the California statute providing exemption from creditors.[35]

Understanding

As a tax attorney, one of the important lessons I had to learn is that finding and reading the relevant statute usually did not lead to immediate understanding or resolution of the problem. Moreover, I usually found it difficult to place the statute into context. What case, regulation, Revenue Ruling, or other code section, perhaps a thousand sections away, might bear upon the statute? I quickly learned to put tax code sections into context and understand them by utilizing the CCH Standard Federal Tax Reporter,[36] a combined resource that includes the U.S. tax code, its legislative history, implementing regulations, analysis, and commentary (known as "CCH explanations"), and indexed annotations. By linking the code to commentary, I was able to find my way to an understanding of the code, issues involved, and resolution of my research problem.

The lesson I learned with the tax code applies to almost any primary material. How does a researcher make sure that his or her understanding of a particular case, code section, regulation, or statute comports with that of other attorneys and judges? For California, the researcher could look up the applicable case, *In re* Stern[37] in the "Table of Cases" for California Jurisprudence, and see what, if anything, has been said by commentators about it. Likewise, the researcher can look up California Code of Civil Procedure § 704.115 in the "Table of Statutes."[38] Similar research can be done for federal cases in *American Jurisprudence or Corpus Juris Secundum*. If the case is cited or, better yet, annotated in *American Law Reports (ALR)*, there may be a wealth of information leading to understanding the case. If the case is annotated, a researcher would be foolish to ignore what *ALR* has to say about the case (since it is a collection of "slices of the law," based upon most-representative cases). Using citation analysis with Lexis and Westlaw, law reviews, treatises, and other materials can be quickly located to help with understanding statutes, regulations, cases, constitutions, and other primary sources.

CONCLUSION

Experts think differently than novices. By using schemata, they can see patterns and rapidly organize information and problems to reach resolutions. This paper has presented a complex problem and a series of schemata necessary for its resolution as an example of one approach to legal research and analysis. These schemata appeared in three major parts—those designed to help work or see the problem, those dedicated to understanding the terrain of legal resources, and those matching resources to problem types and outlining the legal research process.

The schemata in this article are not meant to be the "be all and end all" of legal research. Rather, they should challenge legal research instructors and librarians to make explicit their own implicit schemata. Hopefully, my colleagues will refine my schemata and introduce their own to the profession. For instance, schemata for institutional, statistical, special, news, and reference searches have not been explored in this article.[39] Ideally, our students will not only adopt and master such schemata for problem solving, but they will also learn to assess and adapt them as needed.

Much of legal academia does not view legal research instruction as anything but training in a mechanical exercise. At a recent faculty meeting dedicated to curriculum reform, a colleague of mine propounded that legal research lacked critical reasoning skills and therefore had lesser priority. Hopefully, this article illustrates that legal research is anything but a mechanical, rote exercise. It requires critical thinking and creativity, including the application of abstract concepts and systems to concrete, complex problems.

I hope the progression of schemata also suggests the possibility of a common hierarchical taxonomy of skills, a Bloom's Taxonomy,[40] to help establish a common vocabulary, define problem-solving skills more precisely, provide a general order for their introduction to students, and set down benchmarks for the improvement and assessment of research skills. Such a project might go a long way toward improving the standing of legal research in the law school curriculum, but it is a project far beyond the scope of this paper and any one librarian. It must be embarked upon by law librarians and research instructors as a collective, organized effort, perhaps under the auspices of the American Association of Law Libraries.

In criticizing the absence of any discussion of legal research in the Carnegie Foundation's 2007 report on legal education, Richard Leiter notes: "The absence of focused treatment of legal research in the modern debate about reform of legal education happens because we don't have an accurate vocabulary and virtually no research of our own to give form to the discussion."[41] Vocabulary is an initial step in creating a Bloom's Taxonomy. It is part and parcel of constructing the schemata that expert researchers use to solve problems. Arranging vocabulary and schemata into a hierarchical taxonomy that defines the progression of necessary cognitive skills is the ultimate objective. Such taxonomy would establish a credible pedagogy, help communicate the indispensible role of legal research instruction in curriculum reform, and most importantly, improve the research skills of the legal profession.

In closing, my plea is that my colleagues take up the challenge of grounding legal research instruction in a common taxonomy of interrelated schemata, technical vocabulary, and progression of cognitive skills. The failure to have done so suggests that we do not take our own field seriously, and if we do not, why should we expect colleagues from other fields to do so? Indeed, this omission may have kept legal research instruction off of the radar of the elite pedagogues already laboring mightily in the cause of legal education reform. At this critical juncture, we must make the effort to add rigor to our pedagogy by finally defining it. Our students and law faculty colleagues do not "first see, and then define." We must first define, and then they will see.[42]

NOTES

1. Walter Lippmann, *Public Opinion* 81 (7th printing, Macmillan 1961).

2. Commission on Behavioral and Social Sciences and Education, *How People Learn: Brain, Mind, Experience, and School* (expand. ed. 31 National Academics Press 2000), available at http://books.nap.edu/openbook.php?record_id=9853

3. *Id.* (note items 2 and 4).

4. *See Types of Thinking: Expert and Novice Thinking*, Encyclopedia Britannica Online, available at http://www.search.eb.com/eb/article-275929 (last visited 22 Jan. 2009). Throughout this paper, I use the term the technical term "schemata" or "schema" for the singular, but I mean it in the broadest sense to include mental constructs, conceptual frameworks, paradigms, and heuristics.

5. Lippmann, *supra* n.1

6. Parts of this section initially appeared in Paul D. Callister, *Working the Problem*, 91 Ill. B.J. 43, 43 (2003).

7. Apollo 13 (Universal Pictures 1995) (motion picture).

8. Precision is a ratio of relevant documents expressed as:

$$\left(\frac{\text{Number of Relevant Documents Retrieved}}{\text{Total Number of Documents Retrieved}}\right) \times 100$$

Recall is defined:

$$\left(\frac{\text{Number of Relevant Documents Retrieved}}{\text{Total Number of Relevant Documents in the Collection}}\right) \times 100$$

F.W. Lancaster, *Precision and Recall*, 2 Encyclopedia of Library and Information Science 2346, 2346 (Marcia J. Bates, Mary Niles Maack & Miriam Drake eds., 2d ed. Taylor & Francis 2003).

9. For the original schema, as used with government documents, see Jean L. Sears & Marilyn K. Moody, *Using Government Information Sources: Electronic and Print* 5–9 (3d ed. Oryx Press 2001).

10. The placement of case digests and *Words and Phrases* as primary materials may seem odd given their topical arrangement as indexes, but the idea is that they provide a subject arrangement of case summaries granting access directly to the case reporters without intervening commentary.

11. *See* Christopher G. Wren & Jill Robinson Wren, *The Legal Research Manual: A Game Plan for Legal Research and Analysis* 6 (2d ed. Legal Publishing 1986); and Christopher G. Wren & Jill Robinson Wren, *The Teaching of Legal Research*, 80 L. Lib. J. 7, 35 matrix A (1988).

12. For a schemata illustrating precedent in the stream of time, see *infra* and accompanying text.

13. By "tables of authority" (sometimes "points of authority"), I mean the sources cited in a case that, together with that case and subsequent cases, make up the "stream of precedent." Tables of authority can be accessed in the Shepard's and KeyCite features of Lexis and West's online services, respectively. *See infra* figure 9 and accompanying text.

14. *See* Office of Information Resources and Research Services, Digest of Decisions of the Federal Labor Relations Authority (1989-).

15. Both term-and-connector searching and relevancy-ranked natural language searching, each of which is offered by Lexis and Westlaw, operate by computer algorithm. In the case of the former, the search interface responds to specific commands (such as "w/5" or "and") to construct its database search. "Terms-and-connector" searching includes Boolean search commands such as "and," "or," and "not." In contrast, relevancy-ranked natural language searching involves a computer algorithm which "resorts" the database with the most relevant documents "on top." The algorithm may favor documents with search terms that are proximate to each other, in certain fields, or which appear multiple times in the same document. The exact operation of a relevancy-ranked natural language algorithm is proprietary and usually not disclosed. See Danny C.C. Poo & Christopher S.G. Khoo, *Online Catalog Subject Searching*, 2 Encyclopedia of Library and Information Science 2218, 2224 (2003) (description of relevancy-ranked natural language searching); Paul D. Callister, *Introduction to Online Legal Research, Westlaw: Natural Language Searches*, available at http://www1.law.umkc.edu/faculty/callister/bootcamp/ot/NL01.html (last visited 26 Nov. 2008) (archived version of Westlaw and Lexis online services tutorial initially prepared for the University of Illinois College of Law in 2002).

16. *Yahoo! Press Room: FAQ*, available at http://yhoo.client.shareholder.com/press/faq.cfm (follow link to "What does Yahoo! Stand for?") (last visited 12 Sept. 2008). Google's name plays upon the mathematical term, "googol" meaning one with one hundred zeros after it. *Google: Corporate Information*, available at http://www.google.com/intl/en/corporate (last visited 26 Jan. 2009).

17. *See Yahoo! Directory Suggest a Site*, available at http://add.yahoo.com/fast/add (last visited 12 Sept. 2008). Students may confuse Yahoo! Directory with its search engine, which is also algorithmic.

18. *Wikipedia*, available at http://www.wikipedia.org/ (last visited 26 Jan. 2009).

19. *Delicious Social Bookmarking*, available at http://delicious.com/ (last visited 26 Jan. 2009).

20. Jim Giles, *Internet Encyclopedias Go Head to Head*, 438 Nature 900 (2005) (reporting study finding 162 factual errors versus 123 such errors in Wikipedia compared with Encyclopedia Britannica); Paulo N. Correa, Alexandro N. Correa & Malgosia Askanas, *Wikipedia: A Techno-Cult of Ignorance*, available at http://www.aetherometry.com/Electronic_Publications/ Politics_of_Science/Antiwikipedia/awp_index.html (last visited 28 Nov. 2008).

21. Paul D. Callister, *Thinking About Legal Research Problems, Putting a Search Together*, available at http://www1.law.umkc.edu/faculty/callister/bootcamp/Survival/tab5.html (last visited 29 Nov. 2008).

22. For Lexis, see Cases: U.S./Federal & State Cases By State/ CA Federal & State Cases, Combined. For Westlaw, see California State and Federal Cases (CA-CS-ALL).

23. *Gill v. Stern (In re* Stern), 345 F.3d 1036 (9th Cir. 2003), *cert. denied; Stern v. Gill*, 541 U.S. 936 (U.S. 2004) (quote from the Lexis Case Summary Overview).

24. *Cheng v. Gill (In re)*, 182 F.3d 1027 (9th Cir. 1999); *Cheng v. Gill (In re* Cheng*)*, 943 F.2d 1114 (9th Cir. Cal. 1991); *In re* Smith, 1998 U.S. Dist. Lexis 22964 (C.D. Cal. 1998), *rev'd on other grounds; Smith v. Kennedy* (*In re* Smith), 235 F.3d 472 (9th Cir. Cal. 2000); *In re* Acosta, 182 B.R. 561 (N.D. Cal. 1994); *McDonald v. Metz* (Metz), 225 B.R. 173 (B.A.P. 9th Cir. Cal. 1998); *Southern Cal. Permanente Med. Group v. Ehrenberg* (*In re* Moses), 215 B.R. 27 (B.A.P. 9th Cir. Cal. 1997); *In re* Witwer, 148 B.R. 930 (Bankr. C.D. Cal. 1992), *aff'd mem; In re* Witwer, 163 B.R. 614 (B.A.P. 9th Cir. 1994).

25. As noted in figure 4 above, researching federal bankruptcy law is really only necessary for background information: to understand that sometimes bankruptcy and federal appellate courts apply state exemptions under 11 U.S.C § 522 (b), and that any interpretive rulings by such courts on California exemption law may be persuasive authority.

26. *See* Stephen J. Krass, *The Pension Answer Book,* ¶ Q 4:26 (2008 ed.) (by searching under "Creditors" in the index, a reference to "qualified retirement plans" can be found, but the discussion in the section is confusing because of the multiple jurisdictions it covers and the fact that it never really goes beyond the issue of whether a plan falls under ERISA and its anti-alienation provisions or whether the plan was properly qualified by the IRS).

27. 1 Pension Plan Guide (CCH) (no paragraph numbering for citing the index, look under "Bankruptcy" in the index).

28. *See* Library of Congress, Thomas, available at http://thomas.loc.gov (last visited 29 Nov. 2008).

29. For search terms, see text accompanying *supra* n. 23.

30. 943 F.2d 1114.

31. California's state exemption statute applies here because under 11 U.S.C. § 522 (b) (2000 & Supp. V 2007) the debtor may use exemptions designated by state statutes rather than those provided in the Bankruptcy Code. Pursuant to Cal Civ. Proc. Code § 703.140 (Deering 2008), debtors may elect to use any exemption from creditors in the California code's chapter, including § 704.115, which exempts "[a]ll amounts held, controlled, or in process of distribution" from a profit-sharing plan. See *id.* at (a)(2) and (b).

32. In the octant schema, this particular Lexis "More Like This" search is a primary, subject, computer algorithm search.

33. *In re* Witwer, 148 B.R. 930 (Bankr. C.D. Cal. 1992).

34. Unlike Lexis' "More Like This" searching, West's "Topic and Key Number" searching is mediated by human beings, and it would be placed in the primary, subject, human-intermediated octant.

35. Citators and annotations are organized by citation (using a combination of subject, jurisdiction, and chronological arrangements) and are located in the third column of table 4, as a category separate from topical or chronological arrangements of law. As such, they are not included as a dimension in the octant schema. It should be noted that Lexis' Shepard's and West's KeyCite are distinguishable on the basis of intermediation. The former is human intermediated, and the latter depends upon computer algorithm.

36. As a combined resource, CCH's Standard Federal Tax Reporter falls both into the primary, subject, controlled vocabulary octant for its arrangement of the tax code, regulations, and annotations of citing cases and IRS rulings (codes, regulations, and annotations follow topical arrangements) and the secondary, subject, controlled vocabulary octant for its CCH Explanations, which are written by editors.

37. *Gill v. Stern* (*In re* Stern), 345 F.3d 1036, 541 U.S. 936.

38. Enforcement of Judgments, 30 Cal. Jur. § 294 (3rd ed. 2000) (discussion of exemptions for private retirement plans in Cal Civ. Proc. Code § 704.115).

39. *See supra*

40. *See* Committee of College and University Examiners, 1 Taxonomy of Educational Objectives: Cognitive Domain 201–207 (Benjamin S. Bloom ed., 31st prtg. Longman 1987).

41. Richard A. Leiter, *The Missing Lawyering Skill, A New Book on Legal Education Demonstrates the Lack of Attention Paid to Legal Research Training,* AALL Spectrum, 22, 25 (July 2008). *See also* William M. Sullivan, et al., Carnegie Foundation for the Advancement of Teaching, *Educating Lawyers: Preparation for the Practice of Law* (Jossey–Bass 2007) (as Leiter has pointed out, note the lack of any reference to "legal research," "library," or "research" in the index).

42. *See* Lippmann *supra* n. 1

Teaching Advanced Legal Research: Philosophy and Context

ROBERT C. BERRING and KATHLEEN VANDEN HEUVEL[1]
Berkeley Law School, University of California, Berkeley, California, USA

Is there a philosophy that grounds the teaching of advanced legal research (ALR)? Can a coherent identity be found? The authors draw upon the experience of twenty-five years of teaching ALR to large numbers of students to puzzle this question out. Are we teaching a mechanical skill? Are we offering a course in jurisprudence? Are we simply forcing the students to teach themselves? Has the information revolution changed the whole enterprise? Basing the discussion on the context of legal information, the students, and the law, the authors try to find an answer to these fundamental questions.

THE SETUP

Writing an article that sets forth a philosophy of teaching Advanced Legal Research (ALR) is a presumptuous exercise. Articulating a philosophy of law librarianship itself has been enough of a challenge.[2] At least the field of law librarianship has the ethos of a profession with its own professional association that grapples with standards and issues of identity. While there is a rich literature about teaching legal research, complete with a healthy subset of writings about teaching ALR,[3] there is no developed professional cohort. There is no center to the enterprise.

Each person who offers a course in ALR may have her own ideas and concepts as to what she is doing. In this age of empirical research, we would not presume to venture a guess as to what others think they are doing when they teach an ALR course without the use of a well-designed survey instrument. (Trust us, we do not intend to create one, but would love to see it done). But our experience tells us that ALR courses take many forms. One of the weaknesses of the field of teaching legal research has been the failure to identify an intellectual structure for it. Courses sprang up to meet a growing need, often on an *ad hoc* basis. Some focus on special topics; some center on Boolean skills; some are tied to other parts of the curriculum. Viewed by an outsider, there is no unifying thread. To borrow a quotation from Gertrude Stein, there is no there there.[4]

Part of this problem is rooted in the fact that ALR is usually identified on the law school curriculum as a skills course. At top tier law schools, skills courses are at the intellectual margin.[5] They are seldom taught by regular faculty members; in fact, most faculty members at the prestigious law schools lack the real-world expertise to teach them. Skills courses do not lead to the production of academic law review articles, which is the coin of the realm in the world of legal education. Though we think that the ground will soon shift, for now publishing abstract, heavily footnoted pieces in academic law reviews is the path to promotion and status for faculty in the best law schools. While skills courses can be central to the experience of law students, they seldom appear on the radar of the tenure-track faculty.

Given this state of affairs, most observers would contend that a course in ALR has never needed a philosophy. Besides, what could be philosophical about doing research? The answer is, of course, that teaching ALR can be the most deeply philosophical of endeavors. Our approach to a philosophy of ALR parallels the pedagogy that we employ when teaching it. That is the course that we will follow in this article. A bit of perspective on the relation of legal information to ALR will be the start. Then we will reflect on the way the world was, the way the world is, and what the world may be. Following that, we will provide some functional descriptions of what we do and why we do it. Somewhere in there, a philosophy will emerge.

LEGAL INFORMATION AND ALR

Legal information, its classification, and forms of retrieval are at the heart of legal thinking. Legal information informs legal structure. It dictates how law students, law professors, and lawyers think. Understanding legal information can only be accomplished by learning how to use it. Legal research connects legal information to its user. It is not just a process; the researcher is not just performing an action. In carrying out legal research, one brings legal information to life. Legal research is not just a vehicle for gathering data. The way research is done profoundly affects the information itself. Anyone who understands the inner structure of the soul of legal information understands the workings of the substantive law.

We have been teaching ALR at Berkeley for 23 years. One of the reasons that we started a course in ALR was because it was frightening to us to realize how little most law school graduates knew about the materials that were the basic tools of their profession. Contrary to what most law students thought (that is if they thought about it at all), the forms in which legal information appeared were not divinely ordained or historical inevitabilities. They resulted from editorial choices, market forces, and social pressures, translated through the life cycle of profit-making enterprises. When we began teaching ALR, there were long-standing referents in the process of legal research. Everyone used the same set of tools; the cognitive authority of legal research was mapped out. It had been mapped out for so long that no one even noticed it any longer. This well-established galaxy of legal sources made life easier, but it also made many researchers uncritical consumers. One of the reasons that top tier schools tolerated horrendous first-year legal research programs was that the pathways for the researcher were so well worn that it was assumed that everyone would just "catch on."[6]

THE WORLD WHEN WE STARTED

Take the old paper sets of Shepard's Citators, in the days before KeyCite as an example. Everyone used Shepard's Citators to ascertain the validity of a case. Getting students to use the paper Shepard's correctly was a challenge in itself, but our goal was to make the student see ***why*** everyone used Shepard's and how to make the ***best*** use of it. Our goal was to prevent the student from just blindly Shepardizing his case; we wanted him to understand how the citator was assembled, to recognize what the superscript letters and numbers meant, to question what algorithm the Shepard's editors used to produce the tool. (Of course, we would not have used the word algorithm then). One of our mantras has always been, "Use what they give you." Understand the tool. The folks at Shepard's Citators have built in special features that are designed to assist you. Use those features.

Shepard's was not alone. It was part of a fixed universe of tools. We struggled to help our students understand the blueprints for this world of legal information. Our mission was to wake them up, to shake them out of their comfortable assumptions, and to compel them to take research seriously.[7] It was a worthy quest, one we enjoyed. But the tectonic plates of legal information shifted. As the paper culture in which we had grown up began to fade away, the problems changed. The students changed. The tools changed. ALR changed too.

Over the past decade, most of the time-honored sources of information have been swept away or deeply changed by the information revolution. In 2008, teaching ALR is not a matter of explaining the soul of long-established tools. The problem today is not the need to wean students from the existing systems or to make them at least see the value of the existing systems. Today we have to work hard to make our students perceive that there are systems at all. The nature of legal authority is up for grabs.

THE WORLD WE TEACH IN TODAY

Two things have dramatically changed in teaching ALR. The first is the students. The second is the information.

The law student of 1983, that person who used the deeply rooted paper system, is quite different from her counterpart of today. The law student of 2008 is a practiced user of Google and Wikipedia. They communicate via text messaging and Facebook. They own an iPhone that allows them to download videos directly from the Internet. They expect to type a search term into a box and get a result. Many are loath to use indices at all. The idea of a two-step look-up as a part of the research process is an anathema to them. Hyperlinks are an inalienable right.

None of the preceding paragraph is written with a fist shaken in anger at the sky. Resenting change is a fool's errand. That paragraph simply describes the way things are in 2008. The student of 1983 had grown up using libraries and books. He had a deep understanding of how the print culture worked, even if he did not know that he did. Even if he would use a library catalog only when in extremis, he could do it if pressed. For many students in our 2008 ALR class, the utility of a library catalog has to be established through logical argument. Nor do we claim that our logical argument always prevails. These students live in a different world.[8] Anyone who has shown the online version of the Index to Legal Periodicals to a law student and who has seen the look of befuddlement come over her face when she is told that the full text of each indexed article is not linked to its citation, knows whereof I speak. Whether one admires or fears the law student of 2008, one cannot change her.

It is not just the law students that have changed. The whole field of legal information is shifting. We do not just refer to the format in which the information is used. The very nature of the information itself is changing. Today's Supreme Court debates what materials may be cited as binding. Do legislative histories count?[9] What about international and foreign law?[10] The Courts are grappling with the true nature of precedent as the very question of what judicial authority undergoes analysis.[11] The role of legislative materials and how they relate to Presidential power is festering at the federal level. The role and authority of administrative materials is shifting with the change in formats brought on by the omnipresence of laptops and the Internet. As individual administrative agencies experiment with their own Web sites and forms of information distribution, the old templates for publication are gone. These questions of what constitutes the law and legal authority are not new, but they are getting more central each day.

The old paper sets stagger on as mortally wounded dinosaurs. But no one pays them much mind any longer. Reality lies in Lexis and Westlaw; searching grows from the roots of Google. New for-profit players like Bloomberg nibble at the edges. Heroic altruistic efforts like Jurist and the venerable Legal Information Institute try to offer an alternative. As Lexis and Westlaw have been bought up and conflated with other information products, it is hard to say what the legal research landscape will look like in 2010, let alone 2018. Ten years down the road is a lifetime. We view our role as teachers of ALR to prepare the students for whatever happens down that road. We tell our students that each of them will be an important consumer of legal information. ALR is about training in critical thinking about information. We are not simply instructing them in how to carry out legal research—we are trying to assist them to become a generation that will demand high-quality legal information. A good deal is at stake.

There was a need for an underlying philosophy for ALR in the time of paper information. Today the need is even more acute. Rather than setting forth an abstract set of principles, we have decided that the best way to set out our philosophy of teaching ALR in the wild days of 2008 is to set our ideas in the terms that we present it to our students. We urge them to see legal information and the process of legal research in terms of context. The pedagogy of Paolo Freire has always influenced us.[12] Freire would say that one does not transfer bits of knowledge, one teaches a process of thinking and discovery. When it works, the students learn with us, and the teaching is an exciting process. That is how we will present it here.

CONTEXT 1.0

When teaching ALR, it is crucial to provide the context of the legal information that is discussed. Some term this a *functional* approach to legal research. Our premise is that rather than instructing the student in how to find a particular piece of information, we offer the student an understanding of the information itself. This idea was rooted in the world of paper, when we wanted students to understand what to do if a familiar book was off the shelf. It is even more important today.

For example, when teaching about carrying out research using judicial decisions, it is vital to make clear how judicial opinions are produced, how they come to be written and distributed. The opinion of the judge does not emerge fully formed from the heavens. It is the product of a creative process, a process imbued with editorial and intellectual, as well as commercial and mechanical, elements. The judge reacts to the briefs of counsel, argues with other judges on the panel, responds to the record from below, and may have a clerk author the actual opinion. The judge decides if the opinion should be published so that it enters into the stream of precedent. Publishers, both official and commercial, add editorial value to the opinion via a syllabus, headnotes, and a research system. If the student can see this process of creation, she can deal with the information that is part of it, no matter how it is formatted. She can also be prepared for the changes in the mix of information that may come. The only thing that we are sure of is that change ***will*** come.

One way we attempt to get the student to work through these ideas is by means of an exercise where we ask the students to construct the perfect tool for researching a judicial opinion. On a good day, when we push and the classroom comes alive, the students come to see the value of trial court proceedings, discovery materials, and briefs as leading to the opinion. They can also see the utility of citators, commentary, law review articles, expertise from practice, and connections with statutes, regulations, and nonlegal sources leading from the opinion. The judicial opinion is not just a static bit of precedent, it is the center of an information universe. It can be sliced and diced.

We perform an exercise where an opinion moves from the judge's idea, through a clerk's draft, through a judicial conference, to the Thomson Company, through the editing, headnoting, and digesting system, into the Westlaw system, complete with hooks and links. Now the student can see the opinion as one element in an information stream. What she sees on her Westlaw screen or on the printed page is just one step in a process.

If the student comes away with an understanding of how the information is generated and how the form of the information that she sees is produced, then she can handle format changes and new media. The form of the information is not determinative. It is the information itself that matters. Functional understanding of legal information is the start.

This concept is equally important in dealing with statutory material and administrative rules and regulations. Due to the strange structure of legal education, many law students have very little knowledge of these sources. In a sense, this makes it easier to discuss the concepts with them. We do not have to overcome sloppy research habits; we begin with a blank slate. But the same rules apply. We take as an example a piece of enacted legislation, in recent years the U.S.A. Patriot Act. We then work through each step in the legislative process. It is worth noting that many of our highly intelligent second- and third-year law students have either never learned, or have forgotten, the basic high school civics lessons in how a bill becomes law. Step-by-step review of the law-making process, using the Patriot Act, is necessary. In the fall of 2008, we queried our class of 70 as to how many knew what the Statutes at Large might be. Five responded that they knew. This was a salutary reminder of the real state of law school research skills. One of the tricks to teaching ALR over an extended period of time is the need to remember how much the students do not know. We sometimes chuckle at the fact that the course is titled "Advanced Legal Research." Isn't reviewing how a bill becomes law the most basic of legal research tasks? We are teaching them an advanced method of understanding the materials, but you need a foundation before you can build. One can never forget the basics.

When examining a piece of legislation, the student should see the evolution of documents and commentary that lead to the passage of a new law. A textured understanding of legislative history can assist the student in understanding both the realities of statutory research and the best way to find sources. We do not just present a stack of documents—we show the students tools like *CQ Weekly*, *Roll Call*, and the *National Journal*. We want them to see the context of how the law is passed. How is it that a statute comes to be codified? How is an annotated code constructed? How does all of this tie into the process of amendment?

The student with a grasp of this information stream understands legislative materials, and she can put it in context. She comprehends how the world of legislation works. This functional approach will serve her well.

CONTEXT 2.0

Students tend to view ALR as an exercise in acquiring and practicing a skill. They are not wrong. We do teach a skill. But we understand that legal research consists of much more than knowing what database to use or what search engine to employ. We want the students to see the information in its intellectual context. The jurisprudential influence of legal information lies at the center of this enterprise.

If the context of legal information is blended into the story of the development of the common law, learning about legal research becomes an exercise in learning about the internal structure of the law itself. Many students approach legal research with the idea that it will be little more than advanced Lexis and Westlaw training. By placing legal information into the frame of the development of American law, the course can be elevated for them. These roots in legal history and jurisprudence are not simply tacked on to the course; they form part of its core. What are the Restatements? Why are law reviews so important? What accounted for the death of the monumental treatise? Why do people still care about the Key Number System? What does the doctrine of precedent really mean? Scholars from Holmes to A.W.B. Simpson have seen the central role of legal information.[13] The law student of 2008 should know that the centrality of legal information is not new. Is the use of legislative history in arguing a case legitimate? These are all important questions. Weaving each of them into a tapestry of intellectual legitimacy can give the student a framework to hang the research concepts on.

ASSIGNMENTS

Some elements of carrying out high-quality legal research involve the careful development of skill and judgment. They cannot be explained; they must be learned through experience. No matter how clearly we present the information on how to perform a research task, unless the student does it herself, the skill will not take hold. For this reason, we have concentrated our research training efforts on second- and third-year law students via the course in ALR. Most first-year law students do not have enough context to apply the skills that they learn in research and writing. In any case, most of those classes now emphasize writing skills. But even if research was a focus, the first-year law student, immersed in the classic first-year curriculum, has no way to employ the new skills.[14] The second-year student has much more background and may well have the added incentive of a harrowing summer employment experience during which she was asked to find a recent letter ruling of the Internal Revenue Service or to do a quick legislative history of a newly enacted statute and had no idea how to proceed.

The motivated student with sufficient background can, with our help, teach herself how to do legal research. This is the tricky bit of the way that we conceive ALR. There is only so much the instructor can do before the limits of time and energy intrude. If we want to teach classes of 75, and we do, we cannot offer one-on-one tutoring. The student must be required to use the new skills in a realistic environment. To this end, we assign open-ended questions which require the students to do real-world research. Put simply, they teach themselves. We grade the assignments and return each one before the next one is due. To make this system work, we must grade the assignments with dispatch. If the assignments that we return are to be of any use, we must write comments on each one. Since we use four problem sets each semester, we are required to invest considerable time in grading and commenting on student work. Using teaching assistants does not work for us. Each of us, and there are three of us who team teach the course, must commit to reading and commenting on one question on each assignment. It is not a simple regimen for the instructors, but we have found no other way to accomplish our goal. Until we can devise some way to leverage our efforts, extensive investment of time and energy is required. Sweat equity is a component in our philosophy of teaching ALR.

CONCLUSION

Our philosophy of teaching ALR does not admit to a simple summary. However we put it will be both too grandiose and too simplistic. It is one part information theory, one part jurisprudence, five parts critical thinking, and fifty parts student-generated learning. The course is odd from the start because we recognize that we are not as deft at using many of the online search engines and databases that we discuss as our students are. But we want them to be more than nimble—we want them to understand what they are doing and the nature of the information with which they are working. They are the future. Decisions about the quality and integrity of legal information will be made in the coming decade. Those decisions will not be made by us; they will be made by our students. If we can make them critical judges of the new formats and search engines (and whatever currently inconceivable things that are to come), if we can make them demand more than just speed and ease of use, we will have done our job.

NOTES

1. The royal "we" is used throughout this article. Bob taught the ALR course for a few years before Kathleen who, after having taken it as a student while getting her J.D., joined him, but we are no longer able to disentangle who came up with what, so the "we" is a convenient choice. Michael Levy is the third part of our teaching team in ALR and is the one who has kept our heads above water concerning issues of technology. His ideas are blended into what is said in this article, but he bears no responsibility for our errors or pomposity.

2. The most famous attempt was that of Professor Morris Cohen in his piece on the President's Page column of the Law Library Journal. It is worth noting that this page with its potential for philosophical rumination no longer appears. Morris L. Cohen, *Towards a Philosophy of Law Librarianship*, 64 L. Lib. J. 1, 1 (1971). Professor Richard Danner has made notable contribution in this field. *See e.g.* Richard A. Danner, *Contemporary and Future Directions in American Legal Research: Responding to the Threat of the Available*, 31 Intl. J. Leg. Info. 179 (2003).

3. For an excellent introduction to the literature of the field, see Gallacher, *Forty-Two: The Hitchhiker's Guide to Teaching Legal Research to the Google Generation*, 39 Akron L. Rev. 191 (2006). The extensive footnotes that are a part of this article offer citations to the complete world of literature on the subject.

4. Ms. Stein's famous quip, made in her classic *Everybody's Autobiography* (1937, reprinted Exact Change 2004), describes what she found when she visited her childhood home in Oakland, California.

5. For the past several years, the Registrar at Berkeley Law School, when dividing up course offerings by subject and type, placed ALR into a category called "Miscellaneous." The only other course so listed is an ungraded course formerly taught by the Assistant Dean of Students called "Spanish for Lawyers."

6. When Bob went to Harvard Law School to work in 1978, legal research instruction for first-year law students was entirely in the hands of the Board of Student Advisors, a student-run group. Since no one had trained the Board of Student Advisors in how to carry out legal research, and no one on the Harvard Faculty cared, training was primitive at best.

7. The Commando Legal Research video series grew out of these years. In the world of paper, where everything was taken as a given, sometimes one had to wave a rubber chicken to keep the students engaged.

8. John Palfrey & Urs Gasser, *Born Digital* (Basic Books 2008) is a very readable description of the student of 2008. Authored by Professor John Palfrey, a cyberlaw expert who has been recently appointed director of the Harvard Law Library, the book is not only a fine source, it is a lovely irony that its author is head of what may be the world's greatest law library.

9. For an informed discussion of the differing opinions of Supreme Court Justices on the use of legislative history, check the Concurring Opinion blog, available at http://www.concurringopinions.com/archives/2007/11/early_reflectio.html.

10. A fine discussion of Justice Scalia's opinions on the use of foreign law by the Supreme Court can be found at the Opiono Juris, the highly regarded blog, available at http://lawofnations.blogspot.com/2006/02/justice-scalia-on-foreign-law-and.html.

11. Two brilliant expositions of the problem of precedent can be found by reading *Anastosoff v. United States*, 223 F.3d 898, vacated as moot on rehearing en banc (8th Cir. 2000) and *Hart v. Massinari*, 266 F.3d 1165 (9th Cir. 2001). There is no precedential value here, but there is wonderful discussion of the nature of precedent.

12. Paolo Freire, *Pedagogy of the Oppressed*, (Myra Bergman Ramos trans., Continuum 2000) has informed our teaching for years. "Authentic education is not carried on *for* 'A' by 'B' or by 'A' *about* 'B,'

but rather by 'A' *with* 'B,'..." p. 82. It is a wonderfully coherent way to think about the entire first year of law school education.

13. A.W.B. Simpson, *The Rise and Fall of the Legal Treatise: Legal Principles and the Forms of Legal Literature*, 48 U. Chi. L. Rev. (1981) is an elegant statement of the interaction of legal publishing and legal principles. For elegant prose in the service of law books consider this passage: "The means of the study (of law) are a body of reports, of treatises, and of statutes, in this country... these sibylline leaves are gathered the scattered prophecies of the past... " Holmes, *The Path of the Law* (Yale electronic publication 1897, reprinted Thomson Gale 2004) This beautiful essay has been reprinted many times. The easiest place to find this passage is in Project Gutenberg, available at http://www.gutenberg.org/catalog/world/readfile?fk_files=223748. We are quoting from the second paragraph of the essay. Only Holmes could use the word sibylline.

14. The argument about when and how to teach legal research led us into an exchange of views with Christopher and Jill Robinson Wren. *See* Christopher G. Wren & Jill Robinson Wren, *The Teaching of Legal Research* 80 L. Lib. J. 7 (1988); Robert C. Berring & Kathleen Vanden Heuvel, *Legal Research: Should Students Learn It or Wing It?*, 81 L. Lib. J. 431 (1989); Christopher G. Wren & Jill Robinson Wren, *Reviving Legal Research: A Reply to Berring and Vanden Heuvel*, 82 L. Lib. J. 463 (1990); Robert C. Berring & Kathleen Vanden Heuvel, *Legal Research: A Final Response*, 82 L. Lib. J. 495 (1990).

A Motivational Perspective on First-Year Legal Research Instruction

KRIS GILLILAND

University of Mississippi School of Law, Oxford, Mississippi, USA

This article examines some recent pedagogical concepts and trends, such as signature pedagogy and student-centered learning, and their application to legal research instruction. Law librarians and other legal research instructors have long utilized a core instructional model known as the bibliographic method. But, given a rapidly changing information environment and today's born digital students, we must question whether its traditional teacher-centered approach can still motivate students and provide them with the authentic experience necessary for effective learning.

For nearly a century, librarians have taken the lead in legal research education, and, generation after generation, most have remained faithful to a core instructional approach known as the bibliographic method.[1] It survives in law schools across the country, even as the books that have traditionally defined it fall into disuse and the integrated first-year legal research and writing course becomes the norm.[2] But as the information environment grows increasingly complex, everyone who teaches legal research must question whether a pedagogy born in the print era can engage today's "born digital" law students and prepare them for future practice.[3]

WHAT ARE "SIGNATURE PEDAGOGIES' AND WHY DO THEY MATTER?

Signature pedagogies are characteristic sets of teaching and learning practices that are distinctive to professional education and include law's case-based method and medicine's clinical rounds.[4] They emerge and evolve because they "help students connect thought and action in ways that are accepted in the profession."[5] They are multidimensional and facilitate "the learning of theory, the mastery of practice, [and] the formation of professional identity."[6] They are also pervasive and determine "what counts as knowledge in a field and how things become known [and] how knowledge is analyzed, criticized, accepted, or discarded."[7] They "define the functions of expertise in a field, the locus of authority, and the privileges of rank and standing."[8]

Most importantly, signature pedagogies are engaging and require students to become active learners.[9] Signature pedagogies create learning spaces that make students feel visible and accountable. In this way, they signal that the professional must be prepared to act even when the situation is uncertain and information is lacking.[10] By providing students with the opportunity to learn in realistic contexts, pedagogies of engagement lead students to the deep learning that is necessary to acquire the professional's habits of mind and heart.[11]

CREATING A SIGNATURE PEDAGOGY FOR FIRST-YEAR LEGAL RESEARCH

For the newest generation of law students, expectations about information finding and research are shaped almost exclusively by experiences online.[12] With Google and other more familiar tools readily available, these students' motivation to learn to use traditional research tools (i.e., the books) as well as more sophisticated computer-assisted legal research services like Westlaw and Lexis is often slight. Many, if not most, new first-year students will enter their legal research and writing courses confident in the adequacy, even the superiority, of their existing research skills.[13]

Unfortunately, "[h]igh confidence coupled with low 'competence' is a dangerous combination for the prospect of future learning."[14] The legal research instructor's challenge is thus twofold: first, to craft an instructional approach that will help students learn the difficult process of integrating the print paradigm's coherent and authoritative research systems with fluid, even vaporous, online sources, and in the process, to motivate students to undertake, and persist at the task.[15]

This article's objective is to address the second of these challenges. Although scholars in a variety of disciplines have studied learner motivation extensively, this complex topic remains poorly understood.[16] However, as the following discussion suggests, recent theory and research offer useful insights for legal research instructors who are seeking ways to make classroom-based practice and the learning environment more engaging and effective. An added benefit will be students who are not only better legal researchers, but also students who are self-regulated learners, able to monitor and adjust their own motivational levels and learning strategies, skills critical to the deliberate practice that expertise requires.[17]

Student-Centered Instructional Strategies

For adult learners, especially when instruction is compulsory, student-centered instructional approaches that satisfy their expectations for autonomy, authenticity, and immediacy of course resources (e.g., instructor's feedback) and applicability of course content are likely to be most successful.[18] The adult student's motivation to learn is shaped in part by outcome expectation, or belief in the personal consequences from learning, and in part by self-efficacy, or the confidence in his or her ability to accomplish necessary learning tasks.[19] Even when students find a learning task less than enjoyable, if they believe in its value, they will feel that learning is their choice and thus be more likely to persevere.[20]

Most fundamentally, then, the instructional approach should increase the students' sense of control.[21] Teachers who not only provide meaningful explanations for course materials and activities but also allow students to try things in alternative ways, encourage initiative, or are simply perceived to support student autonomy are also more likely to have intrinsically motivated students who learn for the sake of learning and not simply for academic results.[22] These students are, in turn, more likely to stay interested, feel competent, persevere when they encounter obstacles, and model values associated with the course.[23]

Traditional directed teaching methods, in which "the teacher prescribes and the students perform," have been shown to deter intrinsic motivation and self-efficacy.[24] At the same time, while student-centered, active-learning techniques are considered more engaging, extensive research also suggests that lecture is one of the most efficient ways to help students learn basic knowledge in a new discipline; similarly, classroom demonstrations and worked examples are excellent for helping students apply this newly acquired knowledge.[25] For more advanced problem solving, different instructional approaches will be needed and, thus, the instructor will need to balance materials-based, curriculum-oriented strategies with "innovative interactions" that require the student to experiment and to reach for solutions beyond the immediately known.[26]

For decades, behavioral psychologists have viewed learning in six levels of increasing complexity.[27] According to Bloom's widely used taxonomy, the learner first must master basic knowledge (i.e., the ability to name, define, and list) and only then is the student ready to comprehend, apply, analyze, synthesize, and ultimately, to evaluate (i.e., have the ability to assess and judge) knowledge within a new discipline.[28] A recently updated version has further expanded the first level, suggesting that the novice's initial learning objectives must be to "remember" the following:

- factual knowledge (e.g., terminology, elements);
- conceptual knowledge (classification and categories, principles and generalizations, and theories);
- procedural knowledge (specific how-to skills and techniques and criteria for appropriate strategies); and
- metacognitive knowledge.[29]

From this perspective, the best instructional method depends primarily on the learner's prior knowledge and thus it is "crucial to ask what learners bring to a situation as they begin their learning . . . because it will profoundly affect what they learn."[30]

On the other hand, self-efficacy is a primary objective of various experiential-learning methods, which have long been popular in medical and business schools and are now increasingly seen in upper-level law school skills courses.[31] These student-directed methodologies are the essential pedagogies of engagement: the teacher gives up center stage to empower the students.

Problem-based learning, for example, features projects that are centered on a "driving question that is worthwhile, meaningful, and feasible."[32] The students, working in small groups, are responsible for planning, designing, and conducting the necessary "real-world research," including "asking questions, designing experiments, collecting and analyzing ideas, and drawing inferences."[33] The students collaborate with the teacher and outside practitioners who pose and answer questions, but it is they who are primarily responsible for monitoring and controlling the learning process and for determining and reflecting on its results.[34]

When they work properly, experiential-learning methods are said to create "flow," or the "state of consciousness associated with intense concentration, effortless control, and deep enjoyment."[35] The outcome is not only increased motivation to learn and better problem-solving skills, but also improved self-regulated learning skills.[36] Self-regulated learners, in turn, are able to "make sense of the learning task, to create goals and strategies, and to implement actions" that are necessary to learn a discipline's deep structures.[37]

Because of their intrinsic demands, however, problem-based learning and similar learning models are not appropriate, at least as fully implemented in advanced courses, for students who yet lack the requisite knowledge base.[38] But an instructor can easily incorporate their core principles into a more traditional methodology like the bibliographic method. For example, the course might be structured around small-group problems that are open-ended and multipart as well as student-led classroom demonstrations.[39]

Good metacognitive skills can, and should, also be incorporated and assessed in the legal research course just as any other content.[40] Instructors can help students begin by providing clear and manageable learning goals (e.g., a syllabus that includes specific, discrete learning objectives for each class meeting) and by suggesting learning strategies, such as mnemonic devices (e.g., TARP [Thing, Action, Remedy, Party]) for a research problem's preliminary analysis and flowcharts for mapping various basic research paths. Also very useful are research journals and similar exercises that require the students not only to record their research paths but also to reflect upon their thinking and their choices along the way.[41]

Situated Learning

Experiential-learning methodologies are also premised on constructivist theories that suggest learning is essentially social and that knowledge is inextricable from its context. Thus, the learning environment must reflect to a sufficient degree the unpredictability and uncertainty of "real-world" practice, and the profession's culture and its environment should define desired learning outcomes.[42] Authentic hypothetical problems and typical research tasks, using research tools that are commonly available in law firm offices, will better prepare students as well as be more engaging. Observation and emulation are also important learning techniques, and each student should be given the opportunity to express ideas and model behaviors as well as to see and hear others.[43]

Expertise studies and recent advances in the cognitive science of human learning underscore the importance of a realistic experience and prior knowledge: "Experts are experts because they have learned many more examples than novices."[44] Similarly, advanced learning is believed to be built by "revisiting the same material, at different times, in rearranged contexts, for different purposes, and from different conceptual perspectives."[45] It is this experience, and the refined and elaborated cognitive architecture that it produces, that enables experts to "perceive meaningful, interconnected patterns" among the "problem-relevant details" more rapidly and more accurately than novices.[46]

But it takes time to build expertise.[47] The instructor must select reasonably achievable learning goals and should begin new learning processes with activities that are efficiency oriented, i.e., that emphasize consistency, speed, and accuracy, like well-crafted closed-end library exercises and worked examples, because they build critical automatic routines and schema.[48] To facilitate this process, it is "crucial" for the instructor "to ask what learners bring to a situation as they begin their learning . . . because it will profoundly affect what they learn."[49]

Excellent Teaching

Successful learning is not simply a matter of a well-designed curriculum and a student-centered instructional approach; excellent teaching is often the critical motivational factor.[50] It is axiomatic, however, that teachers teach as they were taught, and all who first learned their research skills via the bibliographic method and now teach the same must be careful to design their courses for their students and not themselves.[51]

Scholars have studied those teachers judged to be among the best by their students and their peers extensively. Invariably, these teachers are described as warm, welcoming, engaging, enthusiastic, and caring.[52] They treat students with respect and, perhaps most critically, model professional behavior, including good metacognitive skills.[53] They also share a common set of pedagogical practices: They

- offer frequent personal interaction with students;
- encourage cooperation among students;
- encourage "active learning;"
- set clear goals;
- give prompt feedback;
- emphasize learning over grades;
- have high expectations; and
- accommodate diverse talents and ways of learning.[54]

CONCLUSION

If the first-year research course's most important learning objectives are to help students remember the sources of law and their roles in the research process, then the bibliographic method's typical "show-and-tell" approach is an efficient, although perhaps not very enjoyable, way to learn.[55] On the other hand, its reliance on teacher-centered methods will require rigorous use of external motivation to encourage students to learn; diminish intrinsic motivation, already in short supply; deter self-efficacy; and, at best, produce only so-called routine expertise.[56] In a "'whitewater world' where change is the norm," students also need to be prepared to adapt and to think creatively.[57]

Thus, the first-year legal research instructor should employ a mix of instructional approaches, including:

- lecture and classroom demonstrations;
- a series of objective exercises that are designed to build upon prior knowledge and to reinforce newly acquired knowledge;

- interactive exercises like computer-assisted legal instruction (CALI) lessons and research journals that encourage reflection and other self-regulatory processes;
- visual aids (e.g., flowcharts and PowerPoint presentations);
- assignments and course materials that provide realistic research tasks and communicate community practice and values;
- collaborative work (e.g., small-group work that features peer coaching and peer evaluation); and
- frequent student-teacher contact and substantive feedback.

But, above all, perhaps, an engaged-learning experience in first-year legal research will require a respectful and caring instructor who is genuinely enthusiastic about the subject and the learning process.

Like other faculty, librarians and legal research instructors are now tasked "with the great challenge of meeting the needs of learners who come from cultures that are foreign to themselves and who often have very different abilities and experiences than originally assumed."[58] Librarians are also no longer the gatekeepers of legal information and the only instructors of legal research skills. But if we persist in utilizing a teaching method that does not accommodate new ways of thinking about information and research, we risk our credibility as the subject's experts.

As libraries transform themselves into organizations defined as much or more by their services as their collections, it is clear that teaching good research skills in the classroom will be one of our most important roles. The popularity of advanced legal research courses demonstrates that law students who have experienced the real world are eager to learn more about research. But finding a pedagogical approach that motivates first-year students to learn good research habits is a challenge that we cannot afford to avoid.

We can begin by working more closely with our legal writing colleagues. In the last decade, they have built an impressive and enviable body of scholarship devoted to good pedagogy for first-year legal writing and analysis and have explored alternatives to the bibliographic method.[59] Together, perhaps, we can soon devise a new signature pedagogy for legal research and writing that is both pervasive and engaging. (See Appendix A infra, describing a first–year legal research program, in which many of these ideas are now being incorporated).

NOTES

1. *See* Paul Douglas Callister, *Beyond Training: Law Librarianship's Quest for the Pedagogy of Legal Research Education*, 95 L. Lib. J. 7 (2003). While this label is typically used disparagingly, here it is intended as a convenient shorthand for the source-based teaching methodology that grew from Frederick Hicks' pioneering efforts to Columbia Law School students' use of law books in the early 1900s. *See also* Ellie Margolis & Susan L. DeJarnatt, *Moving Beyond Product to Process: Building a Better LRW Program*,

46 Santa Clara L. Rev. 93 (2005) (observing "[t]hat this approach is common is evident from a survey of research texts.")

2. At least 151 law schools in the United States now teach research and legal writing skills together in one integrated course. At ninety-eight schools, LRW faculty and other non-librarian instructors take primary responsibility for research teaching; at 52 schools, librarians are the research instructors; and at another 66 schools, faculty and librarians share responsibility. *See* Association of Legal Writing Directors/Legal Writing Institute (ALWD/LWI), *2008 Survey Results*, available at http://www.alwd.org/surveys.html.

3. *See* John Palfrey & Urs Gasser, *Born Digital: Understanding the First Generation of Digital Natives* (Basic Books 2008).

4. *See* Lee S. Shulman, *Signature Pedagogies in the Professions*, 134 Daedalus 52 (2005); William M. Sullivan et al., *Educating Lawyers: Preparation for the Practice of Law* (Jossey–Bass/Wiley 2007); and Judith Welch Wegner, *Educating Lawyers*, 13 AALL Spectrum 20 (Stylus Publishing 2009). The concept is rapidly gaining attention across the higher-education spectrum. *See e.g.* Regan A.R. Gurug et al., *Exploring Signature Pedagogies: Approaches to Teaching Disciplinary Habits of Mind* (2008); Chris M. Golde, *Signature Pedagogies in Doctoral Education: Are They Adaptable for the Preparation of Education Researchers?* 36 Educ. Researcher 34 (2007).

5. Gary Poole, *Academic Disciplines: Homes or Barricades*, in *The University and Its Disciplines* 55 (Caroline Kreber ed., Routledge 2008).

6. William M. Sullivan, *Markets versus Professions: Value Added?* 134 Daedalus 19, 23 (2005).

7. Shulman, *supra* n. 4, at 54.

8. *See id.*

9. *See* Stephen Bowen, *Engaged Learning: Are We All on the Same Page?* Peer Rev. 4 (2005). *Active learning* is a common umbrella term for student-centered teaching techniques that promote student engagement. *See e.g.* Ellen R. Wylie & Krista Auster, *Creating Active Learning in the Classroom: A Systematic Approach*, 30 J. Mgt. Educ. 333 (2006); Robin A. Boyle, *Employing Active-Learning Techniques and Metacognition in Law School: Shifting Energy from Professor to Student*, 81 U. Det. Mercy L. Rev. 1 (2003); and Gerald F. Hess, *Monographs on Teaching and Learning for Legal Educators*, 35 Gonz. L. Rev. 63 (2000).

10. *See* Lee Shulman, *The Signature Pedagogies of the Professions of Law, Medicine, Engineering, and the Clergy: Potential Lessons for the Education of Teachers* (Math Science Partnerships Workshop at the National Research Council's Center for Education, 6–8, Feb. 2005) (available at http://hub.mspnet.org/index.cfm/11172.)

11. *See id. See also* Bowen, *supra* n. 9, at 7.

12. Approximately two-thirds of law students were born after 1977 and are often described as just-in-time, rather than just-in-case, learners. *See 2007 Law School Survey of Student Engagement Annual Survey*, available at http://lssse.iub.edu/index.cfm. *See also* Leslie Larkin Cooney, *Giving Millennials a Leg-Up: How to Avoid the 'If I Knew Then What I Know Now' Syndrome*, 96 Ky. L.J. 505 (2008); Ian Gallacher, *'Who Are Those Guys?': The Results of a Survey Studying the Information Literacy of Incoming Law Students*, 44 Cal. W. L. Rev. 151 (2007); Joanne Ingham & Robin A. Boyle, *Generation X in Law School: How These Law Students Are Different From Those Who Teach Them*, 56 J. Leg. Educ. 281 (2006); Cathaleen A. Roach, *Is the Sky Falling? Ruminations on Incoming Law Students Preparedness (and Implications for the Profession) in the Wake of Recent National and Other Reports*, 11 Leg. Writing 295 (2005); and Tracy L. McGaugh, *Generation X in Law School: The Dying of the Light or the Dawn of a New Day?* 9 Leg. Writing 119 (2003). *But see* B. Glesner Fines, *The Impact of Expectations on Teaching and Learning*, 38 Gonz. L. Rev. 89 (2002).

13. *See* Gallacher, *supra* n. 12, at 3. In Professor Gallacher's survey of 750 incoming law students, only seven percent believed that legal research would be the most important skill that they would learn in law school and more than eighty percent stated that they were already "very" or "somewhat" confident in their research skills. Almost as many reported that they were very or somewhat confident that their use of Internet search engines retrieved the best resources for the information need at hand. *But see* B. Glesner Fines, *The Impact of Expectations on Teaching and Learning*, 38 Gonz. L. Rev. 89 (2002).

14. *See* Daniel L. Schwartz et al., *Efficiency and Innovation in Transfer*, in *Transfer of Learning from a Modern Multidisciplinary Perspective* 8 (2005), available at http://aaalab.stanford.edu/papers/

15. *See e.g.* Sanford N. Greenberg, *Legal Research Training: Preparing Students for A Rapidly Changing Environment*, 13 Leg. Writing 241 (2007).

16. The multidisciplinary literature devoted to motivation in learning is vast and often inclusive, but a good single-volume treatment of educational psychology generally is *The Handbook of Educational Psychology* (Patricia Alexander & Philip Winne eds., Erlbaum 2006). For a helpful overview of major contemporary pedagogical concepts, including motivation, see also Orison Carlile & Anne Jordan, *It Works in Practice But Will It Work in Theory? The Theoretical Underpinnings of Pedagogy*, in *Emerging Issues in the Practice of University Learning and Teaching* 14 (Geraldine O'Neill, Sarah Moore, Barry McMullin eds. All Ireland Society for Higher Education 2005). And, for something a little more cutting edge, see Erica McWilliams & Shane Dawson, *Pedagogical Practice After the Information Age*, 12 J. Future Stud. 1 (2008) (describing "liquid modern learning" as it relates to the knowledge creation cycle and noting that the time to communicate with 50 million people has decreased from thirty years during the Radio Age to four in the Web Age).

17. *See* Christopher A. Wolters, *Regulation of Motivation: Evaluating an Underemphasized Aspect of Self-Regulated Learning*, 38 Educ. Psychol. 189 (2003).

18. For an excellent comparison of the major schools of adult learning theory, see Michael Marquardt & Deborah Waddill, *The Power of Learning in Action Learning: A Conceptual Analysis of How the Five Schools of Adult Learning Theories Are Incorporated Within the Practice of Action Learning*, 1 Action Learning: Research & Prac. 186 (2004).

19. Barry J. Zimmerman, *Becoming a Self-Regulated Learner: An Overview*, 41 Theory into Prac. 66 (2002), at 68 (citing Albert Bandura, *Self-Efficacy: The Exercise of Control* (W. H. Freeman 1997)). *See also* Ellen L. Usher & Frank Pajares, *Sources of Self-Efficacy in School: Critical Review of the Literature and Future Directions*, 78 Rev. Educ. Research 751 (2008).

20. *See* Gerald F. Hess, *Collaborative Course Design: Not My Course, Not Their Course, But Our Course*, 47 Washburn L.J. 367, 369 (2008).

21. *See e.g.* Edwin A. Locke & Gary P. Latham, *Building a Practically Useful Theory of Goal Setting and Task Motivation: A 35-Year Odyssey*, 57 Am. Psychol. 705 (2002).

22. *See e.g.* Kennon M. Sheldon & Lawrence S. Krieger, *Understanding the Negative Effects of Legal Education on Law Students: A Longitudinal Test of Self-Determination Theory*, 33 Pers. & Soc. Psychol. Bull. 883 (2007); Kennon M. Sheldon & Lawrence S. Krieger, *Does Legal Education Have Undermining Effects on Law Students? Evaluating Changes in Motivation, Values, and Well-Being*, 22 Behav. Sci.& L. 251 (2004) (excellent bibliography).

23. *See e.g.* Leah Christensen, *Predicting Law School Success: A Study of Goal Orientations, Academic Achievement, and the Declining Self-Efficacy of Our Law Students* (Thomas Jefferson School of Law Legal Studies Research Paper No. 1235528 2008), available at http://www.ssrn.com. (quoting Ruth Ann McKinney, *Depression and Anxiety in Law Students: Are We Part of the Problem and Can We Be Part of the Solution?* 8 Leg. Writing 229, 234 (2002)).

24. *See* Young, *infra* n. 37, at 25. Recent empirical studies indicate a disturbing decrease in law students' self-efficacy and motivation after the first year of law school. *See e.g.* Christensen, *supra* n. 23; Sheldon & Krieger, *supra* n. 22.

25. *See* J. D. Walker et al., *A Delicate Balance: Integrating Active Learning into a Large Lecture Course*, 7 Life Sci. Educ. 361 (2008). *See also* Paul A. Kirschner, John Sweller & Richard E. Clark, *Why Minimal Guidance During Instruction Does Not Work: An Analysis of the Failure of Constructivist, Discovery, Problem-Based, Experiential, and Inquiry-Based Teaching*, 41 Educ. Psychol. 75 (2006) (discussing worked examples).

26. Schwartz et al., *supra* n. 14, at 31.

27. *See* Benjamin S. Bloom & David R. Krathwohl, *Taxonomy of Educational Objectives: The Classification of Educational Goals: Cognitive Domain* (Longmans, Green 1956).

28. *Id. See also* Christine M. Venter, *Analyze This: Using Taxonomies to 'Scaffold' Students' Legal Thinking and Writing Skills*, 57 Mercer L. Rev. 621 (2007).

29. *See* David R. Krathwohl, *A Revision of Bloom's Taxonomy: An Overview*, 41(4) Theory Into Prac. 212 (2002). The learner can then proceed to understand (i.e., to interpret and explain), apply, analyze, evaluate, and create knowledge. *Id.* at 215.

30. *See* Schwartz et al., *supra* n. 14, at 12. "[W]hat one notices about new situations and how one frames problems has major effects on subsequent thinking and cognitive processing." *Id.* at 9. For more about the importance of prior knowledge to transfer and the cognitive science of learning, see National Research Council, *How People Learn: Brain, Mind, Experience, and School* (John D. Bransford, Ann L.

Brown & Rodney R. Cocking eds., National Academics Press 1999), available at http://www.nap.com. *See also* Susan M. Barnett & Stephen J. Ceci, *When and Where Do We Apply What We Learn? A Taxonomy for Far Transfer*, 128 Psychol. Bull. 612 (2002).

31. *See* Roy Stuckey et al., *Best Practices for Legal Education* (Clinical Legal Education Association 2007), available at http://www.cleaweb.org/resources/bp.html.

32. *See e.g.* Cindy E. Hmelo-Silver, *Problem-Based Learning: What and How Do Students Learn*, 16 Educ. Psychol. Rev. 235 (2004).

33. *Id.*

34. *Id.*

35. Scott G. Paris & Alison H. Paris, *Classroom Applications of Research on Self-Regulated Learning*, 36 Educ. Psychol. 89, 94 (2001).

36. A growing number of scholars believe that the learner's ability to monitor and regulate his or her own (1) cognitive learning skills (e.g., problem-solving strategies and critical thinking), (2) "metacognitive" skills, and (3) motivation is fundamental to expertise. *See e.g.* Michael Hunter Schwartz, *Expert Learning for Law Students* (2nd ed. Carolina Academic Press 2008). If self-regulated learning is "the fusion of skill and will," then metacognition is the glue. Paris & Paris, *supra* n. 35, at 98. Usually defined as an awareness and control of one's own thinking during the learning process, it is an expert's "habit of mind" and thought to be especially important "during initial learning, while trouble shooting and while teaching others to use strategies." *Id.* at 91. *See also* Paul R. Pintrich, *The Role of Metacognitive Knowledge in Learning, Teaching, and Assessing*, 41 Theory Into Prac. (2002); and Anthony S. Niedwicki, *Lawyers and Learning: A Metacognitive Approach to Legal Education*, 13 Widener L. Rev. 33 (2007).

37. *See* Mark R. Young, *The Motivational Effects of the Classroom Environment in Facilitating Self-Regulated Learning*, J. Mktg. Educ. 24 (2005).

38. *Id.* at 255. Some scholars question experential learning's effectiveness for more advanced students, too. *See* Kirschner, Sweller & Clark., *supra* n. 25; Richard E. Mayer, *Should There Be a Three-Strikes Rule against Pure Discovery Learning?* 59 Am. Psychol. 24 (2004); Jerry Gosen & John Washbush, *A Review of Scholarship on Assessing Experiential Learning Effectiveness*, 35 Simulation & Gaming 270 (2004); and Jeroen J. G. van Merrienboer et al., *Taking the Load Off a Learner's Mind: Instructional Design for Complex Learning*, 38 Educ. Psychol. 5 (2003).

39. *See e.g.* Elizabeth G. Cohen et al., *Teaching Cooperative Learning* (State University of New York Press 2004); David W. Johnson & Roger T. Johnson, *Learning Together and Alone* (5th ed. Prentice Hall 1998); and Robert E. Slavin, *Research for the Future: Research on Cooperative Learning and Achievement: What We Know, What We Need to Know*, 21 Contemporary Educ. Psychol. 43 (Prentice Hall 1996).

40. These skills include setting goals (e.g., memorize a list of definitions for a quiz), creating study strategies (e.g., flashcards); and systematically reflecting on performance outcomes. *See* Zimmerman, *supra* n. 19; Pintrich, *supra* n. 36, at 223.

41. *See e.g.* James B. Levy, *Practice and Procedure: Better Research Through 'Point of Need' Library Exercises*, 7 Leg. Writing 87 (2001).

42. *See* John Seely Brown et al., *Situated Cognition and the Culture of Learning*, 18 Educ. Researcher 10.

43. Albert Bandura, *Social Learning Theory* 22 (Prentice Hall 1977). For a helpful summary of Bandura's influential theory, see Raymond B. Miller & Stephanie J. Brickman, *A Model of Future-Oriented Motivation and Self-Regulation*, 16 Educ. Psychol. Rev. 9 (2004).

44. *See* Laurel Currie Oates, *Did Harvard Get It Right?* 59 Mercer L. Rev. 675, 684 (2008).

45. R. J. Spiro et al., *Cognitive Flexibility, Constructivism and Hypertext: Random Access Instruction for Advanced Knowledge Acquisition in Ill-Structured Domains*, 31 Educ. Tech. 24 (1991). Research on expert cognition indicates that experts use deductive reasoning, creating a mental model for the task at hand using both abstract principles and the relevant data available. Novices, on the other hand, employ inductive reasoning to identify solutions, using strategies derived from "surface-level features," rather than deeper principles, and "trial-and-error tests of constantly changing hypotheses." *See* David F. Feldon, *The Implications of Research on Expertise for Curriculum and Pedagogy*, 19 Educ. Psychol. Rev. 91 (2007).

46. Michael Hunter Schwartz, *Teaching Law by Design: How Learning Theory and Instructional Design Can Inform and Reform Law Teaching*, 38 S.D. L. Rev. 347, 355 (2003).

47. *See* National Research Council, *supra* n. 30, at 56–58.

48. *See* Schwartz et al., *supra* n. 14, at 36. *But cf.* Margolis & DeJarnatt, *supra* n. 1, at 6 (arguing that "treasure hunt" exercises "feed the common student illusion that there must be a 'right' answer.")

49. *Id.* at 12. "[W]hat one notices about new situations and how one frames problems has major effects on subsequent thinking and cognitive processing." *Id.* at 9. The bibliographic method's most significant drawback as traditionally implemented is perhaps its presuppositions about students' prior knowledge, experience and expectations (e.g., the purpose and use of an encyclopedia or an index, recursive research).

50. *See* David Lavoie & Andrew J. Rosman, *Using Active Student-Centered Learning-Based Instructional Design to Develop Faculty and Improve Course Design, Delivery, and Evaluation*, 22 Issues Acctg. Educ. 105, 105 (2007).

51. "Many faculty members describe an ideal learning environment as one in which they receive a lot of information upfront and have the opportunity to read and reflect upon that information, followed by an opportunity to apply and test out new ideas or skills. By contrast, undergraduates' commitment to learning is maintained by a preference for a more active, experiential mode [and] topics that allow them to engage immediately . . . and then comprehend how the material relates to their lives and experiences." Mathew L. Ouelette, *Faculty Development and Universal Instructional Design*, 37 Eq. & Excellence Educ.135, 137 (2004). The literature associated with "instructional design," an emerging professional discipline sometimes described as "applied learning theory," is particularly useful. *See* Schwartz, *supra* n. 46; Steven J. Bell & John D. Shank, *Academic Librarianship By Design* (American Library Association 2007); Robert Gagne et al., *Principles of Instructional Design* (5th ed. Thomson/Wadsworth 2005).

52. *See* Jeanne Nakamura & Mihaly Csikszentmihalyi, *Engagement in a Profession: The Case of Undergraduate Teaching*, 134 Daedalus 60, 62–66 (2005). *See also* Deborah Jones Merritt, *Legal Education in the Age of Cognitive Science and Advanced Classroom Technology* 14 (Ohio State Public Law Working Paper No. 94 2007), available at http://www.ssrn.com (describing studies that have addressed immediacy's effects on student motivation and demonstrated that "students learn more from a humanizing, conversational style than from an overly formal one.")

53. *See* Stuckey, *supra* n. 31 at 80–95.

54. *See* Arthur W. Chickering and Zelda F. Gamson, *Applying the Seven Principles for Good Practice in Undergraduate Education* (Jossey–Bass 1999); Ken Bain, *What the Best College Teachers Do* (Harvard University Press 2004) (suggesting attitude, not teaching method, is the key to great teaching).

55. *See* ALWD/LWI 2008 Survey Results, *supra* n. 2, at 26.

56. Schwartz et al., *supra* n. 14.

57. *Id.* at 12, 28–29.

58. Roderick Sims, *Rethinking (E)learning: A Manifesto for Connected Generations*, 29(2) Distance Educ. 53 (2008).

59. *See e.g.* J. P. Oglivy, *Clinical Legal Education Bibliography*, 11 Clinical L. Rev., Special Issue No. 2 (2005). *See e.g.* Amy Sloan, *Step Right Up: Using Consumer Decision-Making Theory to Teach Research Process in the Electronic Age*, 60 S.C. L. Rev. 123 (2008). *See also* Anna Marie Johnson & Sarah Jent, *Library Instruction and Information Literacy*, 35 Ref. Serv. Rev. 137 (2007) (an extensive annotated bibliography of recent articles and monographs devoted to teaching information literacy); Pat Hutchings et al., *The Scholarship of Teaching and Learning in Higher Education: An Annotated Bibliography* (2002), available at http://www.carnegiefoundation.org/dynamic/downloads/file_1_196.pdf.

APPENDIX A

AN EXAMPLE OF AN EVOLVING LEGAL RESEARCH PROGRAM.

At the University of Mississippi, our guiding principles are cooperation, immediacy, and a pragmatic approach to the fundamentals. We want the course to reflect the realities of the practices in which most of our students will find themselves, whether it be in small rural law firms, large regional firms, governmental agencies, or other. To this end, we talk with local practitioners and upper-level students about their summer experience after the first year and invite alumni into the classroom several times each term. We solicit feedback from the students continuously and experiment with course structure, types of assignments, and other course features, tweaking and discarding old ones every year.

Ole Miss has a two-semester integrated first-year legal research and writing program that is required for all students. The library director has been its co-director since inception, but the law library's four public service librarians have only recently assumed primary responsibility for first-year research instruction. Each year, we also hire at least one practicing attorney to join the teaching team.

Each research instructor is paired for the year with one of the four writing instructors. The writing instructors meet with larger sections of students for an hour twice a week. They also discuss research in their class meetings with their students but leave more detailed instruction on research resources and strategies to the research instructors who meet with smaller sections of approximately twenty to twenty-five students in the classroom one hour each week.

Each fall. the legal research instructors create five hypothetical problems that provide the framework for the semester's curriculum. For reinforcement purposes, these problems are carefully designed to be similar, but slightly different (to provide more practice) from the hypothetical problems that the legal writing faculty use for closed- and open-end memoranda as well as other writing assignments. Each week, there are also group exercises, which students are given the choice to complete in class or outside class, which scaffold the students' introduction to the major types of secondary sources, codes, and case-finding tools.

Some assignments are completed individually for assessment purposes, but most are collaborative. With approximately twenty students per section, each section is usually divided into approximately five "practice groups" that make up the class "law firm." Each instructor, in term, serves as a law firm "partner," and any student who needs assistance can approach that instructor. Students, individually and in their groups, and instructors meet frequently outside of class, keeping frustration in check, bolstering confidence, but not directing the students' work.

Lecture is limited to twenty minutes each week, and the remainder of class time is spent largely on group assignments prepared and distributed by the instructor each week. (These assignments are designed to require some work outside of class each week.) In the past, we have occasionally required student presentations with mixed results.

We remain committed to the bibliographic method's orientation to the sources of law and their publication patterns, features, and finding aids, but online research has a slightly larger profile in the curriculum and full access to Westlaw and Lexis is provided within the first month. However, we emphasize strategies that integrate print- and computer-aided legal research. As noted above, library exercises are designed specifically to replicate the kinds of research tasks that first-year summer associates are likely to encounter, including finding and updating primary and secondary sources and commonly used practitioner materials (e.g., form books), using low-cost research services like Casemaker, and reporting research results in brief memo, letter, or motion form.

We recommend Amy Sloan's *Basic Legal Research* as a very useful supplement but use CALI lessons for most assigned readings to provide an additional active-learning component. (To show that they have completed the lessons, each student must submit a score certificate showing eighty percent of the questions were answered correctly.) We have found our students are much more likely to read online and they have responded especially well to the interactive nature of the CALI lessons and retain more basic knowledge.[1] Recently, when given the choice between a return to an assigned textbook or to remain with CALI in the second semester, the students voted overwhelmingly in CALI's favor despite some annoying technical problems.

Professionalism is a major instructional point and is a significant percentage of the final grade. We emphasize "punctual, polite, and professional" and cooperative work. Peer evaluations, based on group work, also contribute to the final grade.

In conjunction with the class' professionalism component, the library has developed a speaker series that we call "Lawyer in the Library." Practicing attorneys from various traditional and nontraditional workplaces are invited to the law school several times each term to talk informally with students about practice and, more particularly, about the role of legal research in their work. While we provide some incentive to attend at least one session (i.e., extra-credit points), we find most students attend all sessions voluntarily. Both speakers and students have given the program uniformly high marks, and the research instructors feel that it is now one of the most important aspects of the course for all involved.

Judged by objective standards, including an assessment we give at the beginning and the end of each year, and student evaluations, which went from universally dismal to overwhelmingly positive almost overnight, the program is a success. The key to future success, we believe, is to treat legal research pedagogy as a dynamic process that requires constant reflection and adjustment.

1. In past years, students were required to purchase a textbook (one widely adopted around the country) and to read at least one chapter each week. To reinforce the reading, i.e., to make sure that they did the reading, we posted biweekly quizzes on the course Web site that comprised half of the research grade. Wildly unpopular with the students, the quizzes were also time consuming to create and administer and, ultimately, as a year-end assessment revealed, not terribly effective in the long term.

Best Practices: What First-Year Law Students Should Learn in a Legal Research Class

NANCY P. JOHNSON
Georgia State University College of Law Library, Atlanta, Georgia, USA

Legal research instructors seldom have adequate class time to teach students the print and online sources needed to complete a research task successfully. However, there are core principles that first-year students should learn in a legal research class. The author discusses best practices in teaching the legal research process, along with the important research sources, including judicial opinions and reporters, digests and finding cases, statutes, administrative publications, citators for updating research, and secondary sources.

INTRODUCTION

During the past twenty-five years, I have taught legal research to first-year law (1L) students in a law school whose curriculum includes legal research and legal writing as two distinct courses. In reviewing the classes taught between 1982 and 2007, I noted that the topics I teach have remained the same; however, the format of the materials available to students has changed drastically.[1] Currently, students implement research strategies using a combination of print and electronic resources.[2] In light of this, and from my assessment of topics, I realize that there are definitely core principles that first-year students should learn in a legal research class regardless of the research format they use. This article discusses these essential core principles and includes the main points that I emphasize in my classes.

Portions of this article are borrowed from Nancy P. Johnson, Elizabeth G. Adelman & Nancy J. Adams, *Georgia Legal Research* (Suzanne E. Rowe ed., Carolina Academic Press 2007); and from Suzanne E. Rowe, *Oregon Legal Research* (2d ed., Carolina Academic Press 2007). The author acknowledges the permission of Carolina Academic Press, her coauthors, and Suzanne Rowe to include material from those books.

Librarians and attorneys lament the poor research skills of new attorneys.[3] The need for improved legal research skills prompted the American Association of Law Libraries (AALL) to explore what it can do to foster and support legal research as a subject specialty in law schools and in practice.[4] In 2008, Thomson West conducted a survey of law firm librarians and attorneys on the skill levels of new associates in completing legal research tasks.[5] The findings are no surprise to legal research professors. However, it was refreshing to read about collaborative efforts by academic and law firm librarians on teaching summer associates effective research skills. It is also imperative that teaching librarians keep both their teaching skills and their legal research skills current by routinely reading several excellent journals designed for legal research.[6]

THE FIRST-YEAR LEGAL RESEARCH CLASS AT GEORGIA STATE UNIVERSITY COLLEGE OF LAW

At Georgia State University (GSU) College of Law, 1L students are required to take a two-semester first-year legal research course and a research, writing, and advocacy course (RWA). The legal research course is one-credit hour, pass/fail offered in the fall semester and includes twelve class sessions. Students must complete all assignments from a standard assignment book[7] and pass an exam. The librarians use The West Educational Network (TWEN) for class materials, and there is not a textbook. We refer students to several excellent legal research textbooks;[8] unfortunately, students do not usually read the texts. In addition to readings and assignments, we assign appropriate legal research Computer Assisted Legal-Instruction (CALI) lessons.[9] Students find CALI lessons helpful on a weekly basis and as a review for the exam. At GSU, students generally enjoy the class. Since they receive weekly feedback on their assignments, they can chart their progress. Although it is pass/fail, not all students pass the class; hence, students tend to take the class seriously.

During the semester, we cover the core principles discussed in this article. We instruct the students on what they need to know to excel in their writing class, plus other materials, such as Georgia legal research and administrative legal research, which they may use in their summer jobs. We do not teach citation format in class; however, we request that students use proper citation format to complete their assignments. We also do not touch on international law and other very important topics.

The five librarians who teach the class start at different places in the materials to avoid a large number of students hovering over the same books. Therefore, we begin the semester studying either cases, statutes, or secondary materials. Since the material is new to the students, they have not expressed a preference as to the learning order of the material. During the semester, we discuss the most efficient way to begin a research project, but the order of teaching the material has never been a factor on how students learn the materials.

We realize that we cannot expect students to just stumble on indexes to multi-volume treatises or know how to locate cases that have interpreted statutes without an instructor mentioning these tools in class. We discuss the process of legal research and research strategies and discuss how the materials connect to each other. However, all legal research professors face the challenge of students who have neither the experience nor the vocabulary to understand the process of legal research. Furthermore, we have one hour each week for twelve weeks to teach students not only the process of legal research but also the materials needed to conduct legal research. In other words, our students learn basic legal research, and these basic skills will improve with practice during law school and in their professional positions.

LEGAL RESEARCH PROCESS—BEST PRACTICES

Nationwide, legal research professors teach the legal research process in their own unique ways.[10] The most effective way we have found is an integration of electronic and print sources.[11] Students may feel that this method is more time consuming, but using both types of sources allows for more effective, efficient research. It also prepares students for all types of legal careers where the availability of legal sources will vary depending on the type and size of the practice or workplace.

Obviously, students first have to analyze their facts. Next, students have to determine whether their issue is state law, federal law, or both. Students should also think about other classifications applicable to the facts, such as civil or criminal, or procedural or substantive. These issues become easier to grasp as students move through the first year.

Many professors strongly recommend that students use secondary sources first to understand the subject area, identify issues and terms, and obtain citations for primary sources. Students are already familiar with texts from their undergraduate days and feel more comfortable in secondary sources than they do diving into statutes or digests. Secondary sources will also help students identify whether statutory or case law is the basis for their issues. Since it is important for students to learn the vocabulary of their research projects, they should begin with secondary sources. From these sources, they will generate a list of research terms. From the research terms, they can then move to either statutes or cases. At this point, students will be tempted to jump on the Internet and Google the search terms. Hopefully, students will soon learn that legal research involves types of materials found more easily through law-specific databases. It is difficult to convey to new students the necessity of evaluating what they find online. However, professors should help students distinguish material found on Wikipedia or other Internet sources from material found on reliable legal databases.[12]

Next, students have to read the entire text of primary law. Attorneys complain that students rely on headnotes or summaries and miss important parts of the entire case. Of course, students must make sure cases are still good law and that statutes are current. In practice, lawyers stop their research when they run out of time and when the cost exceeds the benefit. In law school, students stop their research when their assignment is due. Students should feel comfortable to stop researching when they use both secondary and primary resources and locate the same authorities in both.

For students to relate to legal research, they must know how and when to use the materials. It is very important that students know why they would want to update a code section, use an *American Law Reports* (*ALR*) annotation, or find an administrative regulation. One way to teach the material is to use a few real-life plausible research issues throughout the semester. By relating the material to their writing problem or some current cases, students can see the utility of learning new research skills.

The topic of print versus online materials is a battle no longer worth fighting.[13] There are effective materials in both print and online. When discussing the various research tools, professors must point out the differences between print and online and then urge students to decide the best medium. If professors have adequate time, they could ask students to analyze both methods and come to their own conclusions on which method works best for their research projects.

CASE LAW RESEARCH

All 1L students grasp the concept of case law within a few weeks of law school; however, reading and understanding the meaning of cases is very difficult for new students. Students soon learn that case law research refers to opinions written by judges, usually on the appellate level, which resolve litigated disputes. Judges base their reasoning on statutes or previously decided cases. In their 1L research class, students should gain an understanding of a generic court system, the doctrine of precedent, the parts of an opinion, how to read a case citation, and the names of the reporters.

It is easiest to explain court hierarchy using a generic model. Students should refer to Table T.1 of *The Bluebook*[14] for specific court hierarchy. Professors can use this opportunity to explain that *The Bluebook* is a useful tool for not only learning about citation format but also for learning about the federal and state court systems. Court systems have one or two tiers of appellate courts. The judges of the intermediate court, typically called the *court of appeals*, review trial courts' handling of cases for reversible errors. The justices of the highest court, typically called the *supreme court*, conduct a secondary review for errors by focusing primarily on the development of the legal doctrine. Typically, appeal to the intermediate court is a right, while the Supreme Court affords discretionary review.

Most case reporters only publish appellate court cases—courts of appeal and supreme court cases. Simply stated, the trial court provides a forum for presentation of the facts to a jury or judge, determination of the facts in dispute, and application of the law to the facts to yield an initial resolution of the dispute. A party that loses in the trial court may appeal. Students become frustrated when they discover that they cannot locate most materials from trial courts. In fact, most trial-level cases are not reported, and a written opinion is often unavailable.

The federal court hierarchy is easy to understand on a very basic level. Typically, civil procedure courses will explain court structure in detail. The federal trial courts are the United States District Courts. Each state has one to four district courts, each covering part or all of the state. The intermediate appellate courts are the United States Courts of Appeal. There are eleven numbered circuits, each covering several states, and the District of Columbia Circuit and the Federal Circuit. The United States Supreme Court hears cases on discretionary review from the lower federal courts (the federal courts of appeal and the federal district courts) or judgments of state courts of last resort that deal with questions of federal law. Specialized trial and appeal courts exist in such areas as bankruptcy.

Precedent and Authority

Past decisions in appellate cases are predictors of what the courts are likely to do in future cases given a similar set of facts. Students should understand two basic principles when they read cases. One is *precedent*, and the other is *authority*. Precedent is an earlier case that is relevant to a case to be decided. If there is nothing to distinguish the circumstances of the current case from the already decided one, the earlier holding is considered binding on the court. Authority can be either mandatory or persuasive. *Mandatory* authority is law that is binding on the court deciding the case. A case is only a precedent as to a particular set of facts and the precise legal issue decided in light of those facts. If the case is not a precedent, but contains an excellent analysis of the legal issues and provides guidance for a court, it is a *persuasive* authority. Such issues as precedent and authority are explored in writing courses that cover case analysis. Legal research classes never have adequate time to cover how cases apply to individual issues, whereas legal writing and analysis classes describe these concepts.[15]

Sources for Case Law Research

Students read cases online on LexisNexis, Westlaw, or free online sources. Students no longer mob the stacks for volumes of *case reporters*. However, students must know how to locate cases in the print sources called case reporters so they are prepared for any kind of research environment. The cases are generally published chronologically as they are decided. Reporters do not include transcripts of court proceedings or the text of documents submitted by the parties.

There is a distinction in case reporting between official and unofficial reporters. *Official reporters* are simply those reporters that a statute or a court order designates as official. The text of an opinion as it is published in an *unofficial reporter* is the same as the text of the opinion as it is published in the official. However, unofficial reporters, most notably those published by West Publishing Company, include helpful editorial enhancements, such as headnotes and topic/key numbers as aids to researchers.

One concern that new researchers may stumble upon is the issue of integrity of electronic documents, including documents issued by courts, agencies, and legislatures. The emergence of online *official* legal resources is a positive development, provided that the publications are trustworthy. To be trustworthy, digital materials vulnerable to lapses in management and control, corruption, and tampering must be equivalent to print *official* legal resources. To be equivalent, they must be *authentic*. The AALL issued a comprehensive study entitled *State-by-State Report on Authentication of Online Legal Resources*.[16] The study found that state online resources are not authenticated and do not afford ready authentication by standard methods. Additionally, in February 2004, the American Bar Association (ABA) House of Delegates approved Standard 1.65, Court Use of Electronic Filing.[17] This standard addresses the issue of integrity and trustworthiness of electronically transmitted and stored information.

A citation to the same case published in more than one reporter is a *parallel citation*. Parallel citations are different citations to the same case in official versus unofficial reporters. New researchers have a difficult time grasping the concept of a parallel citation. The truth is that there is great duplication of cases in the field of legal publishing, and professors should take the time to explain the different legal publishers; however, in an electronic age, it is very difficult to explain why there is still so much duplication of print sources.

It is interesting for students to learn about unpublished opinions,[18] but they generally learn about them later in law school. Students are surprised to learn that the great majority of federal and some state judicial opinions are not reported at all. Sometimes an opinion is not reported because the court deems it redundant with previous decisions; other opinions are not reported because they are determined to lack precedential value. Court rules in each jurisdiction indicate when reporting of an opinion is necessary or desirable, and the rules vary among jurisdictions. Nearly all the decisions of courts of last resort within the state and federal system are reported in full. Students run across unpublished opinions on LexisNexis, Westlaw, and the

Federal Appendix, a case law reporter published by West Publishing. The *Federal Appendix* publishes judicial opinions of the United States courts of appeals that have not been selected for publication. Previously, *unpublished* cases were apparently without value as precedent. However, the Supreme Court made a change to the Federal Rules of Appellate Procedure in 2006.[19] Now, Rule 32.1 says that federal circuit courts are not allowed to prohibit the citation of unpublished opinions issued on or after January 1, 2007.

Reporters

Professors should introduce different publishers in the context of what they publish and the editorial enhancements offered. West Publishing Company is the major publisher for reporters and digests, but other legal publishers are strong in providing secondary sources. West developed the National Reporter System, a system of case reporters that provides court opinions from all states. There are seven regional reporters and a separate reporter for each of two large states—New York and California. Students should not spend time trying to understand the system because it was devised at the end of the nineteenth century, and it no longer makes any sense. Some states still have reporters of their own state opinions. The tendency has been to rely increasingly upon the National Reporter System for print versions of cases from the states, even when official reporters still exist. Federal cases are reported in their own reporters. The U.S. Supreme Court cases are printed in the *United States Reports* (official, but slowly printed and not useful), the *Supreme Court Reporter* (West), and the *United States Supreme Court Reports, Lawyers' Edition* (LexisNexis). The U.S. Court of Appeals decisions are published in the *Federal Reporter* (West), and the U.S. District Court opinions are published in the *Federal Supplement* (West). First-year students simply must memorize these titles for the federal reporters and their own state reporters.[20]

Details of a Case

Understanding the structure of a case will help students analyze cases more effectively. While they seem apparent to seasoned researchers, first-year instructors need to explain all the elements of a decision to students.[21]

Case Name or Party Name. The name of a case includes the names of the parties. Most cases are named for the parties involved to indicate who is suing whom (e.g., *Brannon v. Brannon*). Some cases may have only one name with a Latin phrase attached (e.g., *In re Seiferth*). In a criminal case, because the state brings the action, the first party will often be the state itself (e.g., *State v. Birditt*).

When a case begins in the trial court, the first name is the plaintiff, or the party suing, and the name after the *v.* is the defendant. On appeal, the name of the petitioner or appellant will be listed first; the name of the respondent or appellee will be listed second. Therefore, if the defendant in the trial court brings an appeal, his or her name may be listed first in the appellate case. The case name that appears at the top of the page in the reporters is not in correct citation format and should not be followed as an example of proper citation format.

Docket Number. When a case is filed with the court clerk, it is assigned a docket number that remains with the case and is used to keep track of all documents filed in the course of the litigation. If a case is appealed to a different level court, it will receive a new, different docket number for that court. Each court issues its own docket numbers, and the sequence of letters and numbers used to identify the case will vary from court to court.

Date. A case report will include the exact month, day, and year that it was decided. For citation purposes, only the year the case was decided should be used.

Synopsis and Summaries. Attorney-editors at West and attorney-editors at LexisNexis write a synopsis or brief description of each case. The synopsis includes the background and the holding. The synopsis also includes the name of the judge writing the opinion. If students have many cases to read, they can quickly scan the synopses to weed out the irrelevant cases, but students should be advised that the synopsis is not part of the opinion. Moreover, students must never cite the synopsis (except where state rules allow for it, as in Ohio) even when it gives an excellent summary of the case, because it is not authoritative.

Disposition. The *disposition* of the case is the court's decision to affirm, reverse, remand, or vacate the decision.

Headnotes. Court decisions contain at least one legal issue. An issue is the question raised when the facts of the case intersect with the rules of law. West attorney-editors identify the legal issues in the cases and discuss each issue in a *headnote*. Each headnote is usually one sentence. In reporters, headnotes appear between the synopsis and the opinion. A headnote in a West reporter begins with a number in boldface type followed by a topic name and key number. Headnotes are numbered so students can use them as they would a table of contents to the case. Numbers corresponding to the headnote numbers appear inside brackets within the text of the opinion. The bracketed number indicates the portion of the text summarized by a particular headnote. The headnotes in a LexisNexis case contain texts pulled directly from the case itself. The headnotes are also numbered. Students must recognize that West headnotes are different from LexisNexis headnotes.

Topics. In a West reporter, immediately following the headnote number is the broad legal topic under which a West attorney-editor has classified that particular headnote. *Topics* are the main headnote classification. After the topic in a West reporter, a key number is given. The key number represents a specific aspect or subsection of a topic.

Digests. Headnotes from West cases are grouped in books called *digests*, in which they are arranged by topics and key numbers. The lines of text in the digest are actually the headnotes themselves. The two things combined—the topic/key number and the summary of the issue—are consolidated into a headnote. Some cases have only one headnote, while others have dozens, depending on the number and complexity of the issues in the case.

Attorneys or Counsel. Immediately preceding the text of the opinion, students will find the names of the attorneys of record, along with the name of the attorney's firm. Students will later learn that searching for attorneys involved in cases is invaluable in their interviewing process for a job.

Opinion. The actual text of the decision in a case is called the *opinion*. The structure of an opinion generally includes a description of the nature of the case, a statement of the issues presented, the facts, the errors assigned if the case is on appeal, and the disposition.

If the judges who heard an appellate case do not agree on the outcome or the reasons for the outcome, there may be several opinions. The opinion supported by a majority of the judges is called the *majority* opinion. An opinion written to agree with the outcome but not the reasoning of the majority is called a *concurring* opinion. A dissenting judge disagrees with the opinion and judgment of the majority and writes a *dissenting* opinion. While only the majority opinion is a binding precedent, the other opinions provide valuable insight and may be cited as persuasive authority.

FINDING CASES

Locating cases on point is probably the most difficult task for a new researcher, yet all students must find cases relatively soon in their law school careers. Students can locate cases by using various tools, such as digests, annotated codes, online databases, and secondary sources.

Most instructors introduce students to West digests to locate cases. It is important for first-year students to be familiar with digests and know how to use them, but it is a difficult task. Legal research professors appreciate the incredibly efficient method of organizing and indexing virtually every printed decision.[22] Unfortunately, most students do not share the professors' passions for the West key number system. Some students never really understand digests, which is unfortunate because digests provide an effective and efficient method for finding cases.

Digests are indexes to case law. Digests contain abstracts or *digests* of cases organized by subject. West has the largest system since it is the only one that covers all American jurisdictions. Students will often obtain the best results by using digests in conjunction with Westlaw, which has the digests online. Once they discover digests online, students become more interested in the digest system.

The digest system contains a comprehensive list of legal topics that remains an amazing classification system. Each legal topic is subdivided into issues, and each issue is assigned a digest classification number called a key number.

Listed under each key number are headnotes from reported cases addressing the issue. Remember that West attorney-editors create headnotes by isolating and summarizing every issue of law that appears in the opinion and by assigning topics and key numbers to each headnote. Each headnote is assigned at least one topic and key number, and some headnotes are assigned several. Students do not necessarily need to know how West organizes its digest, but they do need both the topic and the key number to find cases.

Professors should stress the relationship between the headnotes and the digests because it is crucial for using the digests. The paragraphs in the digests are the headnote paragraphs from the cases in the reporters, rearranged according to subject. Headnotes from different cases that discuss the same point of law appear together in a digest, and the same headnote may appear in two or more places in the digest. Although the language is usually copied loosely from the text of the case, headnotes are written by West attorney-editors, not judges, and should never be cited. In a digest or any source, students should locate the most recent cases first and then work back in time.

Many times, a student will have a useful case that he or she found in a secondary source or one recommended by a professor. If students are lucky enough to know one relevant case, they can easily expand their research by using the West key number system in the West digests. From the case, students can determine the relevant topic and key numbers and then look in the appropriate jurisdictional digest to find cases that have headnotes classified under those topics and key numbers. All West digests use the same topic and key numbers, so "one good case" can be from any jurisdiction.

If students do not have one good case by which to find other cases, their gateway into the digest can be the descriptive word index (DWI). The DWI is a substantial list of everyday words, legal terms, and phrases. Under these DWI terms, students can find relevant topics and key numbers. Unfortunately, most students do not master the DWI, and they miss West's extraordinary indexing system for cases.

If students do not use digests, what do they use? For the most part, they use full-text searching on Westlaw and LexisNexis.[23] Students can use either Boolean (sometimes referred to as relevance-based searching) or natural language searching on either system. If students take advantage of the classes offered by librarians or LexisNexis and Westlaw representatives, they can become proficient searchers. Without training, students waste numerous hours with poorly crafted search terms.

In addition to digests and online searching, another effective way to locate cases is to begin with a state or federal statute and find the cases that interpret that particular statute. However, if there is no statute involved in the research project, then students have to search exclusively for case law. Of course, there are other ways to locate case law without a statute. There are excellent treatises and other secondary materials that cite cases.

Finding Cases Online

LexisNexis and Westlaw are the largest commercial providers of computerized legal research. However, there are less expensive and even free systems available.[24] LexisNexis and Westlaw offer very good training programs for law students on almost all aspects of legal research. Students should take advantage of the training while they are in law school. This is not to suggest that legal research professors should turn over online instruction to the vendor representatives. There is a place for vendor instruction in the first-year research program, but it should be in collaboration with the librarians. If legal research professors have a good relationship with their vendor representatives, students will learn from both instructors and vendor representatives.

LexisNexis and Westlaw offer two search methods: *natural language* and *terms and connectors*. The search method that is best for the user's needs is determined by several factors, including the type of information a student is looking for. Librarians prefer searching with connectors, but some studies show effective results with natural language. Students may use natural language searching if they are searching for broad concepts, if they are searching databases containing large numbers of documents, if they infrequently search online, or if they are not retrieving the information by using terms and connectors. On the other hand, if students are searching for particular terms or for a particular document, then they should use the terms-and-connectors type of search.

CITATORS

First-year students both grasp the concept of citators quickly and, if they take not only an introductory course to citators but also advanced training courses from either librarians or representatives, they will use the systems effectively. Students hear the horror stories about lawyers that have been sued for malpractice for the failure to update a case. They also hear unpleasant moot court stories about upper-class students who failed to find the latest changes in the status of a case. Therefore, they are usually anxious to use the online systems as often as possible. Students are especially pleased to hear from their professors that they should use the online systems exclusively and not the print citators. In fact, students should not use print citators except in the most limited of circumstances.[25] The print citators are not current, and the electronic format has many time-saving features.

Before using any legal authority to analyze a problem, students must know how that authority has been treated by later actions of a court, legislature, or agency. A case may have been reversed or overruled; a statute or regulation may have been amended or repealed. Pocket parts in digests and annotated codes provide access to newer law, but they do not indicate the status of older authority. Ensuring that the cases, statutes, and other authorities students rely on represent the *current* law requires an additional step. The generic term for this step is *updating*, though it is often called *Shepardizing* because the first major updating tool was *Shepard's Citations*. Of course, now there are two tools that are predominately used for updating: Shepard's (LexisNexis) and KeyCite (Westlaw).

When discussing citators, professors usually focus on cases, because cases are the authorities most often updated. Other authorities—including statutes, constitutional provisions, regulations, and some secondary sources—can also be updated, but those topics are usually discussed in advanced courses.

It is very important that students take the time to interpret the information presented and read the later authorities to determine how those later authorities affect their analyses. When students update a case, their main goal is to determine whether the case has been overruled or reversed. If it has been overruled or reversed, students must determine whether it was overruled or reversed for the same issue or point of law on which they are relying. First-year students rely too much on the colored signals found in the online citators and must be instructed repeatedly to understand the actual meaning and extent of affect noted by the signal.

Updating can be a valuable research tool at several points in the research process. Some researchers update cases as soon as they find them. A researcher following this method knows immediately whether a case is still respected authority. At the same time, the researcher also finds other cases and secondary sources that discuss the same points of law as the first case.

Others update cases later in the research process. In this instance, a researcher would begin by finding cases in annotated statutes and in digests, reading the cases, outlining an argument, and then updating only the cases that will likely appear in the memorandum. This researcher will have to update fewer cases but may have started to develop a line of analysis that is no longer "good law." In this case, the researcher may need to do additional research or rethink the argument.

There are a few differences in the way that Shepard's and KeyCite organize their information. For example, Shepard's organizes cases by jurisdiction; KeyCite organizes cases by treatment and then by depth of analysis. Students will quickly prefer one system to the other; however, for cases central to their arguments, students should check both systems because they will refer to different secondary sources.

Citators were designed primarily as an updating tool. However, once a student finds a relevant case, the citators can be used to find other cases dealing with the same issue.

STATUTES

During the first year of law school, most students will read and research cases, but not necessarily analyze and find *statutes*. In practice, students will definitely read and research statutes along with cases. When a student reads a statute, he or she must also read the cases that have interpreted the statute, because the wording may be ambiguous. The case law takes on a life of its own, but the statutes remain, and the legislators can modify or repeal them over the years.

Codes

When teaching new researchers about statutes, it is best to begin with a discussion of *codes*, particularly annotated codes. Starting state and federal statutory research with an annotated code is a very smart way to begin research. The concept of a statutory code is difficult for first-year students; however, once they are introduced to the arrangement and indexing of codes, students understand quickly how to use them.

First, students must understand that laws are classified—that is, codified—by subject or topic in volumes called codes. These codes group the laws by subject and show all subsequent amendments. Each subject matter is in a different title. Students will use an annotated code when they want to locate statutes with all of their amendments and deletions, along with notes of decisions applying to the statute.

Because some laws apply to more than one subject, students may have to check more than one place in the code. In addition to placing similar laws together under topics, codes also incorporate amendments and indicate repealed laws by stating that the law was repealed by a different code section.

To use the codes, students must use the index. The code indexes are detailed and easy to use. Students should not stop reviewing the index after finding just one statute reference; several statutes may address an issue. Sometimes a research term will be included in the index but will be followed by a cross reference to another index term. Referring to that term may lead students to relevant statutes.

Attorneys state that the next step is the most important: *read* the statute very carefully. Too many researchers fail to take the time necessary to read the language of the statute and consider all its implications before deciding whether it is relevant to the research problem. Moreover, because few statutes are so clear that they can be understood in one reading, careful research will likely require researchers to read a statute several times before they understand its meaning and relevance. Also, researchers should watch for the definition of terms. There is often a separate definitions section that appears with the code section. For all these reasons, new researchers should at least begin with the print codes. It is easier to scan ahead using the print format than it is on an online database.

Statutes seldom remain unchanged for very long. A future legislature may amend or repeal a statute for any number of reasons. Students should be wary of a statute that has not been altered in some way. Therefore, the constant possibility of change in legislation means that students must always check a law for recent changes. Look at the publication date (copyright date on the back of the title page) of the hardbound volume of the code to determine whether a law needs updating.

To check for amendments and deletions that have appeared since the bound volume was published, refer to the pocket parts inserted in the back of each volume and the supplementary pamphlets shelved at the end of the set. New students often forget to check the pocket parts. They are arranged by the same section numbers as the bound volume. Even though it is easier to work with print codes, students should be concerned with the currency of annual pocket parts. Even if students check the pocket parts, it is safer to update statutes online by checking the currency note of the document in online systems.

It is rare for researchers to locate a relevant statute and apply it immediately to the facts without first researching case law. Legislatures write broad statutes to apply to a wide array of circumstances. To be able to predict how a court may apply a statute to the facts, researchers must know how the courts have interpreted the statute and applied it in the past. Listed in the code under Notes of Decisions are short summaries of cases that have interpreted and applied that statute. In addition, annotated codes include extremely useful references to law reviews, treatises, and other secondary sources.

Every state has a statutory code, and some states have two. There are three federal codes; United States Code Annotated (U.S.C.A., West) and United States Code Service (U.S.C.S., LexisNexis) are quite similar. In general, the state and federal codes are available in print and online. United States Code (U.S.C.) is the official code for federal laws. Do not use the U.S.C. because the recompilations are slow, it has no annotations, and researchers using it will miss current laws, amendments, and deletions. A small library may have either U.S.C.A. or U.S.C.S. and using either one is appropriate.

The U.S.C.A. (available on Westlaw) is an example of the West publishing philosophy. West believes in providing as much information as possible and giving researchers tools that help them use that information efficiently and effectively. The U.S.C.A. includes more than 300 volumes and provides researchers with citations to cases and a wide variety of other references. Because each statute is followed by editorially enhanced notes and references to other research materials, the U.S.C.A. is easy to use and is an entry to finding cases.

U.S.C.S. (available on LexisNexis) also includes annotations to cases and other useful materials. U.S.C.S. fills 235 volumes and has numerous cross references to the Code of Federal Regulations (C.F.R.), treatises, and law review articles. U.S.C.S. has better coverage of citations to administrative decisions than U.S.C.A.

Session Laws

At the end of each session of Congress, the laws for that session are compiled and published in numerical order in bound volumes. *Session laws* are useful for looking for the original version of an act, as it existed prior to its codification by subject in the U.S.C., before amendments were added, or when students require the language of a particular amendment. First-year students will most likely not need to read session laws. However, they should know that, if needed, they could locate session laws in the United States Statutes at Large and the U.S. Code Congressional and Administrative News.

Legislative History

As much as some 1L professors feel that locating legislative intent is an important research skill, my years of experience in teaching legal research and have led me to conclude that 1L students do not need to know how to conduct a legislative history. I do not teach this. Hopefully, students will receive instruction in an advanced legal research course and learn about this topic then. If needed in practice, lawyers would be wise to learn this skill from a law librarian.[26]

ADMINISTRATIVE PUBLICATIONS

Currently, in the first year of law school, most students will not use or read administrative materials; however, the lack of administrative law in the 1L curriculum may be changing after the Carnegie Report[27] and the curriculum reform efforts underway at various law schools. Regardless, using administrative rules and regulations and the decisions of administrative boards is central to the practice of law. Therefore, in a first-year legal research class, our professors introduce students to the C.F.R. and the Federal Register. Students tend to forget what they learn about these publications as soon as possible, but at least they have heard of the resources if a partner in a law firm mentions them. During the same lecture as they learn about the C.F.R., students can also learn about looseleaf services, both in paper and online. Since looseleaf services concentrate in highly regulated areas, they are more commonly used than the official C.F.R. and Federal Register. First-year students quickly grasp the concept of looseleaf services, but rarely understand how to use them either in print or online until later in their law school career or in practice.

As an introduction, administrative law is the law created by administrative agencies in the form of rules, regulations, orders, and decisions. Regulations are not laws because they were not created by the legislature. However, regulations have the force of law. If students remember the two most important publications for regulations—the Federal Register and the C.F.R.—they will be ready for their first professional position. States also publish regulations, but each state has its own peculiar publication of regulations.

Federal regulations are published in the C.F.R., which is published by the U.S. Government Printing Office (G.P.O.) The C.F.R. is a codification of regulations issued by federal agencies. The index to the C.F.R. is challenging because there are almost no subject entries. In order to research regulations efficiently, a user should know the agency involved, along with the subject area.

C.F.R. volumes are updated and replaced annually. This is a major drawback of the C.F.R., and students should use caution when researching the print version. The C.F.R. on LexisNexis and Westlaw is up to date, and the current date is noted. The G.P.O.'s Electronic Code of Federal Regulations (e-CFR) is a free, currently updated version of the C.F.R. It is not an official legal edition of the C.F.R., but the e-CFR is an editorial compilation of C.F.R. material and Federal Register amendments all in one place. The current update status appears at the top of all e-CFR Web pages.

Students will find that an efficient way to begin federal administrative research is in an annotated statutory code that contains references to related regulations for each statute. After finding a statute on point, students should review the annotations following the statutory language for cross references to relevant regulations. Students may notice that the U.S.C.S. tends to provide more references to regulations than does the U.S.C.A.

New regulations and proposed changes to existing regulations are published first in the Federal Register. The Federal Register is the official daily publication for rules, proposed rules, and notices of federal agencies and organizations, as well as for executive orders and other presidential documents. Its continuous pagination means that page numbers in the thousands are common. A user must have a volume (or year) and page number because the "index" is impossible to use. Updating regulations refers to the process of determining whether the text of a regulation has changed or whether the regulation has been repealed. Print updating is cumbersome and should be avoided. If students use the C.F.R. on LexisNexis or Westlaw, they will feel confident that their regulation is current.

Looseleaf Services

Practitioners rely heavily on *looseleaf services*, in either print or online.[28] These services pull together both primary and secondary materials in an updated format. Looseleaf services are published in highly regulated areas, such as tax, environmental law, and securities. Looking in one place for both primary materials and explanations saves time for attorneys. Students will need guidance on how to use both the print and online versions of looseleaf services. Professors in legal research courses seldom have time to teach students how to use the services. However, 1L students should know their importance to them as practitioners.

There is a great deal more that students could learn about federal administrative law research, but it will not happen in the first year. Once students take tax courses or other administrative courses, they will quickly learn the importance of administrative research.

SECONDARY MATERIALS

Researchers have previously analyzed many of the issues that students will face in law school and in practice. Many have published their legal analyses in legal encyclopedias, treatises, law review articles, and other secondary sources. These sources are *secondary* because law professors, practicing attorneys, legal editors, and even law students write them. In contrast, as previously mentioned, legislatures, courts, and administrative agencies write *primary* authorities.

Often, beginning a new research project with a secondary source will be more effective for a novice researcher than beginning immediately to search for statutes or cases on point. In fact, the less information students know, the more valuable secondary resources are. By locating and understanding secondary sources on point, students can more easily comprehend the analysis of the problem and more quickly find pertinent primary authorities. The text of a secondary source will likely explain unfamiliar terminology and concepts, and secondary sources will make it possible for them to develop a more effective list of research terms. Secondary sources will also help students understand the cases and statutes when they read them.

Secondary sources often provide a shortcut to researching primary authorities by including numerous references to cases, statutes, and rules.

First-year law students will be introduced to the most commonly used secondary sources, including treatises, legal periodicals, legal encyclopedias, *ALR*, and Restatements. During the second and third years, students will use other secondary sources, such as practice materials, forms, and looseleaf services.

New students need to know "what the law is." It is very difficult for most students to understand the law just from reading the casebooks. An excellent place for them to begin researching "what the law is" is with treatises, which include hornbooks, nutshells, and multi-volume works. There are hornbooks and nutshells on all 1L subjects. Most treatises have very good indexes, and many treatises are available on LexisNexis and Westlaw. The advantage of using treatises online is the ability to click through to the cited sources. However, students will find using print treatises easy, especially if they want to see a particular section in its surrounding context. Students should pay particular attention to the copyright date of the main volume and the pocket part of the treatise. If it is old, students should move on to another, more recent title.

Novice researchers should not begin with law review articles unless they already know something about the subject area. Law review articles generally cover narrow legal topics in great depth. Therefore, law review articles are excellent resources for more advanced research on narrow topics, but not necessarily for beginning researchers.

One of the most important things that a 1L student can learn is how to use the library's online catalog. For example, most online catalogs include references to both print and online sources. Students often do not use the online catalogs,[29] and once discovered, students are amazed at the wealth of information. In a legal research class, instructors should stress the importance of online catalogs both in the law library and in other libraries.

Encyclopedias

All 1L students are introduced to the two major national legal encyclopedias, but there are other, superior secondary sources, for example, *ALR*, that introduce new researchers to a topic. The text of encyclopedia entries is cursory because the goal of the writers is to summarize the law. Encyclopedia entries will identify any variations that exist between different jurisdictions, but they do not attempt to resolve differences or recommend improvements in the law. New researchers should use caution when they use the two national encyclopedias, *American Jurisprudence 2d* (Am. Jur. 2d) and *Corpus Juris Secondum* (C.J.S.), due to the date of the volumes and the necessity of remembering to use the pocket parts, which themselves can be a year or more old. Additionally, encyclopedias emphasize case law and generally do a poor job with statutory or administrative law subjects. On the other hand, several state encyclopedias are written for attorneys and provide a practical approach to a topic.

Law Reviews

Law reviews publish scholarly articles written by law professors, judges, practitioners, and law students.[30] Each article explores in detail a specific legal issue. Freed from the constraints of representing a client's interests or deciding a particular case, an author is able to explore whether the laws currently in force are the best legal rules and to propose changes.

Law review articles are good at identifying weaknesses or new trends in the law that might address a client's situation. The many footnotes in law review and law journal articles can provide excellent summaries of relevant research. Students should pay particular attention to the date of the article. It usually takes at least a year for an article to appear in a journal from the time it was written. The sources cited in the footnotes are generally at least one year out of date and will likely need updating.

Articles written by students are called *notes* or *comments*. Although not as authoritative as articles written by recognized experts, student articles can provide clear and careful analysis, and their footnotes are valuable research tools.

By using a controlled list of subject headings in periodical indexes, researchers can focus on the articles that are on point. Using periodical indexes is always a more precise research method than searching journal articles in full-text databases. New and veteran researchers should not use the full-text databases on LexisNexis, Westlaw, or HeinOnline to find articles. It is a waste of time compared to using the online and print indexes. Therefore, researchers should first use the indexes and then read the full text of the article either in print or online on LexisNexis, Westlaw, or HeinOnline.

The indexes to periodicals include the *Current Law Index* (CLI) and the *Index to Legal Periodicals and Books* (ILPB). The database version of the CLIis called LegalTrac. If the library subscribes to both indexes, either online or in print, researchers should use both. Researchers will get different results from the two indexes.

HeinOnline offers the full text of a large number of law review titles. Most law review articles are available on HeinOnline within a year or two of publication. Because articles in HeinOnline are in portable document format (PDF), when one prints out a page or an article, it looks exactly as it would in the hard copy books. This is a major advantage over printing articles from Westlaw or LexisNexis, which are not paginated like the books and which place footnotes at the end of documents.

American Law Reports

Serious legal researchers are huge fans of *ALR*. If researchers have a very specific topic (and that is how lawyers practice), *ALR* is an excellent tool for finding pertinent cases. Then, the researcher can use the West topic and key numbers to find additional cases.

ALR in print offers both commentary on certain legal issues and the full text of major, published cases on those issues. *ALR* online offers the commentary and links to all cases discussed. The commentary articles are called *annotations*. They tend to focus on very narrow topics, take a practitioner's view, and provide a survey of the law in different jurisdictions. Thus, an annotation on the exact topic is likely to be extremely helpful.

If a student can locate an *ALR* annotation on his or her topic, it can save a considerable amount of research time. The only tricky thing about using *ALR* is that one must pay attention to the series; there are six for state cases plus two federal *ALR*s. Students should be cautioned not to waste time with an early numbered series because the annotation will most likely be rewritten. If students are using *ALR* in print, they should spend an extra minute and check the annotation citation in the Annotation History Table that is located in the index volumes. If the annotation has been superseded, it will give the citation in a later series. *ALR* is available on LexisNexis and Westlaw.

Restatements

First-year students will find Restatements cited in their contracts and torts casebooks. A Restatement is an organized and detailed summary of the common law (i.e., case law) in a specific legal area. Restatements are the results of collaborative efforts by committees of scholars, practitioners, and judges organized by the American Law Institute (ALI). These committees, led by a scholar called a *reporter*, draft text that explains the common law in rule format (i.e., they are written with outline headings similar to statutes, rather than in the narrative form of cases). The committees circulate the drafts for review and revision and are ultimately debated and approved by the entire ALI. The Restatement that is published by ALI includes not only the text of the rules that embody the common law but also commentary, illustrations, and notes from the reporter.

Restatements were originally intended simply to restate the law as it existed in an effort to build national consistency in key common law areas. Over time, Restatements grew more aggressive in stating what the authors think the law should be. First-year students should be aware of what a Restatement is when they read the excerpts in their casebooks. Some faculty may emphasize the importance of Restatements in their substantive law courses.

CONCLUSION

One of the greatest challenges legal research professors face is persuading students to connect with legal research materials in a manner that encourages them to learn. If 1L students acquire new knowledge about new research tools in context and not in isolation, they are more comfortable using the materials. Legal research professors have to decide the best way to put the material in context for their students.

It is also difficult for some professors to connect with students who feel that books are a less effective way to find answers to their legal research questions. Students feel that electronic research is the most successful strategy. If the legal research professor demonstrates the pros and cons of both print and online materials, students will be better prepared for most research situations.

During the years, various legal research professors have attempted to cover more topics than what is included in the core principles. This is usually a fatal error since students become overwhelmed with information that they do not need during their first year. If professors teach the core principles of legal research in a clear and understandable manner, students will easily grasp the subject matter. Students want to learn the material and gain a real sense of accomplishment by finding a case on point, using a code index to find a statute, and updating a case. Their satisfaction with these tasks is immediate and they are grateful to perform these tasks quickly and with little frustration.

Many law schools are undergoing curricular reform, which may or may not include changes in teaching legal research. Many challenges remain for teachers of legal research. As stated at the beginning of this article, we make it clear that we teach our students basic legal research skills. As students progress through law school and become new lawyers, we are hopeful that their research skills become more sophisticated and build on the foundation given to them during their first-year course.

NOTES

1. Donald J. Dunn, *Why Legal Research Skills Declined, or When Two Rights Make a Wrong*, 85 L. Lib. J. 49, 61 (1993) (explains legal research as a concept, rather than a course).

2. Ian Gallacher, *Forty-Two: The Hitchhiker's Guide to Teaching Legal Research to the Google Generation*, 39 Akron L. Rev. 151 (2006) (the author states that books are less important to our students and electronic research is a successful strategy for the Google generation).

3. This is not the place to discuss again the poor research habits of new law school graduates. Suffice it to say, there are several excellent articles detailing the problems associated with poor legal research skills. Joan Howland & Nancy Lewis, *The Effectiveness of Law School Legal Research Training Programs*, 40 J. Leg. Educ. 381 (1990); Robin K. Mills, *Legal Research Instruction in Law Schools, The State of the Art or, Why Law School Students Do Not Know How to Find the Law*, 70 L. Lib. J. 343 (1977); Thomas A. Woxland, *Why Can't Johnny Research? or It all Started with Christopher Columbus Langdell*, 81 L. Lib. J. 451 (1989); Thomson West, *Research Skills for Lawyers and Law Students,* White Paper (2007), available at http://west.thomson.com/pdf/librarian/Legal_Research_white_paper.pdf

4. *See* Special Committee on Fostering Legal Research as a Subject Specialty, AALL, *Final Report* (Oct. 2006), available at http://www.aallnet.org/committee/reports/FosterLegalResearchCmteReport-Oct.pdf.

5. Thomson West, *Partnership and Solutions for Preparing Job-Ready Attorneys*, White Paper (July 2008), available at http://west.thomson.com/support/librarian/event/AALLwhitepaper.pdf.

6. *Perspectives: Teaching Legal Research and Writing,* published by West three times a year; *Legal Reference Services Quarterly,* published by Routledge, Taylor & Francis; *Law Library Journal,* published quarterly by AALL. An example of a seminal article on the pedagogy of teaching legal research: Robert C. Berring & Kathleen Vanden Heuvel, *Legal Research: Should Students Learn It or Wing It?* 81 L. Lib. J. 431 (1989).

7. Students at Georgia State University use Nancy P. Johnson & Susan T. Phillips, *Legal Research Exercises, Following the Bluebook* (10th ed. Thomson/West 2008).

8. To name a few of the excellent recent research textbooks: Amy E. Sloan, *Basic Legal Research: Tools and Strategies* (4th ed. Aspen Publishers 2009); Christina L. Kunz, *The Process of Legal Research* (7th ed. Aspen Publishers 2008); Roy M. Mersky, *Berkan, Mersky and Legal Research Illustrated* (9th ed. Thomson/West 2008); Morris L. Cohen, *Legal Research in a Nutshell* (9th ed. Thomson/West 2007); Ruth Ann McKinney, *Legal Research* (5th ed. Thomson/West 2008); and books in the Carolina Academic Press Legal Research Series, including *Georgia Legal Research* (Carolina Academic Press 2007).

9. Deborah Hackerson, *Legal Research: A Guide to Online Tutorials for First-Year Law Students*, 25 Leg. Ref. Servs. Q. 153 (2006); Elizabeth G. Adelman, *CALI Lessons in Legal Research Courses: Alternatives to Reading about Research*, 15 Persps. Teaching Leg. Research & Writing 25 (Fall 2006); CALI Lessons are available at http://www.cali.org (there are currently over 75 CALI legal research lessons).

10. There are several articles detailing different teaching methodologies and styles: Dennis S. Sears, *The Teaching of First-Year Research Revisited: A Review and Synthesis of Methodologies*, 19 Leg. Ref. Servs. Q. 5 (2001); Charles J. Ten Brink, *A Jurisprudential Approach to Teaching Legal Research*, 39 New Eng. L. Rev. 307 (2005); James B. Levy, *Better Research Instruction Through 'Point of Need' Library Exercises*, 7 Leg. Writing 87 (2000).

11. Carrie W. Teitcher, *Rebooting the Approach to Teaching Research: Embracing the Computer Age*, 99 L. Lib. J. 555, 564 (2007) (the author describes one law school's adoption of a fully integrated legal research curriculum); Michelle M. Wu, *Why Print and Electronic Resources Are Essential to the Academic Law Library*, 97 L. Lib. J. 233 (2005) (discusses the pros and cons of the two formats).

12. Beth Simone Noveck, *Wikipedia and the Future of Legal Education*, 57 J. Leg. Educ. 3 (2007).

13. Barbara Bintliff, *Context and Legal Research*, 99 L. Lib. J. 249 (2007) (explains the shift from digests and print resources to electronic information and how basic communication theory is used to understand how the changes affect the shared context).

14. *The Bluebook: Uniform System of Citation* (18th ed. Harvard Law Review Association 2005); Mary Whisner, *The Dreaded 'Bluebook'* 100 L. Lib. J. 393 (2008) (discusses students' anxiety level in using *The Bluebook*).

15. Christina L. Kunz, *The Process of Legal Research* 158–159 (7th ed. Aspen Publishers 2008) (explains that the distinction between mandatory and persuasive precedent is critical).

16. The AALL study is available at http://www.aallnet.org/aallwash/authen_rprt/AuthenFinalReport.pdf.

17. ABA Standard 1.65 (a)(xiv)

18. William R. Mills, *The Shape of the Universe: The Impact of Unpublished Opinions on the Process of Legal Research*, 46 N.Y. L. Sch. L. Rev. 429 (2002).

19. Fed. R. App. P. 32.1.

20. Thomson West also issues a number of other reporters in specialized subject fields of federal law, including *Military Justice Reporter*, *Bankruptcy Reporter*, *Federal Claims Reporter*, and *Veterans Appeals Reporter*.

21. Orin S. Kerr, How to Read a Legal Opinion: A Guide for New Law Students, 11 Green Bag 51 (2007).

22. Robert C. Berring, *Legal Research and Legal Concepts: Where Form Molds Substance*, 75 Cal. L. Rev. 15, 22 (1987).

23. Lee F. Peoples, *The Death of the Digest and the Pitfalls of Electronic Research: What is the Modern Legal Researcher To Do?* 97 L. Lib. J. 661 (2005).

24. Lisa Smith-Butler, *Cost-Effective Legal Research Redux: How to Avoid Becoming the Accidental Tourist, Lost in Cyberspace*, 6 Fla. Coastal L. Rev. 101 (2008).

25. For some historical codes and an eclectic range of other materials, Shepard's includes coverage only in their print Shepard's Citations. However, for most research needs, the online citators are invaluable and the only source students will need.

26. Fortunately, legislative history is an easier task with the help of one of the several good online sources: Hein Online Legislative Histories, LexisNexis Congressional, LexisNexis Serial Set Digital Collection, Thomas, and G.P.O. Access.

27. William M. Sullivan, *Educating Lawyers: Preparation for the Profession of Law* (Jossey–Bass 2007).

28. Available looseleaf services in a subject arrangement and by publisher are listed in *Legal Looseleafs in Print*, published by Infosources Publishing. The information is also available online on LawTRIO Database, available at http://www.infosourcespub.com/cdlinks/search.cfm.

29. Scott Matheson & Stephanie Davidson, *The Evolution of Providing Access to Information: Is the Online Catalog Nearing Extinction?* 26 Leg. Ref. Servs. Q. 57 (2007).

30. Cameron Stracher, *Reading, Writing, and Citing: In Praise of Law Reviews*, 52 N.Y. L. Sch. L. Rev. 349 (2008) (exhaustive discussion of various aspects of law reviews).

On Teaching Advanced Legal Research

CHRISTOPHER A. KNOTT

Donald L. Garbrecht Law Library, University of Maine School of Law, Portland, Maine, USA

This article addresses the issues faced by instructors of courses in advanced legal research. Everyone teaching in this area must have a strategy for organizing the subject matter, drafting problems and assignments, constructing a syllabus, and planning and delivering a course designed to meet its stated goals. Most importantly, the instructor must give serious thought to the desired outcomes at which he or she aims. In this article, Professor Knott has categorized outcome targets into three levels: competency, fluency, and mastery. The instructor's decisions about desired outcomes will have implications for all aspects of course design and delivery. The article identifies and discusses these issues and provides a framework instructors can use when designing their own courses. Attached as appendices are specific examples of many of the kinds of materials discussed in the article, all drawn from material prepared for use in the author's advanced legal research classes.

INTRODUCTION

Advanced legal research (ALR) courses are taught at many law schools in the United States.[1] The content and format of these courses vary from institution to institution, and there is no national standard by which to measure one's own course. What, then, to teach in such a course? How best to teach it? How to measure success or failure? This article examines the range of practice in law schools and suggests ideas and approaches to consider. At some level, however, each ALR instructor bears the final responsibility for deciding what will be the experience of students, the desired outcome, and the methods of measuring achievement in his or her own classroom.

What seems undeniable is that the need for such instruction is greater than ever before. General information literacy among law students has been shown to be inadequate to the task of successfully negotiating the increasingly complex legal information environment.[2] Online keyword-based systems have supplanted carefully ordered intellectual systems in the minds of many beginning researchers, and the sources and access to material has exploded to such an extent that even specialists find keeping current a challenge. ALR instruction, carefully designed and intelligently executed, can arm law students with the knowledge and skills necessary to solve real research problems efficiently and with confidence. Law librarians, with their long experience with ordered systems and constant contact with faculty, students, and lawyers in the process of research and information seeking, are best suited to deliver such instruction.

DECIDING WHAT TO TEACH

A commonly held view is that legal research is different in many, if not most respects, from what it was even ten years ago. That may or may not be true (and I am inclined to believe that things have changed far less radically than is commonly supposed), but the idea of change is certainly today's currency. It is well worth examining what ALR courses have traditionally sought to teach students, and assessing whether these lessons remain relevant, or whether the Web, Google, Lexis, and Westlaw, and online access to a vast array of legal material has so altered the intellectual landscape that an entirely new pedagogy needs to be developed. As in most things, the answer probably lies somewhere in between the view that everything has changed and the view that nothing has.

Accepting for the moment that the ubiquity of the online environment has changed not only the production and presentation of legal information, but also the ways in which lawyers will search for and make use of that information, how can that change be described? What exactly is different, and does it matter for the ALR instructor? More to the point, what effect does this change have on what law schools should expect graduating students to know about legal information and legal research?

Starting with the obvious first, the explosion of information on the Web has dramatically altered the expectations and information-seeking behaviors of law students. Undergraduates, and much of society, have become accustomed to finding what they need to know on the Web. Law librarians know how much of the best and most useful legal information exists in print format only or is best used in print, but the law students librarians serve are skeptical, if not in open disbelief, when told this. Whatever other goals the instructor brings to the course, of paramount importance is to help students understand the difference between a retrieval search using one search engine or another and real legal research. Retrieval is not research, and finding something is no substitute for finding everything or finding the right thing. Law students should be taught how indispensible context is to their work and that legal information systems already in place are structured specifically to provide that context.

An undeniable and profound change from the law students of a generation ago is the degree of experience with libraries many law students bring to an ALR class. Instructors used to be able, for example, to explain legal periodical indexes with an offhand comparative reference to the *Reader's Guide to Periodical Literature*, confident that every student in the school would have used this resource at some point in junior high school, high school, or college. It is simply no longer the case that most students will have long experience in libraries, working with catalogues, indexes, and other finding aids. The practical upshot of this is that the instructor must be prepared to explain systems of classification, the mechanics of basic research, and other topics once considered remedial.

If it is true that today's younger students have come to the study of law lacking depth of experience with research strategies and tools generally, how does the ALR instructor adjust to this new reality? Teaching ALR as if nothing has changed in the past generation or so is simply not realistic. Innocent as many younger law students are of the basic tools of library research, one must wonder how best to approach this population when teaching ALR. The normative position, insisting that students must conform to older tropes of practice and training, is almost certainly doomed to failure. Long discredited—and in my view, completely outmoded—the view of legal research instruction that considers a thorough grounding in processes and methodologies that would have been familiar to lawyers of prior generations as a necessary if painful part of the socialization of new lawyers is a brutalizing and essentially self-defeating view of the world.

However, it is critically important that students be taught ideas and practices that may be entirely foreign to their Google-based information-seeking experience: the power of a classified and structured system of information. As an example, researching case law with only keyword searching is, as every law librarian well knows, fraught with pitfalls.[3] The ordered intellectual outline of the law found in West's American Digest System (to name only the best known of a number of ordered legal information systems) overcomes the vagaries of vocabulary, conceptual drift over time, and other problems that beset the committed keyword-only searcher. Driving this point home in an ALR class involves a good deal of pointed discussion and illustrative problem solving but is necessary to produce effective researchers.

Another result of the information and technological revolutions of recent years is that libraries and librarians are no longer the gatekeepers for most information. This is as true in the law library as in any other kind of library. Not too long ago, a student or faculty member needing, for example, a statute from another state, had no practical option other than to visit the library. The librarian's job was to gather the best resources, according to standards carefully worked out over generations, and to be ready to teach others how to locate and use that information in the library. Researchers were forced into a transaction of some sort with the library and its staff, but on the positive side, the researcher was required to know little or nothing about selecting or evaluating the available resources. With the advent of Lexis, Westlaw, the Web, and electronic databases, that arrangement is forever altered. One can say that the responsibility for evaluating resources has been decentralized, residing now with each researcher instead of with the librarian. Put another way, the researcher is no longer forced into a transaction with the library in order to find that statute, but the cost of that convenience (if convenience it is) is that the researcher bypassing the library must make evaluation decisions on his or her own. To say that students in any setting are not being taught to take on this obligation hardly begins to describe the state we are in. Very few students can accurately evaluate the information they find online. Whether ALR courses can meaningfully teach this discrimination remains an open question.

A final reality that instructors of ALR must take into account is that the explosion and variety of formats, coupled with the expectation of instant access to all information and the inexperience of many younger students with the basics of libraries and research, have all conspired to make legal research—real and creditable legal research—harder to perform. During the past few decades, the drive of librarians to conquer the access issue has been successful; a library can offer instant or nearly instant access to more or less anything related to law (and most of the rest of the disciplines nearly as easily). In order to do so, however, libraries, abetted by publishers and governments, have created systems of a high degree of complexity. I am not making the claim that the complexities of our research and information systems have contributed to the resistance of some law students to learning the details of thorough legal research, rather, I believe there has been a confluence of several related trends. Less rigorous and thorough training in research methods and sources in secondary and post-secondary education, easily accessed, keyword-based Web searching, and the fact that effective use of even a small law library is more difficult to master than ever, are an unhappy and unfortunate coincidence.

Exacerbating this state of affairs is that the otherwise salutary professionalization of the legal research writing instructor in American law schools has resulted in the slow evolution of these courses into remedial writing courses. No criticism of the emphasis on writing is intended here, but when law schools set out to improve the writing ability of their students and hire instructors for the first-year programs who consider themselves writing instructors first, the inevitable result is that first-year students receive correspondingly less instruction in legal research. This leaves students entering the second and third years of law school with lower levels of training in legal research sources and methods than might have been true at earlier times. The ALR instructor must, I think, remedy this situation by seeking first to demystify the library and its systems, or the rest of the message is likely to go unheard.

DECIDING HOW TO TEACH

Knowing what to teach in an ALR course can be as difficult as the teaching itself. Establishing goals is probably the first step in effective teaching. What does the instructor want the student to know at the end of the course? In my own teaching, I keep a list of ideas or principles[4] that I consider to be indispensible for the researcher. I update it every time I teach and design my course around those ideas. This list can be quite simple. For instance, students must, in my view, understand the purpose, meaning, and value of annotation. Why do annotated codes exist? Why do publishers produce them, lawyers use them, libraries buy them? What do they include, and how are they useful? And perhaps most importantly, why would a researcher need an annotated code when the statutes themselves are available via the Web? A student who clearly understands the answers to these questions can attack a statutory research problem in an entirely different way and on a much higher level than one who does not.

Once the instructor has outlined the course goals, the rest of the teaching is designed in service of achieving those goals. This is, of course, much more difficult than it sounds. An important piece of information is the starting point: what does the individual student in the class know, and what is the level of knowledge in the class as a whole? Pretesting can help establish this baseline and can help the instructor plan a route from this intellectual starting point to the desired outcome.

Establishing a Baseline Through Pretesting

Conducting pretesting at an early stage in an ALR class can give the instructor a much clearer idea of the baseline knowledge and skills upon which he or she has to build. However designed and administered, an effective pretest allows the instructor to both gauge the skill set of each individual student and get a sense of the class as a whole. Based on the results, the instructor can determine, for example, how much base knowledge of sources, of the interaction of cases, of statutes and secondary material, and so on, to count on when addressing the class.

Pretests can be of several different types, but the idea is to test student knowledge on multiple levels and on a variety of topics related to legal information. One idea is to ask students to complete a series of short-answer questions before the first class.[5] When I have used this style of pretest, I stress that this is only a pretest and will be ungraded. I usually distribute an answer key when I hand back the papers after examining them to see which questions students did well answering and which they were unable to answer.

A second type of pretest, comprised of simple multiple-choice quiz-type questions[6] might be prove an effective way to determine whether students come to the ALR course in command of the basics of the federal and state court systems, what a digest is used for, why annotated codes are superior to non-annotated versions, and so on. This format has the advantage, of course, of being easy to draft and quick to grade, no small consideration at the beginning of a semester.

The first two styles of pretest are designed to elicit answers illustrating the degree and depth of the students' understanding of legal resources and perhaps inevitably focus on the bibliographic. The instructor seeking to understand whether his or her students are able to construct and execute an effective search should pretest using a different approach. This third approach involves asking students at the beginning of the class to research a particular problem and keep a detailed log of their process, allowing the instructor to not only analyze the almost certainly inadequate strategy and performance of his or her students, but also allowing the instructor to describe the typical process to the class and to use that summary as a point of comparison and a point of departure throughout the rest of the semester.[7] This more active pretest also allows students to compare their progress over the course of the semester. It is often with a shock, and with no small embarrassment, that students look back at how they attacked the pretest problem after the end of the class. This dramatic proof of the effect of a little knowledge on their own effectiveness and confidence is often the single most important lesson ALR students take away from the class. The drawback to this approach is that the answers given by students before the beginning of the ALR course are generally so inadequate, and so predictable in strategy and execution, that the instructor often learns very little that is new or particular to any specific class of students. The decision of which approach to use in pretesting students is, not surprisingly, entirely dependent upon the instructor's methods and goals. Regardless of which type of pretest is utilized, I have found pretesting has always produced information I find useful throughout the rest of the semester.

Once the instructor has an idea of the strengths and weaknesses of particular students or the class in the aggregate, he or she can set about adjusting lectures and assignments to ensure that the students learn what they need to learn and that no valuable time is wasted repeating ideas or information the students already have well in hand. It almost certainly makes no sense to attach letter grades to these pretests that will count in the final grade or even to make extensive remarks or corrections on any individual response. The point is to create a picture of the state of student skills before the class begins.

Constructing a Syllabus

Designing the topics to be covered in ALR courses and the sequence in which they are introduced is a subject on which there is no profession-wide consensus, although there are several standard patterns. These patterns correspond roughly to the underlying philosophy or goal of the ALR course. ALR courses having a bibliographic orientation, i.e., those in which a thorough grounding in the sources and their use is the primary aim, tend to focus on categories of sources. Statutes are taught in week one, cases in week two, and so on. This is probably the most common approach and is a time-tested way to cover all of the basics in a one-semester course.

Some ALR courses are taught with an emphasis on process, establishing an approach to legal research that can be employed in many or most research situations. Such a course may be structured in the same way as the bibliographic course but will stress different things—namely, the ways in which a researcher moves from one source to another using intrinsic cues. Often offering a template for conducting research and leaving students with a comforting sense that they are learning how to approach novel problems, this approach is often used in first-year legal research and writing courses as well.

The third type of ALR course, the approach I use in my own teaching, focuses on the structure of legal information. This structuralist approach can be taught in any number of ways—source by source as in the above, or by describing the evolution of legal information sources over time, or by describing the action of governments and asking students to imagine how best to report the results of that action. This last approach, describing legal resources as having grown more or less organically from need, rather than developing by whim or by accident, allows the instructor to introduce some fairly complex ideas in a straightforward way; namely, the legal information system that has developed has done so in its current form because it is useful, it solves the problems of governments and lawyers, and the structure itself carries meaning and intellectual content.

As an example of this structuralist approach, imagine introducing the annotated federal code to a class of ALR students. Simply describing this resource, its constituent parts, its uses, and its online versions is necessary but not very enlightening. The students are left accepting the existence, description, and function of the annotated code, but they have not been given enough of the story to truly understand why this resource evolved in the way it has. How to provide the missing understanding? I start with a thought experiment. I ask the student to imagine a legal system like ours, but without any publications to memorialize what the courts, the legislature, and the executive branch are doing. The legislature would be passing laws, and eventually it would occur to someone that it would be very useful to have a record of these laws. Published in order as they are passed, and in their original and official language, this publication, the session law, becomes the publication of record for legislative action. Very quickly, though, the volume of chronologically arranged laws becomes such that it is impossible to find all of the different laws on a specific subject. In order to determine the law on any particular topic, the researcher has to page through each act to find relevant language, determine which later language supersedes or contradicts earlier language, and so on. Eventually, the idea of arranging all of the session laws by subject will become necessary for researchers; this is the code. The session laws are still the official statement of the legislature, but the code is what researchers need. But even that innovation is not sufficient, because in our legal system the statutory language alone is not enough to learn what the law is on any specific subject, since the statutes are subject to review, interpretation, and explication by courts. In addition, legal scholars often write articles and books that influence the interpretation or application of statutes. In short, to determine what a statute means, the researcher has to consult a variety of resources. As useful a shortcut as the code may be, even better from the researcher's standpoint would be a code that also provided citations to and/or summaries of the relevant related material. Out of this need, the annotated code was born.

This story is, of course, second nature to the law librarian and the ALR instructor. However, I have come to believe that presenting the resources in this way, as having grown naturally and organically out of the requirements of government and the needs of researchers, gives students a depth of understanding of legal information and an expectation that legal information is ordered and arranged in logical, predictable patterns. A law student thus armed is prepared to think critically about resources and will approach legal research in a completely different way from a student who has no such understanding of why legal information resources developed as they did and exist in the form they do.

The course syllabus may not, and I would argue, need not, reflect the approach described above. Teaching the course as an extended narrative of how legal information develops and evolves as a response to the needs of governments and researchers does not on its face dictate the ordering of topics or even the topics covered. However constructed, the ALR course syllabus should provide the student with an intellectual framework sufficient to place each lecture, each research assignment, and each reading assignment in its proper context. The instructor should require students to work, to think, to strive, and to seek understanding, but this process is not helped in any way by hiding the ultimate goal. Students can benefit from being told and shown from the beginning exactly what is expected of them and what they will know at the end of the course if they are successful. The syllabus is the place to start this. A good syllabus contains the outline of the student's development and not just times, dates, and assignments.

In my own teaching, I have chosen to distribute a syllabus that ignores most of the advice given above. My syllabus has class meeting times, the general topic for each class, readings, and other mundane information. I couple that document with a separate student outline[8] for each class meeting. This student outline contains a more detailed outline of what I intend to cover that day, goals for the class, major and minor concepts I plan to stress, and so on. By breaking the syllabus down into thirteen class-specific documents, I find I can deliver more content and can adjust my focus as the semester progresses.

Selecting Readings and Drafting Research Assignments

Central to any ALR class are the readings and research assignments to be completed during the semester. Selecting readings is often a very difficult process. There are several standard texts in common use in law schools (I have co-authored one, there are other excellent choices from which to pick), but many instructors choose instead to assign shorter readings from a wide variety of sources. The bibliography of legal research is extensive, and librarians are generally willing to exchange ideas, but in the end, the selection of reading material for an ALR course will come to reflect the predilections of the instructor. There is no substitute for reading widely in the field and collecting articles and other works that seem instructive or useful.

It is typical that the course work will include a number of research assignments to be completed, graded, and discussed during class. Indeed, many instructors have chosen to fashion their classes along the lines of a lecture and laboratory model, with research problems acting as lab work. This accomplishes multiple goals; it provides a reinforcement of lessons learned, offers practical experience working with materials and techniques discussed in class, offers diagnostic information to the student and the instructor, and gives the student ongoing feedback about progress and understanding. Designing effective research assignments is frankly difficult, but there are many sources available that contain problems an instructor can tailor. The same exchange among instructors, formal and informal, that exists for compiling reading lists is also a useful place to turn for assignment ideas.

Over the years, I have experimented with just about every type of research assignment there is. Some kinds of problems work reasonably well, some kinds work less well, but every research assignment involves a compromise. No matter how carefully designed, no classroom assignment can avoid being fundamentally artificial and abstract. That said, the research assignments should be an important, if not a central, component of the course. The research assignment should accomplish two goals: to reinforce and make as real as possible the content of lectures and readings and also to give the students experience in facing the challenges posed by legal research in practice.

The problems I use in my classes are very similar to the problems found in Appendix D, below. I draft them myself and use state and federal advance sheets to find interesting opinions. I work backward from the holding to derive an initial question that is similar in nature to the kind of question a client or a senior lawyer might give to a young lawyer to handle. (Often, the question I compose bears only a casual relationship to the actual opinion from which I have borrowed facts and holding. With a legal question prepared, I ask the students to perform specific tasks or steps. Almost invariably, this involves requiring them to prepare a research plan, which forces students to think about what kind of question this is, what area of law is implicated, what jurisdiction is involved, and so on. The most important part of the process is to ask the students to use their research plans to outline their initial approach to the research. In other words, I ask the students to demonstrate an understanding of how to proceed once they have provisionally decided what the question is about.

Students are introduced to this method slowly over time. For the first few weeks of the course, I pose these questions as thought experiments only and we discuss them in class. The questions I pose during this introductory period are intended to signal what I expect them to think through for themselves later. For example, if a student believes that the answer to a particular question will be found in a regulation, I then ask what steps the student intends to take that are designed to find relevant regulations. I am trying to instill in students one way to think about research; the research plan, the estimate of the answer's form or source, the initial steps in the plan, and the resources the students will consult are all related. These steps are all connected by the researcher's conception of what the question is really asking. We then talk about how to adjust the plan and the approach if the initial idea bears no fruit. Throughout the semester, the students progress from answering these questions together in class, to writing out all the plans and steps individually, and later in the semester, to actually completing the research. This involves a great deal of problem drafting and assignment correcting, but the results are, in my view, well worth the effort.

Other instructors employ radically different kinds of problems, and every good teacher has developed his or her own method of helping students put knowledge gained from readings and lectures into action. For the beginning instructor, my advice is to try a wide variety of approaches until something seems to fit and produces answers that are close to the goals for the course. I am always searching for better problems and better methods of getting students the experience they need, and I am convinced there is no one best approach.

Blending Sources, Process, and Structure

As discussed above, the syllabus and the conduct of the course will depend to some extent on the philosophical orientation and goals of the instructor. For purposes of illustration, I have presented the three types of course in very broad terms, and it is unlikely that seasoned instructors will find their particular approach described precisely by any one of the three categories. What can be stated with confidence, however, is that any successful course will include elements of all three ideas.

Regardless of emphasis or organization, any successful ALR course must impart to students a knowledge of the sources of the law, some idea of a process whereby all the relevant information may be gathered, and an understanding of the shape of any area of law (what sources exist, why are they produced and by whom, what constitutes persuasive evidence in this area of law, can I be sure I have everything, and so on). Armed with sufficient expertise in these three areas of understanding, a student can confidently tackle most legal research problems. Every instructor must seek his or her own ideal balance, but the ultimate goal should be to impart an understanding of what sources exist and how they are used, and a sense of the context in which any specific point of legal information exists.

For example, the instructor can pick a particular area of law—say, federal tax—to illustrate the three different kinds of understanding. Federal tax is considered a difficult field in which to conduct research in part because the sources of law are so diffuse and varied. One simply cannot effectively conduct research in tax without understanding that the federal taxing power stems from an amendment to the Constitution. Congress, armed with the constitutional power to levy taxes, has established the Internal Revenue Code, which is the entirety of Title 26 of the United States Code (U.S.C.). In addition to this direct law making, the Congress has also delegated rule-making authority to the Treasury Department, most importantly to a unit of Treasury, the Internal Revenue Service (IRS). Those regulations are found in Title 26 of the Code of Federal Regulations (C.F.R.). Tax cases can be litigated in state courts, federal courts, the United States Tax Court, and so on. The mass of case law and its scattered venues is another daunting hurdle for the researcher. The IRS produces additional material that is useful in interpreting and applying statutes and regulations. These publications, private letter rulings, field manuals, etc., are important elements of tax research. And the list goes on and on. A catalogue of primary and secondary sources is very useful, even critical, but gives very little insight into how these pieces interact. After the sources are identified (no small task in this case), the researcher needs a process whereby all of the relevant material, regardless of source, may be gathered. Out of this need grows the tax looseleaf, which has as its primary reason for existence the gathering of all related material, regardless of source, into one place. The tax researcher with an understanding of these two ideas—that there are a wide variety of primary and secondary sources that might contain useful information and that the tax looseleaf exists to draw these sources together in one logical package—has a realistic chance of successfully researching a tax problem. The third step, understanding the shape of the subject's literature, is the final step on the road to true mastery. At this stage, the researcher understands the broad outlines of tax, the issues raised in its practice, and how the resources developed and why they exist in the form they do. Mastery involves knowledge of the sources of authority in the field and the resources that contain or describe that authority; a clear sense of what is and is not likely to be found in those resources; and how to efficiently develop a plan to consult the appropriate publications in the proper way to elicit the required answers. Many law librarians know how to quickly master an unfamiliar area of law. Imparting that ability to students is among the most ambitious and difficult goals to achieve in the ALR course.

THE LEVELS OF UNDERSTANDING

The ALR instructor must make another critical decision when designing the course: what level of achievement to aspire to. In other words, what degree of mastery is the course's goal? What will be expected of students? The answer will affect everything the instructor does, from assigning readings to planning how to evaluate student performance.

One can think in terms of three levels of achievement: competence, fluency, and mastery. I will attempt to define these levels in the following paragraphs and to describe what characterizes each. To some extent, the instructor operates within parameters which will influence, if not dictate, the ambitions for the course's students. For example, ALR is taught in a variety of settings under different names. The traditional ALR course is a two- or three-credit hour seminar and workshop class, offering a good deal of in-class time and carrying an expectation of an amount of outside preparation adequate to develop a fairly deep understanding of the course material. Law schools also offer one-credit (or occasionally no credit) ALR courses in the form of "preparing to practice" or "bridging the gap" programs. Valuable and popular as these courses can be, there simply isn't enough time in or out of class to aim much higher than basic competence. In some law schools, ALR is taught as a one-credit addition to a doctrinal course (e.g., a tax law research addition to a tax law course). These courses, focused as they are on one specific area of law, offer little opportunity to develop deep knowledge of legal research but can be a valuable introduction to concepts that a more substantive legal research course might examine in detail.

Competence

Without implying any criticism of legal research and writing instruction in law schools, it is beyond debate that most law students enter their upper class years without any real understanding of legal research, any sense of its importance to their future success as lawyers, nor any real urgency to learn more. Why can't students learn legal research in the first year? There are doubtless many reasons, but it is worth examining a few of the most important and universal. Legal research and writing is usually taught in very large sections, making individualized and flexible teaching difficult to accommodate. There is also a (proper, in my view) emphasis on the forms of legal writing. That said, much writing instruction is remedial in nature. It is hard to imagine a successful law student or lawyer who is unable to write well. Finally, and most importantly, the first year is simply too early in one's legal education to effectively learn much of what ALR seeks to impart. It is relatively easy to explain to beginning law students that cases are important, that they appear in reporters, and that one can use digests to find cases on a particular topic, but first-year (usually first-semester) students simply do not know enough about the law to delve more deeply than that, let alone conduct even simple research effectively.

Given that, the ALR course is really the first chance a student has to achieve something approaching basic competence in legal research. What is basic competence, and of what is it comprised? Basic competence implies an understanding of the sources of law, the publication of the law, and the existence and use of basic finding aids. The competent legal researcher should be comfortable using materials in multiple formats and understand the advantages and disadvantages inherent in each format.

Taking professional responsibility as an example, the competent legal researcher might know that the regulation of lawyers in her state is a matter of state law. These laws are found in the state's code, and the competent researcher is well aware of the advantages of consulting an annotated code. She may also have a vague awareness that the bar of the state is charged with overseeing lawyer discipline and that the attorney general of the state occasionally issues opinions, some advisory in nature, concerning the legal profession in the state. She may also be aware that on occasion there are appeals from these disciplinary proceedings and that it might be well to search for case law on point in the state's reporter. Competence means that the researcher knows, or can find out, which government actors have authority to make laws or rules, decide cases, and so on, and can match those actors with the resources that contain reports of their actions.

Fluency

Beyond mere competency lies fluency. Fluency in legal research means knowing the categories of sources of legal information, their use, and their relative authority. Able to work in print or electronic form, the fluent legal researcher is familiar with resources and techniques, has confidence when beginning a research problem, and knows when to seek help. Perhaps it is best to say that the fluent legal researcher is a critical consumer of information. Lexis and Westlaw natural language searching seems easy and will always return some answer to any query, but the fluent researcher knows, or at least suspects, that there may be a better or a different way.

Fluency lies between competence, which may be said to be a minimal set of skills and basic understanding of how legal information fits together, and mastery, by which the researcher can see the entire field before him or her and has an expectation of what exists, what is likely to be found, and what use can be made of the results. Many practicing lawyers never attain fluency, but a law school should aspire to graduate as many students as practical with at least this level of achievement.

To return to the example of professional responsibility, the fluent researcher knows all the competent researcher knows and more. She knows that her state's laws regulating lawyers were derived from a model or uniform law and knows that this has implications for the breadth of case law and related research. In fact, there are multistate reporters, keyed to the underlying uniform or model sources that can provide opinions from other jurisdictions which might have more persuasive value than extra-jurisdictional case law in other areas of law. Similarly, the fluent researcher knows that the relevant Restatement is more authoritative and will probably be accorded more weight by readers than almost any other secondary source.

Mastery

Mastery in legal research is the highest goal to which the ALR instructor and student can aspire. A student who has mastered legal research (and I do believe this is possible for the intelligent and hard-working law student taught by a skilled instructor) knows much that most lawyers do not. At the highest levels of attainment, a student will have a deep understanding of the larger framework of legal information and can accurately place any particular question in its proper context. This student will be indifferent to format and will be able to articulate sound reasons why keyword searching or human ordered searching is most likely to produce the best results. A student with mastery will have internalized the principles of source evaluation and can readily assess the authority, reliability, currency, etc. of any resource encountered.

Why would any ALR instructor not aim for mastery? It may be that there are simply too many students to teach to propel all of them to this advanced level. This is the case in law schools that require some ALR course work for all students. It is very difficult to muster the human resources to ensure that each student is progressing towards mastery. It may also be the case that the ALR course offering is one credit, which is probably not enough contact time to patiently unwrap unfamiliar systems, explain difficult and complex intellectual concepts, and carefully lead students to a deeper understanding of legal information. There is no shame in producing new lawyers who are competent and/or fluent in research. One works within existing systems at the highest level available.

Returning once more to professional responsibility, the researchers who have achieved true mastery will know all of the available sources, will understand the implications of their genesis and development, know how to weigh their relative value and authority, and can develop a plan designed to lead to an answer. Additionally, the master researcher can move freely among formats, has a clear understanding of why and when to choose keyword searching over a human-ordered arrangement like a digest, or the reverse. The master researcher knows where to go to find new developments, how to identify trends, and how to construct a winning (or at least a plausible) argument in the face of adverse authority. A researcher with mastery of the field knows what sources and what answers are likely to be found, and it is just this expectation that sets the master apart. With a client facing a disciplinary proceeding for an alleged violation of the state's professional ethics rules, the competent researcher knows how to find the statutes and cases. The fluent researcher knows what opinions or articles or ideas courts are likely to find authoritative, knows how to craft an argument in a case of first impression by cobbling together authority from related factual situations or other jurisdictions. The master can derive the general principles or spot the general trends in the case law or disciplinary board enforcement. The master can find and recognize useful analogies from related areas of law. Finally, the researcher who is a master can gather and use all of the relevant material, while simultaneously distilling what she has found into arguments, ideas, and principles to be deployed as needed. The master can, to put it colloquially, see the entire field.

MEASURING OUTCOMES

ALR instructors must wrestle with the difficult question of how to evaluate student performance in the class. There are a variety of methods, none perfect. For the beginning ALR instructor, no part of the teaching experience is more fraught with uncertainty. Even among seasoned instructors, very, very few are completely comfortable with the method they have chosen to evaluate student performance. There are several different possibilities.

A final exam is one popular method for assessing how well or poorly students have performed. Often difficult to construct, a final exam in ALR works well for testing how well students understand important concepts, or at a lower level, to test whether students have successfully mastered the details of particular resources. The disadvantage is that there is little opportunity in this format to test the ability of students to conduct actual research.

Many ALR instructors assign a pathfinder or other final project in order to allow students to demonstrate their knowledge of a particular area of law and to demonstrate an orderly and methodical approach to conducting research. Using pathfinders and similar final projects as evaluative tools is relatively common, but there are several drawbacks to doing so. This approach does not directly test a student's ability to solve actual (or at least realistic) research problems and these projects are not something practicing lawyers do, which can make the exercise seem too far removed from the skills teachers seek to impart. The artificiality of the project, and its disconnectedness from actual legal research conducted to solve a problem, lead some instructors away from this kind of assessment tool, although many excellent instructors value the opportunity the pathfinder or similar project affords the student to delve deeply into the literature of an area of law. This fact outweighs any potential problems in using the project for assessment.

Some ALR courses conclude with an actual legal research problem, assigned to students for completion within a certain time period, along the lines of a take-home examination. Although very difficult to administer (A different problem for each student? Is that fair? The same problem to each student? How to ensure that each student does his or her own work?), this approach is the choice in some ALR courses because it directly examines the ability of the student to perform actual research, which is, after all, the ultimate goal of the course.

Regular research assignments throughout the semester are a routine feature of most ALR courses. Some instructors assign a letter or number grade to each of these assignments and assign a final grade based on the cumulative score achieved, dispensing with any other method of testing student achievement. This approach has the obvious advantage of forcing students to be as diligent as possible when completing the research assignments but carries the disadvantage of not allowing for the opportunity for one climactic summary exercise, whether exam or project. There is something galvanizing about the preparation for an exam or final paper or project, and the instructor should not lightly dismiss the value of the capstone experience for student learning and satisfaction.

Oral examinations in ALR courses also have advocates. Time consuming and subjective, oral examinations also provide the instructor with the clearest evidence of the state of a student's knowledge of the material covered in the course or so say the method's proponents. It is not unlikely that oral examinations might meet with resistance from students, but the idea is certainly intriguing.

There are doubtless other methods being practiced which are not listed here. Some instructors give a midterm exam, many do not. Some count things like attendance and class participation in the calculation of the final grade, and some do not. The best method of assessing student performance is, of course, open to debate. It is relatively easy to separate the best students from the worst, but the gradations in between are quite fine, and ALR instructors may find it difficult to design a method of evaluation that both adequately tests what the students have learned, while allowing the instructor to assign appropriate grades. This is the case in almost every law school course, however, and struggling with examination and evaluation is part of every law teacher's responsibility.

CONCLUSION

Teaching ALR is a challenging but rewarding undertaking. Teaching effectively requires an accurate assessment and understanding of the level of knowledge and experience students bring to the class. The instructor must be able to articulate how legal information is structured, how it differs from the literature of other disciplines, and how an entire toolbox of skills and techniques is required to research effectively. Whether aiming for basic competence, fluency, or mastery, the instructor must be prepared to introduce students to a collection of concepts many students will find unfamiliar, counterintuitive, and even bizarre. The message should be that legal research involves much more than simply finding something and that a deeper understanding of how legal information is produced, arranged, and consumed will afford students and lawyers profound competitive advantage in practice.

Law librarians have had the field of ALR instruction to themselves for decades. I believe this is entirely appropriate, given that librarians bring a wealth of experience and an awareness of the research needs of students and new lawyers that others are simply not in a position to develop. The ALR challenge is changing, as tools change and the skills and experiences of students change, and even as the expectations and practices in the legal marketplace change. Some things, however, endure. And it is on this enduring body of knowledge and practice that ALR courses should concentrate. A well-designed and executed ALR class prepares a student for today's information and research climate and for information innovations yet to come, as well as grounding that student in the long-established patterns of publication and research that still constitute best research practices today.

NOTES

1. *See*, for example, Ann Hemmens, *Advanced Legal Research Courses: A Survey of ABA-Accredited Law Schools* 94 L. Lib. J. 209, 220 (Spring 2002) (where nearly 64.9% of a large sample of law schools offered at least one ALR course in the 2000–2001 academic year).

2. An excellent recent examination of the current state of information literacy in beginning law students is Ian Gallacher, *'Who Are These Guys?': The Results of a Survey Studying the Information Literacy of Incoming Law Students* (July 31, 2007), available at http://papers.ssrn.com/sol3/papers.cfm?abstract_id=1004088 (among the findings are that not only do law students lack adequate information literacy skills, but they also have an unrealistically positive view of those skills).

3. I often ask students in one of the first classes of a given semester to compose a Google, Lexis, or Westlaw query designed to find all of the cases in a particular jurisdiction dealing with capital punishment. When asked to do so, most students can navigate successfully to the appropriate Web

site or database and enter a search for "capital punishment" without considering all of the variety of synonyms (e.g., "execution," "death penalty," etc.) that are used in opinions even within one jurisdiction. As the semester progresses, students thus prepared are better able to recognize and understand a risk of keyword searching far more difficult to overcome; the literal nature of the keyword search destroys context in many cases. In other words, the human mind can impose an order on concepts and ideas that transcends vocabulary. Finding all of the opinions from New York that mention Hamlet using a keyword search is easy; but using a keyword search to find all of the opinions from New York in which some instance of jury misconduct was found to be harmless is exceedingly difficult, if not impossible.

4. See Appendix A for an example of a list of principles or concepts compiled during a recent semester. I wrote short explanatory paragraphs for each point I wished to emphasize and distributed this document to the students at the last class meeting. In my view, this does not constitute spoon-feeding students answers or insights, rather the document memorializes and amplifies what I have worked to impart throughout the semester.

5. See Appendix B for an example of a short-answer pretest I administered in a recent semester.

6. See Appendix C for an example of a multiple-choice pretest.

7. See Appendix D for an example of a research problem pretest.

8. See Appendix E for an example of a student outline.

APPENDIX A
LIST OF KEY PRINCIPLES OF CONCEPTS

Major Concepts

FIRST CHRONOLOGICAL, THEN BY SUBJECT

Legal publications are only arranged according to a few different patterns. This has been true for centuries. You would readily recognize the legal materials available to the Tudor or Stuart or colonial American lawyer: statutes, reporters, digests, treatises, other secondary sources, etc. The dominant pattern is the one described here. Many publications are twinned; they appear first in chronological order, then are arranged by someone into subject order. The reasons for this are obvious: all branches of government act in real time, performing work in chronological order. This results in material that is official and accurate, etc. but very difficult to use for research. After the chronological printing, then, someone has to rearrange all that material into subject order as an aid to practitioners and researchers. Remember the analogies:

Chronological Order	Subject Order
Session laws—	Codes—
United States Statutes at Large	U.S.C.
U.S.C.C.A.N.	U.S.C.A.
State session law	State code
Reporters—	Digests—
Texas Reports	Texas Digest
Pacific Reporter	Pacific Digest
Administrative Register—	Administrative Code—
Federal Register	Code of Federal Regulations
State administrative register	State administrative code

Human Ordering Versus Machine Recall

The idea here is to keep constantly in your mind that you have a choice of sources and to know which source, or which kind of source, best suits your needs. Keyword searching is very powerful, allowing you to search for specific factual situations or names or phrases, etc. The ability to search through full-text databases using keywords has changed legal research forever. The dangers in this power stem from the fact that the success of this method of searching depends upon your understanding and control of vocabulary. The literal nature of machine recall (i.e., the keyword search) means that you sometimes sacrifice recall in favor of precision. That's fine, just so long as you are conscious that that is the choice you are making. Using human ordering as in an index, a table, a table of contents, or especially a digest, the opposite is true. You get improved recall (for example, all the cases on an issue, regardless of vocabulary) at the expense of precision (you have to wade through all the warrantless search cases to find the ones that were searches of car interiors). The point is not that one method is better than the other; the point is that they are different, and it is up to you which to reach for.

Official Publications Often Less Useful

This isn't very complicated. Official publications often come with two distinct disadvantages: (1) they are usually not current, and (2) they are not annotated. A good example is the *United States Statutes at Large*. It is always at least two years out of date. In addition, the *Statutes at Large* contain only a fraction of the finding aids, tables, and indexes available in the commercial version, United States Code Congressional and Administrative News (U.S.C.C.A.N.), let alone all of the legislative history material U.S.C.C.A.N. prints. The U.S.C.C.A.N. is up to date within two or three weeks. This is a very typical pattern with official and commercial versions of the same material.

It is Very Difficult to do Effective Statutory Research Online. Know Why That is True

There are a few reasons why I believe this is true. Typically, statutory research involves using a variety of tabular or columnar material. This material, tables of contents, conversion tables of various kinds, indexes, outlines of titles, etc., are available in the online databases, but I find them difficult to locate in the services and unnecessarily hard to use in electronic form. You may disagree, which is fine, but I've never seen anyone able to make quick use of, for instance, an online version of an index. Also, codes are arranged in outline form, with titles, chapters, subsections, and sections, and with notes and appendices added. This structure can be very hard to visualize online. If you do a keyword search for a particular term or phrase, click on the likeliest looking hit, and determine that this section is relevant, it is tempting to conclude that your research is over. However, at that point you need to place that section in its larger context to ensure that language in some other, related section doesn't control or alter the interpretation of what you've found in the section your search turned up. I'm not telling you not to do your statutory research online; I'm only counseling you to be careful.

Know Exactly What Legislative Histories Are and What They Are For

A legislative history is an attempt to determine the intent of the legislature. The intent of the legislature is one of the arguments you can use when arguing how a facially ambiguous statute should be interpreted. It is not controlling or binding on a court. A legislative history is compiled from all of the published evidence of legislative deliberation. In the federal setting, much of what Congress does is published. Understand, though, that the importance of the major committee report (reprinted in U.S.C.C.A.N.) dwarfs the importance of everything else you might find. Remember, too, that many courts and many judges are hostile to the legislative intent argument.

Precision Versus Recall for Online Searching. Know the Distinction, Know That They Are a Zero Sum Game, Make Your Decisions Carefully and Deliberately

This was discussed above. Recall means getting a large result, including some hits that may not be relevant. Precision means getting a narrowly defined, specific result, and running the risk of missing some relevant material. Every technique, every source, every approach you take involves a trade-off between these two. Ask yourself what compromise you can afford to make at any particular point in your research and what you might do to minimize the risk, then pick your source. It's not that complex, just something to keep in the back of your mind as you reach for a digest or an online source or whatever. If you have the luxury of a little time, you can use two different sources for balance. For example, if searching for cases, you might begin with a keyword search in Lexis or Westlaw, then gather the key number(s) from the cases you find, and check the completeness of your result in a digest to see if there is anything you missed. You won't always have the time to do that, of course.

Let Someone Else Do the Work For You

There is nothing more satisfying than finding out that some scholar or publisher has already compiled the information you need. Before you dig in to a long research problem, try to think whether it is likely that someone has already done this for you. Federal legislative histories for the past twenty years are easy if you know about the Congressional Information Service volumes, for example. Digests gather all the cases on a particular issue together in one place. Many treatises are filled with information that would be very time consuming to gather from scratch. Always try to find the easiest way to do a thorough and accurate job. Librarians can help you find out if someone has done your work for you. Make use of them.

Stare Decisis and Binding Precedent Are Fairy Tales. You Must be Able to Make an Argument, Even in the Seemingly Hopeless Case

Remember, nothing is binding, nothing is controlling, and there is always an argument. You should drop the phrase "binding precedent" from your vocabulary as of today. There's just no such thing. You have to train yourself to make the distinction, resist the temptation to say there's nothing out there, work to craft an argument even where the case seems hopeless. And remember, novel arguments are successfully put forward all the time. Just because nobody has made an argument or a distinction before doesn't mean that it's a loser argument or baseless distinction.

Your Strategy Will Depend Upon Your Starting Point. What Do You Know Now?

You should know how to start from a known case or statute or article or issue and move from your starting point to gather all the rest of the relevant material on your topic. As an example, starting with a known case, you can use a citator to update it, use its headnotes to find its place (and other similar cases) in a digest, use the citation in the tables of cases in secondary sources to find where in a treatise or encyclopedia or wherever your issue is discussed. The finding aids and other tools in law books allow you to start anywhere and move forward or backward in time or laterally to encircle all the sources relevant to your issue in your jurisdiction. There is a real art to framing the issue, imagining the possible arguments, etc., but there are simple mechanical procedures to follow once that is done to gather all the material that is relevant.

Estimate Your Answer

By this, I don't mean guess whether your client has or has not broken the law (or whatever the ultimate issue is); I mean something different. By estimate your answer, I mean that when you are beginning your research, you should ask yourself what form the answer will take. Is your answer likely to be a statute, a regulation, an article, a definition in a dictionary, a line of cases, or something else? You might have to revise your estimate as you go along (in many instances, it is nearly impossible, for example, to predict whether any particular state issue is addressed in the statutes or the regulations), but there's no harm in that. By focusing on what **form** your answer will likely take, it will help you choose your approach. I find it helps me think clearly about my research strategy. Surprisingly, making a guess as to the ultimate, substantive outcome of your research before you begin is almost never helpful, and in fact, can prejudice your search. I suppose everyone begins research with at least a hunch about the outcome, but don't let it cloud your process.

Finding Aids, Finding Aids, Finding Aids

Anything worth saying once is worth repeating, evidently. What I mean here should be obvious. The more you know about the kinds of finding aids that exist, the better the odds that your work will be thorough, accurate, and timely.

Learn to Evaluate Sources Like an Expert

You know more than you think. Next time your work takes you to a new source, take a minute and pick it apart like you have done in class. Look at the organization of the source, the publisher, the date, the table of contents, the finding aids, and tables. If there is an instructional preface, read it. Even if you've never seen this source before, you'll find that it falls into one of a very few types. You're ready to get from the source what it has to offer you.

The Less You Know, The More Certainly You Need Secondary Sources

Context is king in legal research. When faced with a new area of law or a new concept, begin your research in the secondary sources, using them to help you understand the general framework in which your issue can be placed. If you get an assignment related to admiralty law, and you don't know the first thing about admiralty law, you need to start with secondary sources. After you understand a little about your area, then you can proceed to the primary sources you need to solve your problem. Just jumping straight into primary sources with no context is dangerous.

Secondary Leads to Primary, But There Are Other Ways Around the Circle

The main use for secondary sources is to steer you to primary sources. Sometimes, though, secondary sources lead to other secondary sources. Or you might use a primary source (say, a known case) as a way into a secondary source (looking up that case in the table of cases in a well-respected treatise or maybe a Restatement) which will then lead you to primary sources. All I mean here is that you often have to use a variety of sources in different combinations to get from where you are to where you need to be.

Minor Concepts

Look for the finding aids; there are only a few varieties out there.
Know the advantages and disadvantages of print and electronic sources.
Almost every issue is covered by a statute or regulation at some point.
Research should most often begin by looking for that statute or regulation and working from there.
Not everything an administrative agency does is published.
Secondary sources lead to primary sources.
Know what law review articles are and are not.
Remember the distinguishing points of looseleafs.
Asking the right question is half the battle.
Be flexible as you progress.
Make a plan, have contingencies lined up.
In statutory research, know your tables.

The minor concepts listed above need little or no explication. They are, or should be, self-explanatory. I could have listed a dozen more, or even a hundred more. There's a lot to keep in mind, but you understand the basic principles, and you know to ask for help when you're stuck. Wherever you work, make friends with the librarians right away. They know a great deal about sources and how they work, and their job is to help you. Let them.

APPENDIX B
AN EXAMPLE OF A SHORT-ANSWER PRETEST

Case Law

1. Can you find federal cases in regional reporters?
2. Where are Missouri trial level court reports published?
3. Does the government publish its own federal courts of appeals decisions?
4. What are the four main print sources for U.S. Supreme Court opinions?
5. If there are no cases on point in my state, would I rely more heavily on cases from states in the same regional reporter than those in other regional reporters?
6. How are case reporters arranged?
7. How are digests arranged?
8. The government began printing Supreme Court cases in 1817. Where were the earlier cases, including *Marbury v. Madison* and other important early cases, published?

9. I have a citation to an old New York opinion in something called *Johnson's Reports*. Where can I find out whether these opinions have been reprinted in the New York Reports?
10. Why is the Descriptive Word Index in every West digest exactly the same?
11. I have a Michigan opinion that discusses my issue. How can I find New Jersey opinions that are on the same topic?
12. I know that Exxon sued Amoco in 1999. Can you think of at least three reasons why I can't find an opinion in this case?

Statutes

1. Since session laws are published first and contain all the language enacted by the legislature, why would the government or a commercial publisher bother making a code out of the session laws?
2. What is the official version of Congressional session laws called? What is the commercially published version called?
3. Can you name at least two advantages of the commercial set over the official set?
4. Do states have session laws? If so, where are they in our library?
5. What part of an annotated code would I use to find out the Public Law number of the Federal Lawn Sprinkler Act of 2008?
6. I am interested in a statute with the Public Law number of 103–211. What does the 103 stand for? What about the 211?
7. Is the U.S. Constitution part of the U.S.C.? If not, why not?
8. Who puts the Congressional session laws in code order?
9. I read an opinion that refers to Immigration and Naturalization Act (INA) section 204A. I know that Title 8 of the U.S.C. is about immigration, but section 204A isn't on point. What else could 204A be referring to? How can I translate that into the code section I need?
10. Congress passed a law two weeks ago I want to read. How many different places can you name where I might find it?
11. Are the Titles of the U.S.C. in any particular order?
12. I know that Title IX has something to do with discrimination, but U.S.C. Title 9 seems to be about something else. Where is the Title IX I want? How can I find it?

Legislative History

1. Describe the situation(s) in which the legislative history of a statute is useful.
2. In the case of a facially ambiguous statute, does proof of the intent of the legislature control the court's interpretation of the statute?

3. Where can you find the number of the House or Senate bill that eventually became any particular law?
4. How might you use the library's online catalogue to see if the library owns a particular published legislative history?
5. Can you name at least five Congressional sources that could be used in compiling a legislative history? Of these sources, which one is overwhelmingly the most important?
6. Put the following source in declining order of importance: floor debate from the Congressional Record; Committee Report; bill versions; hearing testimony; Senate or House Documents; Senate or House Reports; President's signing or veto statement.
7. What is a committee print?
8. What is in the United States Congressional Serial Set?
9. How does one compile a legislative history of a state law?

Administrative Law

1. What is in the Federal Register? How often is it published?
2. How can I see an official version of the text of today's Federal Register?
3. From where does an executive branch agency get the power to make regulations that have the force of law?
4. How many agencies have such power? Where might I find a list of them?
5. What is published in the Federal Register every October and April that lawyers in heavily regulated areas of law find very useful?
6. What is the relationship of the Federal Register to the C.F.R.? Can you name two other sets of primary materials that have the same relationship to one another?
7. What kinds of things in the Federal Register don't find their way into the C.F.R.?
8. If a regulation is found to be unconstitutional is there a notation to that effect in the Federal Register or C.F.R.?
9. Why does C.F.R. Title 3 have a spine colored differently from the rest of the set? What is different about Title 3? What kinds of things are in Title 3?
10. What is the state equivalent of the Federal Register? The C.F.R.? What source would you use to find out the names of these state publications?

Secondary Sources

1. What is *American Law Reports,* and how is it different from *American Jurisprudence* and *Corpus Juris Secundum?*
2. Is there something special about the case *American Law Reports* uses to illustrate each annotation?

3. Is the *Index to Legal Periodicals* available in print? By subscription via the library's Web site? On Lexis? On Westlaw?
4. What is a Restatement? Is it more or less authoritative than *American Jurisprudence, Corpus Juris Secundum*, and *American Law Reports?* Which of these four sources would you be most likely to cite in a brief?
5. What are the two types of looseleafs? Can you give an example of each one?
6. Where might you look to see if there is a looseleaf published about labor law in Pennsylvania?
7. How would you use the library's online catalogue to find all the books in the library about drafting insurance contracts?
8. How would you use the library's online catalogue to find a book when all you know about it is that it was written by Smith and Jones?
9. How would you use the library's online catalogue to find all of the books in the library about administrative law published in French?
10. How would you use the library's online catalogue to find all the books in the library about Iowa law that were published before 1900?

APPENDIX C
AN EXAMPLE OF A MULTIPLE-CHOICE PRETEST

1. Where can one find the texts of Congressional bills?
   a. U.S.C.C.A.N.
   b. United States Congressional Serial Set
   c. Thomas
   d. United States Statutes at Large
2. Which of the following statements is false?
   a. About half of the titles of the U.S.C. have been enacted into positive law
   b. The entire C.F.R. is reprinted each year on January 1.
   c. One can Shepardize and/or Keycite law review articles.
   d. HeinOnline allows keyword searching of law review articles.
3. Which of the following best describes the third series of Restatements?
   a. Normative, not descriptive
   b. Usually descriptive, occasionally normative
   c. Occasionally descriptive, usually normative
   d. Equally normative and descriptive
4. Which is not a reason why a Court of Appeals opinion might get published?
   a. The opinion harmonizes a split of authority.
   b. The opinion criticizes an existing rule.

c. The opinion makes a new rule.
d. The opinion explains an existing rule.

5. Which was published first in the American colonies?
   a. Session laws
   b. Codes
   c. Constitutions
   d. Case reports
6. Why might it not matter that there is no Southern Digest?
   a. There is a state digest for every state in the region.
   b. The key number system in Westlaw includes every case in every state in the region.
   c. Both a and b are reasons why it might not matter.
   d. Neither a nor b are reasons why it might not matter.
7. Given that the Supreme Court makes it opinions available on its Web site, why does the *United States Law Week* still get published?
   a. Quicker access to opinions
   b. Better coverage of key numbers and headnotes
   c. Analysis of opinions and other legal matters
   d. Important cross-references to secondary sources
8. Which of the following statements is false?
   a. President Bush is the first president to issue Presidential Signing Statements.
   b. Presidential Signing Statements are found in U.S.C.C.A.N.
   c. Presidential Signing Statements do not get reprinted in the U.S.C.
   d. Presidential Signing Statements do not get reprinted in the Statutes at Large.
9. Which of the following statements about the U.S.C. is true?
   a. Updated every six years
   b. Updated every year, reprinted every six years
   c. Updated and reprinted every year
   d. Positive law titles reprinted on a different schedule than the rest
10. Which of the following is updated with pocket parts?
    a. U.S.C.
    b. U.S.C.C.A.N.
    c. U.S.C.S.
    d. Stat.
11. Which of the following statements is false?
    a. *American Law Reports* treats subjects in greater depth than *American Jurisprudence*.
    b. U.S.C.S. contains more cross-references to regulations than does the U.S.C.A.
    c. Hornbooks are primarily aids for students.
    d. Electronic research renders *The Bluebook* less important.

12. Which of the following statements is true?
    a. Keycite is usually considered to be more accurate than Shepard's.
    b. Law firms trust Shepard's more than Keycite.
    c. Shepard's in print is considered more trustworthy than the electronic version.
    d. All of the statements above are false.
13. Which of the following can be found in the United States Congressional Serial Set?
    a. House documents
    b. Senate bills
    c. Conference reports
    d. Floor debate
14. Which of the following statements about the U.S.C.A. Popular Names Table is false?
    a. It is a reprint of the one produced by the Office of Law Revision Counsel.
    b. It is compiled by editors at West.
    c. It provides citations to amendments of named statutes.
    d. It differs from the U.S.C.S. table.
15. Which of the following statements is true?
    a. Looseleafs all follow the same basic organizational structure.
    b. Looseleafs are usually organized by statute.
    c. Looseleafs are usually organized by topic.
    d. Looseleafs have a structure determined by the particular subject matter covered.
16. Which of the following statements is false?
    a. Hearing transcripts are rarely important for legislative history.
    b. Hearings are published in the Serial Set.
    c. Selected hearings are available via Thomas.
    d. Selected hearings are available via Lexis.
17. Why are appropriations acts not codified?
    a. They are not laws.
    b. They are not of general application and permanent duration.
    c. They are printed in the Federal Register.
    d. They change too often.
18. What would you expect to find in the Unified Agenda?
    a. Meeting notices
    b. Plans for new regulations
    c. Notices of open comment periods
    d. Agency hearings
19. Which of the following statements is true?
    a. Religious legal systems rarely have session laws.
    b. Civil law systems rely as heavily on case law as common law systems.

c. Common law and civil law systems are growing more alike all the time.
d. The European Union has no judicial branch, leaving trials to member states.

20. Which of the following statements is false?
a. High precision is better than high recall.
b. High precision implies low recall.
c. Keyword searches can be high precision or high recall.
d. At the beginning of a research project, one would probably choose a high recall search over a high precision search.

APPENDIX D
AN EXAMPLE OF A RESEARCH PROBLEM PRETEST

1. A report from a few years ago (pre-Iraq war) claimed that the four governments who execute the most teenaged offenders were (in descending order): Iran, Iraq, China, and Texas. I'd like to find out about the bases of appeals for Texas executions of teenaged prisoners in the past ten years, appeals that were successful, and those that weren't. Outline for me your strategy in a detailed research log. Start with your definition of the issue, the jurisdiction, the time, etc. Then think about which sources you might use and tell me which order you would approach them, and *why you would choose that order*. Then, in your log, describe what you have found.
2. In Massachusetts, the agency in charge of environmental protection established a whistleblower program that allowed citizens to anonymously report violations of prohibitions on industrial dumping in river systems. That agency delegated to county and municipal boards to oversee and administer the program. One town, Truro, laid out procedures by which they will only investigate claims made by whistleblowers willing to identify themselves. We represent citizens who object to Truro's requirement that they give up their anonymity. Assume that there is nothing in the Massachusetts regulations that directly forbids Truro's policy and focus instead on case law. Please lay out your strategy for attacking this (very difficult) research problem. Keep a research log, in which you keep a detailed record of what sources you used, the technique of vocabulary you used in your search, and what you found. Don't be frustrated if you cannot find a definitive answer, I am much more interested in your approach.
3. The 7th Amendment to the Constitution guarantees a right to a jury trial in certain circumstances. Our client had a jury award for punitive damages drastically reduced by a federal appeals court. Was our client improperly

denied his/her right to a jury trial because the judge reduced the award that the trial court jury returned? Please outline your research strategy in a detailed research log, as above.

4. Does Iowa law forbid passing retroactive tax statutes? Has the issue ever been litigated? Pretend you are a state legislative counsel to the tax committee (whatever they call it in the Iowa legislature) and are asked to render an opinion as to the constitutionality of a bill that proposes to retroactively tax state teacher pensions. What would your strategy be? How would you conduct research sufficient to render an accurate opinion? Lay out your strategy in a detailed research log, as above.

APPENDIX E
EXAMPLE OF A STUDENT OUTLINE FROM A RECENT CLASS MEETING

Class VI—Case Law, Part II
Student Outline, Concepts and Additional Readings

Danby article (*Universe of Thinkable Thoughts*)—What does it mean? Is he right? Does it matter?

Topics in case law research

What is case law? What is it for?
Stare decisis and binding precedent: Once upon a time . . .
Fencing the universe: making cross-references work
Asking the right question: the transformational nature of legal research
Gaming the game: judges, arguments, philosophy, types, and analogies

Strategies

How to begin: are you starting with a subject, a case, or a statute?
Estimate your answer—this means estimating the form the answer will take
Legal research as discussion
Drawing your circle—scope is all-important
Keywords or controlled vocabulary? (back to Dabney)
Precision vs. recall
What if you find nothing?
How and when to stop: what constitutes closure?

Sample problems for class discussion: Applying what you've learned

Class VI Goals and Concepts

By the end of Class VI, students should:

- Know the factual material presented; know what is published and in what manner it appears.
- Have a sense of different case law research strategies.
- Understand digests, citators, case reporters, keyword searching, etc. fluently.
- Be able to formulate strategies for researching a variety of types of problems.
- Understand what source to reach for first, and why.

Major Concepts

- First chronological, then by subject.
- Human ordering vs. machine recall.
- Official publications often less useful.
- It is very difficult to do effective statutory research online. Know why that is true.
- Precision v. Recall for online searching. Know the distinction, know that they are a zero sum game, make your decisions carefully and deliberately.
- Let someone else do the work for you.
- *Stare decisis* and binding precedent are fairy tales. You must be able to make an argument, even in the seemingly hopeless case.
- Your strategy will depend upon your starting point. What do you know now?
- Estimate your answer.

Minor Concepts

- Look for the finding aids; there are only a few varieties out there.
- Know the advantages and disadvantages of print and electronic sources.
- Almost every issue is covered by a statute or regulation at some point; Research should most often begin by looking for that statute or regulation and working from there.
- Not everything an administrative agency does is published.
- Secondary sources lead to primary sources. Always.
- Know what law review articles are and are not.
- Remember the distinguishing points of looseleafs.
- Asking the right question is half the battle.
- Be flexible as you progress.

Reading: *Where the Law Is*, Chapter 5. Read Chapters 2 and 14 for next week.

The Skills They Need: International and Foreign Legal Research

MARY RUMSEY
University of Minnesota Law Library, Minneapolis, Minnesota, USA

Law schools should offer classes in international and foreign legal research (IFLR) because the increasing globalization of law practice requires new skills of lawyers. Moreover, internationalized law school programs and curricula, including human rights clinics, exchange programs, and transnational law courses, require complementary research skills. Currently, few schools offer a stand-alone IFLR class. This article describes an ideal IFLR class, which would cover public and private international law, foreign law, and selected topics, and provide students with basic IFLR skills. The author notes that librarians are best suited to teach such a class because of their extensive knowledge of IFLR resources and usage.

INTRODUCTION

This article outlines the reasons why law schools should offer classes in international and foreign legal research (IFLR) and proposes a model for such classes. The first section notes the increasing globalization of law practice and its impact on law school programs and curricula. The second section describes the current state of IFLR teaching. The third section outlines the subjects and structure of an ideal IFLR class. I conclude by explaining why IFLR should be taught by librarians.

I would like to dedicate this article to Marci Hoffman for her endless generosity in sharing her expertise with me and with many others.

GLOBALIZATION OF LAW PRACTICE

To state that law practice is increasingly global is to go beyond cliché into the realms of those truths we hold to be self-evident. "[T]he pace of global commerce now requires lawyers to facilitate transactions and resolve disputes in an environment that spans a wide array of legal systems with vastly different traditions."[1] International law now affects domestic law in myriad and sometimes unexpected ways: the Convention on the Law Applicable to International Sale of Goods[2] and its successor Convention[3] may override the Uniform Commercial Code;[4] child custody and support decisions may be affected by the Hague Conventions;[5] and trade law extends its tentacles everywhere.[6]

According to a recent survey, in the past seven years, the 250 largest U.S.-based law firms have dramatically increased the number of attorneys working abroad.[7] In addition, foreign law firms have begun opening offices in the United States.[8] More striking than large-firm activity, however, may be the change in small-firm, small-town practice. One attorney who heads a three-lawyer firm in St. Paul, Minn., states:

> I consider myself as only having a Minnesota practice. Yet in the last year, I have found myself having to research Russian probate law and Hong Kong real estate law in order to decide how to proceed or advise local clients. Since I do not know Russian or Mandarin, let alone read Cyrillic or Chinese characters, it was quite a challenge. This was in addition to more ordinary experiences like needing to have a witness testify who only spoke Spanish or reading a letter from a Swiss Bank that was written in French or interview and advise clients who mostly spoke Somali.[9]

Further, a small-firm lawyer in Madison, Wis. observes:

> The amount of work I do that has international elements has grown significantly. Our clients realize that globalization presents both increased competitive threats and new market opportunities. There's also more interest among foreign companies in locating manufacturing and distributing facilities in the Midwest. This is especially true of European companies, as the U.S. dollar has declined in value against the Euro. My business/intellectual property (IP)-oriented practice has become increasingly international in just the last five years.[10]

These are just two examples of the impact international and foreign law has on the everyday practice of law. The challenge to law schools is to craft an adequate curricular response to globalization that does not take emphasis away from the many educational needs of students whose legal careers will focus on U.S. law.

GLOBALIZATION OF LEGAL EDUCATION

Law schools have begun to reflect these changes. They have added classes: a 2001 study by Judith Wegner found that one of every six new courses was international or comparative in scope, and eighty-four percent of schools responding had added at least one new international or comparative course.[11] Some schools, such as the University of Michigan, have moved from offering such courses to requiring them.[12] Harvard's recent curriculum revision also makes some exposure to foreign and international law mandatory.[13]

Law students routinely express interest in foreign and international law.[14] In part because of such interest, many law schools have expanded summer-, semester-, or year-abroad programs; recruited more foreign exchange students; and launched or enlarged their LL.M. programs.[15] Other schools have established branch campuses abroad[16] or entered into joint ventures with foreign law schools to grant degrees in other countries.[17]

In addition to doctrinal classes, law schools have begun incorporating foreign and international law into their clinical programs.[18] A study by Deena Hurwitz found only three clinical programs on human rights in 1992 but found more than a dozen of them, along with more than twenty human rights centers, ten years later.[19] The number of such programs has increased even more rapidly since 2002.[20] Moreover, clinical programs without a specifically international focus, such as domestic violence clinics, now see many clients who bring foreign and international issues through their doors.[21]

Law schools' increasingly global perspective also shows up in the growing number of transnational law reviews. One scholar found a more than 450 percent increase in the number of such reviews during the twenty-five-year period ending in 2001.[22] "Law schools in the United States currently publish over 330 specialized law journals edited by students, the most common of which, numbered at over 70,[23] are about transnational law. That translates into about forty-five percent of all accredited law schools publishing a student-edited transnational journal."[24]

The increased internationalization of U.S. law schools was well summarized by Catherine Valcke in 2004:

> Course offerings in international and comparative law abound; student and faculty exchanges are proliferating; transnational recruitment of faculty and students is expanding; international student initiatives such as mooting, journals, and internships are multiplying rapidly; [and] visitors' programs and transnational collaborative research projects are ubiquitous.[25]

WHY IFLR?

Exposing students to international or foreign law will not help them much if they have no tools to research the law in those jurisdictions. All U.S. law schools teach U.S. legal research; learning to research is part of becoming a lawyer. Preparing students for modern law practice requires not only a doctrinal component but a research component, and this requirement applies to international and foreign law.

INADEQUACY OF FAMILIAR RESEARCH TOOLS

For legal research purposes, if foreign countries were just another jurisdiction like a U.S. state, no one would advocate special classes on how to research their laws. But we have no West Digest system for Mongolia (or even for France), no Shepard's Citators for Nigerian case law, and no annotated statutes for China.[26] Foreign legal systems and the international legal system invoke different sources of law, may lack familiar institutions such as jury trials, and have the unnerving habit of using languages other than English.

These differences matter enormously in IFLR. If students learn only U.S. research tools, they will be unprepared to tackle modern legal practice.

As law librarians and others have documented, law students overwhelmingly use computer-assisted legal research (CALR) during law school.[27] Yet experts agree that Westlaw and LexisNexis, the two main CALR vendors, do not meet researchers' foreign or international law needs.[28] Equipping a student to use CALR will not solve the problem of global legal research.

INADEQUACY OF FAMILIAR RESEARCH TECHNIQUES

Not only does IFLR require different tools from U.S. research, but it requires different techniques. Lee Peoples writes:

> A lawyer from a civil law jurisdiction will begin researching most issues by looking for the appropriate article in one of her jurisdiction's codes. In contrast, a lawyer from a common law jurisdiction usually begins his or her research by searching for relevant cases. Foreign, comparative, and international law (FCIL) research projects often involve aspects of international, foreign, and domestic legal research. For example, a question about the North American Free Trade Agreement (NAFTA) might also implicate Mexican legislation implementing the NAFTA agreement, Canadian case law interpreting the agreement, and regulations issued by a U.S. administrative agency implementing the NAFTA requirements.[29]

International law, particularly international customary law,[30] requires a wholly different type of research from that used in domestic law. To show the existence of a rule of customary international law, a lawyer musters examples of state practice, whether manifested in treaties, national legislation and court cases, diplomatic correspondence, or other miscellany. While treaties can be roughly analogized to statutes in the sense that they both create binding rules, treaties, unlike statutes, are usually drafted in indefinite and sweeping language. Thus, to discern obligations under a treaty, a lawyer must often explore other sources, such as the *travaux préparatoires* (preparatory works), interpretive commentary from the body charged with treaty implementation, scholarly analyses, and national legislation.

Research in civil law countries takes equally unfamiliar paths. As the major statutory codes in civil law jurisdictions (most typically civil, criminal, commercial, civil procedure, and criminal procedure codes) are designed to address comprehensively all potential legal issues, the researcher there aims to find a code section, or a principle derived from the code, to apply to her research question. Civil lawyers rely heavily on scholarly commentaries or doctrine to interpret code sections and understand their application. Case law has little or no role in legal research in most civil law jurisdictions, which lack digests of case law[31] that common law researchers use to organize cases and expound on legal rules. Interestingly, even civil law professors agree that researching civil law is more difficult than researching common law.[32]

CURRENT IFLR TEACHING

Currently, U.S. law students are exposed to IFLR, if at all, in one of three ways: 1) in an elective, stand-alone class; 2) as part of an advanced legal research (ALR) class, nearly always elective; or 3) within a doctrinal class or seminar, such as international human rights law, comparative constitutional law, or trade law. In the latter case, a faculty member allots some time during class in which a librarian guest-lectures to introduce IFLR techniques, or the faculty member teaches research herself.

According to an e-mail survey, thirty-two law schools offer a stand-alone IFLR class without incorporating any IFLR instruction into their ALR class. Twenty schools incorporate some IFLR into their ALR class but offer no separate IFLR class. Fifteen schools offer both a stand-alone class and an ALR class that incorporates some IFLR instruction.[33]

Incorporating IFLR instruction in doctrinal classes may elevate its perceived importance in students' eyes. Nonetheless, this option is probably the least successful method. The session is usually designed to prepare students to research international or foreign law so they can write a paper about it; most students will not begin their research immediately and will not retain the information for long. Rarely do professors assign research exercises in conjunction with the session, so students have no opportunity for hands-on reinforcement.[34]

Including IFLR into ALR classes qualifies as better than nothing. In most ALR classes, students complete exercises that force them to use the tools they learn about. Thus, students whose ALR classes incorporate a lecture on IFLR will at least use the tools shortly after their exposure to them in class. Nonetheless, spending one class on IFLR basics, as is the most common practice, cannot equip students with much more than an awareness that research will be different "across the border."

THE STAND-ALONE CLASS

For students to gain a foundational understanding of IFLR, they should take a stand-alone class. The number of schools offering such classes has increased in the past few years.[35] Among specialized research courses, an IFLR course is the most common class that schools offer.[36] Although it is unrealistic to expect law schools to *require* all students to take IFLR courses,[37] it is reasonable to expect every U.S. law school to offer one as an elective. In that case, at least those students who expect to seek out or take on international or foreign legal problems can prepare themselves to do so.

While a few schools require international law as a prerequisite to IFLR classes, I have found students manage to pick up the necessary background if exposed to it briefly in class. In other words, students do not need to complete a class in public international law before they understand such concepts as treaty reservations or the amorphous nature of customary international law. The only prerequisite should be the completion of first-year legal research training; I have had LL.M. students who floundered without such training.[38]

SUBSTANTIVE COMPONENTS

While course content varies among schools, all IFLR courses share a common core.[39] This core forms the minimum content of an adequate research course. First, every class deals with treaty research, including finding treaties, determining their status and any relevant reservations, and researching the *travaux préparatoires*—documentation of the treaty's drafting history. Second, all courses cover customary international law—the rules of international law that most nations follow most of the time, out of a sense of legal obligation. Third, every class examines at least one intergovernmental organization (IGO) (e.g., the United Nations) with an eye toward understanding its structure and its documentation. Fourth, every course covers foreign law. Fifth, nearly every course looks at the European Union: finding directives and regulations (secondary legislation), cases, and perhaps national implementing measures—i.e., the laws or regulations enacted at the member-state level to implement an E.U. directive. Sixth, nearly every course looks at the World Trade Organization (WTO) (and, in some cases, NAFTA).

While most courses do not cover cross-border business transactions, I have concluded that the likelihood of students needing to know how to research them is high enough that the ideal IFLR course will cover this topic. Thus, the class should introduce students to sources for information on joint ventures, foreign licensing, contracts for the sale of goods or services, dispute resolution, and related matters. Students need cross-border more than public international legal skills—not many will work in public international law; more will work on business matters.

In addition to the common core described above, some existing FCIL courses include sessions on particular jurisdictions, such as Canada or the United Kingdom as paradigmatic common law countries, or France as a paradigmatic civil law country. Certainly, examining a country in depth—particularly a civil law country—is an excellent way to convey the major differences between legal systems. An alarming proportion of law students and lawyers assume that foreign legal systems must mirror the U.S. system. As the only foreign and international law librarian in Minnesota, I get phone calls from lawyers wanting sources like "civil jury instructions for Germany" (which has no civil trial system); "forms and explanations of how to probate a will in France" (which has no probate); and "just one or two key cases on the law of insurance contracts in the Netherlands" (leaving aside the lack of English translations of Dutch court decisions, it would be hard to identify "key cases" in a system in which cases are not primary legal sources). Although doctrinal classes might alert students to some differences, it is the practical task of finding legal sources that makes the differences sink in.

While treatment of foreign law may vary in depth, students must learn some of the key ways in which civil law jurisdictions differ from common law ones. Examples include the difference between public and private law, the lack of *stare decisis*, the greater participation by civil law judges in court cases, and the overarching structure and philosophy of the civil codes. Each of those differences affects how a lawyer conducts research. For example, court actions in public law (criminal law, for instance) typically are heard within a separate court system from private law actions (commercial disputes, for instance). As civil law systems incorporate the principle of *stare decisis* only in limited ways, if at all, tools, such as citators, are completely lacking. In part because of the more active role in litigation of civil law judges, discovery is conducted on a much more restricted scale than in common law systems, particularly in the United States.

Many IFLR instructors also examine subject areas, such as human rights, IP, and cross-border dispute resolution. While acquaintance with these topics may not be essential, the instructor can use the topics to reinforce important concepts and familiarize students with commonly used IFLR tools. While teaching IP research, for example, the instructor may ask students to find relevant treaties, determine whether a particular country is a party, and then find an English translation of that country's copyright or patent act. Teaching cross-border dispute resolution, similarly, might call for students to get acquainted with tools, such as the State Department's Judicial Assistance Web pages,[40] which provide information on foreign service of process, discovery, and related topics.

Beyond the core topics, it is impossible to predict what subjects a student may encounter as a practitioner. Instructors may choose, then, to explore topics that reflect student interest, while reinforcing skills and concepts. A law school with a strong maritime law program, for example, might cover research on that topic. At the University of Minnesota Law School, the IFLR course includes human rights because many of the students express interest in it. At the first session of the class, I survey the students about their interests and sometimes adjust the syllabus to reflect those interests.[41]

ESSENTIAL TOOLS

Just as an ideal course must cover the common core identified above, it must also introduce students to a set of essential tools. Some of these, such as legal periodical indexes, including the Index to Foreign Legal Periodicals, can be introduced and then re-used at various points in the class. Instructors must also emphasize the efficiency and utility of secondary sources, particularly to students whose principal idea of research is searching for cases in a Westlaw or LexisNexis database. Regardless of the substantive topic, students can be asked to identify useful legal encyclopedias and law review articles. Similarly, students must learn to identify and use research guides, journal index headings, Library of Congress subject headings, and other finding aids. Any session on IFLR, no matter how brief, should include exposure to Globalex,[42] the online collection of foreign and international legal research guides, and similar collections from the Law Library Research Xchange (LLRX).[43]

Other tools are more closely tied to specific course topics. In learning treaties, for example, the students should use the U.N. treaty database, Westlaw and LexisNexis treaty databases, and perhaps some of the specialized or national treaty collections, such as the *United Nations Conference on Trade and Development* (UNCTAD) database of bilateral investment treaties,[44] or the French national treaty database, Base Pacte.[45] Sources for treaty status information and for *travaux préparatoires*[46] should also be covered at this point. Once students are introduced to the tools, exercises should reinforce their use throughout the course.

For locating rules of customary international law, the focus should be on secondary sources, such as treatises and the *Restatement of Foreign Relations Law*,[47] because for most researchers, these are adequate tools. The instructor should introduce sources for more detailed research on customary international law—the digests of state practice, yearbooks of international law, and the underlying documents—treaties, diplomatic correspondence, resolutions, and other documents of IGOs. Because few students will go on to work intensively with public international law, however, one "brutal choice in curricular design"[48] is to settle for some acquaintance with these sources, rather than extensive work.

Examining at least one IGO gives students an essential grounding in these major transnational law players. Students should understand the typical features of IGOs—secretariats, quasi-legislative organs (e.g., the U.N. General Assembly), and—often—dispute resolution bodies (e.g., the International Court of Justice). From a research perspective, students should be able to find charters, resolutions, reports, and the decisions of dispute resolution bodies. Exercises can then ask students to apply what they have learned about one IGO to researching another.

Teaching foreign legal research necessarily focuses on materials in English. In any particular class, some students will know no foreign language, and others will have varying degrees of proficiency in a number of languages. Few, if any, have "legal proficiency" in a foreign language, similar to most U.S. practitioners who do not know a foreign language well enough to feel comfortable using legal materials in that language. Thus, most of the demand is for English-language materials. Purists may object that relying on English-language sources for foreign legal research has many pitfalls—translations lack authority, usually lack currentness, and may not be entirely accurate; key terms have no real English equivalents; secondary materials are often incomplete or unavailable. All true. Nonetheless, U.S. attorneys will continue to demand and use these materials for lack of anything better.

The foreign research part of the course, then, should include warnings about the risks of operating in a jurisdiction without reading its legal sources in the original language. To reinforce advice about translations, the instructor may want to demonstrate the difficulty of reading foreign legal materials and the inadequacy of software translation programs. One way to do this is to collect versions of legislation in translation for several languages—i.e., locate both the English and the vernacular and start by giving each student a few sections of a code or law in the vernacular.[49] Students who know a foreign language can be asked to try making a rough translation. The students who read no other language can be asked to use popular online translators such as Babel Fish on similar sections. (EUR–LEX [http://eur–lex.europa.eu] is an excellent source for translations, but samples of laws from many other languages can be collected from various free Web sources.) Having students take five to ten minutes to try translating foreign law and then giving them professional translations usually convinces them that foreign law cannot be easily translated. In my experience, students are usually amused by the failure of online translation programs to handle legal language; ideally, the experience will arm them against reliance on such programs.

If students learn only one thing during coverage of foreign legal research, they should learn about sources for English-language translations, especially Reynolds & Flores' *Foreign Law Guide*.[50] This listing of major legislation and codes, including references to English translations where available, deserves repeated use in class exercises. Another key tool is the Law Library of Congress' Multinational Collections Database,[51] pointing researchers to treatises with both primary law and commentary that cover multiple jurisdictions. In discussing these collections, instructors should convey the concept of "subject collections." Organized by subject rather than jurisdiction, these resources include well-established print sources, such as *Investment Laws of the World*, and databases, such as World Intellectual Property Organization's Collection of Laws for Electronic Access (a successor to WIPO's print collections of IP laws). Although many subject collections (e.g., *Digest of Commercial Laws of the World*, *International Joint Ventures*) focus on summaries and commentary rather than providing complete translations of statutes, for some jurisdictions, these sources are the best available information.

The E.U. component of the class offers a chance for instructors to reinforce LexisNexis and Westlaw skills, as many students have little idea of how to find a database, determine its scope, or formulate an efficient search. The free E.U. sources, such as the invaluable EUR-Lex,[52] also belong in this section. Students should learn how to find directives, regulations, national implementing measures, and European Court of Justice cases. Moreover, students should be asked to explore the Directorate-General sites (analogous to U.S. federal agency sites) for various topics, because of the wealth of useful information on E.U. law these offer.

Covering the WTO and perhaps NAFTA gives the instructor the chance to reinforce lessons on IGO structure and research techniques. Availability of WTO/NAFTA materials on Westlaw and LexisNexis gives students another chance to refine their skills, but the course should also cover online finding tools like the WTO Analytical Index: Guide to WTO Law and Practice.[53] Because of the proliferation of current awareness sources, such as *Inside U.S. Trade*,[54] trade works well as a vehicle to teach students how to use blogs and other current awareness sources.

The final core topic, cross-border business transactions, may be harder for instructors to define. Some instructors may even want to lump international trade under this heading. Others may decide to include or exclude cross-border dispute settlement. Useful sources to introduce include the Case Law on UNCITRAL Texts (CLOUT) database on U.N. Commission on International Trade Law (UNCITRAL) cases,[55] the concept of "doing business" guides (some of which are available on LexisNexis), *Worldwide Tax and Commercial Laws* (formerly *Commercial Laws of the World*; available by subscription through Research Institute of America Checkpoint), *Martindale-Hubbell's International Law Digest*, Transnational Law Digest & Bibliography,[56] and similar tools. Reinforcing the use of finding tools (research guides, library catalogs, periodical indexes, etc.) at this point works well.

Anyone with experience in IFLR could add resources to this list, but to ensure that students learn the tools well enough to remember them, it is better to make some brutal choices and offer enough opportunities for the students to become familiar with the chosen tools.

INSTRUCTIONAL FORMAT

After years of experimentation, I believe the best approach for teaching IFLR is to lecture briefly, usually with presentation software and screen captures, spend time in class having students work through sample exercises, and then assign exercises for students to complete outside of class. The in-class exercises need not cover every question on the weekly exercise but should introduce major databases and other tools. Inevitably, exercises will use a "scavenger hunt" format, describing the type of information needed. I have found students benefit from exercises that move from specific "known-item" finding (e.g., "Find a bilateral investment treaty between Argentina and Germany") to more open-ended questions (e.g., "Find a book that covers licensing patents in foreign countries"). While I score exercises rather than using a pass/fail approach, I sometimes include questions that I would hardly ever mark "wrong." For example: "Using the library catalog, identify what you think would be the most useful book for a lawyer who wants to set up a joint venture for his client in China and explain why you chose it." The instructor's feedback on this question is a chance to help students learn how to spot useful materials, for example, recent or recently updated practice-oriented, comprehensive treatments. To get students in the habit of looking at Help documentation (both in print and electronic resources), exercises should include questions on how to use particular tools—e.g., how to search for synonyms in the EUR-Lex database.

My class meets once a week, with exercises required for all but the first class.[57] I also encourage students to ask for help (by e-mail, phone, or in person) during the week if they have trouble with the questions. Some students require much more help than others, but nearly all of them can master IFLR skills with enough repetition. In reading years of student evaluations, one strong theme that emerges is the effectiveness of repetition in teaching research skills. It is exciting to see a student gain the confidence later in the course to say promptly, "I'd start with Reynolds & Flores," or "I'd look in HUDOC."[58]

READINGS

It is possible to cobble together suitable reading materials from a combination of online research guides, journal articles, and text chapters. Sample syllabi, along with many other useful exercises, PowerPoint presentations, and other class materials, are freely available at the "Syllabi and Course Materials" Web page[59] of the FCIL Special Interest Section of the American Association of Law Libraries (AALL). In late 2007, Marci Hoffman and I published *International and Foreign Legal Research: A Coursebook*,[60] designed for IFLR classes. Another publication librarians may want to consider is *Legal Research Methods in the U.S. and Europe*, by J. Paul Lomio and Henrik Spang-Hanssen.[61]

ASSESSMENT

To assess students' ability to perform IFLR *efficiently*, a take-home exam (due perhaps eight to twenty-four hours after receipt) works well. A timed take-home exam separates those who have learned how to select the right tool for each question and to use that tool efficiently from students who may have managed to complete the weekly exercises by spending a disproportionate amount of time on them. Students in my course generally approach the final exam with some trepidation, but after completing it, they tell me, "I didn't realize how much I've learned!" Creating the exam need not be difficult; the best approach is to take typical questions from earlier assignments and change one aspect (e.g., the jurisdiction, the topic of an IGO resolution, or the subject of an E.U. directive).

Some IFLR instructors prefer to require a research guide or pathfinder as a final product, usually centered on a foreign jurisdiction or an international law issue, such as international criminal law, NAFTA, or international taxation. Pathfinders have the advantage of forcing students to dig deeper into relevant sources for one country or topic. After a few years of requiring pathfinders, however, the lack of connection between pathfinders and legal practice convinced me to bulk up on exercises and add an exam instead. My own experience in law practice, coupled with my experience fielding research requests from attorneys and law librarians, convinced me that creating a pathfinder is much more suited to future law librarians than to future lawyers. As a practical matter, with country and topic guides increasingly available online at Globalex, LLRX, and various law library Web sites, it is also getting harder to know whether students really conducted their own investigation into research sources, or relied on existing guides instead.

LAW LIBRARIANS MUST BE THE TEACHERS

Generally, experts agree that librarians should teach legal research.[62] The landscape of available research sources changes quickly. Web sites come and go, databases are abandoned, print tools become online only; librarians are best suited to monitor these changes. Librarians have been trained to understand the principles that underlie research tools—indexing; database concordances, fields, and document breaks; Boolean connectors; and bibliographic control. Librarians track and evaluate new and evolving research tools in their day-to-day work. Moreover, only librarians, as research specialists, can teach students the flexibility they will need to use a universe of varying Web sites, commercial databases, and hard-copy sources. Students should emerge from the FCIL class with strategies for learning what a database or other resource contains, how current and complete it is, and how to use it effectively.[63]

Law professors whose primary focus is substantive tend to be the "one-trick ponies" of international and foreign research—they may know how to find U.N. resolutions or European Court of Justice cases using their favorite tool but are unlikely to know of or seek out alternatives. Professors should teach the substance of foreign or international law—for example, how E.U. legislative powers are divided—but they lack the skills and the class time to cover finding information and analyzing its provenance and quality.

For different but obvious reasons, Westlaw and LexisNexis vendors also fail to expose students to the whole range of tools they need. I experimented early on with having guest lectures from Westlaw and LexisNexis trainers but found that they lacked enough understanding of international and foreign research to present their resources usefully. They also suffer from a tendency to make research look easier than it is, to the point that the techniques and examples they use in class will not necessarily work on real problems. Librarians can expose students to the valuable resources on Westlaw and LexisNexis while reminding them of the cost and limitations of these services.

CONCLUSION

The globalization of law practice imposes obligations on law schools. To prepare students for practice, schools must give them the right tools. A well-designed IFLR class will enhance American law students' ability to function and compete in the global marketplace. Do students themselves see the value of such courses? Based on several years of enthusiastic course evaluations, I believe they do. And I treasure the comment of one former student, who filled out a class evaluation form which asked, "Would you recommend this course to a friend?" In response, he printed neatly, "I would recommend this course to GOD!"[64]

NOTES

1. William D. Henderson, *The Globalization of the Legal Profession*, 14 Ind. J. Global Leg. Stud. 1, 2 (2007).

2. *Convention on the Law Applicable to International Sale of Goods* (signed 15 June 1955), 510 U.N.T.S. 147.

3. *Convention on the Law Applicable to Contracts for the International Sale of Goods* (signed 22 Dec. 1986), 24 I.L.M. 1575.

4. Harold Hongju Koh, *Is There a 'New' New Haven School of International Law?* 32 Yale J. Intl. L. 559, 568 n. 57 (2007).

5. *Hague Convention on the Civil Aspects of International Child Abduction* (signed 25 Oct. 1980), 1343 U.N.T.S. 89; *Hague Convention on the International Recovery of Child Support and Other Forms of Family Support* (signed 23 Nov. 2007), U.N.T.S., http://www.hcch.net/index_en.php?act=conventions.pdf&cid=131 (visited 14 May 2009); *see also* Barbara Handschu & Mary Kay Kisthardt, *Family Law, International Disputes*, Natl. L.J. 13, 13 (9 June 2008).

6. Christian Tietje, *The WTO Sanctions Regime and International Constitutional Political Economy*, 2008 U. Ill. L. Rev. 383, 386 (2008); Frank J. Garcia, *Building a Just Trade Order for a New Millennium*, 33 Geo. Wash. Intl. L. Rev. 1015, 1049 (2001) ("Trade law and trade institutions are impacting more and more areas of traditional domestic concern, such as environmental protection, labor, and employment standards, and cultural identity.") (footnotes omitted).

7. John Flynn Rooney, *E-Discovery, Globalization Top List of Tests*, Chi. Daily L. Bull., 1 (17 Dec. 2007) (stating that since 2000, "the 250 largest U.S.-based law firms have increased their attorney rosters in Europe by sixty percent and in Latin America by forty-two percent.")

8. Georgina Stanley, *The British Are (Still) Coming*, 10 Law Firm Inc. 14 (2007), available at Westlaw, Legal News, ALM New. Some British firms, such as Linklater's, have New York offices. Josh Berick & Jennifer Katz-Hickman, *How to Offer Law Students the World: Entry-Level Recruiting Poses Unique Opportunities and Challenges for Global Law Firms*, Fulton Co. Daily Rep., S9 (2 June 2008).

9. E-mail from Karen L. Tarrant, partner, Tarrant, Drummer & Liska, to Mary Rumsey (4 Sept. 2008, 4:08 p.m. CST) (copy on file with author).

10. E-mail from Erik W. Ibele, attorney, Neider & Boucher, to Mary Rumsey (19 Sept. 2008, 1:36 p.m. CST) (copy on file with author).

11. Judith W. Wegner, *The Curriculum: Patterns and Possibilities*, 51 J. Leg. Educ. 431, 433 (2001).

12. Janet Koven Levit, *Sanchez-Llamas v. Oregon: The Glass Is Half Full*, 11 Lewis & Clark L. Rev. 29, 35–36 (2007); *Washington & Lee Becomes Eighth Law School to Require International or 'Transnational' Law*, Am. Soc'y. Int'l. L. News 7, 7 (April/June, 2008).

13. Luke Bierman, *The Administration of Justice a Century after Roscoe Pound: Future Directions and Emerging Trends*, 48 S. Tex. L. Rev. 1051, 1061 (2007) (stating that Harvard's revision of its mandatory curriculum reflects impact of globalization).

14. Anita Bernstein, *On Nourishing the Curriculum with a Transnational Law Lagniappe*, 56 J. Leg. Educ. 578, 578–579 (2006) ("Admissions officers in law schools have told me that 'international law' is consistently one of the top two curricular interests that prospective students check off on survey forms . . . ").

15. Joan Mahoney, *The Future of Legal Education*, 33 U. Toledo L. Rev. 113, 116 (2001) ("The number of summer study abroad programs has increased exponentially, as have semester abroad and foreign exchange programs."); Julie M. Spanbauer, *Lost in Translation in the Law School Classroom: Assessing Required Coursework in LL.M. Programs for International Students*, 35 Intl. J. Leg. Info. 396 (2007) (stating that "[a]s of 2007, 114 law schools admitted foreign students to a total of 179 LL.M. programs.")

16. Teresa C. Stanton, *Foreign and International Law Librarians—One and All*, 16 Austrl. L. Lib. 124, 125 (2008) (stating that in October 2008, Georgetown will open the Center for Transnational Legal Studies in London); Richard Lloyd, Letter from London, *World Class Georgetown University Law Center Unveils Its Take on Global Expansion*, Am. Law. 77 (April 2008) (stating that Yale is considering similar ventures).

17. *E.g.* Northwestern Law School, *Executive LL.M. in Seoul*, available at http://www.law.northwestern.edu/graduate/llmkorea (last accessed 3 Dec. 2008).

18. Scott L. Cummings, *The Internationalization of Public Interest Law*, 57 Duke L.J. 891, 911 (2008) (noting the emergence of asylum-oriented law school clinical programs); Oona A. Hathaway, *The Continuing Influence of the New Haven School*, 32 Yale J. Intl. L. 553, 558 (2007) (stating that "[l]aw school clinics focusing on issues of international law have proliferated during the last several decades.")

19. Deena R. Hurwitz, *Lawyering for Justice and the Inevitability of International Human Rights Clinics*, 28 Yale J. Intl. L. 505, 527 (2003).

20. Martha F. Davis, *Essay, The Pendulum Swings Back: Poverty Law in the Old and New Curriculum*, 34 Fordham Urb. L.J. 1391, 1407 (2007).

21. For example, the Conservation Clinic at the University of Florida Levin College of Law advises international and nongovernmental organizations on international and foreign conservation projects. Jon Mills & Timothy McLendon, *Law Schools as Agents of Change and Justice Reform in the Americas*, 20 Fla. J. Intl. L. 5, 18 (2008).

22. Carole Silver, *Studying Singapore: Internationalizing the U.S. Law School Curriculum*, 51 J. Leg. Educ. 75, 77–78 (2001).

23. A more recent count of foreign/international law journals from John Doyle's Web site at Washington & Lee University School of Law puts the total at 112. Washington & Lee University School of Law, *Law Journals: Submissions and Ranking*, available at http://lawlib.wlu.edu/LJ/index.aspx (last accessed 5 Jan. 2009).

24. Donna E. Arzt, *From Soviets to Saddam: Introduction to the Thirtieth Anniversary Symposium*, 30 Syracuse J. Intl. L. & Com. 181, 185 (2003) (footnote omitted).

25. Catherine Valcke, *Global Law Teaching*, 54 J. Leg. Educ. 160, 160 (2004).

26. Lee Peoples, *Strategies and Sources for International Legal Research*, 60 Consumer Fin. L.Q. Rep. 412, 413 (2006) ("Some research tools familiar to the U.S. law researcher are missing in FCIL research. There is no huge database of every treaty or decision of international tribunals that may be quickly searched on LexisNexis or Westlaw. There are some digests in FCIL research but no West key number system organizing the entire corpus of FCIL into a massive subject outline. Shepard's is another research tool that is not always found in FCIL research. Jurisdictions that share the common law tradition of *stare decisis* will usually have some tool for verifying the status of case law and other sources of legal authority. In the United Kingdom, the equivalent of Shepard's is called the Noter Up. Most civil law jurisdictions do not formally recognize the concept of *stare decisis* and have no Shepard's citator equivalent. There is also no Shepard's citator equivalent for verifying and updating the decisions of international courts and tribunals.")

27. Thomas Keefe, *Teaching Legal Research from the Inside Out*, 97 L. Lib. J. 117, 118 (2005).

28. *See e.g.* Peoples, *supra* note 26; Mary Whisner, *Practicing Reference, Researching Outside the Box*, 95 L. Lib. J. 467, 470–471 (2003) (noting absence of Westlaw and LexisNexis databases for researching customary international law); Lyonette Louis-Jacques, *Essay, Gaps in International Legal Literature*, 1 Chi. J. Intl. L. 101, 104 (2000) (noting lack of foreign law databases on Westlaw and LexisNexis).

29. Peoples, *supra* n. 26 (footnote omitted).

30. Customary international law is "international law that derives from the practice of states and is accepted by them as legally binding." *Black's Law Dictionary* 835 (Bryan A. Garner ed., 8th ed., West 2004).

31. Most court decisions in civil law countries do not constitute primary law, because precedent does not have controlling effect in these systems (with certain exceptions). *See* John Henry Merryman & Rogelio Pérez-Perdomo, *The Civil Law Tradition: An Introduction to the Legal Systems of Western Europe and Latin America* 47 (3d ed. Stanford University Press 2007) (noting the lack of a formal rule of *stare decisis* in civil law systems, while recognizing the influence of previous decisions on courts); Ken Gormley, *Judicial Review in the Americas: Comments on the United States and Mexico*, 45 Duq. L. Rev. 393, 403 (2007) (stating that in "civil law countries, judicial precedent is not the driving force of the legal system.")

32. Liana Fiol Matta, *Common Law and Civil Law in the Legal Method of Puerto Rico: The Transmission of Legal Discourse*, 64 Rev. Juridica U. Inter. P.R. 501, 523 n.69 (1995) (reporting that a survey of Puerto Rican law professors revealed "substantial agreement [eighty-seven percent] on the proposition that civilian research sources are not as easy to use as Anglo-American sources.")

33. Survey conducted on the electronic discussion lists "law-lib" (open to any law librarians) and "fcil-sis" (the Foreign, Comparative & International Law Special Interest Section of the American Association of Law Libraries) during April 2008 (results on file with author).

34. Some of my statements about FCIL research instruction are based on yearly attendance at the FCIL Special Interest Section's Teaching Foreign & International Legal Research group meetings during the AALL's annual meetings. I have attended each yearly session for the past several years and am grateful for the information provided by other attendees.

35. Several of the respondents to the survey cited in *supra* n. 33 stated that their schools were just starting to offer a stand-alone class.

36. Stacey L. Gordon, *Specialized Legal Research: My Experience in Developing Courses*, Leg. Info. Alert 1, 4 (April 2007) (noting increase in specialized research courses and stating that IFLR courses are the most common).

37. Very few U.S. law schools require students to take advanced U.S. legal research. In Ann Hemmens' careful survey of law schools, she found only four that required ALR. Ann Hemmens, *Advanced Legal Research Courses: A Survey of ABA-Accredited Law Schools*, 94 L. Lib. J. 209, 226 (2004).

38. If the instructor is able and willing to provide extra help for such students, even the lack of first-year legal research training should be no barrier. As with most prerequisites, an instructor can choose to waive that requirement, and LL.M. students bring useful experience and education to the class.

39. *See e.g.* syllabi for FCIL research courses collected at the Web site of the Foreign, Comparative & International Law Special Interest Section of the AALL, available at http://www.aallnet.org/sis/fcilsis/syllabinewsite.html.

40. U.S. Department of State, *Judicial Assistance: Country-Specific Information*, available at http://travel.state.gov/law/info/judicial/judicial_2510.html.

41. For example, I always offer to teach international environmental research, and every year, to my chagrin, students express little interest. I then remove it from the syllabus. At a school with a stronger focus on environmental law, student preferences would probably differ.

42. *Globalex*, available at http://www.nyulawglobal.org/globalex/index.html.

43. *Comparative and Foreign Law*, available at http://www.llrx.com/comparative_and_foreign_law.html; *International Law guides*, available at http://www.llrx.com/international_law.html.

44. *UNCTAD database*, available at http://www.unctadxi.org/templates/DocSearch______779.aspx.

45. *Base Pacte*, available at http://www.doc.diplomatie.gouv.fr/pacte.

46. Sources and techniques related to *travaux préparatoires* are ably described by Jonathan Pratter in the Globalex guide, *À la Recherche des Travaux Préparatoires: An Approach to Researching the Drafting History of International Agreements*, available at http://www.nyulawglobal.org/Globalex/Travaux_Preparatoires1.htm (2008).

47. *Restatement (Third) of the Law, The Foreign Relations Law of the United States* (1987).

48. An aptly titled feature of the journal *Perspectives: Teaching Legal Research and Writing*.

49. During the first few weeks of my class, I hand out a survey to find out what international or foreign legal experience students have, what foreign languages they read, and what their areas of topical interest are.

50. Thomas H. Reynolds & Arturo A. Flores, *Foreign Law Guide: Current Sources of Codes and Basic Legislation in Jurisdictions of the World*, available by subscription at http://www.foreignlawguide.com.

51. *Law Library of Congress Multinational Collections Database*, available at http://www.loc.gov/mulp. After a hiatus, this database is once again being updated. E-mail from Shameema Rahman, Library of Congress Legal Reference Specialist, to Mary Rumsey (6 Jan. 2009, 2:12 p.m. CST) (copy on file with author).

52. "EUR-Lex provides direct free access to European Union law. Here you can consult the *Official Journal of the European Union,* as well as the treaties, legislation, case law, and legislative proposals." EUR-Lex, *About This Web Site*, available at http://eur-lex.europa.eu/en/tools/welcome.htm (last accessed 5 Jan. 2009).

53. *Analytical Index: Guide to WTO Law and Practice*, available at http://www.wto.org/english/res_e/booksp_e/analytic_index_e/analytic_index_e.htm.

54. *Inside U.S. Trade* is available on LexisNexis, via the path Area of Law - By Topic/International Trade/Search News/General News.

55. *Case Law on UNCITRAL Texts (CLOUT)*, available at http://www.uncitral.org/uncitral/en/case_law.html.

56. *Transnational Law Digest & Bibliography*, available at http://www.tldb.net.

57. Peter Schanck, among others, has emphasized the need for students to complete enough exercises to "[assure] sufficient practice using the sources, [keep] the students involved in the class, and [maintain] a certain level of rigor." Peter C. Schanck, *Mandatory Advanced Legal Research: A Viable Program for Law Schools?* 92 L. Lib. J. 295, 299 (2000).

58. HUDOC is the free database of European human rights jurisprudence, available at http://cmiskp.echr.coe.int.

59. Syllabi and Course Materials, available at http://www.aallnet.org/sis/fcilsis/syllabinewsite.html.

60. Marci Hoffman & Mary Rumsey, *International and Foreign Legal Research: A Coursebook* (Martinus Nijhoff Publishers 2007).

61. J. Paul Lomio & Henrik Spang-Hanssen, *Legal Research Methods in the U.S. and Europe* (DJOF Publishing 2007).

62. *See e.g.* Joyce Manna Janto & Lucinda D. Harrison-Cox, *Teaching Legal Research, Past and Present*, 84 L. Lib. J. 281, 281 (1992). *See also* Hillel Levin, PrawfsBlawg, *Teaching Research: Next in an Ongoing Series on LRW*, http://prawfsblawg.blogs.com/prawfsblawg/2008/10/teaching-resear.html (19 Oct. 2008) (noting that librarians "bring a huge amount of knowledge and information to the table, and ... can introduce students to a whole range of resources"), and the further comment by Anonymous, PrawfsBlawg, *Teaching Research: Next in an Ongoing Series on LRW*, http://prawfsblawg.blogs.com/prawfsblawg/2008/10/teaching-resear.html, (20 Oct. 2008) ("Get the reference librarians in your law schools teaching legal research, because they are the people who know how to do legal research.")

63. Readers will notice that these skills translate well into U.S. research; many of my students have observed that their overall research skills improved greatly from the FCIL research course.

64. Student evaluations on file with author.

State-Specific Legal Research Instruction: Curricular Stepchild or Core Competency?

VICTORIA K. TROTTA and BETH DiFELICE
Ross Blakley Law Library, Sandra Day O'Connor College of Law, Arizona State University, Tempe, Arizona, USA

The authors argue that proficiency in state-specific legal research is a competency all law students should attain in law school, for the primary reason that many (if not most) students begin practice in the state where they attend law school, a reality of even those who attend so-called national law schools. Ten state-specific legal research courses currently offered are discussed by the authors, who also present a model syllabus for a one, two, and three unit state-specific legal research course.

INTRODUCTION

Legal research instruction is a time-honored activity of law librarians everywhere. Through publication, formal coursework, workshops, brown bags, online tutorials, and podcasts, our law students, new associates, and non-law professional colleagues are the beneficiaries of our expertise in planning and delivering instruction. We teach how to find the law, how to make sure it is current, and how to interpret the law that is found. Traditional formal legal research instruction usually emphasizes the federal system of law creation, leaving law students to fend for themselves when their practice requires legal research in the state jurisdiction of their practice. Although sources of state

The authors wish to thank all our colleagues who took time to answer the survey and to those instructors of state-specific legal research courses who agreed to be interviewed for this article and to share their syllabi. We also wish to thank our library secretary, Sara Lipich, without whose assistance this article would not have been completed. Thanks to Deb Quentel at CALI for updating the online list of state exercises.

law are frequently included in textbooks and in some lectures and exercise sets of first-year or advanced legal research (ALR) courses, the sources and methods of conducting state research usually receive short shrift, particularly in law schools that consider themselves "national." This level of instruction is not adequate. We must prepare our law students to practice in whatever state jurisdiction they find themselves and that includes instructing them in identifying sources for state jurisdictions and specialized areas of the law, evaluating legal authority regardless of format, and conducting cost-effective electronic research. Our research reveals that providing a state-specific legal research course as one of a series of legal research courses is a popular and well-attended opportunity for students that enhances research competencies and builds confidence. Every law school should include meaningful state-specific legal research content as part of its formal research curriculum.

THE EVOLUTION OF ALR CLASSES

We have come a long way since Frederick Hicks urged adoption of formal legal bibliography courses in 1918.[1] Law librarians are active leaders and advocates in legal research instruction. They know that the students need and value this instruction. Legal research instruction has taken a variety of forms, from informal lunchtime brown bags and "bridge the gap" type programs to legal bibliography within the required first-year (1L) legal research and writing courses and providing guest lectures in substantive law classes. Additionally, there has been a documented increase in the number of formal courses given for academic credit.

Several major articles have chronicled the growth in the number and content of ALR courses offered by American Bar Association (ABA)-approved law schools.[2] In 1983, Robin Mills reported that nine of the twenty-eight law schools responding to her survey offered an ALR course. A 1986 study by Blair Kaufman gathered responses from 151 law schools. At that time, twenty-seven law schools had at least one formal ALR course and another forty law schools had a course in the planning stages.[3] Kaufman identified the "classic topics" of legal research instruction in 1986 as being computer-aided legal research, administrative sources, statutes, federal and state legislative histories, and interdisciplinary resources and databases. State legislative histories are the only state materials mentioned in Kaufman's list. Kaufman also included so-called special topics that are sometimes the focus of their own specialized ALR course: foreign and international, securities, tax, and labor. By 2002, Ann Hemmens reported that the number of courses was seventy-two, and the list of topics covered in the courses had expanded from Kaufman's list.[4] She identified the following additional topics: Internet research, secondary sources, legal research strategies and approaches, comparison of paper and online versions of sources, citators, practice materials, and cost comparison of research approaches. Moreover, "state-specific materials" is listed as a topic by sixty-four (ninety percent) of the respondents in Hemmens' survey.

The increased number of formal legal research course offerings, along with the expanded list of topics covered in these courses, reflects trends in legal education. The landscape in legal education has changed dramatically in its complexity, and in many respects, the universe of legal bibliography and research is emblematic of that change. Our graduates must be equipped with substantive knowledge that includes even more emphasis on specialization. Law schools increasingly offer a curriculum that reflects the growing complexity of this reality. Moreover, as businesspeople, new graduates must quickly become efficient in the ways of practice and savvy consumers of legal information. They are faced with a growing and sometimes bewildering smorgasbord of options when it comes to delivery of legal information. They need exposure to the full spectrum of all those information options, knowledge of how to evaluate the information they discover, and practice in cost-effective and accurate research techniques. More than ever, formal instruction in legal research in all its forms and processes is necessary. Although frequently dismissed as merely "skills" courses, formal legal research instruction is gaining ground in law schools, even among "elite" schools, indicating an acknowledgement of its importance. Law librarians have always understood its importance, and just as importantly, so do our students. Students flock to informal sessions and oversubscribe to our research seminars. When asked, students ask for more.[5] Are our law schools doing enough to ensure that law students receive the instruction they need to be marketable and effective in today's competitive legal market?

WHERE WE ARE WE NOW: RESULTS OF THE SURVEY

How Many Law Schools Are Offering What Courses?

The authors sent a short survey to the members of the Academic Law Libraries Section of the American Association of Law Libraries (AALL) on the extent to which state-specific information is included in the ALR curriculum of their institutions.[6] The survey is included as Appendix A, *infra*. One hundred and eleven responses representing ninety-six law schools were received. To supplement the survey, the authors reviewed the Web sites of all 200 ABA-approved law schools for course descriptions of ALR courses, and the two lists were cross-checked. Four categories of ALR courses were identified: ALR courses that expressly include state-specific content; ALR courses that do not specifically mention the inclusion of state-specific content; ALR courses dedicated to state-specific legal research; and ALR courses that cover a specific topic or format. If a survey respondent clarified that state-specific content was in fact included in courses but did not include that information in the course description, the category designation was changed to conform to the survey respondent's information. Follow-up e-mail correspondence and phone calls were conducted with the instructors of every state-specific legal research course that was identified in this manner.[7] Results of the survey and the study reveal that 152 law schools report at least one formal course in ALR. The study identified a total of 162 courses, which fall into one of four categories:

ALR courses that included state-specific content: sixty-six (32.7%)
ALR courses that are dedicated to a special topic: twelve (6%)
ALR courses that provide no information about state-specific content: seventy-five (36%)
ALR courses dedicated to state-specific content: nine (4%)[8]
Law schools with no ALR courses listed on the law school Web sites: forty-eight (23%)

Why Are Existing ALR Courses Including State-Specific Content?

Seventy-seven of our survey respondents provided rationales for including state-specific content in their ALR curricula. Some respondents listed multiple reasons. Their reasons were consistent across all four categories of ALR courses identified:

Most of our students end up clerking and/or practicing here: fifty-five (71.4%)
The ability to successfully conduct state research is an important competency for law students to possess: eighteen (23.3%)
Students need to be able to conduct state and federal research: eight (10.3%)
Students need to know the sometimes unique resources and idiosyncratic research methods of our state: eight (10.3%)
Including state-specific content reinforces the concept of jurisdiction and provides students the opportunity to see how state authority and research can differ from the federal arena: four (5.1%)
Strong staff preference for including state-specific content: one (1%)
Students expressed an interest in learning about state legal research: one (1%)
State-specific topics such as legislative history and administrative law that are not included or are given cursory treatment in first-year legal research and writing courses due to time constraints can be included and even emphasized: one (1%)

Why Are Some Law Schools Not Providing State-Specific Content?

The survey asked respondents to give reasons for not providing state-specific content in their formal courses. As most of the respondents reported the inclusion of state-specific content, understandably there were fewer reasons for excluding that content. The responses included:

- "National" law schools pride themselves on asserting the principle that they prepare students to practice anywhere and in a variety of environments.
- Once a student learns the federal system and the system of publications and methods required to discover, update and interpret federal authority, students will easily apply that knowledge to any state system once they start to practice.
- The legal bibliography of the federal government, both in print and electronic, is discoverable and robust, and access to the sources of primary and secondary authority is ubiquitous. Therefore, the federal system of publication and research is easier for instructors to teach and for students to understand and master.
- There are serious time constraints in any legal research course. The courses preceding the digital era focused on a closed universe of print resources and emphasized bibliography and the processes for using those resources. Today's course demands time to explore other important topics, including the nature of authority in an electronic world, evaluation of information regardless of format, cost-effective search techniques, consideration of the many paid and free electronic resources that now contain information of potential usefulness to legal researchers, and the demands of specialized areas of law, such as international, foreign, tax, and securities. Given course units of one to three credits, choices must be made.

WHY STATE-SPECIFIC INSTRUCTION IS A CRITICAL COMPETENCY FOR LAW STUDENTS

After evaluating the reasons given by our survey participants for including or not including state-specific legal research instruction, we concluded that law students do need in-depth instruction on researching the law of the state where they will practice. Although many "national" schools argue against this instruction because their graduates relocate after graduation, our conclusion from the data we were able to obtain is that many law students do practice in the state (or at least the region) where they attend law school. Further, we disagree with the argument that a student who knows how to research federal law will be able to easily apply that knowledge to state research. Federal research is quite different than state research, and the states themselves vary.

We realize that in a world of finite resources, choices between course offerings must be made, and to some extent, exposure to one system of legal research sources can begin to inform lawyers of what they might expect when conducting research in another jurisdiction. But these arguments only take one so far. They may have been valid in the days before Westlaw, LexisNexis, and the Internet transformed the landscape of legal information. It might have been true in the past with its comparatively closed and finite print universe of the West National Reporter System and Shepard's that once a lawyer learned a "system" of legal research, she might have been able to transfer that knowledge and skill set to another state jurisdiction. In the past, new lawyers might have had the leisure to discover the state sources of primary and secondary authority once on the job.

The current environment surrounding legal practice is completely changed. These days, the universe of legal research skills that lawyers need to master is expanding. Today, lawyers have many more alternatives and options for conducting legal research. Many law firms are now national and practice in many jurisdictions. Clients increasingly resist paying for legal research. The demands of sophisticated legal practice require cost-effective research skills. Law firms expect their associates to come to them with a certain level of competence in legal research skills.

Some "national" law schools may argue that they do not need to teach their students state-specific legal research skills because their students scatter after graduation. Under this line of thought, the students would just pick up what they need to know once they begin practice, absolving the institution of supplying competent instruction in conducting legal research "somewhere." Our study underscores that graduates from so-called "national" law schools may indeed find themselves practicing anywhere in the United States—all the more reason to supply some amount of formal state-specific legal research instruction. However, while conducting state-specific legal research may have some similarities from jurisdiction to jurisdiction, the breadth and scope of available resources vary greatly, and some attention to the differences in various systems of legal information is necessary for competency to be insured. For example, the resources for conducting legal research in California or New York are worlds away from those available to researchers in Arizona.

These rationales simply no longer serve the needs of our law students, regardless of the law school they attend. Today, the challenge for legal research instructors must center around determining the skill sets and competencies law students need to be effective and productive legal researchers in today's legal environment where the cost of access to legal information is skyrocketing, and the array of options in locating legal information continues to expand and develop. Legal research instructors must include state-specific research content in formal classes because newly minted lawyers simply do not have the time to get themselves up to speed on the particulars of their practice state. A formal class in state-specific legal research offers law students the opportunity to focus on the increasing number of sources for primary and secondary authority and to become accustomed to the idiosyncrasies of state research.

WHERE DO GRADUATES BEGIN PRACTICE?

Before conducting their survey, the authors hypothesized that state-specific legal research courses would be more prevalent at law schools where a good percentage of the school's graduates practiced in that state or at least accepted their first positions there. It proved difficult to find the data to support this position. Although law schools are required to report their employment data to the National Association of Law Placement, this information is confidential. The authors initially surveyed the registrars of the ABA-approved law schools to determine this information, but we received virtually no response. We inspected the Web sites of the 200 ABA-approved law schools and learned that many law schools post their employment statistics online in a prominent place, usually targeted to prospective students.[9] While some law schools state the percentage of graduates accepting jobs in their state, the majority of law schools express their graduation employment statistics in terms of regional employment. Regional statistics may or may not be broken down into the employment figures for the states within the region.

The study of the law school Web sites was revealing. Only forty law schools (twenty percent) disclosed specific employment locations. The remainder of the law school Web sites either did not disclose employment location statistics at all or provided narrative that was not responsive to geographic location.

Eleven (5.5%) law schools disclosed that more than fifty percent of their recent graduates accepted positions in the state in which the law school is located.

Twenty-nine (14.5%) law schools disclosed that more than fifty percent of their recent graduates accepted positions in the region in which the law school is located.

Anecdotal information about the general percentage of law students remaining in the state to practice does exist. Thirty-one (15.5%) of the ALR survey respondents stated that the reason they included state-specific material in their ALR curriculum was that some significant percentage of their graduates did in fact practice in the state. The respondents described this circumstance as "many" (eight responses); "most" (fourteen responses); "many if not most" (three responses); "a majority" (four responses); "high" (two responses).

Readers may interpret those characterizations any way they choose, but even conservatively speaking, there is evidence that forty-two percent of the nation's law graduates begin their legal careers in the state in which they graduated. If you consider that students remaining in the regional vicinity of their law school might also have a need for competency in legal research for some state, the number jumps to fifty-one percent. However, our survey indicates that only four percent of ABA-approved law schools provide a formal course dedicated to state-specific legal research.

WHAT IS UNIQUE ENOUGH ABOUT STATE-SPECIFIC LEGAL RESEARCH TO WARRANT SEPARATE INSTRUCTION?

Even given that a large percentage of the graduates of many law schools remain in the state, what is so unique about state-specific research that requires its own course? How does state research differ from federal research, and how does research differ from state to state? Good attorneys should be well versed in the workings of the state constitution, the legislature, and the major agencies of the state in which they practice, all of which can vary greatly from state to state. Attorneys should be knowledgeable about the publications and law-making processes of the local jurisdictions. As the providers of legal research instruction in law schools, it is our job to provide our students with this knowledge to help prepare them for the practice of law. Exposure to the bibliography and methods of the state can underscore the importance of consulting state materials for students who might not otherwise think to consult those resources.

Our arguments that state research is unique enough to merit its own course can be summarized by the following points:

- There are customs that are particular to various state legal communities. For example, in South Carolina, master in equity courts exist to hear lawsuits dealing with real property. In Colorado, the court of appeals has come and gone several times. The City and County of Denver keep creating and abolishing trial level courts, such as drug courts, juvenile courts, and probate courts. Nebraska has a one-house legislature which makes bill tracking and legislative history research in that state unique. Some Arizona agencies are lax about complying with the publication requirements when adopting new regulations.
- Some areas of practice are grounded in state law. In some states, certain practice areas are very important, largely a matter of state law, and can vary from state to state. For example, the area of water law is critical in western states such as Arizona, Nevada, and California. Tribal law is important in states like Arizona and Oklahoma. Local law resources would be of interest in states with large urban areas like New York City.
- While the legal bibliography of state jurisdictions is relatively stable and robust when it comes to location and availability of cases and statutes, the legal bibliography of many states diverge in almost every other respect. For example, the availability of state administrative codes is a relatively recent event, and the availability of other materials of state agencies may vary greatly. Sources for state legislative history vary. Some states make legislative hearings available, and some do not. Many states do not have separate digests or encyclopedias, and practice commentary can be left largely to Continuing Legal Education (CLE) providers. The structure and

publication methods of state primary and secondary authority for many states can only be described as quirky, particularly in the area of legislative history.

- The lesson that not everything is available electronically or even easily located can be illustrated forcefully in the state arena. While many states provide Web sites with current agency and court information, their practices of preserving and providing permanent public access vary widely from state to state.
- State and local bar associations are entering into contracts with vendors to provide access to certain low-cost databases. For example, Fastcase is touted as a benefit of bar membership in Arizona and other states. Loislaw contains the state bar publications of Arizona and some other states. Students planning to practice in the states with these arrangements will be more informed consumers of legal information.

While many general ALR courses may touch on some of these topics, the opportunity to more thoughtfully and thoroughly explore them can only strengthen the student's confidence that she will be able to function in the legal community she is about to join.

DESCRIPTION OF COURSES TAUGHT CURRENTLY

The authors discovered nine courses through the survey, supplemented by a search of ABA-approved law school Web sites that focused on state-specific legal research. As a cohort, they reveal a spectrum of topics and approaches that are interesting to note and to consider when planning a course.

Akron[10]

Ohio Legislative Research for ALR (one unit) Students must complete two required and six elective module hours to complete a one-unit ALR credit. There is a state-specific elective module for two module hours on Ohio Legislative History. Description: "This module covers the Ohio legislative process and locating Ohio legislative history materials. Students will begin with a fact scenario and then research for Ohio legislative materials in LexisNexis, Westlaw, an independent subscription-based Web site and free state government Web sites." The self-paced module is conducted completely online and consists of two lessons and exercises. One exercise focuses on reading statutes and locating state legislative history documents. Students compare and contrast coverage on commercial and non-commercial databases. The second exercise exposes students to two commercial Ohio legislative information databases. Instructor uses The West Education Network (TWEN).

Fordham[11]

ALR: N.Y. Legal Materials (one unit) "This course examines the three branches of the New York State government. Students will learn to find statutes, New York legislative history, cases, and administrative decisions. Secondary sources on specific topics will be discussed. Both print and online sources will be examined. The focus will be on research strategies to solve practical questions that an attorney would encounter in a typical New York practice using cost-effective methods." The course is organized around a well-known New York statute that was in the news. Topics include cases, statutes and legislative history, administrative law and decisions, secondary sources, forms, and New York reference tools. New York City sources are also included in each module. There are six assignments administered throughout the semester. Research diaries are required for each assignment. In-class exercises feature teams of students using different legal research services to solve legal problems. No paper or final is required. Instructor uses TWEN.

Golden Gate[12]

California Legal Research (two units) "This course demonstrates the structure and use of legal resources as they relate to California practice. The course goal is research proficiency, especially with electronic California legal materials. Each student is responsible for learning to use the electronic research tools, theories, and strategies presented by the instructors. Weekly exercises are assigned, and students may also be expected to complete either a semester research project or a shorter end-of-semester project to demonstrate a comprehensive grasp of research skills. Paper and online resources will be compared to reveal their respective strengths and weaknesses, so students in this class can also expect to hone their skills in researching California printed legal materials." Topics include introduction to California legal research, cases and court reports, database selection, searching using terms and connectors and natural language, case law searching with fields, statutes and codes, citators, legislative history, administrative and executive branch publications, public records and factual research, secondary sources, news, legal newspapers and newsletters, court documents, research strategies, and cost-effective legal research. A series of six exercises is required. The final project is a pathfinder. Instructor uses TWEN.

Marquette[13]

Wisconsin Law (one unit) Marquette requires one unit of ALR which students can fulfill by any of nine one-unit classes. "This variable topic course focuses on practical legal research strategies leading students to make informed choices about the type and format of resource to use, an efficient method for using resources, and understanding of the costs involved with various resources. Students will complete a series of research assignments demonstrating appropriate research techniques and problem solving. This course satisfies the ALR requirement." Topics include: research strategy; secondary materials; statutory research; legislative history; administrative law; case law; and practice materials. Class length is seven weeks. There is an assignment that corresponds with each class session, and there is a final project. Instructor uses TWEN.

Marquette

State Law (one unit) "This variable topic course focuses on practical legal research strategies leading students to make informed choices about the type and format of resource to use, an efficient method for using resources, and understanding of the costs involved with various resources. Students will complete a series of research assignments demonstrating appropriate research techniques and problem solving for their preferred jurisdiction. This course satisfies the ALR requirement." Topics include: secondary materials including practice materials; use of LoisLaw; statutes; state and federal regulations; case finding, statutory interpretation, and administrative decision making; state and federal legislative history; comprehensive practice problems. There is a final project. The course is seven weeks in length. In this course, the student selects the jurisdiction to study. Students learn about the sources that are available for conducting research in their chosen jurisdiction and to apply the knowledge through a series of exercises. The students share information about how their jurisdiction handles certain legal areas. Typically, there are four to nine jurisdictions represented in any given state law class. Instructor uses TWEN or LexisNexis Web Course.

University of Miami[14]

Florida Legal Research (one unit) "This course is designed to offer you a working knowledge of legal bibliography and research methods in both print and electronic formats. Emphasis will be placed on the strategy involved in evaluating and using resources. The goal of this course is to help you negotiate the complex demands of a rapidly changing legal research environment and to enable you to develop competencies, skills, and appropriate methods for conducting effective and efficient research, both as law students and as legal professionals." The course covers evaluation of resources and authority, secondary sources, including current awareness tools, Internet searching and Florida Web sites, constitutions, session law and statutes, administrative law research, case law research, citators, court rules and court records, legislative materials, and research strategy. Assessment tools include Computer-Assisted

Legal Instruction (CALI) exercises, preparation of a research journal, short, in-class presentations and a pathfinder covering any Florida law-related topic. Instructor uses TWEN.

University of San Francisco[15]

California Legal Research (two units) "Designed primarily for second-, third-, and fourth-year law students who are planning to practice law in California, this overview course will provide practical legal research skills to help prepare students to conduct legal research as clerks, interns, or new attorneys. Assignments, lectures, and regular hands-on in-class exercises will emphasize cost-efficient research strategies, print and online legal materials, and law practice technology. Written assignments will emulate research assignments typically given to attorneys new to practice. Lectures and assignments will focus on California law, court systems, and practice materials." This is a new course for the University of San Francisco, and the development is still in progress. The class may be organized around a complicated hypothetical that might be introduced to the class by a local practitioner. Search strategies for analyzing the problem and planning efficient and cost-effective research techniques will be emphasized. There will be some lecture and student discussion, and this course will emphasize in-class assignments.

University of Texas[16]

ALR: Texas Law (one unit) "This class covers the basic research materials available on Texas law. It is not a class in Texas civil procedure or in the substantive aspects of Texas law except as those aspects related to the finding and interpretation of legal materials." Topics include secondary sources, Vernon's Texas Statutes and Codes and rules of court; Texas legislative history; Texas court structure and reporters, citators, and writ/petition history; Texas administrative materials and attorney general opinions; and additional electronic resources. The class meets for seven weeks only. Three exercises are administered. There is no final paper or examination. Emphasis is on introducing students to the sources they are most likely to use in practice and on those unique characteristics of Texas law and legal practice.

Texas Wesleyan[17]

Texas Legal Research Practicum (two units) "This course will focus on ALR methodologies, costs, and strategies within the context of Texas law.

It includes coverage of the Texas court system, legislation and legislative history, regulations and regulatory history, agency decisions and Web sites, treatises, electronic databases, free online resources, court rules, jury instructions, practice materials, and strategies for making sure that your research is thorough. Students will complete assignments, including drafting using Texas practice materials. A final project is required." Assignments focus on eight research scenarios. Extensive readings are included. The final examination is a four-part exam (research log, a memorandum answering a question, an assessment of what they learned in the class, and a five-minute in-class presentation, one on one with the instructor.) These in-person presentations are held on the day of the written final. In addition, a final research scenario is presented and students have two weeks to complete the assignment.

Western State[18]

California Legal Research (one unit) "This course introduces students to leading resources in California legal and law-related research. Students will learn both print and computerized (including commercial online and free Internet) information resources and techniques by doing directed assignments in the library and online. The course emphasizes research exercises or law practice simulation assignments to help students develop their legal research skills. This course satisfies the advanced professional skills course requirements." This course is offered in the summer session. There are six classes, each of three-hour duration, over a period of two weeks. The class size is kept small (under ten). Topics include: California legal system, research strategies and techniques, electronic versus print resources; secondary sources; case law, court rules and forms, and other court documents; state constitution and statutes, legislative history, ballot propositions, and municipal ordinances; and executive and administrative materials. There are two assignments integrating the content of the courses. There is no final examination or paper requirement. Instructors alternate between TWEN and LexisNexis Blackboard.

OPTIONS FOR PROVIDING STATE-SPECIFIC INSTRUCTION

Now that we have reached the conclusion that we must instruct our students on state legal research, the next question is how this goal might be accomplished. There are at least three options. State-specific instruction can be incorporated into 1L legal research instruction, into existing ALR courses, or taught as its own separate course. Before discussing stand-alone courses, we will discuss the first two options briefly.

First-Year Legal Research and Writing

Incorporating state-specific legal research into 1L legal research and writing courses presents significant challenges. To begin with, the configuration of this required course varies widely between law school programs. Some courses are two semesters; some are three. Some courses focus on legal writing; some provide more or less equal measures of research and writing. Content will also vary depending upon who is teaching the course—legal writing professors or law librarians. It is the authors' view that so long as the teacher of 1L legal research instructs the students on the specifics of the primary sources of law for the three branches of government (federal and state) and both the federal and state constitutions, the students will have a basic framework that could be built upon later. Separate, optional one- or two-hour workshops in the spring semester for students who have secured summer associate positions could introduce students to the sources of state primary authority along with any practice materials that may exist for the jurisdiction. Any workshop of this nature for 1L students should also include general information about search strategies.

ALR Courses

Although this course category is widespread in law schools, it can vary widely in its content. Time constraints due to the pressure to add specialized topics such as international and foreign legal research, topical research such as tax law and Indian law, and federal legislative history can trump state-specific research instruction. When state-specific instruction is introduced into general ALR courses on a limited basis, instructors should emphasize topics that present special challenges to researchers in that state. The legislative process and statutory research should be included, as should administrative regulations and agency decisions. Finally, some exposure to practice materials should be included. For a model syllabus for incorporating state-specific content into a general ALR course, see Appendix D, *infra*.

Stand-Alone State-Specific Legal Research Courses

Limited staff resources and challenges attendant to getting a course proposal past a curriculum committee present some obvious obstacles to implementing a state-specific research course. When deciding to propose one of these courses, instructors will need to determine whether a student taking this course should also be allowed to take a general advanced research course and whether the course should be one, two, or three units. The authors believe that if the institution provides no advanced or specialized legal research courses, a full two- or three-unit course could be developed that is dedicated to state-specific legal research. However, as most of the 200 ABA-approved law schools provide some formal ALR instruction, a state-specific course of one unit is recommended. A one-unit course would have thirteen or fourteen contact hours, which is sufficient to present the sources of legal authority, the full range of options for retrieving the authority, cost-effective search strategies, and special customs and cultural circumstances that might exist in the state government. A sample syllabus for a one-unit course appears as Appendix D, *infra*.

PUTTING A COURSE TOGETHER

Once a decision to offer a state-specific legal research course has been made, how do you put such a course together? What resources are available? In the next part of this article, we will discuss available textbooks and CALI lessons and the responses to our survey about assessment techniques. A model syllabus for a one-credit legal research course appears as Appendix D, *infra*.

Twenty-nine states and the District of Columbia have state-specific legal research treatises or textbooks published within the last ten years. Most of these are published by Carolina Academic Press, several by Hein, and a few by Thomson West and LexisNexis. The William S. Hein series is more like a treatise and tends to take a more thorough historical bibliographic and research view, and the Carolina Academic Press Series focuses on process and highlights limited options for researching. Individual titles in the Carolina Academic Press Series follow essentially the same format.

Out of ninety-six law schools responding to this question on our survey, only fourteen reported using a textbook. Five respondents use the state-specific legal research treatise for their state, seven respondents use a general legal research treatise or nutshell (Mersky or Sloan), and one school, Northern Illinois University, created its own textbook. One respondent does not require a textbook, but recommends one of the state-specific legal research treatises available for the state. For a list of available textbooks, see Appendix B, infra.

Currently forty-six states and the District of Columbia are represented among the bibliographies available in the *State Documents Bibliographies* series published by the AALL Government Documents Special Interest Section (SIS).[19] Each bibliography sets out the most useful source of state authority, and most now include Web-based resources. Many, but not all, include legal research strategies. These are a good tool to use when there is no dedicated treatise to the state's legal bibliography. In addition to their use as course development tools, these have value for law students who wish to familiarize themselves quickly with the authority for the state.

A third resource is state-specific research pathfinders and tutorials which are found on most law school Web sites. Check the Web sites of all the law schools in a particular state to see what is available. A notable collection of state legislative history research guides is available at Indiana University Bloomington Law Library's Web site.[20]

Finally, another potential resource to use in the preparation and execution of a state-specific legal research course is the collection of CALI lessons that cover a specific state.[21] Nine states and the District of Columbia have CALI lessons available. A current list of these exercises is included in Appendix C, *infra*.

CALI

Teachers of legal research in Arizona, the District of Columbia, Georgia, Maryland, Nebraska, Nevada, New York, Pennsylvania, Washington, and Wyoming have the option of using a CALI tutorial to teach students how to research in their state.[22] CALI lessons for primary (and in some cases secondary) legal research sources are available and free for students in CALI-member schools. In addition to being used for a state-specific legal research course, they could also be used as an assignment for a first-year or ALR class or recommended to students who do not take ALR but will be working in that state.

An instructor may decide that the lesson available for a particular state is not quite what the instructor would like to assign. The lesson could be modified to add secondary material if it is not included in the lesson already; add information specific to a particular law library; shorten the lesson; or incorporate hands-on research assignments. These modifications are not difficult to do. The authors have modified the Arizona primary law lesson for their ALR students, adding a page about secondary sources and adding questions requiring the students to periodically leave the lesson to find particular bills, session laws, and statutes from the Arizona legislature's Web site.

Modifying a lesson requires use of the CALI Author software, which can be downloaded by CALI member schools for free from the CALI Web site.[23] A password from CALI is needed to do the modifications. CALI owns the copyright in the lessons, and although users may modify the lessons without seeking the author's permission, CALI asks that instructors note the modification on the opening screen of the lesson and on each modified page. Anyone unfamiliar with CALI Author may want the assistance of someone who has used the software. For someone who knows CALI Author, the modifications are very easy to do.

If there is not a CALI lesson for your state, consider writing one—or two.[24] Generally, primary and secondary sources are covered in separate lessons. Lessons on primary materials should include, at a minimum, the state's statutes, court opinions, court rules, and regulations. Consider including other sources, such as legislative history, attorney general opinions, and ethics rules and opinions. Lessons on secondary sources may cover the state's encyclopedia, state-specific form books, CLE publications, bar journals, etc. Authors of state-specific lessons do not need to repeat instruction that is contained in other lessons but can simply refer the student to the appropriate CALI lesson. For example, rather than including instructions on how to use the digests, simply refer to Brian Huddleston's lesson, "How to Find Case Law Using the Digests."[25]

WHAT ASSESSMENT TECHNIQUES ARE UTILIZED?

The respondents to the ALR survey conducted by the authors revealed a number of assessment techniques used across all courses where state-specific content was included. Thirty-two of ninety-six law schools responded to this question, and many noted multiple assessment techniques, including:

CALI exercises: four respondents (one additional respondent reported he would use CALI exercises if they existed for his state)
Online tutorials: three respondents
Audience response technology: four respondents (and one in planning stages)
In-class exercises: six respondents
Game show format: one respondent
Quizzes and/or final exam: twelve respondents
Graded exercises/practice problems: thirteen respondents
Short paper/memo: three respondents
Final project or pathfinder: four respondents
Pre- or post-test: two respondents

CONCLUSION

Seventy-one of the 200 ABA-approved law schools report either through their Web sites or through anecdotal information from the survey responders that fifty-percent or more of their new graduates remain in their state to practice, and this number may be much higher. The survey and the Web site inspection reveal that although a large number of law schools include some state-specific content in their ALR courses, only nine schools provide a state-specific legal research course.

The authors do not presume to label any law school as "national" or "regional," nor can we verify the employment data that express the percentage of graduates that stay in the state or in the region to practice. Many of the survey responders had some grasp of the general situation in their own law schools, however vaguely expressed as "most," "many," significant," etc. Resourceful course planners will have access to that information from their career services colleagues. If a significant percentage of the graduates in your school are staying in the state to practice, perhaps it is time to include some state-specific content in existing courses or plan a course dedicated to state-specific legal research. Even if your graduates do not remain in your state to practice, there is plenty of justification for providing formal state-specific legal research content in legal research courses. There are many resources to assist in the creation and execution of such a course. A one-unit course in particular would be useful in familiarizing students with the common tools and processes needed for basic research competence. For students who expect to remain to practice locally, state-specific content will boost their confidence and prepare them for research in a local legal practice. For students who practice elsewhere, instruction in state-specific legal research will enrich their legal education and better prepare them for practice wherever they go.

NOTES

1. Frederick Hicks, *The Teaching of Legal Bibliography,* 11 L. Lib. J 4 (1918).
2. Robin K. Mills, *Legal Research Instruction After the First Year of Law School,* 76 L. Lib. J. 603 (1983); S. Blair Kaufman, *Advanced Legal Research Courses: A New Trend in Legal Education*, 6 Leg. Ref. Servs. Q. (3/4) 123 (1986); Gary Hill, *Survey on Legal Research Instruction*, AALL Publications Series No. 56 (W. S. Hein & Co. 1989); Ann Hemmens, *Advanced Legal Research Courses: A Survey of ABA-Accredited Law Schools,* 94 L. Lib. J. 209 (2002).
3. Kaufman, *supra* n. 2, at 123.
4. Hemmens, *supra* n. 2, at 231–232.
5. Kaufman, *supra* n. 2, at 127–128.
6. The eleven-question survey was created using Survey Monkey. The ALL-SIS was selected for the survey because it is a principle vehicle for communications among academic law librarians. That population includes those law librarians most likely to be teaching advanced and specialized legal research courses. The survey was distributed in June 2008 to 1,125 subscribers.
7. Legal research courses for 1L students are excluded from our results because those courses are under the control of the legal research and writing programs at most ABA-approved law schools. According to the survey results, thirteen law schools indicated that they provided state-specific content in the context of the 1L legal research and writing courses. Moreover, nineteen survey respondents indicated that they provided more informal opportunities for instruction.
8. The study revealed one law school that used to offer a formal state-specific ALR course but subsumed it into the new and presumably improved "Advanced Legal Research" in 2007.
9. One hundred and eleven, or 55.5%, do not disclose their employment statistics publicly on their Web sites.
10. The University of Akron School of Law ALR course, available at http://www.uakron.edu/law/library/alr.php (last accessed 13 Sept. 2008). Interview with Lynn Lenart, Asst. L. Libr., Ref. Services, U. Akron Sch. L.
11. Fordham University, available at http://law.fordham.edu/index.htm. Interview with Janis Greer, Ref. Libr., Fordham U. L. Sch.
12. Golden Gate University School of Law Course Catalog, available at http://www.ggu.edu/courses/catalog/browse_law.do?lawType=LAW3. Syllabus available online. Telephone interview with Marisa Diehl, Ref. Libr., Golden Gate U. L. Sch.

13. Interview with Professor Patricia Cervenka, Marquette U. L. Sch.

14. Syllabus for Fall 2008 class supplied by Professor Sally Wise, U. Miami. L. Sch.

15. University of San Francisco, available at http://www.usfca.edu/law/current/ElectiveCourseDescriptions.html#C. Interview with Lee Ryan, Senior Ref. Libr., U.S.F. L. Sch.

16. The University of Texas at Austin, School of Law, available at http://utdirect.utexas.edu/loreg/clap.WBX?ccyys=20089&class_unique_number=28885. Interview with Jane A. O'Connell, Dir. Faculty and Student Services, U. Tex. L. Sch.

17. Interview with Stephanie Marshall, Faculty Services Libr., Tex. Wesleyan L. Sch.

18. Western State University College of Law, available at http://www.wsulaw.edu/current-students/spring2007info.asp. Interview with Scott Frey, Ref. Libr., W. St. U. L. Sch.

19. The states that do not have legal bibliographies in this series at the present time are: Florica, New Hampshire, North Dakota, South Carolina, and Utah.

20. Indiana University Bloomington Law Library's Web site, available at http://www.law.indiana.edu/lawlibrary/research/guides/statelegislative/index.shtml.

21. CALI, available at http://www2.cali.org.

22. More lessons have probably been added since this article was written. To see an updated list, go to http://www2.cali.org/index.php?fuseaction=lessons.subjectlist&cat=LR.

23. CALI Author Information, available at http://www2.cali.org/index.php?fuseaction=teaching.caliauthorinfo.

24. Instructions for submitting proposals for new lessons are available at http://www2.cali.org/index.php?fuseaction=static.lrcap.

25. *Supra*, n. 21.

APPENDIX A
THE SURVEY INSTRUMENT

State-Specific Legal Research Survey

1. Please enter the NAME OF YOUR SCHOOL
2. Do you include state-specific legal research anywhere in your legal research curriculum?
   Yes
   No
3. If YES, which educational offerings contain this content? (check all that apply)
   First-year legal research
   Advanced Legal Research
   A special for-credit course, e.g., Arizona Legal Research
4. (How many credits do you assign to this course?)
   A non-credit workshop or lecture that covers only legal research sources for your state
   Other (please specify)
5. If you do include state-specific legal research anywhere in your legal research curriculum, what are your reasons for doing so?
6. What topics are covered in your state-specific legal research curriculum?

7. Do you use a textbook in conjunction with your state-specific legal research courses?
   Yes (please specify below)
   No
8. Do you require your students to work through any of the CALI state-specific exercises as part of their coursework?
   Yes
   No
9. What other assessment techniques do you employ in your state-specific legal research courses?
   Online tutorials you have created
   Audience response technology
   Other (please specify)
10. If you do NOT include state-specific legal research anywhere in your legal research curriculum, why not?
11. Would you be willing to be contacted by one of us about your experiences with state-specific legal research courses? If so, please fill out the following:
   Name
   Email
   Phone

APPENDIX B
CURRENTLY AVAILABLE TEXTBOOKS

LISTS OF TEXTBOOKS AVAILABLE

Below is a list of state legal research books, arranged alphabetically by state.[1] Some states, such as California, have more than one book.

Alabama:

Laurel R. Clapp, *Alabama Legal Research Guide* (Hein 2006).

Gary Lewis Orlando, *Legal Research in Alabama: How to Find and Understand the Law in Alabama* (Gary Orland Lewis 2001).

Arizona:

Tamara S. Herrera, *Arizona Legal Research* (Carolina Academic Press 2008).

Kathy Shimpock-Vieweg & Marianne Alcorn, *Arizona Legal Research Guide* (Hein 1992).

Arkansas:

Coleen M. Barger, *Arkansas Legal Research* (Carolina Academic Press 2007).

California:

Larry D. Dershem, *California Legal Research Handbook* (2nd ed., Hein 2008).

Hether C. Macfarlane & Suzanne E. Rowe, *California Legal Research* (Carolina Academic Press 2008).

John K. Hanft, *Legal Research in California* (6th ed., West 2007).

Daniel W. Martin, *Henke's California Law Guide* (8th ed., LexisNexis 2006).

Connecticut:

Jessica G. Hynes, *Connecticut Legal Research* (Carolina Academic Press 2008).

Lawrence G. Cheeseman, *The Connecticut Legal Research Handbook* (Connecticut Law Book Co. 1992).

District of Columbia:

John D. Eure, *A Guide to Legal Research in Virginia* (5th ed., Virginia CLE Publications 2005) (covers D.C., Maryland, and Virginia).

Florida:

Betsy L. Stupski, *Guide to Florida Legal Research* (LexisNexis 2008).

Barbara J. Busharis & Suzanne E. Rowe, *Florida Legal Research* (3rd ed., Carolina Academic Press 2007).

Georgia:

Nancy P. Johnson, Elizabeth G. Adelman & Nancy J. Adams, *Georgia Legal Research* (Carolina Academic Press 2007).

Leah F. Chanin & Suzanne L. Cassidy, *Guide to Georgia Legal Research and Legal History* (Harrison 1990).

Idaho:

Tenielle Fordyce-Ruff & Suzanne E. Rowe, *Idaho Legal Research* (Carolina Academic Press 2008).

Illinois:

Laurel Wendt, *Illinois Legal Research Guide* (2nd ed., Hein 2006).

Mark E. Wojcik, *Illinois Legal Research* (Carolina Academic Press 2003).

Iowa:

John D. Edwards, *Iowa Legal Research Guide* (Hein 2003).

Kansas:

Joseph A. Custer & Christopher L. Steadham, *Kansas Legal Research* (Carolina Academic Press 2008).

Joseph A. Custer, Barbara J. Ginzburg & Robert A. Mead, *Kansas Legal Research and Reference Guide* (3rd. ed., Kansas Bar Association 2003).

Kentucky:

Kurt Metzmeier, Amy Osborne & Shaun Esposito, *Kentucky Legal Research Manual* (3rd ed., University of Kentucky College of Law, Office of Continuing Legal Education 2005)

Louisiana:

Mary Garvey Algero, *Louisiana Legal Research* (Carolina Academic Press 2008).

Win-Shin S. Chiang, *Louisiana Legal Research* (2nd ed., Butterworth 1990).

Maryland:

John D. Eure, *A Guide to Legal Research in Virginia* (5th ed., Virginia CLE Publications 2005) (covers D.C., Maryland, and Virginia)

Massachusetts:

Mary Ann Neary, *Handbook of Legal Research in Massachusetts* (Massachusetts Continuing Legal Education 2002).

Michigan:

Pamela Lysaght, *Michigan Legal Research* (Carolina Academic Press 2006).

Richard L. Beer, Michigan Legal Literature: An Annotated Guide (2nd ed., Hein 1991)

Minnesota:

John Tessner, George R. Jackson & Brenda Wolfe, *Minnesota Legal Research Guide* (2nd ed., Hein 2002).

Missouri:

Wanda M. Temm & Julie M. Cheslik, *Missouri Legal Research* (Carolina Academic Press 2007).

Nebraska:

Kay L. Andrus, *Research Guide to Nebraska Law* (LexisNexis 2006)

Nevada:

Jennifer Gross, Thomas Gross& Tom Boone, *Nevada Legal Research Guide* (Hein 2005).

New Jersey:

Paul Axel-Lute, *New Jersey Legal Research Handbook* (5th ed., New Jersey Institute for Continuing Legal Education 2008)

New Mexico:

Michelle Rigual. *New Mexico Legal Research* (Hein, forthcoming)

New York:

Elizabeth G. Adelman & Suzanne E. Rowe, *New York Legal Research* (Carolina Academic Press 2008).

William H. Manz, Ellen M. Gibson & Karen L. Spencer, *Gibson's New York Legal Research Guide* (3rd ed., Hein 2004).

North Carolina:

Miriam J. Baer & James C. Ray, *Legal Research in North Carolina* (Carolina 2006).

Mary Louise Corbett, Guide to North Carolina Legal and Law-Related Materials (2nd ed., AALL 1996)

Jean Sinclair McKnight, *North Carolina Legal Research Guide* (Rothman 1994).

Ohio:

Susan Schaefgen, Melanie Putnam & Katherine Hall, *Ohio Legal Research Guide* (Hein 1997).

Katherine L. Hall & Sara A. Sampson, *Ohio Legal Research* (Carolina Academic Press 2008).

Oregon:

Suzanne E. Rowe, *Oregon Legal Research* (2nd ed., Carolina Academic Press 2007).

Pennsylvania:

Frank Y. Liu, *Pennsylvania Legal Research Handbook* (American Lawyer Media 2008).

Barbara J. Busharis & Bonny L. Tavares, *Pennsylvania Legal Research* (Carolina Academic Press 2007).

South Dakota:

Delores A. Jorgensen, *South Dakota Legal Research Guide* (2nd ed., Hein 1999).

Tennessee:

Sibyl Marshall & Carol McCrehan Parker, *Tennessee Legal Research* (Carolina Academic Press 2007).

Texas:

Brandon D. Quarles & Matthew D. Cordon, *Researching Texas Law* (2nd ed., Hein 2008).

Matthew D. Cordon & Brandon D. Quarles, *Specialized Topics in Texas Legal Research* (Hein 2005).

Vermont:

Virginia Wise, A Bibliographical Guide to the Vermont Legal System (AALL 1991)

Virginia

John D. Eure, *A Guide to Legal Research in Virginia* (5th ed., Virginia CLE Publications 2005) (covers D.C., Maryland, and Virginia)

Leah F. Chanin, Pamela J. Gregory & Sarah K. Wiant, *Legal Research in the District of Columbia, Maryland, and Virginia* (2nd ed., Hein 2000).

Washington:

Julie Cho, *Washington Legal Research* (Carolina Academic Press 2005).

Penny A. Hazelton, *Washington Legal Researcher's Deskbook* (3rd ed., Marian Gould Gallagher Law Library 2002).

Wisconsin:

Theodore A. Potter & Jane Colwin, *Legal Research in Wisconsin* (2nd ed., Hein 2008).

1. See Nancy Adams Deel & Barbara G. James, *An Annotated Bibliography of State Legal Research Guides* 14(1/2) Leg. Ref. Servs. Q. (1994) for historical sources.

APPENDIX C
STATE-SPECIFIC CALI EXERCISES

List of CALI lessons, arranged alphabetically by state

Arizona Legal Research—Primary Sources; Beth DiFelice and Jennifer Murray
Arizona Legal Research—Secondary Sources; Diane Murley

Arkansas Legal Research—Primary Sources; Colleen Williams (in progress)
California Legal Research—Primary Sources (in development)
California Legal Research—Secondary Sources; Jack Schroeder (in progress)
Colorado Legal Research—Primary Sources; Barbara Bintliff, Alicia Brillon, Alan Pannell, Jane Thompson
District of Columbia Legal Research—Primary Sources; Louise Tsang
Florida Legal Research—Primary Sources; Rebecca Trammell, Pamela Burdett, Wanita Scroggs, Julieanne Hartman Stevens, Sally Ginsberg Waters (in progress)
Florida Legal Research—Secondary Sources; Jessica de Perio Wittman (in progress)
Georgia Legal Research—Primary Source Material; Elizabeth Adelman, Nancy Johnson, Nancy Adams, and Terrance Manion
Georgia Legal Research—Secondary Sources (in development)
Louisiana Legal Research—Primary Sources; Brian Huddleston (in progress)
Maryland Legal Research—Primary Authority; Sara Kelley and Susan Herrick
Nebraska Primary Resources—Legislative & Judicial; Sandy Placzek
Nevada Legal Research—Jennifer Gross
New York Primary Legal Research—Joseph Gerken
North Carolina Legal Research—Primary Sources; Maureen Eggert, Shannon Gilreath (in progress)
Ohio Legal Reserach—Primary Sources;, David Fetrow and Nancy Armstrong
Ohio Legal Research—Secondary Sources (in development)
Pennsylvania Primary Legal Research—Brent Johnson, Ed Sonnenberg, Patricia Fox
Pennsylvania Secondary Legal Resources—Brent Johnson
South Carolina Legal Research—Primary Sources; Stacy Etheredge, Terrye Conroy, David Lehmann (in progress)
Utah Legal Research—Primary and Secondary Sources; Shawn Nevers (in progress)
Washington (State) Legal Research—Primary Sources; Kelly Kunsch
Wyoming Legal Research—Deborah Person and Tawnya Plumb

APPENDIX D
MODEL STATE-SPECIFIC LEGAL RESEARCH SYLLABUS—STAND-ALONE COURSE

Sample Syllabus for a One-Credit State Legal Research Lesson. We have not yet offered an Arizona legal research course at Arizona State University, but we are planning one for the very near future.[1] The course is a one-unit opportunity and joins other specialized legal research offerings at the law school. While recognizing the time limitations of a one-unit course, we concluded that students completing this course would be conversant in the structure and methods of the Arizona branches of government, become familiar with the state's publication and citation practices, become proficient in locating and using primary authority and conducting legislative histories, and gain familiarity with some special areas of particular interest to Arizona lawyers. We will use the *Arizona Legal Research* textbook, which focuses on the processes of conducting legal research. Classroom instruction will focus on the substance of sources and format options and will include guest lecturers who will provide some "real-life" opportunities for interaction with local practitioners. The exercises allow the students to discover and explore the sources and methods of Arizona legal research and provide practice in using those sources.

Arizona Legal Research

1 credit, pass/fail. The class meets once a week for an hour.

Textbook: Tamara S. Herrera, *Arizona Legal Research* (Carolina Academic Press 2008)

Week 1: Lecture on Arizona legal history.
Week 2: Lecture on the Arizona legislative process. Guest lecturer from the legislature.
Week 3: Tracking bills. Legislative history.

- Reading for today's class: James H. Kemper, *Legislative History: The Needle in the Haystack*, November 1991 Ariz. Atty. 14.
- Homework assignment: The course will be taught Spring semester, and the legislature will be in session. Students will be assigned two to three bills to track throughout the legislative session.
- Homework assignment: Students will prepare a legislative history for an assigned piece of legislation.

Week 4: Arizona constitution, statutes, and local codes.

- Homework: practice questions on finding statutes.

Week 5: Arizona regulations, agency decisions, attorney general opinions, ethics opinions and rules, and governor's executive orders and proclamations.

- Homework: practice questions on finding these sources.

Week 6: Overview of the Arizona court system. Finding cases, court rules, briefs, and other case information.

- Homework: practice questions on finding cases and court rules.

Week 7: Overview of the role of tribal law in Arizona legal research. Finding the laws of Arizona tribes.
Week 8: Arizona practice materials and other secondary sources.
Week 9: Loislaw, Fastcase, and Arizona materials on Westlaw and Lexis.
Week 10: Putting it all together—the research process.
Week 11: An in-class research problem using Arizona materials to be finished outside of class.
Week 12: A quick overview of federal sources, primarily federal statutes and regulations.
Week 13: An in-class research problem with Arizona and federal issues to be finished outside of class.

We have a thirteen-week semester. If we had a fourteen-week semester we would add an in-class group exercise on creating a cost-effective Arizona law library. Students would provide a budget, and we would have the groups discuss what they would select and why.

Additional content that could be added is researching non-legal information, such as census data, local businesses, and people.

1. A recent survey sent to Arizona State University Law School 2Ls and 3Ls revealed that seventy-eight percent of the respondents would be very interested in a one-credit Arizona Legal Research course.

APPENDIX D

MODEL STATE-SPECIFIC LEGAL RESEARCH SYLLABUS—MODULE WITHIN EXISTING ALR COURSE

Where offering a stand-alone state-specific legal research course is problematic, we recommend that a minimum of two or three hours of instruction within an existing three-unit ALR course be devoted to state-specific research topics. The topics selected for instruction are generally considered advanced topics and focus on information the new lawyer is likely to need or should at least know about at the beginning of practice.

A. Integrate identification and discussion of the sources of state primary law, including a comparison of coverage in the array of electronic fee and free databases throughout the ALR course. According to our survey, this appears to be the standard and favored approach to including state-specific content.
B. In addition to A above, devote a two-hour session to the advanced topics of researching state administrative law and creating legislative histories for recent statutes where an array of electronic resources is likely available.

Assign a take-home exercise that combines statutory and administrative research with compiling an easy legislative history. This might be useful as a group assignment.

C. If a third hour of instruction is available, use it to introduce the range of secondary material available to practitioners in the state: legal newspapers, business newspapers, bar journals, CLE and bar publications, treatises, directories, state bar Web resources, etc. If this hour is not available, consider adding a "show and tell" component to weekly ALR classes by introducing the students to one or two of these sources at the beginning of each class. Show them the tangible version but identify online sources if any contain this information.

D. Integrate identification and discussion of the sources of state primary law and secondary sources throughout the ALR course, as in A, above. As a take-home exercise toward the end of the course, challenge the students to explore and then identify the sources of primary and secondary authority available to the lawyers of the state jurisdiction and set a reasonable page limit. Ask them to evaluate the usefulness and efficacy of the fee and free electronic resources that are available. Spend an hour in class conducting a discussion of what the students found. Discuss cost-effective research tips they might not have discovered and point out some of the idiosyncrasies of conducting legal research in the jurisdiction.

Tubs, Buckets, and a Variety of Lumber: Developing a Strategic Approach to Legal Research

ALLEN MOYE

Rinn Law Library, DePaul College of Law, Chicago, Illinois, USA

Today's instructors of legal research face a number of challenges. With an increasing variety of formats and access points for obtaining information, the landscape of legal research material is fluid and evolving. Teaching students the value of some of the more traditional methods of research in a technology-saturated world focused on instant gratification requires some creativity and innovation. Using simple references and metaphors from everyday life, the author focuses on creative ways of helping students to develop a practical strategy for approaching any legal research problem.

INTRODUCTION

A few years ago, as I was preparing to teach a course in advanced legal research for the first time, I found a range of material on various approaches to teaching legal research.[1] I reviewed several of these methods and spoke with colleagues, and once I felt I had a pretty good command of the subject matter to be covered, I focused on making the topics interesting. One way that I tried to achieve this was by adding context with relevant examples. Particularly when introducing a topic that deals with a process, like developing a strategic research plan, it is important that the students have a sense of why a particular task is done, as well as the best way to do it. Having this information can allow for a more flexible approach that can be adapted or adjusted as needed for different types of research projects. As I taught more classes, trying different approaches and receiving feedback from students, the genesis of this article began to take shape.

This article was written for those instructors who may be somewhat new to teaching legal research or may just be looking for alternate ways to introduce the topic of developing a strategic approach to their students. I begin by discussing the importance of knowing the mission or having an understanding of exactly what the research task entails, including knowing and respecting any given deadlines, having a defined, yet flexible plan, and following it through.

Next, I address breaking down the facts into groups in order to identify the issues. This part of the process helps formulate the issue statements or research questions. These statements or questions determine the scope, focus, and direction of the research and inform the researcher what to look for and where to look. In discussing this process, I try to provide context and some suggestions for making the tasks relevant. Just like the surgeon needs to know when to select scissors over a scalpel or the carpenter chooses a nail gun over the hammer, the legal researcher needs to know how to select the best resources for any given project. Most students understand the idea with the surgeon or carpenter references, which are examples of how I try to use common and fairly universal analogies to make my points.

I refer to tasks typically associated with "wash day" in the title of this article because I believe that developing a strategy for conducting legal research can become as simple as doing laundry,[2] a fairly routine task with which most people are at least somewhat familiar. To get the best outcome from either endeavor—laundry or legal research—requires a little forethought and planning. For example, I compare issue spotting from a set of facts to the task of sorting dirty clothes before washing. It is important to separate light from dark, denim from silk, in the same way that you want to identify your various legal issues in a research problem. Determining which legal resource to use can be like selecting the detergent and fabric softener of your choice. Most will do the same thing, but there may be a particular fragrance (or lack thereof) or ingredient that is preferred. Categorizing and classifying one's research findings is based on the same simple organizational skills learned in preschool, like finding the right "cubby" for one's playthings. It is also similar to sorting, folding, and stacking one's clothes after washing. I also offer the concept of building word ladders and a tried and true pneumonic (Thing, Action, Relief, Persons) to assist with organization and arrangement.

Understanding the legal research process means learning the landscape of legal information resources, which can be daunting for many law students who typically have little or no frame of reference for this type of material. I offer a discussion of how to evaluate legal information sources in an era of multiple formats and mixed media[3] and with the challenges presented as a result of a world increasingly oversaturated with technology.

Using simple references and metaphors allows me to highlight important and often overlooked steps in the research process in a way that many students can relate to and find easy to understand. The goal is to guide the students through the process of developing their own strategy for researching legal topics.

In the last part of the article, I provide some tips on knowing when to stop researching and the importance of leaving enough time for synthesizing and writing.

KNOW THE MISSION

One of the first things I tell the students is to make sure that they understand their given assignment and know what they are expected to produce. It is very important that they know what to look for, so they will recognize it when they find it or can be certain that it does not exist. I advise the students to ask for a case file, which they should take the time to read and summarize. I also advise them to talk to the assigning attorney or someone else at the firm or organization who may have done related or similar research previously. The time to ask questions is before any research begins. Are there any specific recommended sources that should be checked? Are there any terms of art or acronyms that need to be explained or clarified? Also, the researcher should know and respect any deadlines for his or her assignment. If a specific deadline has not been given, I tell the students to suggest one on their own and stick to it.

HAVE A PLAN

Most successful endeavors, from waging war to negotiating peace treaties, are based on carefully executed plans. Legal research in particular *requires* a carefully laid-out plan, because a big challenge for novice researchers is to know when to stop searching. Having a plan and following through keeps the researcher from falling for the first (or fifth) thing that comes along and seems to support a proposition.[4] In addition, a plan establishes the checks and balances needed to avoid unsupported conclusions and creates a structure for logical and orderly documentation.[5]

Throughout the course, one of my goals is to guide the students toward developing their own strategic approach to legal research. I begin by telling them that the following four basic steps should form the cornerstone of their strategy.[6]

First, a thorough analysis of the facts is required in order to identify keywords and terms. These keywords and terms help the researcher to focus on legally significant issues, and they serve as access points to a broad spectrum of legal resources, such as digests, indices, tables of contents, and electronic databases. I will get more into the significance of this later, but it is important that this initial step not be overlooked or downplayed, "because it is the facts of a legal problem that control the direction of the research."[7]

Second, the identified legal issues should be grouped from general to specific. Grouping helps to establish a much-needed sense of order as the various issues are researched. Ultimately, this will form the basis of the issue statement or question for each legal issue raised by the facts.

Third, for each issue identified, a decision must be made as to the appropriate source or sources with which to begin the research. This should be systematic and methodical and requires a good sense of what is available and what each particular resource can provide. This decision not only concerns the physical format of the source but must also take into account the question of authority or authoritativeness.[8]

Fourth, with the law in a constant state of change, the research strategy must include a provision for updating. New statutes are enacted and old ones are repealed, while various courts issue rulings that "create new law, refine, reaffirm, or change existing law."[9] It is imperative that legal research be current and up to date since failure to do so is not only careless and negligent but can lead to sanctions for violating ethical standards of the legal profession.[10]

With the four basic elements of the strategy established, I next turn to the details of implementation. While it is necessary to have a standard outline as part of a strategy for legal research, I remind the students that they should remain flexible in its application. Legal research is a process that can, and with experience will, become natural to them, but it does not have to be rote or uninspired. A full-scale application of a comprehensive strategy typically works best with open-ended questions in unfamiliar areas of law. However, the same level of intensity may not be necessary for certain types of questions, such as finding a specific case, reading a specific statute, or determining if a case is still good law.[11]

ANALYZE FACTS AND IDENTIFY LEGAL ISSUES

'X' Marks the Spot

Issue identification, or "issue spotting," is one of the key and most important skills that students are taught during their first year of law school. Students become more proficient at spotting issues over time by reading and analyzing selected judicial opinions, which represent a variety of situations and circumstances. The student's ability to "issue spot" is then tested in the context of the hypothetical law school exam, the purpose of which is to determine how well the student can identify practical examples of a potential legal issue pertaining to one or more components of a legal rule taught in the course.[12] Theoretically, developing this key skill is the optimum way to help future lawyers identify the issues in a future client's legal problem.

Although many students have been exposed to this process for at least one year before taking an advanced legal research class, they may actually have limited experience identifying and researching legal issues. The reason for this is that in the context of most required research and writing courses in American law schools, students are *given* the legal issues that they are asked to write about. Consequently, there is no need to identify the issue(s) from a set of jumbled facts. I do not question the value or success of this method. It does exactly what it is designed to do—facilitate the development of the students' analytical and writing skills. However, all too often students lack experience identifying AND researching legal issues from what may very well be a convoluted set of circumstances.

Over the years, librarians[13] and other educators,[14] along with lawyers,[15] have lamented the lack of opportunity for substantial training in research and other "lawyering skills" in the law school setting. I mention this fact to the students primarily to reassure those who express frustration at their lack of knowledge about some of the basic resources of legal research. Even if they are somewhat familiar with a source, it is more often a vague memory of a "treasure hunt" assignment from their first year of law school. If time permits, one way to improve the students' awareness of these sources is to provide a historical overview of the growth and development of the American legal publishing industry. Many students find it interesting to discover how this industry arose and the relationship it has to the way that law schools began using the case law method of teaching in the late nineteenth century.[16]

Word Ladders

It is really important to provide students with opportunities to sharpen their ability to analyze facts. In my class, as part of their graded assignments, each student is given a research scenario and a separate jurisdiction. I give no indication of which issues to focus on, but present a series of generic questions about the scenario. The purpose is to get the students thinking about and examining the facts and to begin identifying important terms and keywords. One of the challenges that has become more acute over the years is that students seem less familiar with the concept of a hierarchy of associated words. They are often quite satisfied with and may become wedded to a narrow set of descriptive words or terms and have a hard time thinking of alternatives. The hierarchy of associated terms is important to the research process, because it connects to the subject arrangements that provide access to many legal resources.[17]

During the first year of law school, the students' vocabulary often becomes narrowly defined because the focus is on learning to write effective briefs and memorandums and discussing specific concepts and cases. To avoid ambiguity in meaning, students are taught that once a thing or item has been identified, all future references to that thing or item should be the same as the original. This often presents the greatest challenge to students with backgrounds or experience in creative writing, where use of synonym, metaphor, analogy, and hyperbole are encouraged. When students need a little help in this area, I introduce them to such tools as legal thesauri, encyclopedias, and *Words & Phrases*.[18] Although I initially focused on print-based sources for this exercise as a way of introducing the concept (mainly because this is how I learned), the same result can be achieved by expanding the resources consulted to include the growing number of reliable and robust electronic sources that serve the same function.[19] This can be a very liberating experience for some students. Discovering alternate terms and expressions helps the students to successfully expand their vocabulary, while staying within the confines of standard legal terminology.

Sorting the 'Dirty' Laundry

The law can be intricate and nuanced. Changing one or two facts (such as time of day or someone's age or a legal relationship between the potential litigants) may alter the issues in a legal research problem and raise an entirely new or different rule of law. Successful issue spotting requires the ability to identify facts which raise legal issues. There are a variety of methods for analyzing facts and identifying issues.[20] I encourage students to explore a few in order to decide on one that they feel works best for them. One method that I use to help students to identify legal issues is what I like to call the "dirty laundry" approach. Although its appeal can vary, I think it is a useful frame of reference and can help with the concept of identifying legal issues. Basically, I analogize the facts as presented to a pile of dirty clothes that must be sorted before being washed and dried, then folded and neatly stacked. Sorting clothes before washing them, I tell the students, is similar to issue spotting in a legal problem. In both cases, the job can be done in a few short, discrete steps, once the researcher/launderer knows what to do. Below is a quick comparison of the tasks involved, isolated into four distinct steps, and some similarities are highlighted.

When it comes to laundry there are a number of different ways to effectively separate clothing. Some people sort by color then by fabric. The method and level of sorting can often depend on the size of the particular load and other demands on one's time. However, a few moments to carefully separate and organize your garments before washing can save time and add to the appearance and lifetime of your clothing in the long run.[21] Similarly, when it comes to a student dealing with a legal research problem or an assignment given to a new associate at a firm, the "size" of your facts and other things competing for your time and attention can have an impact on how well you "sort" through and identify legally relevant issues. Just like sorting laundry on the front end, it is a task that can save time and make the most of your efforts if you take the time to carefully identify all of the potential legal issues.

1. Check care labels—Most garments provide you with proper cleaning instructions on an attached label of some kind.[22] What is the correct water temperature to use? Should the item be washed by hand or dry cleaned instead? The terms used on the labels are like key words that one might find in a jumbled set of facts, indicating potential legal issues to be researched. Checking care labels is similar to identifying the most basic of information that is already provided by your legal research problem. For example, if a client comes to you with a broken leg, alleged to be the result of someone else's conduct, you can deduce that the injury places you in the area of law known as "torts," in the same way the clothing label informs you to wash in "cold water." If washing clothes, you would be wise to select a detergent that performs well in cold water, the same way that you would select sources for your research that specifically address issues of tort law. From there, you may want to focus on anything that establishes or negates "duty" (such as adding a color booster); and then any words or terms used to describe the alleged conduct to see where it may fall on the spectrum of "negligence" (fabric softener during the final rinse?). Essentially, looking for keywords in your facts is similar to reading the care label.
2. Turn clothing inside out—In the world of laundry, this is a step that may be overlooked, even though it is often recommended by the manufacturer and something one can learn from reading the care label. (See step # 1 above.) This technique helps to stretch out the fabric, making for a more uniform washing process and ultimately a cleaner garment. In legal research, this is comparable to looking for unanswered questions. Look at your problem from all angles—from your client's perspective, from the opposing party's viewpoint, and from a neutral position. Turn the problem "inside out." In other words, are there any unknown details or circumstances that could potentially put a "wrinkle" in the accuracy of your results? This could be something like a legal defense, such as age or legislated exemption from liability. It can also refer to looking at the facts from the other party's point of view. This helps the researcher gain an understanding of how the other side might see the issues and can be instructive in terms of potential defenses or responses to certain claims.
3. Check pockets—This step can help prevent an entire load of clothes from being ruined. Checking the pockets allows for the removal of ink pens, lipstick, important papers, or tissues. As a bonus factor, you may find something totally unexpected like coins, paper money, or a phone number on a match book (although people probably do not do that much anymore). Similarly, by carefully reviewing the "pockets" of your facts, you

might stumble across something that at first glance did not seem important or legally significant. Check for that "hidden" issue that is triggered by a certain combination of facts, an issue that, like a tissue that remains in your jeans pocket, may complicate the rest of your process if you don't remain vigilant for it.

However, just like a tissue or piece of lint can mess up an otherwise clean wash cycle, small details can become distractions to one's research and should be removed. One fact pattern I have used concerns a young father accused of shoplifting a box of cookies for his daughter. The facts provide a lot of detail about the uniqueness of the cookies and the father's obsessive quest to obtain them. Interesting reading, which may provide insight into the father's state of mind but ultimately immaterial to the legal issues to be researched. Like a "MacGuffin"[23] found in many suspense novels and films, or the proverbial "red herring,"[24] these kinds of details are nothing more than a diversion from the real issues. Nonetheless, they are important to acknowledge as such before moving on.

4. Check for needed repairs and stains—Before washing, garments should be checked for rips or tears, loose threads or buttons, and serious stains should be pre-treated. In other words, the garment should be whole and complete. Similarly, the researcher should have an understanding of the facts, so that they too are whole, complete, and make sense. Try to determine if there are missing facts that may make a series of events more understandable or explain why actions were taken. Ask questions. This is closely related to step 2, in terms of recognizing that there may be some unanswered questions or missing information. I remind students that the facts should be consistent and follow a logical sequence. If not, any questions or concerns should be pursued and answered at some point in the process.

During the sorting stage, I emphasize the importance of recognizing those facts and situations that may have legal significance. In addition, I remind the students that just because the client feels that he or she has been wronged, it does not mean that the law offers a remedy.

Classify and Categorize

At some point early in our lives, perhaps during preschool or day care, we all learned how to arrange and categorize our material world. Toys, games, and other items were placed in the proper storage areas with similar things, and personal items went into our "cubby hole." Learning this skill served two purposes: it kept the play area clear and it taught us that grouping like things together helps us to more easily identify a particular item, facilitating easy access for future retrieval. I reacquaint the students with this simple concept as a means of discussing the task of organizing the facts and legal issues of a research problem.

One tried and true method for organizing facts and any related legal issues uses the pneumonic below, known as T.A.R.P.,[25] where the facts are analyzed and grouped as follows;

T = **Thing** or subject matter—The focus is on identifying the location or tangible item involved in the controversy. If the client has been harmed by a prescribed medication or ingested food, then that food or medicine becomes a significant fact of the dispute.

A = Cause of **Action** or ground of defense—I tell the students to try to name the legal claim or grounds for defense indicated by the facts. Is there a contractual relationship involved or perhaps some unintentional act that results in harm or injury? Most students recognize a potential claim fairly quickly, even if it has to be retooled at some later point. I try to get them to think of any possible defenses as well (like turning their clothes inside out before washing), so that these concerns may be addressed.

R = **Relief** Sought—What do the parties want, money (damages) or to get someone to do something or stop doing something (injunction)? This is important to identify because it requires a clear statement of what the complaining party is seeking and whether this is something that the law can deliver.

P = **Persons/Parties**—Look for legally significant relationships that exist between those involved (i.e., husband and wife, employer and employee) or legal status of an individual (i.e., a minor or person with a legal disability) that might have an impact on how the law is applied.

An added benefit to using this method of grouping is that it works well with most legal resources because the terms and phrases identified can be used immediately in many print indices, table of contents, and digests.[26]

After a careful assessment and grouping of the facts, the students should be able to formulate issue statements or questions that incorporate the facts of their client's particular situation and the legal theory or theories the student plans to pursue.[27] Although each issue is typically researched separately, there often are several interrelated issue statements to be researched in order to complete an assignment. This may not always be easy and may require more than one attempt, but the issue statement(s) should be capable of a logical answer based on the given facts and circumstances.

Table It—Keep a Record of Your Findings

Once the issues have been identified, grouped, and formulated into research questions, the next step is for the students to set up some method for organizing and prioritizing their work. There are a variety of ways to do this, and again I suggest that the students experiment with a couple of options to determine which works best for them. One standard procedure taught before the proliferation of personal computers was to use 3" × 5" index cards and to note full bibliographic information for each source along with a quote or summary of why the resource was being included. Some students may see this method as prehistoric, a relic of a bygone era, much like the huge wooden card catalog of libraries of the past. I point out, however, that the most important thing is to take complete notes and citation references in order to keep track of what has been looked at and why the source is being used. There may be an infinite number of software programs designed to help students keep track of their work on a computer, but I remind them that it is not necessary to use anything specialized or expensive for recording and keeping track of their research.

One useful suggestion is to start a table or grid, as promoted by Professor Peter Honigsberg of University of San Francisco School of Law.[28] The information is filled in as the research progresses; this table is a useful tool at this stage because it allows the researcher to isolate the issues and fill in as a supporting case or rule is found. In addition, this method provides a handy reference point for conveying one's findings.

Authorities	Facts	Issues
State v Sonsimp	Celebrity H accused of W's murder	Pre-trial publicity

With the issue statement(s) or research question(s) developed, and some method set up for categorizing the findings, the next step is to determine where to begin the search.

UNDERSTAND YOUR SOURCES

Learning the Landscape

Traditional legal resources can be very different from the types of research material that today's students are likely to have used. Digests, indices, citators, and other "finding tools" are quite foreign to many first-year law students, because this organizational format is rarely used for undergraduate or even other graduate level research material.[29] Although there has been an expansion of electronic formats available for conducting legal research, the contextual framework for sources in this subject area remains to a large extent traditionally based in print sources.[30] Furthermore, studies in human behavior patterns have shown that when presented with a new or different experience, people tend to look for similarities from their past.[31] This tendency presents additional challenges when trying to introduce the wide variety of resources available in the world of legal research. As noted earlier, most law students have no frame of reference for the structure of legal research materials. While they may have a vague notion about these sources and how they are used, an entirely new universe opens up once they are shown the vastness of the legal research landscape.

When Secondary Comes First

While it is important to know which source is best for any given research project, sometimes it is just as good to know what is available. For all but the narrowest of subject areas, it is nearly impossible to keep up with the variety of sources covering any one particular area of the law. A realistic approach that I advise my students to consider is to develop a working knowledge of some of the basic types of secondary sources that cover the broad areas of law.

I remind students that hornbooks, nutshells, and treatises are good starting points for researching an unfamiliar area of law and obtaining background information. Understanding the substantive law will provide a realistic perspective on what the researcher should be seeking. This perspective typically yields search words and terms of art that may be specific to a particular area of law. Practitioner-oriented material—like form books and sources of Continuing Legal Education programs, known as "CLEs," which include articles, audio, video, and podcast recordings of presentations—are also very helpful since they provide information on the procedural aspects of a case or potential case. Resources, which deal with the mechanics of drafting agreements or pleadings and filing in the proper venue in a timely manner, may be informative and can be considered as part of an overall strategy in planning legal research. A form will follow the tone and structure of a statute or rule, and it helps to know the how, when, and where of filing a lawsuit should that become necessary. To help decide which of these resources to choose for any given project, I suggest that students ask themselves, "How much time do I have to get up to speed on this?" If the answer is a few weeks to work through a complex research issue, then a well-written treatise or two might be the best choice. I tell them to consider the reputation of the author(s) as legal scholar(s) when selecting a title.[32] As a corollary, I suggest checking to see if the text has been cited in any important court opinions.[33] If they have less time, a hornbook or nutshell might be a better option. Both, however, have limitations. Hornbooks tend to be comprehensive but may not adequately address nuances or very recent developments and may not be available for all subjects. Nutshells tend to cover a broader spectrum of subjects than hornbooks. They may be a better source for reviewing the elements of a topic or subject with which the researcher may already be somewhat familiar but are, by definition, concise in coverage.

Additionally, good pathfinders and research guides such as *West's Legal Desk Reference*[34] or Zimmerman's Research Guide[35] cover a wide variety of subject areas and are good for identifying background sources.

Evaluating Sources in an Era of Multiple Formats and Mixed Media

In order to get the most out of all of the legal information tools available, the researcher must understand what each tool has to offer and how best to use it for a given situation. This requires a quick and useful method of assessment that looks at the structure, functionality, and design of a particular source, as well as how authoritative and informative it is in terms of its coverage of a topic.

Prior to the 1990s, printed sources were unquestioned as the most reliable and authoritative format for conducting legal research.[36] These sources were developed in large part due to the need for authoritative control of an expanding amount of legal information. Traditionally, authoritative control has been achieved by the work of specially trained individuals classifying, categorizing, and organizing the various representations of the law. Print embodied in a tangible, fixed, three-dimensional book form, with carefully designed organizational schemes, became the standard context for communication among and between those studying and practicing law.[37]

However, unlike 25 or 30 years ago, today's first-year law student has most likely studied, worked, and played in an environment increasingly dominated by sophisticated electronic devices and expanding technological developments. Of these developments, one of the more ubiquitous is the personal computer, which has revolutionized modern society's communication options, much like the telephone did in the late nineteenth century. Although there may be variations in the level of exposure, it seems fair to say that most students enter law school with a basic understanding of how to use a computer and some experience with browsers, search engines, and finding information on the Internet.[38]

This experience informs and creates a frame of reference for what some students may consider to be "research," with little thought given to evaluating or assessing the source of the information. "Surfing" the Web can be a means of gathering data and if done properly, can produce useful information. Many students, however, are surprised to learn that this activity does not easily meet the threshold required for serious scholarly or professional work.

I tell the students to remember that it is important to verify the source of any purported legal information whether in print or from the Web. Depending on the material, traditional legal publishers may be a safer bet, because they are more likely to have a better reputation for vetting the resources for validation. This is not always the case with some online sources, where responsibility falls to the researcher to authenticate the material and may add additional research time.

I offer students the following checklist of features to look for and balance as part of the evaluation process of a potential resource for legal research.[39]

First, they should do an assessment of the "structure and organization" of the resource. The focus at this stage is on how this particular publication presents the information. I suggest to the students that they ask themselves the following: How well is it put together? Does it have useful features or unique characteristics? If in print, is there an index or table of authorities? If it is a Web site or other electronic source, is there a guide or manual of some kind on how to navigate or use the resource? A thorough assessment requires looking at the "authoritativeness of any commentary, the care with which the information has been indexed and such elements as the clarity of the graphical layout."[40]

Second, a thorough analysis requires an evaluation of the "authenticity "of the source, which basically means verifying the accuracy and truthfulness of the information being represented. This may be established by the relationship between the publisher and the originator of the material. In some instances, I tell the students that they may be one and the same, as in the case of a state legislature publishing and distributing its own statutory materials. In other cases, a commercial publisher may have been delegated or contracted the responsibility by the originator, thereby giving a "seal of approval." For a number of years, the expense and investment required to enter legal publishing limited the field to a few key but well-known players.[41] This is no longer the case, with mergers and acquisitions by and between publishers, the expansion of the World Wide Web, and the ease with which anyone can "publish" by simply posting data to a Web page. In addition, there are indications that the long-standing institutional authority of print sources, exemplified by the likes of West's National Reporter System and Shepard's Citators, is being eroded, as legal publishing moves further into the arena of electronic formats.[42]

Third, this evaluation requires an assessment of "timeliness" or, how current is the information? If the source is in print, I advise the students to check the copyright date and assume that the information is at least one and possibly two years older. Of course, any potential gaps usually can be filled (at least partially) by information in pocket parts or supplements. For some areas of law, there may be significant lapses even with regular supplements. Although currency tends to be one of the presumed advantages to using online sources, it may not always be easy to establish. I advise students to make sure they can determine when a Web site was last updated. For most reputable Web sites, this is usually somewhere on the launch page. Also, depending on what the material covers, they should be able to tell if the information being provided is the most current available.

Fourth, a thorough evaluation has to address "context," which in this case means identifying where a particular resource falls in the legal research universe. This includes the issue of jurisdiction and whether the cases, statutes, regulations, or other material contained in the resource fall within the specific jurisdiction that is controlling for a particular project. I tell the students to think of each research tool as being part of a great "cross hatching" of information,[43] and that they have to make sure they can connect the various information items they find to their specific research problem.

Connecting the Dots

So what does this mean for the student researcher? How does she make use of all of the above information as part of a strategic plan when trying to determine the more reliable and authoritative source? Well, the first thing to consider is availability. Many firms and legal departments are opting out of purchasing and housing huge print collections and instead maintaining very small print collections while licensing more and more electronic databases.[44] There is also a trend toward relying on the much improved variety of free federal, state, and local government Web sites.[45] This dictates that in some instances, an electronic format may be the preferred option. However, I remind the students that if their employer prefers to maintain a narrowly focused print collection to support a specialized area of practice, then it would behoove them to have a working knowledge of the contents of that collection and how best to use the material.

Another question to consider is, "Can I cite to it?" As an example of a potential complication, I mention the fact that, although most people do federal code research using either United States Code Annotated (U.S.C.A.) or United States Code Service (U.S.C.S.) (print or electronic) because they contain annotations and other editorial enhancements, both are "unofficial" codes. The official source is the United States Code, which should be cited to "whenever possible."[46]

The fact that most law schools still maintain more than a core collection in print, in addition to Westlaw, Lexis, HeinOnline, and a variety of other electronic databases, presents an opportunity for law students to become comfortable and proficient using both formats.

I encourage the students to compare sources and formats and suggest that they locate a few cases on their issues using a print resource, such as the West Digest System. I then have them search for cases on the same topic by formulating a search query using Westlaw, Lexis, and maybe Loislaw. I ask that they compare the results for similarities and differences. Invariably, there will be distinctions in the results even between the electronic databases. I use this to discuss the pros and cons of full-text searching using an electronic source compared to using a print-based indexing system.

Full-text searching tends to work better when researching unique terms or descriptions. It is excellent, for example, when researching for cases involving harm caused by a brand-name drug like "Avandia." A search in an electronic database is typically faster and more precise than print when using unique terms, but one downside is that there is a risk of missing relevant material that may be referred to by different terminology.

One of the benefits of using a well-organized print index can be the overall depth of classification and cross-referencing of multiple subjects and subtopics. This tends to be very helpful for providing alternative terms and identifying potentially analogous situations. A downside of print indexes can be that you find too much information and can miss important items or wind up spending more time than you should before finding something useful.

Also, depending on the topic, another difference between print and electronic resources relates to "timeliness." With printed material, there is a lag time of a few months to several years between when the item was written and the publication date, and processing and shipping adds even more time. So much so that, by the time a new freshly bound volume is placed on the shelf, the information in it may already be years out of date or at the least incomplete. Of course that is why pocket parts and supplements were developed—to pick up any cases or relevant material in between publication dates. I point out to students that, depending on the topic being researched and the jurisdiction, even pocket parts and supplements may not be current enough to include all relevant material. With the premium electronic legal databases being updated often within days, if not hours, of a new decision or ruling becoming available, it often makes the decision, at least when it comes to the issue of timeliness, obvious.[47]

I ask the students to reflect on how they located the cases in print and how that process informed their efforts once they went online. This helps them to take advantage effectively of the best of both formats because the print resources can provide a frame of reference and perhaps some alternate terms which, when used online, can make the search results more inclusive.

SHAKE, FOLD, AND STACK

Knowing When to Stop Searching

As mentioned earlier, one of the biggest challenges for the novice legal researcher is to know when to stop searching. This uncertainty is one of the best reasons for establishing a research strategy and following it through. If you have an outline of what should be done, it can serve as a map or checklist to make sure that all necessary bases have been covered. I discuss this by presenting the following three common errors made by many students when it comes to ending their research[48] and offer some suggestions for avoiding them.

1. Stopping too soon—Many novice researchers decide that they are done as soon they find anything that appears to be "on point." This is a common problem for researchers who cannot get away from a narrow interpretation

of the facts. To avoid this, I suggest a review of the "sorting the dirty laundry" analogy and ask the students if they have thoroughly scrutinized the facts and identified all pertinent legal issues. Particularly instructive is to have the students approach the problem from the point of view of the opposing side. This helps to expand their perspective on the potential issues and possible outcome.

2. Not leaving enough time for analysis and writing—A common mistake for many who approach legal research like a treasure hunt—placing more emphasis on gathering data but not enough on determining its usefulness. An example of this would be a novice researcher who reads only the headnotes as a means of compiling a group of cases on a particular issue. He continues down this path until he has accumulated a sizable collection of cases, before deciding to read them. He becomes discouraged to discover that many of the cases are of little or no use, and he has to start again. Time may be running out and frustration running high, so the researcher in this predicament is more likely to make a mistake or overlook something important. This can be avoided by a careful (not necessarily in depth) review of each source at the time it is found to make sure that it can be used to support the premise or proposition.
3. Becoming "fixated" on finding *the* one perfect case—This error is based on the assumption that there *is* one case out there to be found for every potential issue. Again, this is a myth to which many novice researchers fall victim. This often stems from a very narrow interpretation of the facts and legal issues to be researched. To avoid this, I remind the students to think in broader terms before moving to the more specific. They may not find cases that have the exact same facts but they should remain open to similar or analogous cases, which can provide the appropriate application of law.

As a final statement, I remind the students that just like that pile of dirty laundry that had to be carefully sorted before being washed, they began their research with a jumbled-up set of facts and unknown potential legal issues. A virtual universe of possibilities lay before them. Through a series of methodical steps, reading the labels and keywords in the facts, they divided the light from the dark, the denim from the silk, and identified the important legal issues to be researched. Just like selecting the appropriate detergent and additives for the wash, they made the choices about the best resources for researching the issues of their problem.

They analyzed and synthesized the information and eventually developed a crisp, clear, and clean understanding of the applicable law and then arrived at the best possible answer in the least amount of time. They had sufficient authority to support their findings: wrinkle-free, folded, and neatly stacked. Most importantly, they now have a useful strategy for tackling even the most daunting legal research problem or the dirtiest pile of laundry.

NOTES

1. For example, while most legal research texts emphasize the various sources for doing research with all sorts of sample problems, Laurel Currie Oates in her text *Just Research* (Aspen Publishers 2005) uses an approach that attempts to demystify the legal research process by focusing on researching issues based on the governing law as opposed to solely on the types of sources available.

2. *See generally* http://www.whitehouse.gov/history/whtour/library.html. An interesting factoid I discovered while researching this article: The White House library once served as a laundry room and was found to consist of "tubs, buckets, and a variety of lumber" in the first official White House Inventory of 1801.

3. By multiple formats, I mean print, microform, CD/DVD, and electronic. By mixed media, I mean a book that has an accompanying CD, for example. That is, mixed media is one resource that comes in several formats that are meant to be used together.

4. *See generally* J.D.S. Armstrong & Christopher Knott, *Where the Law Is: An Introduction to Advanced Legal Research* ch. 1 (3d ed., Thomson/West 2009). The authors label this the "Eureka!" syndrome, where " . . . [t]he inexperienced legal researcher finds something to support his claim and calls it quits right there." *Id.* at 3.

5. *Id.* According to the authors,"[t]his documentation is particularly important when you do not find anything that satisfies the requested conditions since the worth of your negative findings lies wholly in your testimony of where you looked. This also applies when you do find something, [because] your document trail serves to validate its appropriateness."

6. The following information is distilled from Steve Barkan, *The Legal Research Process* in The Fundamentals of Legal Research 14–20 (J. Myron Jacobstein & Roy M. Mersky, eds., 8th ed., Foundation Press NY 2002).

7. *Id.* at 15.

8. Armstrong & Knott, *supra* n. 4, at 4–5.

9. Barkan, *supra* n. 6, at 19.

10. *See generally* Marguerite Butler, *Rule 11–Sanctions and a Lawyer's Failure to Conduct Competent Legal Research,* 29 Cap. U. L. Rev. 681 (2001–02) (Professor Butler examines a variety of problems related to poor or negligent legal research that were found to be subject to court sanction); *Lopez v. Clifford Law Offices, P.C.*, 841 N.E.2d 465, 476 (Ill. App. 1st Dist. 2005). "It is *prima facie* negligent conduct for an attorney to misadvise a client on such a settled point of law that can be looked up by the means of ordinary research techniques."

11. *See* Stephen Elias et al., *Legal Research: How to Find & Understand the Law* (Nolo Press 2004).

12. Nadia Nedzel, *Legal Reasoning, Research, and Writing for International Graduate Students* 71 (2nd ed., Aspen Publishers 2008).

13. *See generally* Richard Leiter, *The Missing Lawyering Skill: New Book on Legal Education Demonstrates the Lack of Attention Paid to Legal Research Training ('Educating Lawyers')*, AALL Spectrum 22 (July 2008) (Professor Leiter evaluates the Carnegie Foundation text on the American legal education system, noting that while the book advocates for system reform with "better integration of lawyering skills, moral and ethical training and analysis . . . legal research is rarely mentioned as a lawyering skill.")

14. *See generally* William M. Sullivan, Carnegie Foundation for the Advancement of Teaching et al., *Educating Lawyers: Preparation for the Profession of Law* (Jossey-Bass/Wiley 2007). (Commonly referred to as the "Carnegie Report," it is the culmination of a two-year study of legal education involving a comprehensive look at teaching and learning in American and Canadian law schools today.)

15. ("[N]ewer associates almost exclusively use online tools and stay away from the library . . . [senior level] partners complain that younger associates just don't have an understanding of how to use the library . . . [and] they wonder if things are being missed.") Chris Mickus, quoted in Partnership and Solutions for Preparing Job-Ready Attorneys, white paper, available at http://west.thomson.com/support/librarian/event/AALLwhitepaper.pdf (last accessed 14 Sept. 2008).

16. Some useful references for this discussion include Joel H. Cheskis, *Copyright of Legal Materials: From Wheaton to West—Shaping the Practice of Law in America*, 20 Commun. L. 1–38 (1998): Morris L Cohen, *An Historical Overview of American Law Publishing*, 31 Intl. J. Leg. Info. 168–174 (Summer 2003).

17. *See generally* Barkan, *supra* n. 6. Although this hierarchy is traditionally associated with print resources, such as indices and table of contents, it also works well with electronic sources since it may introduce new terms the student had not considered.

18. I find *Words & Phrases* to be a useful resource to introduce to the students. Many of them have never heard of it, and they find the broad range of definitions from state and federal courts an interesting way to see how the terminology has changed over time.

19. In addition to Westlaw and Lexis, several of the more specialized databases are becoming very good at this. For example, Research Institute of America's Checkpoint offers a comprehensive federal, state, and international tax database and includes a robust tax thesaurus. Commerce Clearing House, Inc. offers a very good thesaurus as part of its Internet Research Network covering "Business and Finance."

20. *See generally* Amy Sloan, *Basic Legal Research—Tools and Strategies* 19 (2nd ed., Aspen Pub. 2003). Some people employ the journalist's approach asking, who, what, when, where, why, and how; while others group the information by parties, places, potential claims, and relief sought.

21. *See* Monte Florman et al., *How to Clean Practically Anything* 81–103 (Consumers Reports Books 1993); Cheryl Mendelson, *Laundry: The Home Comforts Book of Caring for Clothes and Linens* (Scribner 2005).

22. *See generally* Mendelson, *supra* n. 21, at 10 (" . . . care labels have become more complicated over the years since there are new fibers, finishes, and fabric constructions to deal with . . . second-guessing [labels] virtually guarantees that you will eventually ruin something.")

23. "MacGuffin: an object, event, or character in a film or story that serves to set and keep the plot in motion despite usually lacking intrinsic importance." Merriam-Webster Online Dictionary, available at http://www.merriam-webster.com/dictionary/MacGuffin (last accessed 8 Nov. 2008).

24. "Red herring: something that distracts attention away from the real issue." *Merriam-Webster Online Dictionary*, available at http://www.merriam-webster.com/dictionary/red herring (last accessed 14 Sept. 2008).

25. The TARP mnemonic is widely used in legal research instruction. *See e.g.* Barkan, *supra* n. 6, at 15–16.

26. *Id.*

27. I usually remind them of the following templates from their first-year research and writing course as examples: Is there a cause of action for ________ when________? Did X commit ________, when she ________?, Does Y________ owe a duty to ________ Z when ________?

28. Peter Jan Honigsberg, *Organizing the Fruits of Your Research: The Honigsberg Grid,* 4 Persps. Teaching Leg. Research Writing 94 (1996) (reprinted in Best Persps. Teaching Leg. Research Writing 71 (2001).

29. The exception might be Library and Information Science programs.

30. *See* Barbara Bintliff, *Context and Legal Research* in Richard Danner & Frank Houdek, ed., *Legal Information and the Development of American Law (A Collection of Essays)* 89, 79–100 (Thomson/West 2008) (discusses the development of this contextual framework and the need to create a new paradigm of subject-based textbooks).

31. *See* Daniel Frey et. al., *The Deciding Factor*, Supp. 1 Mech. Engr. 20–24 (March 2005) quoting Gary Klein, *Sources of Power: How People Make Decisions* (MIT Press 1998) and his "recognition primed" decision model. "[P]eople look for similarities between the current situations and past situations and develop plans of action on that basis."

32. One way to get a sense of the reputation of the author is to look for a review of his or her work. Several book review Web sites offer evaluations of legal treatises, including *Law and Politics Book Review,* available at http://www.bsos.umd.edu/gvpt/lpbr/index.htm; and JURIST's *Books on Law*, available at http://jurist.law.pitt.edu/lawbooks/index.htm. Also, it may be helpful to get the opinion of a professor or law librarian who has written, researched, or taught in the subject area.

33. If possible, I suggest citing to the highest state court if researching a state issue or to the U.S. Supreme Court if researching a federal issue.

34. William P. Statsky et.al, *West's Legal Desk Reference* (West Pub. Co. 1990). While somewhat dated, this remains a good source for background information in many fields.

35. Zimmerman's Research Guide, available at http://www.lexisnexis.com/infopro/zimmerman/default.aspx.

36. *See* Bintliff, *supra* n. 30.

37. *See generally* Robert Berring, *Legal Information and the Search for Cognitive Authority*, 88 Cal. L. Rev. 1673, 1701 (2000) (examining sources of legal information at the end of the 20th century).

38. *Id.*

39. For a similar approach to evaluating sources, compare Armstrong & Knott, *supra* n. 4, at 243.

40. *Id.*

41. *See generally* Berring, *supra* n. 37, at 281 (Professor Berring notes that American legal publishing was dominated for many years by two large companies, West and Lawyer's Cooperative).

42. *Id.*

43. *See* Robert Berring & Eizabeth Edinger, *Finding the Law* 335 (12th ed., Thomson/West 2005).

44. *See generally* Robert Berring, *A Brief History of Law Librarianship,* in *Law Librarianship in the Twenty-First Century* 8 (Roy Balleste, Sonia Luna-Lamas, & Lisa Smith-Butler eds., Scarecrow Press, 2007) ("Many prestigious law firms once took great pride in maintaining an architecturally striking library and impressive collection.")

45. *Id.*

46. *The Bluebook: A Uniform System of Citation,* R. 12.3, at 104 (18th ed., Harvard Law Review Assoc. 2005).

47. Updates to Westlaw depend on the type of material. For example, current awareness databases are updated three times a day: 9 a.m., 11 a.m., and 2 p.m.; major newspapers are updated daily with regional papers being updated every three days; legislation may only be updated weekly.

48. *See generally* Christina Kunz et al., *The Process of Legal Research* 63–64 (7th ed., Aspen Pub. 2008) (where these points are summarized in a larger list of errors typical of novice legal researchers).

Legal Research Assessment

SIMON CANICK
Warren E. Burger Law Library, William Mitchell College of Law, St. Paul, Minnesota, USA

Legal research instructors seek to provide their students with a working knowledge of important research tools, strategies with which to develop a rational research plan, and the skill to conduct research efficiently, among other things. A well-conceived legal research class may utilize short-answer assignments, quizzes, and scavenger hunt exercises as a means to establish a baseline of knowledge with critical sources; a series of research problems, with grading based upon students' ability to describe a coherent and logical progression; and a pathfinder or process-oriented final exam, all depending on the instructor's goals. Ultimately, the variety of available assessment tools suggests room for creativity and the existence of many appropriate alternatives. As long as instructors use a multifaceted approach, selecting assessment tools to suit course objectives, students will be engaged in the process and will become stronger, more confident legal researchers.

INTRODUCTION

At the rate law librarians are now teaching research courses in law schools nationwide, it is hard to believe that a classroom role took so many years to cement. Indeed, librarians' formal teaching loads have reached historic highs.

Association of Legal Writing Directors/Legal Writing Institute figures show that in 2002, librarians taught the research component of first-year courses at seventy-seven institutions (forty solo and thirty-seven as co-teachers).[1] By 2008, that number had increased to one hundred eighteen institutions (fifty-two solo and sixty-six as co-teachers), an increase of fifty-three percent. And the number of advanced courses taught by librarians has risen by eighty-nine percent, from sixty-four courses in 2000 to 121 in 2008.[2]

Several reasons justify the surge. For one, doctrinal faculty rarely showed interest in teaching research,[3] so at most law schools, teaching of the first-year legal research and writing classes was farmed out to adjuncts or professional legal research and writing teachers. Practitioner-teachers, many of whom lack research skills themselves, unsurprisingly steer their courses away from legal research.[4]

More importantly, over the past fifteen years, a call has emerged for legal education to become more practical and skills based. In 1992, the influential MacCrate Report produced an outline of the fundamental lawyering skills to promote at law schools, including problem solving, legal research, factual investigation, counseling, negotiation, and litigation procedures.[5] In 2007, the Carnegie Report issued a sharp critique of legal education, finding that most law schools demonstrate only:

> casual attention ... to teaching students how to use legal thinking in the complexity of actual law practice .... The result is to prolong and reinforce the habits of thinking like a student rather than an apprentice practitioner, thus conveying the impression that lawyers are more like competitive scholars than attorneys engaged with the problems of clients.[6]

The legal academy has begun to recognize its obligation to train students who act like lawyers from the moment of graduation. But perhaps this realization comes from a complaining bar, rather than self-awareness. The legal profession is demanding a change, arguing that even traditional doctrinal courses need practical components. Further, voices inside and out of the American Bar Association (ABA) have called for a formal tie of a skills-based curriculum to accreditation.[7]

Meanwhile, despite the relative practicality of legal research instruction, law firms remain disappointed with the research skills of recent graduates.[8] In part, this dissatisfaction can be explained by the fact that most students receive significant training only during the fall semester of their first year in law school—most assuredly not the point of their need. Advanced legal research (ALR) classes reach only a small fraction of law students.[9]

In this environment, administrators listen carefully to proposals from librarians who seek a more active role in teaching research. The challenge for librarian-teachers is to develop in their students a sound and confident approach to research, so that when they enter practice they can find the law quickly and efficiently. In ten more years, librarians may dominate the teaching of legal research in law schools, but we will have failed if our students still cannot demonstrate effective research skills to law firms and clients.

The goal of this essay is to suggest a method of ensuring good outcomes in legal research training. It begins with a list of skills that students need and follows with a discussion of the means to "test" students' achievement of those skills. It concludes with a proposal for a multifaceted research curriculum.

GOALS OF LEGAL RESEARCH INSTRUCTION AND ASSESSMENT

> In order to conduct legal research effectively, a lawyer should have a working knowledge of the nature of legal rules and legal institutions, the fundamental tools of legal research, and the process of devising and implementing a coherent and effective research design.[10]

The MacCrate report's statement of knowledge necessary for lawyers to conduct research includes three fundamentally different types of skills, and different skills require diverse teaching and assessment techniques. For example, students striving for a working knowledge of the nature of legal rules and institutions should probably complete some background reading, listen to an illuminating lecture, and then engage in dialogue to answer questions that arise. On the other hand, developing facility with one of the tools of legal research, say LexisNexis, may still require some background reading and lecture, but most important is giving students an opportunity to practice—perhaps with choosing the best database or constructing an effective search.

The purpose of assessment in legal research is to "evaluate a student's learning—what the student knows and what the student can do with the new knowledge and skills."[11] We aim to determine whether the student is "getting it" in these lectures, readings, and practice exercises, such that we can build on what we have covered and move on to more sophisticated research techniques.

To determine whether students have a working knowledge of the nature of legal rules and institutions, the teacher may use an assessment tool like Socratic dialogue or give the class a short-answer quiz. Teaching effective use of LexisNexis, on the other hand, likely involves process-oriented assessment, like research logs to accompany research exercises or firsthand observation. In other words, an appropriate curriculum will include assessment tools that are chosen to complement the skill in question.

Keeping in mind that legal research instructors aim for a wide variety of outcomes (e.g., developing and executing a rational research plan, conducting efficient research, knowing when to stop, etc.), this article will review some of the most frequently used assessment tools and a few you might not have considered. When designing your own course, you might appropriately "pick and choose" from these tools, depending on the subject matter at hand, the particular dynamic in the classroom, and the learning objective you are seeking. There is nothing inconsistent or inappropriate about using a variety of approaches within a single class; indeed, as explained below, it is desirable to do so.

Insofar as legal research courses are practice based and use assessment tools that are more precise than the blunt, end-of-semester, all-or-nothing final exam, they are consistent with current thought on best practices in legal education. In the 2007 report, *Best Practices for Legal Education: A Vision and a Road Map*, Roy Stuckey described assessment in law schools as "inadequate," "flawed," and "abominable," but at least partially exempted legal writing and research courses from his critique.[12] It is worth noting, however, that legal research instruction has evolved significantly over the years.[13] (Indeed, it is the perception that doctrinal law courses have failed to progress since the time of Langdell that so frustrates contemporary commentators.)[14]

In a superb article published in 2003, Paul Callister traced the history of the most significant pedagogical split in the hundred years or so of formal legal research instruction.[15] In 1988, Christopher Wren and Jill Robinson Wren attacked "bibliographic" legal research instruction, arguing that "students in legal research courses are given descriptions of law books without adequate instruction about how or when to use the books. Bibliographic information requires a context to make it meaningful for a legal researcher, and the necessary context is how someone actually does legal research."[16] Bob Berring and Kathleen Vanden Heuvel responded the next year,[17] provoking a second article by the Wrens,[18] which in turn compelled a last word from Berring and Vanden Heuvel.[19] The back-and-forth left its mark, and to this day librarians debate how best to design courses with process-based, experiential principles in mind.[20]

As time went on, bibliographic instruction began to sound more old-fashioned. The caricature of this model is a librarian at the front of the classroom with a cart of books. "This is called the Code of Federal Regulations. It's where you can find rules and regulations of administrative agencies as of a certain date. Notice how the color of the cover changes each year. You'll find it in the Federal Room in the library. I'll pass some copies around." Students fall into a trance-like state out of sheer boredom.

> The bibliographic approach does not teach students why legal research is necessary or how it ultimately will be used to solve legal problems, and it rarely gives students a framework upon which to build their knowledge. The amount of information taught in a bibliographic-based course is often overwhelming and detailed and is quickly forgotten because it is learned out of context and is seldom applied.[21]

The assumed methods of assessment for this model include scavenger hunt exercises to find predetermined, correct answers, and an objective, multiple-choice final exam.[22] Teachers determine which students have best memorized information about sources—what is in them and how to use them.

Conversely, process-based research instruction might emphasize students' development of a research process related to an ill-defined set of facts. Class time is devoted to students' attempts to implement their plans by using the resources they deem appropriate. Assessment might derive from post-exercise debriefings, from subjective evaluation by the instructor based on firsthand observation, or from students' narrative descriptions of research processes undertaken to solve take-home research assignments.

I mention these concepts because they play into our perceptions of the assessment tools described in the next sections of this essay. My contention is that there is good and bad in both approaches—a thoughtful variety of tactics might be the best solution of all.

A NOTE ABOUT TIMING

As noted earlier, librarian participation in first-year research and writing programs has increased dramatically in recent years. In describing their pursuit of formal teaching responsibilities for librarians in the first-year program at the University of Richmond School of Law, Joyce Janto and Lucinda Harrison-Cox wrote that, "[a]s librarians, we felt uniquely qualified to teach legal research and appreciated this opportunity to show how legal research should be taught, because we all felt that the instruction we had received in law school was inadequate."[23] But teaching first-year law students (1Ls) is not easy, and factors exist that can lead to disappointing outcomes. First, librarians are often invited as guest lecturers, rather than being designated as co-teachers, or collaborating with named instructors in meaningful ways. Oftentimes, research lectures are scheduled outside of regular class time, irritating students. The primary instructor may make research lectures voluntary or may fail to attend the sessions herself, sending a signal to her students that the content lacks importance.[24]

Second, it is axiomatic that legal research instruction is most successful when it comes at the point of need. First-year students are struggling to manage their doctrinal courses and get good grades which can unlock the doors to law review or a summer position with a big law firm.[25] In this regard, research and writing courses are at a profound disadvantage. "[Law] schools usually do not give significant academic weight to courses in legal writing, lawyering, or clinical education. This tends to undercut, as does the competitive climate, the seriousness of the assessment that students receive in these courses."[26] Unlike 1Ls, upper-class students have self-selected into graded, elective research courses. Most of them have already experienced summer employment in a legal setting, and understand better why research skills are important.

Third, teaching in the first-year program often means working with hundreds of students. Even if you have several librarians to assist, you probably will not have time to offer a significant level of feedback. That means relying on objective assessment tools, like short-answer questions, that are easier to grade.[27]

ALR and similar electives solve some of these problems because motivated students self-select into the courses, and limited enrollments make it feasible for instructors to create process-based exercises with meaningful feedback.

LEGAL RESEARCH ASSESSMENT TOOLS

Whatever the venue, teachers must approach legal research like any other class; intentionally creating coordinated goals, syllabi, readings, and assignments that are carefully designed to convey information and challenge students. Assessment is the last piece, and instructors must choose assessment tools to further course goals.

Objective Homework Assignments and Quizzes

Whether in the first year or an advanced course, one goal is probably to teach students about a group of important sources—what is in them, where you find them, how you use them, etc. Objective assignments, which may take the form of multiple choice, true/false, or short-answer questions, force students to review their notes and memorize important information that can be built upon with further practice.[28] They give instructors a way to evaluate students, while saving a huge amount of time in grading.[29] Students are also "more likely to accept the results and work to improve performance. Students sometimes dismiss poor results on essay examinations as the result of the professor's arbitrary stylistic preferences."[30]

Many librarians reject "scavenger hunt" exercises on the grounds that they bear no resemblance to real-life research problems,[31] ignore connections between sources, and artificially limit students to one type of material at a time.[32]

> When developing materials for the course, we firmly rejected the old "treasure hunt" methodology, which we all had suffered through when learning legal research ourselves. We were unanimous in our agreement that treasure hunts are not only time consuming and frustrating, but also of limited educational value. Because each source is presented in a vacuum, relationships between different types of material are never made clear to students. The only point these exercises drive home to novice

> researchers is an unintended and erroneous one—that a legal question has only one right answer.[33]

Basing an entire class around short-answer exercises would not make sense, of course, because you would ignore students' choices surrounding the research process.[34] But scavenger hunts and other short-answer exercises are not without merit and can be useful as part of a comprehensive program.

Research Exercises

> When several pieces of knowledge or several skills are evaluated simultaneously, a challenging assessment forces students to learn in more complex and effective ways than if each were assessed separately. This is, in large part, why simulation assignments—assignments that place students in the role of a practicing attorney—are superior to traditional "quiz" assignments. Asking students to solve a legal problem through research is more challenging than asking them to provide answers for a series of sterile research questions.[35]

Unlike quizzes and short-answer exercises, significant research exercises are challenging because they test several skills simultaneously. For example, research related to a factual scenario[36] may involve selecting appropriate secondary sources, choosing the format of selected material, deciding to change course upon hitting a roadblock, demonstrating how to use a good case from one jurisdiction to find similar cases in another, and considering whether you are safe to stop, among many other things. Multifaceted problems naturally test students' ability to form a coherent plan. They also allow for creative problem solving and depending on the scenarios involved, may give students a personal connection to the subject matter of the exercise.

Many ALR courses use weekly assignments for this purpose.[37] Students submit responses in the form of "research logs." This diary is designed to tell the instructor, usually in narrative form, what the student did at each step in the process and why. Research logs force students to compose a research plan and (attempt to) follow it through to completion, improvising when necessary to move the process along.[38] They also offer students an opportunity for self-reflection (e.g., "in retrospect, I should have given up at this point and moved on to another source")[39] and enable teachers to offer quick feedback.[40] Instructors may write personal comments in the margin, e.g., "you'd have gotten a better result set by using a field restriction," respond to humorous remarks, and otherwise make a constructive, personal connection with the student. Noticing that several students have made similar errors prompts teachers to cover the right ground when reviewing assignments with the entire class.

Despite some obvious benefits, research logs are probably inadequate if they serve as an instructor's sole method of assessment. That's because the student's narrative does not necessarily describe the process you would see if you watched it yourself. As Brian Huddleston asked, "[w]ould the winner of a piano competition be as renowned if the contestants merely described in an essay how they would style and perform a particular piece?"[41] And of course, students probably misrepresent their research process, leaving out some of their less productive tangents.[42]

The hardest part about using research logs to collect information is the amount of time that it takes to review and provide meaningful feedback. It can take at least thirty minutes to review one research log, meaning that for a class of twenty, you need to find ten hours of review time.[43] As a weekly exercise, this is difficult to sustain. In 2002, Kristin Gerdy proposed the use of group feedback memos. This promising variation employs a memorandum from the teacher to all students in the class, and features a description of recurring problems.[44] Gerdy writes, "[s]uch a group feedback memo is useful not only for individuals who had particular problems but also for students who did not have the problems because it identifies areas where they were successful and helps them avoid the problems should they arise in the future."[45]

Observation & Dialogue

In a perfect world, we could see a student's research process, evaluate that process, and provide quick feedback. Using narrative research logs, prepared by students, is a good but imperfect approach. Fortunately, there are other methods to learn how students see the problem before them and gauge their thought process as they seek to solve it.

One such approach is to engage in Socratic dialogue with students.[46] It is likely that librarians teaching skills courses, such as legal research, hesitate to embrace the techniques of doctrinal law professors, but there can be significant benefits. Asking students to describe their handling of in-class exercises, for example, and then following up with probing questions will help you to develop a list of the kinds of concepts your students do not understand. And knowing they may be called on will encourage a higher level of engagement and attention throughout your classes.

If you want to avoid this route, consider inviting students to try research problems with the computer attached to the classroom projector.[47] So much of teaching legal research involves electronic resources that it is easy to find opportunities for students to demonstrate short projects from start to finish. If they get stuck, others can shout out suggestions.

Better yet, take advantage of technology to capture the entire electronic research process. Teach your students how to use screencasting software like

Captivate,[48] Camtasia,[49] or a free, open-source alternative like CamStudio,[50] and have them use it to solve a research problem. Students should include audio commentary to add context—e.g., "I'm starting with a Westlaw natural language search because …." This enables the instructor to view an actual research process, while avoiding the pressure students may feel while performing in front of a class or otherwise being watched.

Peer Assessment

Students can more fully participate in the educational process by critiquing the work of their peers. But unlike undergraduate institutions, where a tradition of formal peer assessment and grading has developed, there is no similar model in law schools. In part, this is because the case method dominates, but even in skills courses we hesitate to use peer assessment because students are not comfortable being graded by their peers.[51] In particular, students believe peers are not competent to assess their work.[52]

Students can, however, gain significant benefits from a program of peer feedback. "By peer feedback, we mean a communication process through which learners enter into dialogues related to performance and standards."[53] The practice entails establishing the criteria for assessment and rating peers in terms of those criteria.[54] Setting feedback standards requires agreement between students and teacher during a class dialog.

> Once we begin asking questions about how assessors arrive at marks we are involved in a process of defining learning outcomes and the criteria for assessing those outcomes. This intellectual engagement with outcomes, criteria, and standards is at the heart of student involvement in assessment and can lead to great clarity about the nature of high-quality performance.[55]

Critiquing peers gives student reviewers insight into what it takes to achieve success themselves. That understanding stimulates valuable self-assessment (e.g., "Am I achieving these standards myself?"; "How has my own process fallen short?")[56]

The process also teaches students how to provide constructive feedback to colleagues and friends who they might ordinarily find difficult to criticize because of personal connections. And the reviewers' knowledge that roles may reverse (and they will face criticism later) lends the evaluation process greater seriousness.

Legal research instructors might want to establish a peer feedback regime as a way to engage students. And as teachers know from experience, the process of offering careful critiques stimulates further learning by demonstrating limitations in one's own understanding.[57]

To some extent, legal research teachers already take advantage of peer feedback during the regular give-and-take of class discussions. During lectures, one might introduce a problem and then ask a student, "What would you try first to solve this?" Rather than critiquing the response, the instructor could give others in the class an opportunity to comment. These explanations are chances for students to practice articulating their research processes—a skill they are likely to need in practice.

Another obvious application is to institute peer feedback into process-oriented or longer term projects. As described earlier, many instructors use research logs as assessment tools for assignments. Rather than providing direct feedback, teachers could incorporate an intermediate feedback step, in which each student is assigned the task of critiquing the process employed by one of his or her peers. Student authors would be required to utilize feedback received in producing a final draft the next week, while the instructor could rate the quality of reviewers' comments.

Similarly, instructors might assign reviewers to critique preliminary drafts of final assignments, such as pathfinders. Both students in each designated pair would benefit—the author from the substantive observations given, and the reviewer by absorbing and understanding types of resources the author had selected.

END OF SEMESTER ASSESSMENT

Pathfinder

Since I began teaching ALR, I have required students to prepare pathfinders for their final project.[58] The idea is that students choose a subject of interest and develop a pathfinder (sometimes called "research guide" or "annotated bibliography") that would help another researcher starting out in that topic. Students bring to bear all of the skills they learned during the course while building the guide. A brief, in-class presentation is the final component.

Other instructors reject the pathfinder:

> The final component of the Advanced Legal Research course originally involved the use of a pathfinder. This tool ... is quite common among the advanced legal research courses. This component, however, did not work well in the course because development of the pathfinder is not an exercise with direct practical value. Its most significant weakness is that it fails to integrate problem-solving skills with the research process.[59]

While I disagree with the contention that pathfinders lack practical value, I accept the general point. Many research instructors pursue a practical curriculum, designed to give students the ability to handle all kinds of research problems with confidence and skill. The pathfinder project serves this purpose only indirectly.

To be fair, preparing an excellent pathfinder can be fun and requires a high degree of judgment.

> We tell them not to be comprehensive. We do not want to see every case or journal article; we only want to see the ones that are significant. This is because we want them to practice using their judgment, not just their ability to collect resources. When they are practicing law, they will have to make research choices based on cost and deadlines. The pathfinder gives them an opportunity to develop the intuition they will need when they are lawyers.[60]

Furthermore, as Berring and Vanden Heuvel argued, the assignment may effectively bridge the gap between "conceptual understanding of the tools and working through of research questions that engenders excellent research skills."[61]

Still, juxtaposed against other assignments (e.g., research projects with assessment focused on the process), the pathfinder seems overly bibliographic and out of place. It belongs, perhaps, as one component but not as the culmination of the course.

Examinations

Exams are an obvious end-of-term assessment tool, but of course teachers can use them at any point during the semester. And although we consider exams as a separate assessment category, in reality they simply give teachers a framework in which to implement their preferred assessment choices. For example, objective questions (generally multiple choice, short answer, true or false, etc.) enable professors to establish a baseline of knowledge that they feel students should commit to memory. They are easy to grade,[62] and students are "likely to spend more time studying and learning the material."[63] However, objective exams do not prove that students can use sources effectively, a fact that frustrates some commentators.[64] Judith Rosenbaum, for example, wrote that:

> While it certainly is true that knowledge acquisition is a necessary foundation for learning, because raw facts have to be absorbed, and often memorized, before higher forms of cognitive activity can take place, the essence of legal research is a search for understanding in which finding and thinking continually cross-fertilize each other and these mental processes cannot be emulated by an objective test.[65]

Douglas Miller states the counter-argument:

> The education theorists who conclude that not every skill can be tested in three hours do not advocate the abolition of examinations: rather, they

> suggest that in-class examinations be used with other kinds of projects. Thus, if we conclude that there are skills taught in our courses that cannot be tested in three hours, it does not necessarily follow that examinations are useless for us, for the simple reason that we might use in-class examinations in conjunction with other kinds of assignments.[66]

One might add to Miller's point that just because one type of exam lacks practicality, that does not mean that we cannot conceive of a different kind of exam, one that focuses on process.[67]

A final examination based on firsthand observation makes more sense. One might structure it by scheduling appointments with individual students sometime during exam period. The time allotted could be used to elicit responses to questions about research processes (an oral exam) and to follow the student as he/she attempts to research an issue. Although extremely time consuming, with this method, the instructor may gain a better understanding of the student's research and reasoning skills.

RECOMMENDATIONS AND CONCLUSION

> We owe it to our students to try to be excellent teachers who skillfully employ a wide range of teaching methods. While poor instructional techniques may not particularly affect the very best students, the average and below average students depend on the quality and effectiveness of our instruction to succeed in law school, on the bar exam, and in practice. Law teachers should expertly employ a wide variety of teaching methods. Unfortunately, many of us do not.[68]

Legal research instructors seek to provide their students a working knowledge of important research tools, strategies with which to develop a rational research plan, and the skill to conduct research efficiently, among other things. Given the range of desired outcomes, it would be difficult to argue for the use of a single assessment tool.[69] "Inherent in the quest for variety is the recognition that some assessment measures are more appropriate for some subjects or skills than they are for others."[70]

A well-conceived legal research class may utilize short-answer assignments, quizzes, and scavenger hunt exercises as a means to establish a baseline of knowledge with critical sources. To follow it, teachers are advised to employ a series of research problems, with grading based upon students' ability to describe a coherent and logical progression. The problems' "answers" are less important than the selection of sources, reasonable use of those sources, and adherence to a plan. The assessment tool for such exercises might be some combination of research logs, Socratic dialogue, in-class presentations, or student-prepared Captivate/Camtasia/CamStudio screencasts.[71]

As a final project, a pathfinder, however practical you might make it, is not sufficiently process oriented to stand on its own. If we believe that the most essential skill that teachers can impart is the ability to handle confidently and accurately research projects on unfamiliar subjects, then you should consider a process-oriented exam or another research project instead of (or in addition to) the pathfinder.

Using multiple assessment tools benefits your class whether you teach 1Ls or ALR. The rationales for variety—e.g., that different students learn in different ways, and that assessment should be tailored to the competencies being developed—are the same for both groups. In any legal research course, our objective is to teach multiple skills, which may include creating a research plan and choosing a source to start off, memorizing the official sources of legal materials (and where/how to find them), evaluating the benefits and drawbacks of indexes and full text searches, knowing when print-based research can still help, researching with a time pressure, selecting the most appropriate databases on Lexis or Westlaw, using natural language or terms and connectors, and assessing free Web sites, among hundreds of others. Some skills, like learning the difference between the Statutes at Large and the United States Code, are well suited for objective assessment tools like quizzes; others, like deciding the best place to start researching a complex issue, can best be evaluated with tools like research logs or direct observation. The administrative burden of teaching large first-year classes may make research exercises less practical, but leaving them out entirely would be a disservice to students.

Ultimately, the variety of available assessment tools suggests that there is room for creativity and that there are many appropriate alternatives.[72] So long as instructors use a multifaceted approach, selecting assessment tools to suit their course objectives, students will be engaged in the process and will become stronger, more confident legal researchers.

NOTES

1. *See* Association of Legal Writing Directors/Legal Writing Institute, *2002 Survey Results*, available at http://www.alwd.org/surveys/2002.html.

2. *See* Association of Legal Writing Directors/Legal Writing Institute, *2000 Survey Results*, available at http://www.alwd.org/surveys/2000.html. *See also* Ann Hemmens, *Advanced Legal Research Courses: A Survey of ABA-Accredited Law Schools*, 94 L. Lib. J. 209, 220 (2002) (finding a 700% increase in the number of law schools offering ALR classes between 1983 and 2000).

3. *Cf*. Maureen Fitzgerald, *What's Wrong with Legal Research and Writing? Problems and Solutions*, 88 L. Lib. J. 247, 252 (1996) (noting that although "most law professors recognize the importance of research and writing, they seem unable as a group to find room for it in the curriculum ")

4. *See id*. at 271.

5. ABA, Section of Legal Education and Admissions to the Bar, *Legal Education and Professional Development: An Educational Continuum: Report of the Task Force on Law Schools and the Profession:*

Narrowing the Gap, Statement of Fundamental Lawyering Skills and Professional Values (1992) [hereinafter MacCrate Report].

6. William M. Sullivan et al., *Educating Lawyers: Preparation For The Profession Of Law* 188 (Jossey-Bass/Wiley 2007) [hereinafter Carnegie Report]. The failure of law schools in this regard appears to be unique in professional education.

> With some important exceptions, the underdeveloped area of legal pedagogy is clinical training, which typically is not a required part of the curriculum and is taught by instructors who are themselves not regular members of the faculty. Compared with the centrality of supervised practice, with mentoring and feedback, in the education of physicians and nurses or the importance of supervised practice in the preparation of teachers or social workers, the relative marginality of clinical training in law schools is striking.

Id. at 24.

7. *See* MacCrate Report, *supra* n. 5, at 267 (concluding that "the statement should be an essential reference in the accreditation process"); Roy Stuckey et al., *Best Practices for Legal Education: A Vision and a Road Map* 17 (Clinical Legal Education Association 2007) (arguing that "[w]ithout clearer guidance from the accrediation [sic] standards and without any significant internal or external motivators to change the *status quo*, law schools have been slow to consider the implications of the ABA's mandate to prepare students for effective and responsible participation in the legal profession.")

8. *See* Joan S. Howland & Nancy J. Lewis, *Effectiveness of Law School Legal Research Training Programs*, 40 J. Leg. Educ. 381 (1990). *See also* Paul D. Callister, *Beyond Training: Law Librarianship's Quest for the Pedagogy of Legal Research Education*, 95 L. Lib. J. 7, 9–11 (2003).

9. Librarians at many law schools have attempted to supplement formal course offerings with brown bag sessions, optional lectures, and "bridge the gap" programs specifically designed to assist summer associates and graduating students.

10. MacCrate Report, *supra* n. 5, at 157. Specifically, MacCrate advocates an understanding of: "various sources of legal rules and the processes by which these rules are made," sources providing "controlling principles for resolution of various kinds of issues . . .," and "[t]he variety of legal remedies available in any given situation." *Id*. at 157–158. With respect to fundamental research tools, lawyers "should be generally familiar with the nature of the tool, its likely location in a law library, and the ways in which the tool is used." *Id*. at 159. Last, lawyers should understand how to formulate issues for research, identify "the full range of search strategies that could be used to research the issues . . .," evaluate the search alternatives before settling on a "research design," and implement that design. *Id*. at 160–162.

11. Kristin Gerdy, *Teacher, Coach, Cheerleader, and Judge: Promoting Learning Through Learner-Centered Assessment*, 94 L. Lib. J. 59, 69 (2002); Stuckey, *supra* n. 7, at 236 (stating that the "primary reason to administer assessments is to find out whether our students are learning what we want them to learn.")

12. Stuckey, *supra* n. 7, at 238–239. "In sum, except perhaps in legal writing and research courses, the current assessment practices used by most law teachers are abominable." *Id*. at 239.

13. *See generally* Joyce M. Janto & Lucinda D. Harrison-Cox, *Teaching Legal Research: Past and Present*, 84 L. Lib. J. 281 (1992).

14. *See e.g*. Stuckey, *supra* n. 7, at 236–238 (concluding that "the end-of-the semester essay exam is neither valid, nor realizable, nor fair."

15. *See generally* Callister, *supra* n. 8.

16. Christopher G. Wren & Jill R. Wren, *The Teaching of Legal Research*, 80 L. Lib. J. 7, 10 (1988)

17. Robert C. Berring & Kathleen Vanden Heuvel, *Legal Research: Should Students Learn It or Wing It?* 81 L. Lib. J. 431 (1989).

18. Christopher G. Wren & Jill R. Wren, *Reviving Legal Research: A Reply to Berring and Vanden Heuvel*, 82 L. Lib. J. 463 (1990).

19. Robert C. Berring & Kathleen Vanden Heuvel, *Legal Research: A Final Response*, 82 L. Lib. J. 495 (1990).

20. Berring recently remarked that "[a]lmost 20 years later one might wonder what the fuss was all about." Robert C. (Bob) Berring Jr., *Twenty Years On: The Debate Over Legal Research Instruction*, 17 Persps. Teaching Leg. Research & Writing 1, 3 (2008). Available at http://west.thomson.com/pdf/perspec/2008-Fall/2008-Fall-1.pdf.

21. Fitzgerald, *supra* n. 3, at 255.

22. *See e.g.* Douglas Miller, *Using Examinations in First-Year Legal Research, Writing, and Reasoning Courses*, 3 Leg. Writing 217 (1997). I hasten to add that I have oversimplified the concepts here in order to set an easy distinction. I am not trying to belittle the bibliographic approach generally or the use of examinations specifically. On the contrary, I find many of Mr. Miller's arguments persuasive.

23. Janto & Harrison-Cox, *supra* n. 13, at 289.

24. Baylor Law School has handled this problem by untangling research and writing. In this system, students take a quarter-long, separately graded research class. *See* Matthew C. Cordon, *Beyond Mere Competency: Advanced Legal Research in a Practice-Oriented Curriculum*, 55 Baylor L. Rev. 1, 8 (2003). Similarly, Kory Staheli argues that making legal research into a separately graded course "provide[s] needed motivation and incentive for students to learn the material and to master necessary skills." Kory D. Staheli, *Motivating Law Students to Develop Competent Legal Research Skills: Combating the Negative Findings of the Howland and Lewis Survey*, 14 Legal Ref. Servs. Q. no. 1–2, at 195, 200–201 (1994)

25. See Carnegie Report, *supra* n. 6, at 173.

26. *Id.*

27. *But see id.* at 290 ("We stress that the students are being taught research techniques to insure basic competence, and that the students are themselves responsible for building upon this framework during their three years in law school.")

28. *See* Greg Sergienko, *New Modes of Assessment*, 38 S.D. L. Rev. 463, 486 (2001) (concluding that quick, low-stake examinations "encourage students to keep up with work and provide them with frequent feedback on their progress.")

29. *But see* Miller, *supra* n. 22, at 233 (admitting that "this reduction in grading time does come at the expense of additional preparation time. Good multiple-choice questions don't drop out of the sky: they can be devilishly difficult to construct and fine tune.")

30. Sergienko, *supra* n. 28, at 486.

31. *See* Gerdy, *supra* n. 11, at 67. "After all, when was the last time an attorney did research that had been 'sanitized' by a law librarian in advance to ensure that the desired resources and results were available?" *Id. See also* Callister, *supra* n. 8, at 27.

> The neat order presented by the casebook method is illusory, a pedagogical nicety but an oversimplification of the world they will face in practicing law. To prepare for independence and to be weaned from their sterile law school environment of neatly tied case studies, students will need to learn to build their own paradigms. No subject offers a better opportunity to practice making order out of chaos than legal research.

Id.

32. *See* Janto & Harrison-Cox, *supra* n. 13, at 290–91.

33. *Id.*

34. *See* Gerdy, *supra* n. 11, at 72.

35. *Id.*

36. *See id.* at 67 (noting the distinction between well-defined and ill-defined problems).

37. *See* Fitzgerald, *supra* n. 3, at 265–266.

38. *See* David J. Boud & Allen Tyree, *Self and Peer Assessment in Professional Education: A Preliminary Study in Law*, 15 J. Socy. Pub. Teachers L. 65, 65 (stating that lawyers' work is rarely judged formally, except when "something goes terribly wrong ... The lack of effective external assessment directing his day-to-day work means that his own ability to define goals and to self-assess his progress toward those goals must be better than those of most non-professionals.")

39. *See* Sergienko, *supra* n. 28, at 479 (2001) (noting that commentators believe "self reflection is a critical component of successful professional work.")

40. *Cf.* Gerdy, *supra* n. 11, at 78 (noting that first-year students are eager for feedback of the type that they get in none of their other first-year courses.)

41. Brian Huddleston, *Trial by Fire ... Creating a Practical Application Research Exam*, 7 Persps. Teaching Leg. Research & Writing 99, 99 (1999). Available at http://west.thomson.com/pdf/perspec/trl0899.pdf. The response might be that, unlike concert pianists who are trained to perform before audiences, legal research is generally a solitary endeavor. There is little precedent for having a person standing over your shoulder watching you work.

42. Professors tell students that they will not be penalized for wrong turns, but it defies logic to imagine that all of them take that advice to heart. In a similar situation, I would be tempted to clean up my work.

43. Of course, this does not take into account the time necessary to develop the research problems in the first place. Matthew Cordon suggests delegating the task to students. "The difficulty with developing a practical problem has been resolved to a degree by requiring students to draft research problems of their own creation." Cordon, *supra* n. 24, at 34.

44. Gerdy, *supra* n. 11, at 80.

45. *Id*. Gerdy's article includes numerous interesting ideas. Another is the "minute paper," through which students identifying the points they found most confusing in her lectures.

> At the end of a class period, students are told to write for a minute or two on this question: "If you had to explain the most important concepts you learned today to a class member who was absent—and you are her only source of information—what would you tell her?" The papers, which are submitted anonymously, allow the teacher to assess how much the students have learned and to identify any misunderstandings or common questions.

Id. at 82.

46. *See* Callister, *supra* n. 8, at 33 (arguing that the "fundamental use" of the Socratic method is "to force an examination of one's own view of the world, including the mental frameworks one develops for understanding and solving problems.")

47. As an adjunct at Fordham, I taught ALR in a smart computer lab. A control panel allowed me to select any computer in the room and broadcast that student's image through the projector. As a result, if someone had a problem—say, a process was not working correctly—we could all look at his or her work to discover what had gone wrong.

48. http://www.adobe.com/products/captivate.

49. http://www.techsmith.com/camtasia.asp.

50. http://camstudio.org. MediaNotes is another potentially useful tool. http://w.cali.org/mediannotes. Distributed by Computer-Assisted Legal Instruction, MediaNotes allows teachers to annotate videos (created by Camtasia, CamStudio, or another program). Teachers can use it to point out specific points in the video where students made mistakes or could have followed a more straightforward approach.

51. The potential benefit of time saving for the professor is overwhelmed by the controversy it would cause—students in legal education *want* their professors to grade them, not other students. *See* Shirley Rawson & Alan L. Tyree, *Self and Peer Assessment in Legal Education*, 1 Leg. Educ. Rev. 135, 140 (finding "great student hostility to the inclusion of self and peer assessment marks as part of the formal assessment process."); Sergienko, *supra* n. 28, at 485.

52. *See* Sergienko, *supra* n. 28, at 485 ("The work on incompetence in assessment ... raises questions about the ability of students to grade exam answers that do not conform well to a model answer.")

53. Ngar-Fun Liu & David Carless, *Peer Feedback: The Learning Element of Peer Assessment*, 11 Teaching Higher Educ. 279, 280 (2006).

54. *See* Boud & Tyree, *supra* n. 38, at 67.

55. Liu & Carless, *supra* n. 53, at 280.

56. *See* Boud & Tyree, *supra* n. 38, at 65; Rawson & Tyree, *supra* n. 51, at 136.

57. *See* Liu & Carless *supra* n. 53, at 281.

58. In 2000, more than two-thirds (sixty-nine percent) of all ALR classes featured pathfinder assignments. *See* Hemmens, *supra* n. 2, at 234. Some have used pathfinders as the principle component of students' final grades. *See e.g.* Peter C. Schanck, *Mandatory Advanced Legal Research: A Viable Program for Law Schools*, 92 L. Lib. J. 295, 298 (2000).

59. Cordon, *supra* n. 24, at 34. *See also* Wren & Wren, *supra* n. 18, at 487 (identifying pathfinder projects as "training in legal reference, not legal research.")

60. Berring & Vanden Heuvel, *supra* n. 17, at 446.

61. *Id*. at 445.

62. Easy to grade, though quite hard to write. *See* Miller, *supra* n. 22, at 233.

63. Staheli, *supra* n. 24, at 201.

64. *See e.g.* Fitzgerald, *supra* n. 3, at 267 (complaining that quizzes "test students' ability to find a source but do not assess whether a student knows when to find a source.")

65. Judith Rosenbaum, *Why I Don't Give A Research Exam*, 11 Persps. Teaching Leg. Research & Writing 1, 5 (2002). Available at http://west.thomson.com/pdf/perspec/Fall&202002/Fall021.pdf

66. Miller, *supra* n. 22, at 219.

67. *See generally* Huddleston, *supra* n. 41. Huddleston describes the process of administering a practical examination. It was not designed to test "their ability to perform broad, open-ended research that integrated multiple resources to provide a full answer to a complex legal question." *Id.* at 100. Rather, it sought to assess whether students could "correctly use specific legal bibliographic resources to find material based on given criteria." *Id.* at 101.

68. Stuckey, *supra* n. 7, at 133.

69. *See* Carnegie Report, *supra* n. 6, at 173 (noting that "[i]n law schools, the means of assessing the skills of practice mirror the wide array of pedagogical practices represented in lawyering and clinical courses. This diversity of assessment procedures can be seen as a strength, as reliance on a single format . . . would be both impractical and ill-advised.")

70. Gerdy, *supra* n. 11, at 75.

71. *See infra* n. 49–50, and accompanying text.

72. Students may also enjoy the variety. And because different students will excel at different types of tasks, using a variety of approaches is equitable. *See* Gerdy, *supra* n. 11, at 75.

"Like Sands Through the Hourglass...": How to Develop a Good Legal Research Problem

SUSAN T. PHILLIPS

Texas Wesleyan University School of Law, Fort Worth, Texas, USA

Attorneys have a duty to conduct adequate legal research. Law schools have an obligation to educate students in the standard research techniques. To learn research, students must actually perform research using research problems. Therefore, professors must design appropriate problems for students to learn research skills. The first part of this article discusses the fundamentals of developing a research problem. The second part provides examples of research problems with an explanation of their development.

"You may be guilty of legal malpractice if you do not conduct adequate legal research!" warns the legal research instructor/professor in an attempt to "scare straight" the novice researcher into paying attention to the day's lesson of Shepardizing, KeyCiting, digest searching, statute updating, or any other legal research task.

The professor's attention-getting statement is technically accurate—courts have recognized that an attorney may be liable for malpractice if the attorney fails to conduct adequate legal research when the issue is neither an unsettled nor debatable area of law.[1]

DUTY TO RESEARCH

But aside from intimidating students in their first weeks of law school, this statement emphasizes the importance of learning to conduct legal research. It indicates that learning to conduct legal research is as important as learning the principles of consideration in a contract, negligence in torts, and the personal jurisdiction concepts of *International Shoe*.[2] "A lawyer is expected to possess knowledge of those plain and elementary principles of law which are commonly known by well-informed attorneys and to discover those additional rules of law which, although not commonly known, may be readily found by standard research techniques."[3] As the court noted, legal research is as crucial to the practice of law as the principles of contracts, torts, and civil procedure.

Consequently, it is the duty of law schools to graduate students with not only knowledge from doctrinal classes but also with comprehension of the "standard research techniques" that all attorneys are expected to possess.

RESEARCH THROUGH SIMULATION

The teaching of legal research skills is typically included in the first-year program, usually in conjunction with legal writing or in an upper-level advanced legal research class. Whether the research class is a first-year course or upper-level course, the students must actually perform legal research to learn legal research. Students cannot learn and master how to conduct legal research by reading a legal research text. Nor can the student learn the skill by listening to an expert explain how to conduct legal research. Legal research is a skill that a student can only truly master by actually performing the research. In other words, legal research classes must be taught through simulation by the student actually performing the research task.

A simulation or skills class requires that the professor design research problems for the students to hone their skills. This article's goal is to aid the professor in developing a legal research problem that will be effective in teaching the student the "standard research techniques" needed for the practice of law. This article will specifically address the writing of a problem for teaching the tools and methodology of legal research. The first part focuses on the fundamentals of developing a research problem and the second part provides two examples of research problems with annotations explaining their development.

FOCUS ON RESEARCH

In many, if not most, first-year legal writing and research courses, the component of legal research is incidental to the legal writing. Instructors focus on the written work product to be produced by the law student and not on the components of legal research. For example, a writing instructor's goal is to have his or her students write a memorandum explaining a specific area of law for a particular jurisdiction, such as the law of holographic wills in

Texas. The professor's main focus will be on teaching the student the components of the legal memo—the question presented, statement of the facts, brief answer, legal analysis, and conclusion, as well as proper grammar and citation. If the focus was on or included legal research, the professor would look to see whether the problem was teaching the students the fundamentals of the legal research process. For a statutory problem, the professor would write a problem that required the students to determine whether there was a relevant statute, whether the statute was updated, what cases interpreted the statute, and whether the cases were still good law through verification. The skill of legal research has its own uniqueness that is separate from the skill of legal writing. A student can conduct legal research without incorporating the results in a written work, just as a student can write a legal memorandum without personally completing the research. Consequently, it is imperative for a professor whose goal is teaching legal research to focus specifically on research.

Before the professor begins the actual writing of the research problem, he or she must first determine what the teaching outcome of the assignment will be. What tools or aspects of legal research are the most important for the students to learn in the given time period? The answer is that the professor must first equip the students with the basics of legal research. To determine these "basics," the professor should answer the question, "What are the research skills that every attorney is expected to possess?" Although open to debate, the core of the basics includes the following: case finding, case updating, statute finding, and statute updating. In a first-year class, a professor may also include secondary sources as part of the basics because these tools aid the students, particularly the novice, in not only finding both cases and statutes but also understanding the law. If time permits, the professor could also include locating and updating administrative rules, regulations, and decisions; finding practice and form material; finding court rules; and finding legislative history. Such decisions will depend on the number of classes the professor will have with the students and the amount of information that can be covered in that time period. For example, a professor can cover more information if teaching ten fifty-minute classes than if he is teaching six fifty-minute classes.

TREASURE HUNT PROBLEMS

The professor must also determine what type of problem he will be giving to the student. In teaching legal research, there are two different types of questions used for teaching legal research, the "treasure hunt" question and the contextual or process question. The first type, the treasure hunt question, asks the student to go look for the answer to a question. The end product focuses on the answer to the question without the student providing the steps as to how he found the answer.[4] The question can be about the legal research tool itself (What states' cases are included in the Pacific Reporter?), about a feature of the primary authority (What is the name of the case found at 367 U.S. 643?), or about the law (What is the maximum fine permissible under 16 U.S.C. § 4307?).

Typically, treasure hunt questions work well to acquaint students with the fundamental elements of legal research tools and resources—what the resources themselves look like, what the features of the resources are, and what the law in the resources looks like. Treasure hunt questions do not explicitly show the process of legal research or how to move through the steps of research. In other words, treasure hunt questions do not show the student how the research tools fit into the context of legal research, at least not in an obvious way. However, treasure hunt problems do have their place in teaching the student the fundamental tools of legal research as a foundation before moving into contextual problems.

To write a treasure hunt problem, the professor begins with the resource that the student will use to answer the question. The professor determines the answer that the student will need to find and writes the question to lead the student to that answer. By their very nature, the treasure hunt questions have answers. In developing these questions, the most important aspect is the question itself. The question should provide the student with enough information to find the answer. The author should include relevant keywords in the question that will lead the student to the answer. For example, if the question requires a student to use an index to find the answer, the indexing terms or a very close synonym should be provided in the question. The concept of giving the student the identical or near-identical terms in the question is particularly helpful the first time or two that a student conducts research in a particular resource. This method minimizes the student's frustration as he navigates the resource and permits him to concentrate on using the source instead of being frustrated by terms or keywords.

In addition, the question should eliminate any ambiguity by communicating to the student the specific answer that is required. If there are multiple answers to the question asked, the question should limit the student to the answer the professor is wanting. Does the professor want the student to supply all of the answers or just one specific answer? For example, the professor wants the student to use an index to find an article that discusses trademark parody. If he writes the question as, "Find a law review article whose subject is trademark parody," the student will find dozens of articles on this topic. This question certainly will work if the professor is not concerned with checking all of the possible answers that may be submitted. However, leaving the question open ended causes many students frustration and uncertainty in having to select an answer. A better question would include direction to a specific article by limiting the selection by date, law review, year, or author. "Find the 2004 *Santa Clara Law Review* article that discusses trademark parody." This question gives the student direction by including the date and law review as well as the indexing terms under which the article can be found either on LegalTrac or in *Index to Legal Periodicals and Books*.

Some might criticize this approach to writing treasure hunt questions as being "spoon feeding." But those who criticize should remember the goal of the assignment is to have the student gain hands-on experience with using a research tool to find an answer. By directing the student to a specific answer, the student gains familiarity with the research tool and gains confidence in his research skills. The idea is not to frustrate the student by hiding the ball or making the questions impossible to answer. Professors should foster the idea that research is a much-needed skill that can be mastered by the student.

TREASURE HUNT LIMITATIONS

One limitation of treasure hunt questions is that the questions typically have a short life span. It is the nature of legal publishing to frequently replace print resources, which can have a detrimental effect on the research question. Consequently if any significant time has elapsed since the initial writing of the question, it is imperative to check the questions before assigning them to determine if the question still works with the currently available print resources. In addition, students often mark the answers in the volumes as a "favor" for future researchers or circulate the answers to other students. Treasure hunt questions can also be hard on the library's collection. Seventy students pulling the same volumes create wear on the library collection. Because of these factors, there is an inherent need to replace the treasure hunt questions on a regular basis.

CONTEXTUAL PROBLEMS

The second type of research question is the contextual research problem. Contextual problems show the process for conducting legal research. The professor provides a fact pattern to the students and then takes the students step by step through the process of researching that fact pattern. Contextual problems simulate real life research. The contextual problem can be accomplished by using a new fact pattern for each step or by using one fact pattern for all of the research steps. For example, if the professor wants to show the process of finding a case, then updating that case, then looking up the statute cited in the case, and finally updating the statute, the professor can write one fact pattern that moves the researcher through each of these steps, whether as one assignment or as four individual assignments based on the one fact pattern. Teaching this process could also be accomplished through the use of four separate fact patterns, each fact pattern having its own assignment for one of the steps in the process.

Contextual research problems provide students with a more "real world" experience than do treasure hunt problems. The students are able to experience the type of research they will be conducting as attorneys and will learn how the pieces of the research puzzle fit together. Besides requiring the answer to the legal question posed in the problem, the professor could also require the student to submit a research log detailing his or her steps in the research process, as well as an invoice for the time spent researching. While it may be easier for the professor to write individual problems for each research step since the questions are independent from each other, the use of one fact pattern provides the students with a more realistic experience of the research process. The one fact pattern is more difficult to develop because the facts must permit the researcher to experience each step. For example, a problem that requires the student to research a statute that does not have any interpretative cases will not allow the student to conduct research in case law. If the goal of the problem was to research both statutory and case law, the problem would fail.

DEVELOPING THE CONTEXTUAL PROBLEM

To develop a contextual problem, the professor must first determine the research process he wants the students to experience. The steps of legal research vary as to whether the problem is a statutory problem or a common law problem, so the professor must select an area of law that corresponds to either statutory law or case law. For example, whether an individual qualifies as an innocent spouse under federal tax law is a statutory problem. With such an issue, the student's research can either begin in the federal statutes and then progress to interpreting case law or begin in the cases and move on to the federal statutes. However, if the student was researching whether a child is liable for the intentional tort of battery, the student would be looking for case law since the issue is a common law problem and statutes are not applicable. After deciding on the process, the research begins for the professor, who looks at the law in the selected area to find an issue for the student to research. The issue need not be a complicated one. Since the student is a beginning researcher and a novice as to the law a basic issue will suffice. One common mistake made by authors of legal research problems and writing problems, for that matter, is the tendency to compile a problem that is too complicated due to its over-reaching cleverness for the student. Here, the familiar phrase of "keep it simple" should be followed, at least for new researchers.

Regardless of whether your research goals include statutes or not, case law will almost always be a part of the research. Therefore, researching in cases is a good place to get an understanding of the law in regard to the facts that precipitated the problem. The facts from the case provide the author with a foundation upon which to write the "story" of the research problem. The professor can combine the facts of two or more cases or modify the facts of a single case to create the fact pattern that will be given to the student. Modifying the facts serves a significant purpose. Beginning researchers often believe that there is a specific case *exactly* on point as to facts and as to law, and it is their job to find that *one* case. This scenario is rarely the case. Researchers are more often looking for analogous cases. Consequently, modifying the facts will help the researcher grasp the idea of looking for similar cases.

After compiling the cases and the statutes, if applicable, the professor can then narrow the question that the student will be asked to research and can begin writing the fact pattern. The writing of the fact pattern can be as straightforward as the professor wants. Sure, clever and cute fact patterns are entertaining to the student but the professor should not lose sight of the ultimate goal, to teach the process of legal research and not to win points for creativity. That being said, simple techniques can be employed to make the fact pattern engaging: name the characters in the fact pattern after historical figures, literary characters, or television characters; and use settings to correspond with those figures or characters.

One of the final aspects of developing the problem is to write the call of the question that the student will research.[5] Since the professor conducted the research in the area of law, he should have a good understanding of what the law is in this area. From reading the cases, the professor has seen the issues raised in litigation and can craft an issue for the student to research. The call of the question can be one that has a definite answer for the student to find or one that is unsettled or debatable as to the facts given to the student. For a beginning researcher, unfamiliar with the law and researching, it is easier to approach a problem that has a definite answer. The student will be able to use his knowledge to conduct research that not only allows him to find an answer but to see how the research tools work together.

However, real life legal problems do not always, and in fact often do not, have definite answers. To give the student the opportunity to research a problem without a definite answer, the professor can set the problem in a jurisdiction that does not have primary, mandatory authority for the problem. The professor can instruct the student to look for mandatory authority for the problem's jurisdiction; but if none exists, the student should look for persuasive authority, often mandatory authority from another jurisdiction. The important factor is to advise the student as to whether there is mandatory authority for the jurisdiction he is researching or whether he should be looking at persuasive authority to solve the problem. These instructions will allow the novice researcher to focus on the task at hand which is to learn the steps to researching a problem. Once the student has been introduced to the basics of legal research, he can move on to more advanced situations where he is not told up front whether or not there is a definitive answer, but his prior experience will alert him to the possibility that there may not be an absolute answer.

The first several times a professor goes through the process of researching and writing a problem, he should leave significant time to put the problem together. In other words, these problems can take several days to compile, particularly when the professor is new to the process. The most difficult part is finding the particular area of law that will allow the professor to take the students through the steps that he wants the students to learn. As one gets more familiar with the process, it tends to get easier to construct the problems.

TEST THE PROBLEM IN THE HOME LIBRARY AND IN VARIOUS FORMATS

The author of the problem must also be familiar with the library's collection when writing the problem. If he selects a jurisdiction other than the home state of the library, the professor must make certain the library has the materials for the problem's jurisdiction and that the materials are current. Writing a statutory problem based in Arizona when the library does not have a current subscription to the Arizona statutes and the student has not yet received full access to the information on Westlaw or LexisNexis will be a disaster.

Online access brings up another point. The professor must indicate if the assignment is to be completed in paper resources, in online resources, or if it can be completed in either. The professor must test the problem in whatever format he permits the student to use for the research. If the professor wrote the problem using print resources but then either requires the student to use electronic resources or gives the student the option to use electronic resources, the professor must first conduct the research on the electronic resource to ensure that the problem works in that format. The reverse is true as well. If the professor used Westlaw or LexisNexis to research and write the problem but then requires the student to conduct his research in print or allows the student the option to conduct his research in print, the professor must make sure that the problem can be researched in print and that the library subscribes to the print resources needed for the research.

If the professor recycles the contextual problem in subsequent years, he must conduct a research check to determine if the problem still works. Just as with treasure hunt problems, the resources as well as the law can change and nullify the problem. The library print resources may have been marked with the answers or so overused that the resource literally falls open to the applicable page. In addition, students often pass down class information to the group of students coming behind them. These are all factors that may require the retiring of or the significant modification of a good research problem.

CONTEXTUAL PROBLEM I: "LIKE SANDS THROUGH THE HOURGLASS . . . "[5]

The next part of this article provides two examples of how a contextual research problem was developed. In the first example, the student is told he is a law clerk working for the professor's fictitious law firm. The student is given the fact pattern and told to research for an office memorandum whether or not the holographic will is valid.

Phillips & Teller P.L.L.C.
Attorneys at Law
1515 Commerce
Fort Worth, Texas 76102

TO: Law Clerk
FROM: S. G. Finkbeiner, Esquire
RE: Research State law

Please do the research for an office memorandum, based on the following problem:

After a whirlwind courtship filled with passions in the city of Santa Barbara, Beauregarde and Faith Brady were married in November 1997 and lived as husband and wife in Dallas, Texas. Beau had three grown children from a previous marriage. In February 2001, Beau, a doctor at General Hospital in Port Charles, decided that he was no longer one of the young and the restless and that the time had come to execute a will. Being somewhat frugal, Beau decided to forego hiring an attorney to draft the document. Instead, Beau wrote the following will in his own handwriting:

> I, Beauregarde Brady, being of sound mind and health do hereby declare that this is my last will and testament. My loving family, if you are reading this will, then I have obviously followed the guiding light to another world. To you I bequeath the following: To the bold and the beautiful Faith, for her generous support all the days of our lives, I leave my entire estate, including all property, real and personal, minus a token amount for each of my three children. To all my children, I leave you each $1,000 and these words of wisdom—You only have one life to live, so live each day to the fullest.

Beau signed and dated the document and then placed it in his safe.

On June 4, 2007, Beau Brady met with a tragic death when the single-engine Cessna he was piloting to Sunset Beach crashed on takeoff. The preliminary National Transportation Safety Board investigation is looking at pilot error as the cause of the crash since investigators found Beau had worked the night shift on four consecutive days from May 31 through June 3 and was probably suffering from great fatigue. His entire family was devastated by the event. However, when the contents of the will became known, his children were outraged that they were left a pittance and their stepmother inherited the bulk of the estate. They have challenged the validity of the will, particularly since there were no witnesses and it was handwritten except for one typewritten provision, the last sentence (*To all my children, I leave you each $1,000 and these words of wisdom—You only have one life to live, so live each day to the fullest.*). **Is the will valid?**

Research the question under Texas law. For this problem only, we are unsure in which trial court we will file. Consequently, assume all Texas Court of Appeals decisions as well as Texas Supreme Court decisions are binding.

BONUS: What daytime soap opera currently on one of the major networks is not mentioned in the problem?

COMMENTS ON THE DEVELOPMENT OF THE CONTEXTUAL PROBLEM I

First, the author determined the research steps that the problem would cover: state statutes and interpreting case law. The goal of this problem is to have the student conduct research in state statutes, update the statute, find interpreting cases, and update the cases. This problem tests the student's ability to research and update statutes, as well as the student's ability to find cases that have interpreted the relevant statute.

Next, the author looked for an area of law that is governed by state statutes and had cases interpreting the statutes. Initial research was conducted in Texas law since the home library's collection included several copies of the Texas statutes and codes. In looking through the subject areas of the Texas statutes, the author decided to look at the law of wills and found the Probate Code section concerning holographic wills. The plain language of the statute gave the impression that the law was unambiguous, but upon reading the interpretive cases, the courts have interpreted the statute quite uniquely. The interpretive cases gave rise to the issue of the validity of a handwritten will that contains some part that is not in the testator's handwriting. The author found appealing the fact that the issue would afford the student the opportunity to research specific law with, arguably, no definitive answer. Before proceeding, the author updated the statute to make sure it was still good law and updated the cases as well.

After reading and updating the statute and cases, the author then synthesized the law from the statute and cases. This process allowed the author to determine the call of the question: whether or not a holographic will with one sentence typewritten would be probated as a valid will under Texas law. The author next wrote the fact pattern of the problem. The problem obviously needed to reference a handwritten will that contained a typewritten portion. Because the class that would be using this problem was set up as a fictitious law firm with the student acting as the firm's law clerk, it was a logical step to write the problem as if a client with the holographic will issue had walked into the firm. The problem's fact pattern required certain elements: a dead person, a holographic will with a typewritten portion, and people fighting over the validity of the will. The story was written with the main characters named after soap opera characters. The idea to incorporate the soap opera theme simply came to the author on one of her very limited creative days.

The author then tested the problem both in paper resources and on Westlaw and LexisNexis. The author uses this problem annually and retests it every year to make sure it is still valid. The date of the decedent's death is updated every year so the student does not go down the statute of limitations trail. Over the years, as the major networks added new soap operas, the titles were incorporated into the problem. Soaps that were cancelled remained in the problem! The students get a chuckle out of the problem and its pop culture references which sets them at ease for the class.

The soap opera problem is a good gauge of the student's research skills at the beginning of the semester. The Texas statute dealing with holographic wills states that a holographic will must be "wholly" in the handwriting of the testator.[7] Some students end their inquiry upon reading the statutory language. Those students who delve further into the case law discover that there are several applicable cases that interpret typewritten portions of wills. The question then becomes whether the will will be probated, and if so, whether it will be probated with or without the typewritten sentence. From the cases, it seems that the court will allow the document to be probated. The student is then faced with the question of what will happen to the typewritten sentence. Students then see that there are arguments on both sides and must argue the facts.

This problem can be modified to fit other jurisdictions.

P.S. The answer to the bonus question is *As the World Turns*.

CONTEXTUAL PROBLEM II: EDDIE'S COPYRIGHT ROYALTY DILEMMA[8]

In the second example, the student is again a law clerk working in the professor's fictitious law firm. The student is given the fact pattern at the beginning of the semester. The fact pattern is used throughout the semester. Each week, the professor assigns a different step of the problem to research.

Phillips & Teller P.L.L.C.
Attorneys at Law
1515 Commerce
Fort Worth, Texas 76102

TO: Law Clerk
FROM: S. G. Finkbeiner, Esquire
RE: Class Problem

Tina Rickles has come to our law firm seeking advice for a legal situation involving her young son, Eddie. Ms. Rickles has related the following information concerning the problem: Ms. Rickles met Tom Corbett on October 14, 1999. The two shared many common interests, and soon a romantic relationship developed. The couple tried unsuccessfully for over a year to have a child. After seeing several fertility specialists, Tom and Tina conceived a child through artificial insemination using Tom's sperm and Tina's egg. They agreed that they were going to raise their child together. With Tom present, Tina gave birth to Eddie Corbett on December 30, 2002. The two were ecstatic over the birth of their child. The couple never married but did live together. Tom provided Eddie with financial support as well as paternal emotional support. Tom always referred to Eddie as his "son" whenever speaking of the child in conversation.

During the entire time of the above relationship, Tom Corbett was married to Crissy Drummond. Tom and Crissy met in 1966 and subsequently married on December 1, 1968. The couple never had children. On January 27, 1977 after years of work, Tom's novel *People, Let Me Tell You About My Best Friend* was published by FWT Publishing Co., a Tulsa, Oklahoma company. Tom retained all intellectual property rights to the novel. The book was a huge commercial success making it to the top of *The New York Times* Best Seller list and garnering many literary prizes. The work continues to sell briskly as it is often required reading in high school and undergraduate college English courses.

In April 1999, Tom and Crissy came to the realization that they had grown apart as a couple and amicably agreed that each was free to enter into other relationships. The couple never bothered to divorce.

On March 14, 2004, Tom Corbett died tragically in a single car accident when he lost control of his convertible Corvette and hit a telephone pole. Everyone was devastated by the event, particularly Tom's housekeeper, Mrs. Livingston. Since Tom's death, Crissy, Tom's widow, has been collecting the royalties from his book. Tina has come to us seeking help in obtaining Eddie's share of the royalties.

Note: All of the events in this problem took place in Fort Worth, Texas.

Assignment 1

Please begin researching our client Tina Rickles' case by looking for a secondary source that will help you determine the duration and renewal scheme for Tom's copyright. As you may remember, one of the places you can start your research is in secondary sources. Why? Because you may not understand enough about the issue and need that Encyclopedia Britannica background to start; or, if you do understand the area of law, you may save time by finding material where someone else has done the research for you!

REMEMBER: Your main research objective is to find primary, mandatory authority for your jurisdiction! If no mandatory authority exists, then find primary, persuasive authority.

A relevant secondary source should provide you with the citation to the federal law that answers the following question: What is the applicable federal law regarding copyright renewal of Tom Corbett's 1977 novel? Using proper citation, give the answer to this question. Your next step after using the secondary source is to go look at the primary authority since that is your ultimate goal.

Assignment 2

The firm continues to work on Tina Rickles' case. As you know, she is trying to get her son Eddie, his share, if any, of the royalties from Tom Corbett's book. Tom's widow, Crissy, claims that as Tom's widow, she is exclusively entitled to the copyright renewal.

Please research federal law and find the statute that indicates who is entitled to renewal when the author is deceased. Update the statute. Provide the proper citation to the applicable federal statute. According to the relevant case law, is Crissy's claim accurate? In proper citation format, provide one case that is mandatory authority and supports your explanation.

Assignment 3

We now know who is entitled to the renewal term based on the nondiscretionary hierarchy set forth by statute. We need to begin our research into whether or not Eddie will fall within the definition of "child." Two years ago, an attorney with our firm conducted research on this topic. He had pulled all of the federal cases that had been assigned the topic and key number that includes that point of law regarding transfer of copyright due to death and children. He claims to have put all of the cases he found in a file folder. Unfortunately, the attorney is not known for his organization, and when we sent him to retrieve the file, the only case in the folder was *Fitch v. Shubert*, 20 F. Supp. 314 (S.D.N.Y. 1938). The attorney does remember some pertinent information—the topic and key number for headnote #2 has been reclassified. The new topic and key number given this headnote is the topic and key number assigned to the point of law that we are researching.

Please find all of the federal cases that have been assigned a headnote with the new topic and key number.

1. What is the new topic and key number?
2. How many federal cases have been assigned this topic and key number?
3. Which of the federal cases that have been assigned this topic and key number will be most useful to us as to the "child" issue? Use proper citation form.

Assignment 4

NEW FACTS: Prior to Tom's death and under the original term of the copyright, Tom granted a license to Hollywood producer George Templeton of Hill Country Productions to make a motion picture based on Tom's novel. Tom even agreed to assign the motion picture rights to Templeton for the renewal period. The movie version of *People, Let Me Tell You About My Best Friend* was a big success and included a cast of big name actors. The film was nominated for several top prizes and made its international debut at the Cannes Film Festival. As we know, Tom died before filing for the renewal of the copyright in the novel.

I would like you to research whether or not under the renewal term performances of the motion picture or sales of the DVD are infringements of the copyright in the underlying work. Please find the case that is mandatory authority for our jurisdiction regarding this issue.

There is a catch—the firm is in a dispute with both Westlaw and Lexis regarding our contracts for those services. We are unable to use either service until the dispute is resolved. Consequently, you may only use the appropriate paper digest to find the case in question. Use either the topic analysis method or the descriptive word method to find the relevant topic and appropriate key number in the digest.

Please identify the case using proper citation and provide the topic and key number under which you found the case.

Assignment 5

After reading the cases we have found so far, it seems that the controlling question as to whether Eddie will be considered a child under the renewal section is whether under state law Eddie is an heir of Tom entitled to claim under intestacy statutes. Please research state law and determine the best way for Eddie to establish his paternal parentage. Begin your research in statutes and also look at applicable case law. Often times, the text of one statute refers to another statute. Make sure you look at all of the applicable statutes.

What is the proper citation to the Texas intestacy statute in question? Provide a brief narrative (no more than a page) setting forth your legal strategy for establishing Eddie's paternal parentage. Please include the citations to two Texas state cases supporting your position.

Assignment 6

Please anticipate Crissy's best argument against finding Eddie to be the child of Tom under Texas state law. I am certain that there is a code provision that provides Crissy with a good argument against finding Tom to be Eddie's father due to the unique nature of Eddie's conception. I seem to recall that there is also a Texas case that does not allow the above provision to completely shut the door on our case—it gives us hope that the statute is not strictly interpreted.

Please research this area for me. There is one catch—Tina is unwilling to pay for any electronic research charges; therefore, you will not be able to use Westlaw or Lexis for this assignment as our firm will not absorb the cost as overhead. Remember subsequent history if applicable.

Provide me with the proper citation of the statute/code and case I am seeking.

Assignment 7

As you may know, the federal statute that provides the nondiscretionary hierarchy for copyright renewal is silent as to the exact proportion of the renewal interest that vests in each eligible party. Some cases have interpreted the statute to give disproportionate shares, meaning the surviving spouse gets fifty percent undivided interest and the children take the remaining fifty percent in equal shares. Other courts have held that the widow and surviving children share equally.

It appears in our problem that proportioning is not an issue since we believe Eddie is an only child. However, Tina has just called our office and indicated that there is a rumor that Tom has another child from a marriage that occurred before Tom married Crissy. This marriage ended in divorce.

I would like you to conduct some legislative history research to see if Congress addressed the issue of proportioning the renewal interest in any of the documents associated with the Sonny Bono Copyright Term Extension Act of 1998.

Please print off the summary of the legislative history for the Sonny Bono Copyright Term Extension Act of 1998 (go to the record marked legislative history, hit enter, and then print this document) and submit a copy of the first page (title page) of the House Report listed under the 105th Congress **from the microfiche version of the report**.

Assignment 8

While we know that Tom's book fell under the automatic renewal provision for copyright, I would appreciate it if you would find a copy of the copyright renewal registration form. We need to keep a copy in our file. Make sure you get the renewal form for works registered during their original term and the necessary form for works that were not registered during their original term. *(STUDENTS: You may submit these forms from either a print or electronic source.)*

Due to your excellent work on her case, Tina has decided to have our firm draw up her will. Please find me a form for a Texas will. Don't bother to retype it, just photocopy it, and I'll fill in the blanks. I appreciate you doing this work for me and will remember you when it comes to voting on extending offers to law clerks. (*STUDENTS: After finding the form in hard copy, please also find it from an electronic source other than Lexis or Westlaw and print it out.*)

Assignment 9

Thanks for finding the copyright renewal forms and the Texas will forms. I need a little more research before the partners vote on which clerks to whom they will offer summer associate positions.

FWT Publishing Co., as holder of the royalties generated from Tom's book, has filed an interpleader action to determine its payment obligations.

I need to know the federal court rule for interpleader (not statutory interpleader) and if the appropriate diversity of citizenship requirement is met under rule interpleader (not statutory interpleader). It may help to look at a practice guide to obtain this information.

1. Please provide me with the proper citation to the federal court rule for interpleader.
2. What is the necessary diversity of citizenship requirement for federal court rule interpleader, and is it met here?
3. Also, if we lose at the trial level, I plan on appealing to the court of appeals. I need you to tell me how many days I have to file the notice of appeal after the judgment or order is entered. Provide me with the answer and the proper citation to the rule. In counting the days that I have to file the notice of appeals, do I count Saturdays and Sundays, and assuming Columbus Day falls within the time period, does it count? Provide me with the answers and the proper citation to the rules.

COMMENTS ON THE DEVELOPMENT OF THE CONTEXTUAL PROBLEM II

This problem was certainly more challenging to develop than the soap opera problem. First, the author determined the research steps the problem would cover: secondary sources, federal statutes and interpretative cases, West's topic and key numbers, paper digests, state statutes and interpretive cases, legislative history, form books, and court rules. Each step in the research process would be discussed in class prior to the particular assignment being given to the student.

Next, the author looked for an area of law that is governed by both federal law and state law, particularly statutory law that has interpretive cases. Through experience, the author knows that there are certain areas of federal law that look to state law to resolve specific controversies. For example, bankruptcy law and federal tax law often look to state law to determine whether certain property is community property or not. To find these areas of intersecting law, the author will conduct an electronic search for federal case law using one of the following searches: "federal w/5 law w/5 looks w/5 state w/5 law," "refer! w/5 "state law," or "state law" w/5 control!"

After running the search, the author then skims through the results to determine if any of the resulting cases include both federal and state statutory law. If so, and the topic appears promising, the author then begins researching both the federal issue and the state issue in the case. The author looks at the interpretive cases in particular and notes the jurisdiction of the cases to determine which jurisdictions will have primary authority and which will have persuasive authority.

When conducting the research for this problem, the author found at least one federal case dealing with the nondiscretionary hierarchy of persons entitled to copyright renewal when the author is deceased. The case involved the illegitimate child of the author suing the author's widow for his share in the copyright. In the case, the court looked to the state inheritance laws to determine if the child falls within the federal copyright statute for renewal. Because the federal case was from the United States Supreme Court, the author knew this case would be controlling in all jurisdictions. The author then turned to research the state law issue. Again, the author selected to begin the state law research in Texas since the home library's collection contains plenty of Texas resources. The Texas inheritance statute referenced the Texas Family Code in determining whether a child is the child of his biological father. The Texas Family Code provides the means for establishing paternity. The interpretative cases further provided the author with the fact situations that had been adjudicated under the statutes. Again, before proceeding further, the author updated all relevant statutes and the cases as well.

After reading and updating the statute and cases, the author then synthesized the law from the statute and cases. This process allowed the author to determine the call of the question: whether or not under federal and state law, a child born out-of-wedlock is entitled to a share of the copyright that was renewed after the author/father's death. The author next wrote the fact pattern of the problem by first listing the required elements of the problem: a dead author, the author's widow, the author's child born outside of a marriage, and circumstances of the conception that put the child's paternity in question. The author penned the story in draft form and then decided to name the characters after a 1960s movie and television show, *The Courtship of Eddie's Father*.[9]

Because the author was using this fact pattern for multiple assignments, the author then looked at each step of the research process and created the call of the question for each step/assignment. Copyright law is actually quite a complicated area of the law. Consequently, the author created the first assignment so that the student began his research in secondary sources in order to obtain an overview of the law of copyright. The assignment asked the student to identify a specific federal copyright statute. The second assignment asked the student to look up that federal statute, update the law, and provide his interpretation of the law supported by a case that is mandatory authority. The third assignment introduces the student to expanding his case law research through the West topic and key number. The student can conduct this assignment in paper or on Westlaw. The fourth assignment gives the student new facts and asks the student to find a case that will answer a specific question; however, the student is not permitted to use electronic resources. In the fifth assignment, the student researches state statutory law and corresponding state case law. The next assignment takes the student from the Texas Probate Code to the Texas Family Code. Again, the student is unable to use electronic research and must find interpretative case law along with the statutory section.

The above assignments essentially get the student through the substantive legal aspects of the fact pattern. The seventh assignment provides the student with the experience of retrieving a document from a legislative history of one of the recent federal copyright laws. In the ninth assignment, the student is introduced to form books and must retrieve a form related to copyright as well as a form for a state will. These individual assignments permit adding new facts when necessary! The final assignment covers court rules and, again, introduces new facts tangentially related to the problem. These individual assignments taken from one fact pattern allow the student to follow the research process in a step-by-step manner.

During and after the creation of each assignment, the author tested each assignment in paper and on Westlaw and LexisNexis if the problem allowed the student to use the electronic resources. In the event the author uses the problem in subsequent years, she will certainly check to make sure the law, as well as the resources, are still valid. Typically, it is easy to make adjustments to a fact pattern when there are changes in the substantive law.

CONCLUSION

Developing good legal research problems takes planning and patience. The professor should leave sufficient time to properly consider the research goals that he wants to impart to the student, as well as sufficient time to determine the appropriate area of law to meet these goals. Our responsibility as professors is to introduce the student to the standard legal research techniques that are commonly known by well-informed attorneys. In doing so, we must provide the students with a research experience that will allow them to learn the research process needed for the practice of law. Research is a skill that must be learned by doing. Professors should not expect students to learn to properly research on their own or figure it out after graduation. We have an obligation to prepare our students for the practice of law, of which research is a critical component. As such, professors must create research problems that will lead the students through the research steps that they need to master. These problems should be well planned and tested with the goal to teach the students research. The skill of writing the research problem is one that any professor can master. It simply takes familiarity and an attention to a systematic process whose end result is to impart to the students the skill of conducting research.

NOTES

1. *See e.g. Dixon Ticonderoga Co. v. Est. O'Connor*, 248 F.3d 151 (3d Cir. 2001); *Wash. Elec. Coop., Inc. v. Mass. Mun. Wholesale Elec. Co.*, 894 F. Supp. 777 (D. Vt. 1995); *TCW/Camil Holding LLC v. Fox Horan & Camerini LLP*, 330 B.R. 117 (D. Del. 2005); *Smith v. Lewis*, 530 P.2d 589 (Cal. 1975), *overruled on another point*; *Janik v. Rudy, Exelrod & Zieff*, 14 Cal. Rptr. 3d 751 (App. 1 Dist. 2004); *Stanley v. Richmond*, 41 Cal. Rptr. 2d 768 (App. 4 Dist. 2003); *Lopez v. Clifford L. Offs., P.C.*, 841 N.E.2d 465 (Ill. App. 1 Dist. 2005); *Clary v. Lite Mach. Corp.*, 850 N.E.2d 423 (Ind. App. 2006); *Kempf v. Magida*, 832 N.Y.S.2d 47 (App. Div. 2 Dept. 2007); *Shopsin v. Siben & Siben*, 702 N.Y.S.2d 610 (App. Div. 2 Dept. 2000); *McCoy v. Tepper*, 690 N.Y.S.2d 678 (App. Div. 2 Dept. 1999); *Copeland Lumber Yards, Inc. v. Kincaid*, 684 P.2d 13 (Or. App. 1984); *Fiorentino v. Rapoport*, 693 A.2d 208 (Pa. Super. 1997); *Collas v. Garnick*, 624 A.2d 117 (Pa. Super. 1993).

2. *Intl. Shoe Co. v. Wash.*, 326 U.S. 310 (1945).

3. *Metzger v. Silverman*, 133 Cal. Rptr. 355, 361–362 (Super. App. Dept. 1976) (citing *Smith v. Lewis*, 530 P.2d 589 (Cal. 1975), *overruled on another point*).

4. The treasure hunt problem is the basis of Nancy P. Johnson & Susan T. Phillips, *Legal Research Exercises, Following the Bluebook: A Uniform System of Citation* (10th ed., Thomson West 2008). Recent editions have attempted to combine the treasure hunt questions with the process of conducting legal research.

5. The "call of the question" is what the question asks the students to do or what issues the students should address. For example, the call of the question could ask the student to research how a court would

rule on a particular matter, to determine what the defendant's best argument is, or to research the current law in a given area.

6. Problem reprinted with permission from Susan T. Phillips. Copyright 2008 by Susan T. Phillips.

7. Tex. Prob. Code Ann. § 60 (2003).

8. Problem reprinted with permission from Susan T. Phillips. Copyright 2008 by Susan T. Phillips.

9. Much to the author's chagrin, none of the students in the research class had any clue that the characters and setting of the research problem were taken from *The Courtship of Eddie's Father*.

Teaching Legal Research Online

SUSAN HERRICK
University of Maryland School of Law, Thurgood Marshall Law Library, Baltimore, Maryland, USA

SARA KELLEY BURRIESCI
Georgetown University Law Center, Edward Bennett Williams Law Library, Washington, DC, USA

Online instruction has great potential for accommodating the learning styles and preferences of Millennial law students, as well as for the effective teaching of legal research in the digital age. While integrating instructional technology into a face-to-face classroom legal research course is highly desirable and relatively easy, designing and teaching a purely distance or hybrid distance course provides some unique challenges as well as some distinct benefits for both instructors and students. This article will first evaluate individual instructional technologies independently of each other, since any of them could be used to supplement traditional face-to-face research instruction, whether formal or informal. Consideration will then be given to special problems of teaching a graded legal research course entirely or predominantly online. Legal research instruction presents some opportunities for experimentation and innovation with online learning techniques that may serve students better, accommodate the librarian's technology skills and abilities and her time constraints, and inspire others at our law schools to follow suit.

The authors would like to thank Susan G. McCarty, research fellow, Thurgood Marshall Law Library, University of Maryland School of Law, and Erie Taniuchi, interlibrary loan assistant, Georgetown University Law Library, for their assistance in preparing this article.

INTRODUCTION

This article will consider the benefits and challenges of using various online technologies to provide legal research instruction. Individual technologies will first be evaluated independently of each other, since any of them could be used to supplement traditional face-to-face research instruction, or even to replace less formal types of instruction such as guest lectures or library tours. Consideration will then be given to special problems of teaching a graded legal research course entirely or predominantly online. We conclude that using online technologies to teach legal research has many practical benefits, especially for teaching the Millennial generation of learners. However, there are also potential pitfalls a legal research teacher should explore before making a commitment to teach wholly or partly online.

WHY USE ONLINE TECHNOLOGIES TO TEACH LEGAL RESEARCH?

In deciding whether to adopt any new technology for teaching, legal research teachers should ask themselves several questions: What pedagogical issue or issues does this new technology address? Will the new technology create new difficulties that outweigh its benefits? Will the new technology effectively help students reach the intended learning outcomes?

There are potentially several pedagogical issues that could be addressed by using online technologies as a supplement to or replacement for classroom-based legal research instruction. Online instruction may be used to teach students who cannot come to campus, such as those working out of the area for a semester. It may also be used as a substitute for in-person instruction when either teacher availability or in-class time is insufficient to permit such instruction. All of the technologies discussed in this article could facilitate learning outside of the classroom, but not all could make up for insufficient instructor availability. In fact, as discussed in more detail later in this article, adoption of technologies that have a steep learning curve and the need to meaningfully adapt instruction to an online medium could exacerbate the problem of instructor unavailability. More important is the potential for online technologies to address the need to teach to varying learning styles and to the characteristics of adult learners, as well as the need to engage a generation of students who have grown up with Google, text messaging, and MTV.[1]

Furthermore, each of the online technologies discussed later in this article could add to the instructor's toolbox of alternatives for teaching students with a variety of preferred learning modes, including aural/auditory, visual, and kinesthetic (learning by moving) learners.[2] Besides addressing the issue of students' varying learning mode preferences, online technologies also offer great potential to adapt research instruction to six key characteristics of adult learners. These characteristics include: 1) learners' need to feel that they are engaging voluntarily in the learning process; 2) their need for an environment of mutual respect between instructor and learner; 3) their need to feel involved in a collaborative effort; 4) their need to fit new concepts into past experiences; 5) their need to be actively engaged with new material; and 6) their need for frequent and varied feedback or evaluation.[3]

Another pedagogical challenge that online instructional technologies could address is the problem of recent generations' changed expectations about education. The generation of students born between 1977 and 2003, sometimes referred to as "Generation Y" or as "Millennials,"[4] are now in law school. Millennials perceive technology as "a fundamental facet of life," not as a lifestyle enhancement.[5] The rise of the Web has led to a shift in expectations that affects Millennial attitudes toward the world, including their attitudes toward education. According to Joan Catherine Bohl of Stetson University,

> Not only has the Gen X/Y student come to expect instant gratification from technology, but the perception of the learning experience itself has been fundamentally altered ... [A]s Gen X/Y students matured they experienced education from the vantage point of a consumer, and felt entitled to an educational experience that spoke to them in accessible, even entertaining ways.[6]

Using interactive online technologies may help legal research teachers engage these students in their native environment on their own terms.

EVALUATING SELECTED TECHNOLOGIES FOR PROVIDING LEGAL RESEARCH INSTRUCTION ONLINE

In an effort to help law librarians decide which online technologies to adopt for legal research instruction, this section of the article will evaluate the pros and cons of using several online technologies as instructional tools. Emphasis will be placed on recent interactive technologies, such as blogs and wikis. Where empirical data on the instructional effectiveness of a technology exists, that data will be considered. However, the lack of data on most technologies should provide a fertile area for future researchers on this subject.

Online Tutorials

Tutorials are one of the older technologies discussed in this article, but the recent availability of inexpensive and user-friendly screencasting software, such as Wink,[7] Camtasia[8] , and Captivate[9] has made it possible for almost any librarian to create interactive multimedia tutorials tailored to local instructional needs.[10] Tutorials may be interactive and incorporate text, sound, graphics, video, simulation, and scored quizzes,[11] or they may consist of simpler non-interactive video or audio files.[12] They may be used as replacements for or supplements to course texts[13] and in-person lectures.[14] Ready-made tutorials are available through institutional membership in the Center for Computer-Assisted Legal Instruction (CALI), which has been producing legal research tutorials since at least 1999.[15] In addition, Lexis and Westlaw have long provided free online tutorials that teach various features of their research systems.[16] These readily available tutorials permit even time-challenged teachers to incorporate online instruction into their curricula. It is not surprising, then, that tutorials are one of the online technologies legal research teachers use most.[17]

The use of online tutorials for research instruction has many potential benefits. For example, surveys conducted at Georgia State University in the fall semesters of 2004 and 2005 showed that a large majority of responding law students preferred using interactive CALI lessons over printed texts for learning legal research.[18] Truly multimedia tutorials—those that include sound, graphics or video, simulations, and quizzes—will appeal simultaneously to students with several different preferred learning styles.[19] Tutorials that include interactive quizzes provide students with much-desired immediate feedback.[20] Compared to live lectures, tutorials allow students to learn at their own pace;[21] tutorials also allow students to learn whenever they perceive an immediate need to learn. For example, a student toiling away on a law review note at 2 a.m. who realizes that Google cannot retrieve all the scholarly sources she needs can use a tutorial to learn how to search an unfamiliar database like Academic Search Premier or Public Affairs Information Service. Substituting tutorials for live lectures can reduce library staff- and space-overloads that may result from the need to run numerous instructional sessions at periods of peak demand for guest lectures (e.g., the beginning of the semester).[22] Finally, in a graded course setting, students' compliance with tutorial assignments can often be verified through score reporting.[23]

On the other hand, online tutorials also have a number of drawbacks. Compared with live lectures, tutorials are unable to "emulate instructor enthusiasm" and lack the "ability of the instructor to perceive student confusion and clear it up right away."[24] Students are unable to ask tutorial questions and receive immediate answers as they could with a live instructor.[25] Substituting online tutorials for in-person lectures reduces contact between students and librarians, and may therefore reduce the likelihood that students will seek out librarians for assistance with future research questions.[26] Furthermore, Ms. Burriesci has found, both in assigning CALI tutorials to legal research students at the University of Maryland School of Law and in troubleshooting student complaints about in-house research tutorials at Georgetown Law, that law students often become extremely frustrated by any minor technical glitch they encounter in a tutorial. She has also observed the need to frequently update any in-house tutorials utilizing database screenshots or listing local material locations, because database interfaces and library locations change often.

A primary concern in deciding whether to employ any instructional technology ought to be how effective the technology is. There have been several empirical studies on the effectiveness of online tutorials for teaching information literacy and library skills to non-law students, but we were unable to locate any studies on the effectiveness of such tutorials for teaching legal research skills to law students. We examine three representative non-law studies here.[27]

One study examined the effectiveness of an online library skills tutorial taken by undergraduates enrolled in English composition classes at Ball State University during the spring 2000 semester.[28] Students were divided into two groups. One group, consisting of 104 students, received lecture-based instruction on using the library catalog and a periodicals database; a second group, consisting of ninety students, took an online tutorial covering the same information. The tutorial group worked through the tutorial during in-class sessions attended by a librarian who did not lecture but was available to answer questions. Both groups completed the same, ten-question online quiz after receiving their respective types of instruction. Participants from both groups also completed a comment sheet in which they rated their level of agreement with the statement, "I feel more confident that I can use the university libraries' resources as a result of this instruction session." The study found that quiz scores for both groups averaged around seventy-five percent.[29] However, the comment sheet responses showed that students who received lecture-based instruction subsequently felt more confident in their ability to use the library than did students who only completed the tutorial.[30]

In an Australian study conducted in 2002, investigators divided first-year sociology undergraduates into three groups.[31] Group one, made up of sixty-eight students, independently completed an online tutorial about catalog searching. Group two, consisting of forty-five students, completed the same online tutorial, but with assistance from a librarian. Group three, containing sixty students, had traditional face-to-face instruction in which a librarian demonstrated searching the catalog as students followed along on their own computers and completed a paper exercise sheet. All groups took a pretest and a post-test. While all groups showed improvement between pretests and post-tests, the group that received traditional face-to-face instruction (group three) showed the most improvement.[32] This finding is unique among studies that compare the effectiveness of live instruction and online tutorials for teaching library skills.

A 2005 study evaluated the effectiveness of a library skills tutorial administered to forty-nine graduate-level education students enrolled in three separate classes at the University of Central Florida.[33] Effectiveness was measured not only as to learning outcomes but also as to student self-confidence or "self-efficacy" in their library skills. Group one (containing sixteen students) was an on-campus class that received in-person library instruction; group two (containing nineteen students) was an on-campus class that used a Web-based library tutorial; and group three (containing fourteen students) was a Web-based class that used a Web-based tutorial. All groups completed "pretreatment" and "post-treatment" self-efficacy surveys as well as pretreatment and post-treatment library skills quizzes. The study's authors found no statistically significant difference in library skills quiz score improvement across the three groups.[34] However, they did find a statistically significant difference in self-efficacy improvement between group two (the on-campus class that used a Web-based tutorial) and group three (the Web-based class that used a Web-based tutorial); group two showed the lowest gains in self-efficacy of any of the groups. The authors hypothesize that this difference might be due to group differences in comfort level with Web-based instruction.[35]

A preponderance of the empirical evidence on the effectiveness of online tutorials for library instruction in nonlegal educational settings indicates that tutorials produce similar learning outcomes to live instruction. One possible difference in impact between tutorials and live instruction is that live instruction may be more effective at increasing students' confidence in their own research skills.

It is open to question whether these findings would be transferrable to law students attempting to learn legal research skills via online tutorials, because legal research competency, unlike catalog-searching competency or database-searching competency, involves understanding complex relationships between sources. However, an anecdote from Ms. Burriesci's Georgetown Law colleague Todd Venie illustrates that, for at least some law students, online tutorials can be extremely effective at teaching the basics of searching on Westlaw and Lexis. At the end of Mr. Venie's lecture on beginning computer-assisted legal research techniques, he was approached by an obviously irritated first-year who said, approximately, "You know, most of what you just told us is in the tutorials!"[36] Furthermore, legal research instructors at the University of Maryland, including Ms. Herrick and Ms. Burriesci, have successfully employed online tutorials to teach legal citation to first-year students since 2002. We conclude that there is sufficient evidence of online tutorials' effectiveness for us to recommend their use to teach at least basic research topics such as catalog searching, citation format, and database-specific search techniques. Such usage could free up valuable class time for the discussion of more advanced topics or replace less interactive outside-of-class learning alternatives such as textbooks.

Blogs

A blog, or "Web log," is a frequently updated Web site made up of dated entries, each of which has an individual URL and is "tagged" with various categories.[37] Most blogs allow comments from readers and are created using software that automatically generates an RSS feed to which readers can subscribe.[38]

There are several ways instructors might use blogs in teaching legal research. One common-sense use might be to substitute a blog for the traditional, static, course Web page.[39] Somewhat less obvious instructional uses for blogs include as an installment-based textbook substitute,[40] as a medium for student research or learning journals,[41] and as a forum for student discussion.[42] Students can also be encouraged to monitor or search blogs as part of their research process.[43]

Instructional use of blogging has many positive aspects. For example, instructors may create different types of blogs to appeal to different types of learners: written and video blogs will appeal primarily to visual learners, while audio blogs or "podcasts" will appeal to aural learners.[44] According to at least one blogger, the typing involved in blogging appeals to his kinesthetic tendencies.[45] Written blogs (as opposed to audio or video blogs) have a relatively low learning curve for both teachers and students, because many blog applications provide easy set-up wizards and word processor-like editing.[46] A blog allows its author to "push" information through an RSS feed while simultaneously maintaining a stable, central archive of this information on the Web.[47] Teacher-bloggers can push announcements to students, or student-bloggers can push research journals to teachers and everyone else in the class. Blog-based research journaling, like traditional research journaling, may help students actively engage with studied resources and research techniques. When blog comments are enabled, readers can respond to blog posts with questions or commentary, all blog readers can see these comments, and the comments are archived with the original posts. Because of this commenting feature, blog-based research journals have a major advantage over their print counterparts: not only can everyone in the class read each other's research journals, everyone can also comment on them.[48] Thus, a blog can serve as a platform for both journaling and group discussion. The ability of students to comment on each other's work also has the potential to provide all students with more abundant and more frequent feedback. Furthermore, students' awareness that their writing will be read by their peers, or even by a larger Internet audience, may encourage them to write better.[49]

Despite their versatility, blogs also have some weaknesses. Chief among these is the fact that many students will not use a blog unless they are required to do so, making blogs of limited utility for less formal instruction. In a 2005 study, a librarian who had given information literacy guest lectures to ten classes over two semesters at the Stephen F. Austin State University set up subject-appropriate blogs for each of those ten classes.[50] In these blogs, the librarian wrote about research methods and resources appropriate to the subject matter of each course. The blogs were linked from relevant research guides on the library's Web site, their URLs were included on handouts distributed at the information literacy lectures, and eventually they were promoted through fliers.[51] Visits to the blogs as reported by a hit counter were "overwhelmingly low," and follow-up surveys showed that in the first semester of the study, 73.1% of targeted students never checked their class research blog.[52] In the second semester, only one student out of 101 targeted by the survey bothered to respond.[53]

Even when students are required to blog and their peers are required to comment on those blogs, meaningful discussion may not ensue. Hall and Davison required students in an undergraduate library science course to blog about their learning experiences and also required them to comment on each other's blog entries.[54] They classified the resulting peer comments as "content free" (making no reference to points in the original entry), "non-reflective" (referring to original entry in order to state an opinion, emotion, etc.), or "reflective" (addressing points from the original entry in order to consider its validity).[55] The authors ultimately classified seventy-nine percent of all the student blog comments as either non-reflective or content free.[56]

While the above examples do not involve legal research students, it is reasonable to conclude that law students, who are usually more pressed for time than undergraduates, will be even less responsive to informal research instruction or class discussion conducted via blogs. This conclusion is supported by the findings of a recent survey of Arizona State University law students. Only thirty-two percent of surveyed students responded that they read blogs "some" or "a lot," while sixty-six percent reported reading blogs "a little" or "none."[57] If improving student writing is a course objective, blogs may nevertheless be useful platforms for student research journaling when students are made aware of a potential public audience for their work.

Wikis

Wikis are Web sites that are typically, but not necessarily, open for editing by anyone.[58] In legal research instruction, a wiki could be used as an online textbook written by multiple authors, as a platform for the composition and display of student pathfinders or other student writing,[59] or for students to make collaborative lecture notes.[60]

The strengths of wikis as collaborative writing tools are well documented.[61] According to one author, "[W]ikis are best used by a group of people working toward a consensus, whether it be creating an ultimate list of things or ideas or coming to jointly agreed-upon wording in a document."[62] Wikis allow such collaboration to occur even between physically distant co-authors, and may therefore be useful for group projects in distance education settings. Wikis are often lauded for their ease of editing, which requires no knowledge of HTML.[63] Using publicly readable wikis as a platform for student writing has at least one pedagogical advantage over print-based student papers: students are writing for a public audience when they write for the wiki, and awareness of that audience helps them to develop a professional writing style.[64] When an instructor provides skeletal lecture notes on a wiki for students to fill in together, students gain a collaborative study aid, the instructor can look at the filled-in wiki notes to see what students actually got from the lecture, and the end result will probably better reflect the complete lecture than it would if the instructor merely gave students the presentation slides.[65] Furthermore, it has been argued that "the likelihood that students will encounter wikis in law practice is increasing every day," since attorneys are beginning to experiment with them.[66] One example is the wiki at North Carolina's Rosen Law Firm, which is used to host billing reports, video training, and even employees' personal pages.[67]

Due to the reading and typing involved in wiki use, wikis will most likely appeal to students who are visual or kinesthetic learners; however, this alone makes them no better than traditional writing assignments or reading materials. Wikis are superior to textbooks and other reading materials in their ability to appeal to Millennial students by allowing them to collaborate on the "co-design" of course materials "personalized to [students'] individual needs and preferences."[68] In addition, allowing students to participate in the creation of course readings may also foster a sense of mutual respect between students and instructors that is important in teaching adult learners.[69]

Wikis also have some drawbacks. For those who have never actually edited a wiki, it may be surprising to learn that they are not necessarily easy to edit. Although they require no knowledge of HTML, most wikis do require knowledge of wiki markup language. Some law students (and librarians) may be unwilling or unable to make the modest time commitment required to learn wiki markup.[70] However, editing difficulties may be alleviated by choosing a commercial wiki service such as PBWiki[71] that offers word processor-like editing software. Unfortunately, free commercial wiki services sometimes come with advertising, which may be objectionable to some students and teachers.[72] Another potential problem with wikis is institutional embarrassment or even legal liability. An openly editable wiki poses the risk of embarrassing vandalism.[73] Even if editing capability is limited to the students in a class, they might abuse this capability. For example, they might post language which is defamatory or copyright infringing.[74]

Concerns of a more pedagogical nature include undesired student collaboration, students' sabotage of each other's work, and the difficulty of assessing individual student work when collaboration is allowed.[75] Sabotage and undesired collaboration may be detected in wiki software that requires editors to login and provides a "track changes" feature.[76] Difficulty assessing group work is less easily remedied but is at least as problematic in "offline" group projects. In fact, the wiki's ability to track changes may make it easier to grade individual contributions to a group wiki than it is to grade individual contributions to other group writing projects.

Some of the blessings and difficulties of wikis are illustrated by the experiment of two librarians at the Wake Forest University School of Law, Sally Irvin and Jason Sowards, who employed a wiki as a platform for student writing during the spring 2008 semester. Irvin and Sowards encouraged students in their classroom-based advanced legal research (ALR) class to author topical pathfinders directly on a wiki.[77] The librarians hope to publish librarian-authored teaching materials on more general aspects of legal research at a later time, so that the entire wiki can be used as a collaboratively written text and reference book.[78] In one sense, the experiment was not as successful as the instructors hoped, because many students opted not to use the wiki due to anxiety about technical problems or lack of time to learn wiki markup.[79] Importantly, however, the instructors, who were reviewing the weekly efforts of all students, observed that "[t]he wiki entries [grew] into more robust articles much more quickly than the print pathfinders."[80] Irvin and Sowards speculate that the difference was due to the fact that each week, the wiki-authoring students were producing integrated pieces of a whole work, whereas the print pathfinder students were only producing isolated installments to be assembled later.[81] The instructors were therefore able to comment weekly on the entire work of the wiki-authoring students, but only on part of the work of the print-authoring students. As suggested earlier in this section, the wiki-authoring students' awareness of a public audience for their writing may also have played a role in improving their work product.

Overall, wikis appear to be genuinely superior in certain respects to their more traditional instructional counterparts: they allow students to participate in the creation of course materials, ease the grading of group writing projects with their ability to track who wrote what, and perhaps even contribute to the improvement of student writing. In our opinion, these benefits greatly outweigh the modest learning curve and slight risk of technical difficulties, student abuse, or vandalism associated with the use of wikis whose editing is limited to the members of a single class or institution.

Learning Management Systems & Potential Substitutes

Instructors who decide to use online teaching tools like tutorials, blogs, and wikis will probably want a platform for tying them all together. A traditional course Web site could provide such a platform, but many instructors turn to learning management systems (LMSs)[82] to fulfill this and other important functions.[83] Examples of LMSs include Blackboard[84] (available as a full-featured stand-alone service or in a slimmed-down version on Lexis for Law Schools called "Web Courses"), Westlaw's The West Education Network (TWEN),[85] and the free, open-source Moodle.[86] The numerous LMS software packages on the market each offer a slightly different suite of educational services, but some common features include discussion boards, chat, shared class calendars, quiz and test creation tools, grading tools, and digital assignment drop boxes.[87]

LMSs have several strengths as course platforms. For example, most students coming into law school will already have experience using an LMS. A recent Educause survey found that 82.3% of responding undergraduates had used an LMS during the term in which the survey was conducted, and 69.5% of surveyed students reported that their LMS experiences were positive.[88] Some LMSs, notably Blackboard and Moodle, now allow instructors to directly integrate student blogs[89] and wikis[90] with other LMS functions instead of just linking to them. Further, LMSs provide all of their services behind a password-protected login system, a useful feature for protecting student privacy.

On the other hand, traditional LMSs have been criticized for their "focus on presentation (written documents to read), complemented by basic 'discussion' input from students, [which is] based on traditional lecture, review, and test pedagogy."[91] By default, courses in most LMSs are organized according to content type, rather than topics, dates, or learning objectives. (One exception is Moodle, which orders content by topic or date, much like a regular syllabus.[92]) When a teacher first creates a course on TWEN, for example, that course includes default pages, such as "Calendar," "Syllabus," "Quizzes," and "Web Links." This default architecture may discourage instructors—especially those who are less technologically adept and therefore more likely to accept the defaults—from organizing materials in a more learner-centric manner.[93] These concerns have led some instructors to explore the possibility of using social networking sites (SNSs) and virtual worlds, perhaps in combination with wikis and blogs, as alternatives to out-of-the box LMSs.

Social Networking Sites

SNSs are

> Web-based services that allow individuals to (1) construct a public or semi-public profile within a bounded system, (2) articulate a list of other users with whom they share a connection, and (3) view and traverse their list of connections and those made by others within the system.[94]

Like LMSs, SNSs provide a variety of communication tools, including instant messaging, e-mail, file sharing (including both audio and video files), blogging, and threaded discussion forums.[95] Because they include visual and audio communication technologies, online social networks could be used to reach students with both visual and aural learning styles. To use an SNS as an LMS substitute, a teacher could set up a private group on the site (possible on the most popular SNS, Facebook),[96] or set up a private social network either on a hosted service, such as Ning,[97] or using open-source software, such as Elgg.[98]

SNSs have a few potential advantages over LMSs as platforms for online instruction. First, students are more likely to login to SNSs voluntarily. In fact, because so many students check their SNSs more often than they check their e-mail or LMSs, some instructors have begun to use SNSs to broadcast class announcements to students.[99] Further, SNSs allow users to establish online identities that include profile photos and varying levels of personal information and to interact informally with classmates and instructors. Using online social networks may therefore help compensate for the loss of face time and informal communication that often occurs in distance courses.[100] With their focus on user self-expression and communication, SNSs are designed to be more participatory than LMSs. Finally, they are free for users who are willing to view advertising.

SNSs appear to be similar to LMSs in the number of students who are already using them: An estimated eight-five percent of undergraduates in the United States regularly use the most popular SNS, Facebook.[101] National statistics on law student use of social networks are unavailable; however, a recent survey of Arizona State University law students showed that fifty-four percent used Facebook "a lot" or "some."[102]

Largely because they are designed to be platforms for social and commercial activity rather than instruction, SNSs also have some important pitfalls when used for instruction. For one thing, many instructors and some students will be annoyed by the aggressive advertising found on commercial SNSs. For example, when Ms. Burriesci logs into Facebook, she is usually bombarded with advertising for wrinkle creams and celebrity diets, a depressing reminder of her recent entry into middle age. Presumably this is because she provided Facebook with her gender and birth date upon registration.

Such "targeted" advertising is symptomatic of another unpleasant truth about commercial SNSs: they are inherently less private than traditional LMSs. Even if teachers opt for a secret group on Facebook or a private network on Ning, the service itself will have access to any information published to the network and may use this information for commercial purposes.[103] The fact that services like Facebook give users some control over who else can view posted personal information may only give those users a false sense of security.[104] The probability that students and teachers will reveal personal information about themselves through their course participation increases when the network used for instruction is one they are likely to use for social purposes as well.

Another possible drawback to using a commercially hosted social network for instruction is that students might see this as an academic invasion of their social space.[105] Many students use commercial social networks to comment on their professors or on activities that conflict with their studies (e.g., class cutting); for these students, awareness of a teacher's presence will certainly have a chilling effect.[106] If students welcome instructor participation in online social networks, student-teacher boundary issues may arise. For example, if a student and teacher are "friends" on Facebook, the student might feel more comfortable asking the teacher for academic favors like due-date extensions.[107]

Some of these problems could be alleviated by creating one's own social network using open-source software (such as the previously mentioned Elgg) on an educational institution's secure server. In particular, students would feel less threatened by the presence of their teacher in a single-purpose academic social network, student-teacher boundaries would be easier to maintain, and the privacy of all participants could be more carefully guarded. Unfortunately, one of the major advantages of using commercial SNSs for instruction would be lost in this single-mindedly academic environment; students would have no motive other than class requirements to login. Nevertheless, it is our opinion that privacy issues and instructor-student boundary concerns will usually outweigh the benefits of using commercial SNSs to host required course-related information and activities. At the absolute minimum level of precaution, hosted commercial social networks should definitely not be used to distribute student grades.

Second Life/Virtual Worlds

Like SNSs, virtual worlds such as Second Life[108] are also being explored for their course-hosting potential. Rob Hudson, a librarian at Nova Southeastern University Law School, has held supplemental meetings of his international legal research skills class in Second Life,[109] while teachers of other subjects (including a Harvard Law School extension course) have used it as the primary meeting place for classes held entirely online.[110]

Virtual worlds have numerous attractive features for teachers. Even more than SNSs, worlds like Second Life allow their users to create online personas that may help make up for the lack of face-to-face contact inherent in distance education.[111] These personas are in fact user-designed 3-dimensional (3D) virtual representations with their own names and interact with an equally rich 3D environment. Avatars as well as the overall environment should appeal to visual learners, while the availability of audio chat[112] and other sounds[113] make virtual worlds an option for working with aural learners as well. According to Hudson, another benefit is that "[t]he typical reticence of... law students to speak or otherwise participate diminishe[s] considerably" in a virtual world.[114] In addition, it may be possible to recruit in-world guest speakers from distant locations, or to take virtual "field trips" to in-world libraries and law offices.[115]

Unfortunately, commercial virtual worlds also pose significant difficulties as instructional platforms. These difficulties include high system requirements, frequent service outages,[116] and a steep learning curve.[117] As in commercial social networks, privacy may also be an issue.[118] Another problem is the potential for harassment or even "assault" of students by other virtual world residents.[119] For example, a 2006 CNET interview with a virtual real estate magnate in Second Life was interrupted by an attack of flying animated penises.[120] In a more serious incident, one man was arrested by Japanese authorities for "mugging" other players in the massively multiplayer online game "Lineage II": he used software to beat up their avatars, take their virtual property, and sell it for real money.[121] One commentator has even argued that requiring students to participate in potentially dangerous virtual worlds could be a basis for institutional or instructor legal liability.[122] A less troublesome approach to using virtual worlds for instruction might be that taken in Nova Southeastern Law School's international legal research class: augment a course that meets offline or on a more traditional distance education platform with optional activities to be completed in Second Life.[123] Another alternative is to protect class participants by purchasing a private region in Second Life and limit access to class members. Unfortunately, Second Life's private regions currently cost $700 for an initial purchase by an educational user, plus $147.50 per month to maintain.[124] The private region option will therefore be out of reach for most teachers who lack institutional support for their instructional use of Second Life.

Summing Up

In this part of the article we have considered some potential pedagogical applications of interactive online technologies, such as tutorials, wikis, and SNSs, and have also examined some of their benefits and drawbacks. All of the applications we have examined could be useful supplements to face-to-face instruction in a hybrid legal research course, and some, especially tutorials, might provide useful substitutes for informal in-person instruction such as brief guest lectures.

SPECIAL CONSIDERATIONS IN FOR-CREDIT ONLINE COURSES IN LEGAL RESEARCH

The next part of the article, after briefly describing the current environment for distance learning in legal education, will address the factors to be considered when delivering a graded legal research course solely or primarily through an online or distance format.[125] These factors include course design and choice of instructional methods; assessment and grading of student performance; and evaluation of the effectiveness of distance courses. This section will also suggest strategies for hybrid courses that combine online techniques with face-to-face instruction.

Status of Distance Learning in Higher Education

The concept of delivering online courses is hardly new.[126] In fact, distance learning has been around more than long enough for some commentators to lament its failure to fulfill its initial promise of revolutionizing pedagogy at all levels, from secondary to higher education and into the spheres of postgraduate and continuing education.[127] Despite some notable lapsed initiatives,[128] distance learning undeniably is becoming more commonplace in higher education, which nevertheless trails behind corporate and professional environments in adopting it.[129]

Although currently most students in distance courses are undergraduates,[130] professional accreditation of e-learning programs is beginning to alter the landscape of postgraduate education. Online masters' programs in education, nursing, library science, and public health have made strides in meeting professional accreditation standards.[131] M.B.A. programs also show movement toward acceptance, with programs such as the Global Executive M.B.A. Program at Duke's Fuqua School of Business.[132] Further, fulfillment of continuing education requirements via distance formats has achieved wide acceptance in many professions, including law.[133]

The Millennial generation of students may have come to expect, if not demand, the opportunity to complete some of the necessary credits for various degrees without having to sit in a classroom.[134] Further, it has been frequently opined that Millennials regard education and information in ways that require the integration of new instructional techniques into traditional methods of formal classroom teaching.[135]

Status of Distance Learning in Legal Education: ABA Standards and Beyond

Despite the generally harsh criticism by legal educators and others of all-online law school programs,[136] the American Bar Association (ABA) law school accreditation standards have, over the past decade, moved toward receptivity to distance learning. From its 1997 "Temporary Guidelines for Distance Education" to its current Standard 306 and its interpretations,[137] the ABA has opened the door to law schools' experimentation with distance courses.

ABA Standard 306 currently limits distance education in several ways. Law students may not enroll in distance education courses until they earn twenty-eight credits toward the J.D. degree;[138] students may take a maximum of four credit hours of distance education per term;[139] and a law school may grant a maximum of twelve credit hours of distance courses toward the J.D. degree.[140] However, courses in which two-thirds or more of the course consists of regular classroom instruction are not considered "distance education" for purposes of the standard.[141] This clearly invites the development of "hybrid" courses in which some components are online. The standard also requires curriculum committee approval of course content, method of delivery, and method of evaluating student performance.[142] Law schools must report each year on the distance education courses that they offer;[143] further, "distance education ... requires particular attention from the law school and by the Accreditation Committee for maintenance of educational quality."[144]

Most significantly for those contemplating or planning a distance course offering, the interpretations accompanying Standard 306 stress the importance of providing the technological capacity and staffing to provide necessary support to faculty and students and of providing the technological competence of the faculty providing the courses.[145] The standard also requires "ample interaction with instructor and other students both inside and outside the formal structure of the course throughout its duration;"[146] and "ample mentoring of student effort and accomplishments as the course progresses."[147] Amplifying this standard, the interpretations provide that: "Law schools shall take steps to provide students in distance education courses opportunities to interact with instructors that equal or exceed the opportunities for such interaction with instructors in a traditional classroom setting."[148]

Notwithstanding these parameters for experimentation (or perhaps because of them), distance education is still a relatively untested phenomenon among law schools. Some observers, however, citing the time and cost demands of obtaining a law degree, especially in light of rising student loan debt and a fluctuating job market, predict that legal education will be subject to increasing pressures to relax restrictions on distance learning.[149] Also, the Millennial generation of law students has heightened expectations that their expensive legal education will keep pace with instructional technology as well as prepare them for the technologies they will encounter in law practice.[150]

Further, some have argued that cracks are beginning to appear in the "anti-online education bias of the ABA's accreditation standards," referring to recent changes to ABA Standard 802 suggesting that "experimental programs" may qualify for a waiver of some accreditation requirements under appropriate circumstances.[151] In addition, law professors are showing more willingness to experiment with distance and hybrid course offerings.[152]

Learning Technologies and Legal Research Instruction

If Millennial student attitudes toward education and information suggest the need for adaptation of traditional law school instructional techniques,[153] integration of online methods may be even more important to effective legal research instruction than to other types of law school courses. Teaching research to Millennials presents particular challenges. Joan Catherine Bohl describes Millennials' attitudes toward information in a way that should strike a chord with librarians and legal research instructors:

> Since Internet information appears on one's computer screen with little investment of time or effort, Gen X/Y students have developed a predominantly passive relationship to information and an expectation of instant gratification.
>
> . . .
>
> [They] perceive information as only a few keystrokes away, or at least as available to them as it is to the figure in the front of the classroom.[154]

Bohl also theorizes that the characteristics of adult learners, including needs for voluntariness, respect, collaboration, activity, and evaluation, "mirror many of the generation characteristics associated with Gen XY."[155] The most crucial common element in these factors is the evolution from instructor-centered to student-centered strategies in course design and execution. Although active learning can also be a part of classroom-based instruction, the increased use of instructional technology offers an excellent opportunity to further incorporate active learning into legal research instruction, as well as being appropriate for today's largely digital universe of legal research.

Legal research instruction and online learning methods appear to be a good fit. It is likely that hands-on, problem-based legal research instruction has increasingly eclipsed more bibliographic presentations of legal research materials in many law school research courses. Thus, many legal research courses probably already reflect the adult learning values of student-centered rather than professor-centered pedagogy, with the instructor as facilitator and the student as active participant in learning.[156]

As frequent "early adopters" of new technologies, librarians who teach legal research already may be more inclined than their law faculty counterparts to utilize instructional technology extensively, from LMSs to CALI lessons, blogs, wikis, and beyond. This does not mean, however, that it is a logical or necessarily an effective next step to eliminate the classroom element and convert an existing legal research course to a distance format by merely placing all the course materials online.[157] Nor is it a satisfactory approach to allow the available technology to dictate the learning goals or content of a course. Keeping in mind the need to avoid what has been called the "evaluation bypass,"[158] an enthusiasm for incorporating a new technology should not take the place of a critical evaluation of what the students actually gain from the incorporation of that technology into a legal research—or any other—course. An all-online or even a hybrid course entails many decisions, both in initial course design and in execution, which greatly influence the outcome of the course, regardless of the criteria employed to assess its success or failure.

Considerations in Developing Online Courses in Legal Research

Type of Course

The best candidate for an all-distance offering is probably an Advanced Legal Research (ALR) course, whether general in scope or subject specialized. Many of the decisions involved in designing such a course will be influenced by whether ALR is a required or an elective offering at a particular law school. ABA standards currently preclude a purely online offering for introductory legal research in the first year of law school,[159] although a hybrid model, with one-third or less of the course delivered via distance techniques, could be fashioned under the current standards. First-year law students may be both less receptive to the distance format and less capable of the self-motivation that a distance research course demands; further, it is highly desirable that first-year students have an opportunity to identify the librarians involved in research instruction as information resources. However, a library-developed online introductory legal research course could serve as a useful supplement to any first-year writing and reasoning course, and could offer more thorough research instruction than currently exists in some programs.

Student Enrollment

In designing a distance course, it is important to resist the assumption that a larger number of students can be easily accommodated than in a classroom offering. Ellen Podgor of Stetson University College of Law, who has taught numerous substantive law courses as distance offerings, has estimated that the optimal number of students in a substantive law course taught via distance is twelve to seventeen students, and that no more than twenty-two can be successfully accommodated in any event.[160] Perhaps contrary to preconceptions, the instructor time needed to effectively develop and prepare and to ensure adequate communication with and feedback to students participating in a distance course makes large class sizes unworkable.[161] Team teaching can help with this, but this approach carries its own time demands for planning and coordination. By requiring that opportunities for instructor-student interaction in distance courses "equal or exceed" those available in a traditional classroom course, the ABA Standards appropriately discourage attempts to accommodate very large numbers of students in an online course.[162]

Physical Location of Students and Access to a Law Library

Research instructors must decide whether students must be physically present at the law school or whether they can complete the course from a remote location, such as while participating in a study abroad program or an off-site internship/externship. Even if students are not required to be physically present on site, the research instructor must decide whether they need access to a law library and to the print materials, if any, for which hands-on use will be required during the course. It must also be emphasized to students enrolling in the course that accessible and reliable Internet access is indispensible; this is not generally an issue if students are physically present locally or on campus, but it may be problematic if they are at a remote location, domestic or foreign.

Staffing and Technical Support

A critical decision is the staffing of the course. As already noted, planning time as well as training on and mastery of new instructional technologies can greatly increase the lead time necessary to develop a distance course.[163] Obviously, the involvement and time commitment of members of the information technology staff for training and technical support is essential, during both the planning and execution stages of the course. Backup plans to compensate for the seemingly inevitable technical problems should be established ahead of time and announced to students as part of the course orientation. Also, as discussed later in this article, a distance course requires much greater instructor availability and time to establish and maintain the required online "social presence" that is so essential to success.[164] Ellen Podgor has estimated that teaching a law school distance course requires three times more instructor time than teaching a classroom course;[165] others agree that the time demands on instructors may far exceed those in a traditional classroom course.[166] This must be factored into curriculum planning, teaching loads, and other staffing needs.

Course Platform

Another threshold decision is the course platform. If the institution already utilizes an LMS, such as Blackboard or TWEN, research instructors should consider making it their course platform, since the students may already be familiar with and accustomed to using it. Alternative choices are discussed above under the heading *Evaluating Selected Technologies for Providing Legal Research Instruction Online*.[167] The required learning curves of both instructors and students should factor into this decision.

Synchronous or Asynchronous Methods

A fundamental decision is whether the course will encompass only asynchronous methods, in which students complete all of the course materials on a self-paced basis, or will incorporate some synchronous methods such as

Web casting or virtual classroom sessions via Blackboard, among others. The trade off is that while synchronous methods may provide more immediacy and sense of connection to the instructor and classmates, they also reduce the flexibility that students value so highly. Further, converting a course from traditional to distance format may require rethinking and reorganization of the content. A distance course should aim beyond simply replicating what transpires in the live classroom.[168] Anyone who has sat through a typical videotaped class session realizes that a great deal is lost in translation; further, simply converting standard fifty-minute lectures or PowerPoints into asynchronous formats tend to result in presentations that are too long and too difficult to follow and which fail to meet the adult learning objective of active engagement on the part of the students.

In a completely asynchronous course, a variety of modalities should be employed to meet different learning styles, as well as to avoid boredom and disconnection on the part of the students taking the class. A combination of readings, tutorials such as CALI lessons or "home-grown" lessons, Flash presentations including visual and recorded audio developed with Captivate[169] or Camtasia,[170] and hands-on exercises with grading or feedback can provide variety. Also, even in a fully asynchronous course, there should still be pacing with due dates for the various modalities in order to provide structure. Either an all-distance or a hybrid course permits incorporation of a "cluster of instructional methods," allowing students with different learning styles to tailor the course to best meet their own needs.[171] Because voluntariness and active engagement is so important to adult/Millennial learners, providing students the opportunity to choose between various classroom or electronic methods to satisfy the requirements of a research course can be a satisfying experience for all involved.[172]

Instructor-Student Interaction/Communication

A major consideration in designing an online course is how to compensate for the loss of "face time" inherent in a classroom course. The loss of informal communication with individual students before and after class, as well as classroom interaction, can detract greatly from the experience of both teaching and taking a course; alternate means of contact via establishing a "social presence" must be adopted.[173] "Social presence" refers to the sense of being "connected or engaged" with the other persons involved in the course, a factor which is essential to adult/Millennial learners.[174] It is particularly important that the instructor of an online course maintain an active connection to students in the course. Ellen Podgor recommends that the instructor in a distance course contact each student individually at least once a week.[175] Prompt instructor responses to their e-mails are highly important to students; a distance course can create a student expectation of 24/7 access to the instructor.[176] Virtual office hours via the LMS, which can be held privately with individuals or with groups of students, are also useful and fun. If used, these should be scheduled at various times of the day and evening to encourage students to participate on their own schedules. A blog or discussion board can also be used to post comments, questions, and responses from the research instructor and/or from students in the course. Whatever methods are chosen, they must be realistic and capable of being assiduously followed through; the instructor's "social presence" may be the most essential element of student perceptions of the success of a distance course.[177]

Student-Student Interaction

Another issue is whether an online course should incorporate collaborative work or remain a mainly individual learning experience. Some educators theorize that collaboration enhances student learning and satisfaction in ways essential to a course in which classroom interaction is absent,[178] and that collaboration is a particularly important value for adult/Millennial learners.[179] Others question whether significant interaction occurs even when students are sitting in the same classroom,[180] although clearly this depends on the skill of the instructor in facilitating such interaction. Law student resistance to graded collaborative projects may create obstacles to adopting this approach. Quasi-collaborative efforts, such as wikis where students post individually graded work, even if on the same or related topics, may be more easily implemented and better received by law students. (See the discussions of wikis above under the heading *Evaluating Selected Technologies for Providing Legal Research Instruction Online*.) There is much room for experimentation here; successful collaborative law school courses have been described by Gerard F. Hess of Gonzaga University School of Law and Thomas D. Cobb of University of Washington School of Law.[181]

Another frequently used and simple technique to foster student-student interaction is the discussion board. While many students give low ratings to such boards and to the requirement of posting to them, several techniques can make their use more productive and enjoyable, including active involvement by the instructor, staggering the timing of the postings by each student, and requiring some postings to be responses to other students' postings rather than responses to the instructor's questions, among others.[182]

Methods of Assessment and Grading

A research instructor's choice of assignments and assessment tools in a distance course need not differ substantially from those used in a classroom course. Quizzes or exams, short-answer or open-ended research assignments, and course projects or pathfinders can be adapted for use in a distance format. However, since research instructors in an online course cannot rely on the informal communication that takes place in the classroom to ensure that students are "getting it," other methods may be required to make sure the materials provided are getting the message across. According to Bohl, a quality shared by adult learners and Millennials is the need for frequent give-and-take regarding the course material.[183] Students using asynchronous methods also need more frequent feedback, whether built into the course materials via self-evaluation tools, or through opportunities to communicate directly with the instructor. It may not be sufficient to rely on self-assessment tools, such as tutorials or CALI lessons (even with score reporting), to identify students who are struggling with the material or are not keeping up with assigned work.

Whatever the grading scheme chosen, periodic assessment and feedback seem preferable to one large exam, assignment, or project at the end of the course. Pathfinders, research guides, or other research process papers on topics of the students' own choosing, which are often used in ALR courses, require extra instructor effort to substitute for the informal discussion and paper conferences that occur more spontaneously during a classroom course. At the very least, a one-on-one telephone or "virtual" paper conference is probably a necessity if this type of assignment is used. It may be more desirable in an online course to use a take-home final assignment in which all students work on the same problem. One further consideration in grading is the concern that some have raised about authenticating student work (i.e., preventing cheating) in distance courses.[184] This may or may not be a major worry depending on the type of assignments given.

How to Evaluate Distance Legal Research Courses

Various factors should be considered in evaluating the success of a distance course, including comparison of student learning outcomes; student satisfaction with and perceived effectiveness of the course; and faculty satisfaction and institutional considerations.

Comparison of Learning Outcomes

As rather dryly observed by one researcher, "The rush to implement [Web-based instruction] preceded empirical evidence of its benefits."[185] However, many researchers have attempted to compare the learning outcomes of students in classroom and distance versions of the same courses.

Some studies have found no significant difference between the performance of students in online and classroom versions of the same course.[186] Other studies do suggest differences in student performance,[187] but it has also been suggested that many variables, such as the effects of self-selection into online classes, may make the results of these studies unreliable.[188] It seems safe to predict that there will be ongoing attempts to assess the effectiveness of distance learning;[189] however, the "no significant difference" theory seems to be gaining ground, with growing percentages of academic leaders expressing the belief that online is as good as or better than face-to-face learning.[190] In spite of the proliferation of studies on the topic, it is clear that "student outcomes are not easy to define in higher education, and even experienced researchers have characterized them as 'messy.'"[191] It has also been theorized that it should not even be attempted to compare the learning outcomes of higher education distance courses with classroom versions of the same course, but that distance courses should be evaluated by unique criteria:[192]

> Such comparisons ignore the many factors that influence learning and falsely attribute success (or failure) to the distance delivery medium. Instead of comparing groups on and off campus, student achievement analysis can go to the heart of the issue (and be more effective) by determining whether or not distance students learn what the course is designed to teach.[193]

To the extent that comparative evaluation of the success of an online course with its classroom counterpart depends upon defining and measuring objective learning outcomes, legal research courses may be particularly difficult to assess. If an exam featuring objective or short-answer responses is used, valid comparisons could be made; however, objective measurement of bibliographic knowledge has its limitations in assessing legal research competence. When the main evaluation tool in an ALR course consists of a pathfinder or other research process paper, often on topics of the students' own choosing, objective comparison of outcomes becomes more difficult. The experience in teaching distance versions of ALR courses at University of Maryland School of Law, using both research papers on student-chosen topics and assigned take-home problems as assessment tools, suggests that the range of student performance and grades differs little between an online and a classroom-based course. This area invites further investigation.

Student Satisfaction/Perceived Effectiveness

Recent research suggests that overall student satisfaction with distance courses is high.[194] In a study of undergraduate and graduate students, Walker and Kelly reported that, as might be expected, convenience and the ability to complete the course work at a time and place of one's choosing were among the most highly rated aspects of the courses they studied.[195] Also, among the factors most important to students' satisfaction with distance courses was the promptness of the instructor in responding to questions and providing feedback on student work and the ability to obtain rapid help with technical difficulties. Students were less satisfied with the aspects of the courses aimed at increasing student interaction, such as chat sessions, discussion boards, and peer-to-peer commenting, with undergraduates reacting somewhat more favorably towards these techniques than graduate students.[196] Another significant variable is the students' perception of the amount of work involved in a distance course; although some students believe that online courses are less work, "in actuality, online courses are equal or more challenging than traditional face-to-face courses because the primary responsibility for facilitating learning shifts to the student."[197]

Little information is currently available on student evaluation of distance courses in legal research. Standard law school course evaluations may not be helpful, as they focus more on the instructor than on the materials or the experience. Evaluations of distance courses should at least include student ratings of each type of learning medium presented in the course and might do well to also include open-ended questions or even interviews or debriefing sessions. The available information suggests that legal research distance offerings have been very popular where offered.[198]

Instructor Satisfaction/Institutional Goals

Another crucial element in evaluating a distance learning course is the quality of the experience for the research instructors.

A primary concern in developing distance education courses is the demand such courses make on instructor time. As noted, start-up and development time is significant, particularly in an initial iteration of the course. Instructors may be faced with the need to master new technologies as well as to rethink the usual techniques of presenting familiar content. Preparation must begin farther in advance than in a classroom course; some distance educators believe that an entire course should be available online before the course actually starts.[199] Even if this is not so, preparing tutorials or taped presentations requires extensive advanced planning as well as participation of other staff to record, edit, and publish these presentations, allowing for less flexibility for last-minute changes than a traditional classroom presentation.

Keeping in mind the emphasis placed upon ensuring ample opportunities for student feedback and interaction as required by ABA Interpretation 306–4,[200] research instructors may find it difficult to balance their other responsibilities for faculty and student support, service, and professional activities.[201] High student expectations of online presence and accessibility may be burdensome for some instructors who may also miss the predictability and control inherent in scheduled class sessions and office hours. Some may find troublesome the need to deal with, or refer to others, the inevitable student requests for technical support.[202]

Other more abstract factors may affect instructor satisfaction as well. Some instructors may have difficulty adjusting their role from that of the expert lecturer to that of facilitator (as it has sometimes been put, from being the "sage on the stage" to the "guide on the side").[203] Many may simply miss the classroom atmosphere and the face-to-face contact of a traditional course.

There are also many positive aspects of teaching an online course. Research instructors may need or appreciate the flexibility of not being tied to scheduled classroom sessions. They may also discover that students feel freer to express themselves one-on-one via discussion board or other virtual platform media compared to a classroom or traditional office hours setting, leading to fuller and more diverse participation; further, the online forum may lead to more insightful responses because students have more time to ponder and must commit their thoughts to writing.[204] Students accustomed to interacting virtually may not miss the face-to-face contact as much as the instructor does. Further, students may perceive research instructors who teach an online course as being more savvy and knowledgeable than the garden-variety classroom instructor, thus meeting the adult/Millennial learner's need for respect and collegiality.[205] Another plus for instructors is the stimulation of adopting and integrating new technologies, investigating new strategies that invigorate their teaching, and mastering the tools.[206]

CONCLUSION

Online techniques have great potential for accommodating the learning styles and preferences of Millennial law students, as well as for the effective teaching of legal research in the digital age. While integrating instructional technology into a face-to-face classroom legal research course is highly desirable and relatively easy, designing and teaching a pure distance or hybrid distance course provides some unique challenges as well as some distinct benefits for both instructors and students. It should be emphasized that these benefits cannot be fully realized without institutional support for the additional demands of developing and teaching these courses. Further, there are many issues upon which this article has not touched but which must be considered, such as the accommodation of students with disabilities in using online techniques and issues related to copyright. However, legal research instruction presents some opportunities for experimentation and innovation with online learning techniques that may serve students better, accommodate the librarian's technology skills and abilities and her time constraints, and inspire others at our law schools to follow suit.

NOTES

1. Joan Catherine Bohl, *Generations X and Y in Law School: Practical Strategies for Teaching the 'MTV/Google' Generation*, 54 Loy. L. Rev. (forthcoming 2009), accepted paper available at http://papers.ssrn.com/sol3/papers.cfm?abstract_id=1150925 (last accessed 25 Nov. 2008).

2. Robert F. Wislock, *What Are Perceptual Modalities and How Do They Contribute to Learning?* 59 New Directions for Adult & Continuing Educ. 5, 5–6 (1993) (citing W.B. James & M.W. Galbraith, *Perceptual Learning Styles: Implications and Techniques for the Practitioner*, 8 Lifelong Learning 20 (1985)).

3. Gerald F. Hess, *Listening to Our Students: Obstructing and Enhancing Learning in Law School*, 31 U.S.F. L. Rev. 941, 942–944 (1997).

4. Bohl, *supra* n. 1, at n. 13 and accompanying text. As Ms. Bohl points out, different authors—and sometimes the same author—give varying birth years as the boundaries of the Millennial generation. *See e.g.* Scott Carlson, *The Net Generation in the Classroom*, 52 Chron. Higher Educ. A34 (7 Oct. 2005) (1980–1994); Neil Howe & William Strauss, *Millennials Rising: The Next Great Generation* 4 (Vintage Books 2000) (starting point is 1982).

5. Bohl, *supra* n. 1, at text accompanying n. 24.

6. *Id.* at text accompanying nn. 26–30.

7. *Wink Homepage*, available at http://www.debugmode.com/wink/ (last accessed 29 Oct. 2008).

8. *Camtasia Studio and Screencasting*, available at http://www.techsmith.com/camtasia/screencast.asp (last accessed 29 Oct. 2008).

9. *Adobe Captivate 3: Screen Capture Software, Video Screen Capture Program*, available at http://www.adobe.com/products/captivate/ (last accessed 29 Oct. 2008).

10. Diane Murley, *Tools for Creating Video Tutorials*, 99 L. Lib. J. 857 (2007); Sara Kelley, *Creating Multimedia Research and Software Tutorials with Screencasting Software*, 51 L. Lib. Lights 17–18 (Fall 2007).

11. *See e.g.* the tutorials on the *CALI Lessons Subject List—Legal Research*, available at http://www2.cali.org/index.php?fuseaction=lessons.subjectlist&cat=LR (last accessed 6 Sept. 2008), or those on the Georgetown Law Library Web site, available at http://www.ll.georgetown.edu/tutorials/ (last saved 15 Aug. 2008).

12. *See e.g.* Robert C. Berring, Jr., *Berring's Legal Research Podcast*, available at http://www.berringlegalresearch.com/podcast.asp (last accessed 6 Sept. 2008) (audio-only tutorials); Westminster Law Library, *Case Finding Using Reporters and Digests*, available at http://law.du.edu/index.php/library/research/tutorials (last accessed 6 Sept. 2008) (audio-video tutorial).

13. Elizabeth G. Adelman, *CALI Lessons in Legal Research Courses: Alternatives to Reading about Research*, 15 Persps. Teaching Leg. Research & Writing 25 (Fall 2006).

14. Paul L. Hrycaj, *Elements of Active Learning in the Online Tutorials of ARL Members*, 33 Ref. Servs. Rev. 210, 211 (2005).

15. Adelman, *supra* n. 13.

16. Lexis tutorials are available at http://www.lexisnexis.com/lawschool/content.aspx?articleid=121&topicid=30 (last accessed 11 Nov. 2008); Westlaw tutorials are available at http://lawschool.westlaw.com/shared/marketinfodisplay.asp?code=WT&id=1 (last accessed 11 Nov. 2008).

17. An informal survey conducted by Ms. Burriesci in preparation for this article revealed that 44.2% of the 249 respondents who completed the survey had employed legal research tutorials offered by the Center for CALI in their legal research teaching. Also, 18.5% of respondents had used non-CALI tutorials. In contrast, only 4.8% of respondents reported using wikis and 10.8% reported using blogs. The survey questions, along with summaries of responses, are available at http://www.ll.georgetown.edu/staff/ers/surveysummary.xls (last accessed 1 Dec. 2008).

18. Adelman, *supra* n. 13, at 29.

19. Wislock, citing James & Galbraith, *supra* n. 2.

20. Adelman, *supra* n. 13, at 28; Melissa Muth & Susan Taylor, *Comparing Online Tutorials with Face-to-Face Instruction: A Study at Ball State University*, in *First Impressions, Lasting Impact: Introducing the First-Year Student to the Academic Library* 113, 116 (Julia K. Nims & Ann Andrew eds., Pierian 2002).

21. Muth & Taylor, *supra* n. 20.

22. Marion Churkovich & Christine Oughtred, *Can an Online Tutorial Pass the Test for Library Instruction? An Evaluation and Comparison of Library Skills Instruction Methods for First-Year Students at Deakin University*, 33 Australian & Academic Research Lib. 25 (2002).

23. *CALI Help FAQ—ScoreSave*, available at http://www2.cali.org/index.php?fuseaction=help.faq&topicid=0000000001 (last accessed 6 Sept. 2008). Non-CALI tutorials can be configured to report student scores to a course management system (CMS) if both the tutorial and the CMS are SCORM compliant. *Advanced Distributed Learning—SCORM*, available at http://www.adlnet.gov/Technologies/scorm/default.aspx (rev. 2 Sept. 2008).

24. Muth & Taylor, *supra* n. 20.

25. Churkovich & Oughtred, *supra* n. 22, at 33–34.

26. Elizabeth Blakesley Lindsay et al., *If You Build It, Will They Learn? Assessing Online Information Literacy Tutorials*, 67 College & Research Lib. 429, 431 (2006).

27. Other studies include Carol Anne Germain & Trudi E. Jacobson, *A Comparison of the Effectiveness of Presentation Formats for Instruction: Teaching First-Year Students*, 61 College & Research Lib. 65 (2000); and Lucy Holman, *A Comparison of Computer-Assisted Instruction and Classroom Bibliographic Instruction*, 40 Ref. & User Servs. Q. 53 (2000). Neither of these studies found any significant difference in learning outcomes between students who received live instruction and those who received online tutorial instruction.

28. Muth & Taylor, *supra* n. 20.

29. *Id*. at 114–115.

30. *Id*. at 115.

31. Churkovich & Oughtred, *supra* n. 22, at 28–29.

32. *Id*. at 29–30.

33. Penny M. Beile & David N. Boote, *Does the Medium Matter?: A Comparison of a Web-Based Tutorial with Face-to-Face Library Instruction on Education Students' Self-Efficacy Levels and Learning Outcomes*, 20 Research Strategies 57, 59–60 (2005).

34. *Id*. at 64.

35. *Id*. at 66–67.

36. Interview by Sara Kelley Burriesci with Todd Venie, Ref. Libr., Georgetown U. L. Lib. in D.C. (31 Oct. 2008).

37. Michael Stephens, *Web 2.0 & Libraries*, 42 Lib. Tech. Rep. 16 (July-Aug. 2006).

38. *Id*.

39. Diane Murley, *Innovative Instructional Methods*, 26(1/2) Leg. Ref. Servs. Q. 171, 180 (2007).

40. Priscilla Coulter & Lani Draper, *Blogging It into Them: Weblogs in Information Literacy Instruction*, 45(1/2) J. Lib. Admin. 101 (2006).

41. *See e.g.* Hazel Hall & Brian Davison, *Social Software as Support in Hybrid Learning Environments: The Value of the Blog as a Tool for Reflective Learning and Peer Support*, 29 Lib. & Info. Sci. Research 163 (2007).

42. *Id*.

43. *Blogs*, in *Web 2.0: New Tools for Doing and Teaching Legal Research Wiki*, available at http://library.kentlaw.edu/dginsberg/pmwiki/pmwiki.php?n=Main.Blogs (modified 10 Aug. 2007).

44. Murley, *supra* n. 39, at 176; Wislock, citing James & Galbraith, *supra* n. 2.

45. Sol Lederman, *How Kinesthetic Folks Learn Math*, Articles for Educators, available at http://www.articlesforeducators.com/dir/mathematics/kinesthetic_folks.asp (last accessed 14 Nov. 2008).

46. *See e.g. Blogger*, available at http://www.blogger.com/ (last accessed 6 Sept. 2008); *WordPress*, available at http://www.wordpress.com/ (last accessed 6 Sept. 2008); *LiveJournal*, available at http://www.livejournal.com/ (last accessed 6 Sept. 2008). Unfortunately, most of these services display advertising on hosted blogs unless the blogger pays a fee to remove them. *See e.g.* WordPress.com, *Premium Features*, available at http://wordpress.com/products/ (last accessed 11 Nov. 2008) ("[I]f you'd prefer your readers didn't see ads, you can nix them altogether for $30/year.").

47. Stephens, *supra* n. 37.

48. Hall & Davison, *supra* n. 41.

49. *See* discussion of wikis accompanying n. 60, *infra*.

50. Coulter & Draper, *supra* n. 40, at 103–104.

51. *Id*. at 104.

52. *Id*. at 104–105.

53. *Id*. at 106.

54. Hall & Davison, *supra* n. 41, at 174.

55. *Id*. at 176.

56. *Id*. at 177.

57. Laurie Ralston, Presentation, *Technology Use, Practices, and Desires of Students: What Do They Really Want?* (Balt., Md., 20 June 2008) (PowerPoint slides available at http://wiki.cali.org/calicon08/index.php?n=Sessions.443).

58. Connie Crosby, *The Tao of Law Librarianship: Becoming a Wiki Warrior*, LLRX.com, available at http://www.llrx.com/columns/tao10.htm (15 Jan. 2007).

59. Sally A. Irvin & Jason R. Sowards, *ALR 2.0: When Advanced Legal Research Met a Wiki*, 12 AALL Spectrum 8 (June 2008). Wake Forest's ALR Wiki is available at http://wiki.law.wfu.edu/advancedlegalresearch/index.php/Main_Page (last modified 10 July 2008).

60. Melissa E. O'Neill, *Automated Use of a Wiki for Collaborative Lecture Notes*, 37 ACM SIGCSE Bull. 267 (2005).

61. *E.g.*, Tom Cobb, *Public Interest Research, Collaboration, and the Promise of Wikis*, 16 Persps. Teaching Leg. Research & Writing 1, 7 (Fall 2007); Bo Leuf & Ward Cunningham, *The Wiki Way: Quick Collaboration on the Web* (Addison–Wesley 2001); Crosby, *supra* n. 58; Ashley Jones, *A Case of Collaboration Made Simple*, 31 EContent 44 (Jan./Feb. 2008).

62. Crosby, *supra* n. 58.

63. *E.g.*, Chris Hayes, *Enter the Wiki World*, LLRX.com, available at http://www.llrx.com/features/wiki.htm (25 July 2004).

64. Cobb, *supra* n. 61, at 7.

65. O'Neill, *supra* n. 60, at 268.

66. Irvin & Sowards, *supra* n. 59, at 8.

67. Doug Cornelius, *Wikis at the Rosen Law Firm*, KM Space, available at http://kmspace.blogspot.com/2008/02/wikis-at-rosen-law-firm.html (28 Feb. 2008).

68. Chris Dede, *Planning for NeoMillennial Learning Styles*, 28(1) Educause Q. 7, 8 (2005).

69. Hess, *supra* n. 3.

70. Irvin & Sowards, *supra* n. 59, at 9.

71. *The Editor*, PBWiki Manual, available at http://pbwikimanual.pbwiki.com/The±Editor (last accessed 28 Aug. 2008).

72. For example, *Wetpaint*, available at http://www.wetpaint.com/, places Google AdSense advertising on user wikis. Wetpaint Central Help and Support, *Discussion: Advertising*, available at http://www.wetpaintcentral.com/thread/947869/advertising (last post dated 24 Oct. 2007).

73. Wikipedia's efforts to cope with vandalism are discussed in Lauren Barack, *A Wiki War on Vandals*, 52 Sch. Lib. J. 24 (May 2006).

74. Heather Havenstein, *Companies May Face Lawsuits If Employees Abuse Web 2.0 Tools*, 41 ComputerWorld 36 (19 Feb. 2007).

75. Irvin & Sowards, *supra* n. 59, at 19.

76. *Id.*

77. *Id.* at 8.

78. *Id.* at 19.

79. *Id.* at 9.

80. *Id.* at 19.

81. *Id.*

82. LMSs are perhaps more commonly referred to as course management systems (CMSs). We have opted for the LMS moniker to avoid confusion with a broader type of software product called a content management system (also abbreviated CMS), which can be used to manage any variety of Web site.

83. Seventy-three percent of respondents to Ms. Burriesci's informal survey, *supra* n. 17, reported using an LMS in their legal research teaching.

84. *Blackboard ≫ Educate. Innovate. Everywhere*, available at http://www.blackboard.com/ (last accessed 14 Nov. 2008).

85. *TWEN*, available at http://lawschool.westlaw.com/twen/ (last accessed 14 Nov. 2008).

86. *Moodle—A Free, Open Source Course Management System for Online Learning*, available at http://moodle.org/ (last accessed 14 Nov. 2008).

87. Susan Gibbons, *Library Course-Management Systems: An Overview*, 41 Lib. Tech. Rep. 7 (May-June 2005).

88. Gail Salaway et al., *The ECAR Study of Undergraduate Students and Information Technology* 57 (Educause 2008).

89. *Application Pack 1 for the Blackboard Learning System—Vista Enterprise and CE Enterprise Licenses Features New Capabilities to Support Active Learning*, Blackboard Media Center, available at http://www.blackboard.com/company/press/release.aspx?id=880647 (11 July 2006); *Blogs FAQ*, MoodleDocs, available at http://docs.moodle.org/en/Blogs_FAQ (modified 12 Sept. 2008).

90. *Wiki Module FAQ*, MoodleDocs, available at http://docs.moodle.org/en/Wiki_module_FAQ (modified 30 July 2008). Blackboard still lacks a native wiki function; however, a separate company,

Learning Objects, Inc., sells its own wiki module, Teams LX, that can be integrated with Blackboard. *Learning Objects, Inc.: Teams LX*, available at http://www.learningobjects.com/teams.jsp (last accessed 14 Nov. 2008).

91. Lisa M. Lane, *Toolbox or Trap? Course Management Systems and Pedagogy*, 31(2) Educause Q. 4, 5 (2008).

92. *Id*. at 6.

93. *Id*. at 5.

94. Danah M. Boyd & Nicole B. Ellison, *Social Network Sites: Definition, History, and Scholarship*, 13(1) J. Computer-Mediated Commun. 11 (2007), available at http://jcmc.indiana.edu/vol13/issue1/boyd.ellison.html.

95. Michael Stephens, *Web 2.0 & Libraries, Part 2: Trends and Technologies*, 43 Lib. Tech. Rep. 45 (Sept.-Oct. 2007).

96. *Facebook Help Topic "Groups,"* available at http://www.new.facebook.com/help.php?page=414 (last accessed 6 Sept. 2008). Facebook users can only join "secret" groups by invitation.

97. *Ning Help Topic "Can I Create a Private Group?"* available at http://help.ning.com/ (last accessed 6 Sept. 2008). Ning users must be invited to join a private network.

98. *See Elgg.org*, available at http://www.elgg.org/ (last accessed 13 Nov. 2008).

99. Salaway et al., *supra* n. 88, at 27.

100. Brandi Scollins-Mantha, *Cultivating Social Presence in the Online Learning Classroom: A Literature Review with Recommendations for Practice*, 5 Intl. J. Instructional Tech. & Distance Learning 23 (Mar. 2008).

101. Jennifer L. Behrens, *About Facebook*, 12 AALL Spectrum 14, 15 (Apr. 2008).

102. Ralston, *supra* n. 57.

103. Educause Learning Initiative, *7 Things You Should Know about ... Facebook II*, available at http://net.educause.edu/ir/library/pdf/ELI7025.pdf (May 2007).

104. *Id*.

105. Educause Learning Initiative, *7 Things You Should Know about ... Ning*, available at http://net.educause.edu/ir/library/pdf/ELI7036.pdf (Apr. 2008).

106. Sara Lipka, *For Professors, Friending Can Be Fraught*, 54 Chron. Higher Educ. A1 (7 Dec. 2007).

107. *Id*.

108. *Second Life*, available at http://secondlife.com/ (last accessed 6 Sept. 2008), is only one of many virtual worlds available through the Internet. The Web site, *Virtual Worlds Review*, available at http://www.virtualworldsreview.com (last site update 20 Feb. 2006) lists and reviews twenty-eight different virtual worlds, many of which offer free access.

109. Rob Hudson, *A Little Grafting of Second Life into a Legal Research Class*, LLRX.com, available at http://www.llrx.com/features/secondlife.htm (9 May 2008).

110. For examples of courses taught entirely in Second Life, see Meg Kribble, *A Law Librarian's Second Life*, 12 AALL Spectrum 12 (Nov. 2007); Lucia Graves, *A Second Life For Higher Ed*, 144 U.S. News & World Rep. 49 (21 Jan. 2008); and Andrea L. Foster, *Professor Avatar*, 54 Chron. Higher Educ. A24 (21 Sept. 2007).

111. Kribble, *supra* n. 110, at 14 ("Second Life's sense of presence can also enhance distance education, which often fails to create a real sense of connection among instructors and students.")

112. *Question 39: How to Use Voice, Second Life for Beginners*, https://support.secondlife.com/ics/support/default.asp?deptID=4417 (last accessed 26 June 2009).

113. *Question 12: How Do I Upload Images or Sounds, Inventory Management*, https://support.secondlife.com/ics/support/default.asp?deptID=4417 (last accessed 26 June 2009).

114. Hudson, *supra* n. 109.

115. *Id*.

116. Foster, *supra* n. 110; Hudson, *supra* n. 109.

117. Hudson, *supra* n. 109.

118. *See* Shawn Zeller, *Intelligence Agency Watches Online Gamers*, 66 CQ Wkly. 591 (2008).

119. Michael J. Bugeja, *Second Thoughts about Second Life*, 54 Chron. Higher Educ. C2 (14 Sept. 2007).

120. Daniel Terdiman, *Virtual Magnate Shares Secrets of Success*, CNET News, available at http://news.cnet.com/Virtual-land-magnate-shares-secrets-of-her-success/2008–1043_3–6144967.html (20 Dec. 2006).

121. Alan Sipress, *Does Virtual Reality Need a Sheriff? Reach of Law Enforcement Is Tested When Online Fantasy Games Turn Sordid*, Wash. Post A1 (2 June 2007).

122. Bugeja, *supra* n. 119.

123. Hudson, *supra* n. 109.

124. *Private Region Pricing*, Second Life, http://secondlife.com/land/privatepricing.php (last accessed 1 Dec. 2008).

125. The terms "distance" and "online" are used interchangeably in this part of the paper, since in the law school context, students taking an online course are apt to be also taking classroom courses, and thus are not truly "distance" students.

126. Jon Baggaley, *Where Did Distance Education Go Wrong?* 29 Distance Educ. 39, 42 (May 2008). Baggaley also presents an interesting discussion of how the Internet dominates distance education offerings in the United States and Western Europe, while other technologies, such as satellite broadcasting media, are more common in Japan and China.

127. Robert Zemsky & William F. Massy, *Thwarted Innovation: What Happened to e-learning and Why* 3–5 (Learning Alliance 2004), available at http://www.thelearningalliance.info/Docs/Jun2004/ThwartedInnovation.pdf; Farhad Saba, *Critical Issues in Distance Education: A Report from the United States*, 26 Distance Educ. 255, 258–259 (Aug. 2005).

128. Saba, *supra* n. 127, at 259 (discussing the collapse of Fathom.com, an online for-profit university); *The Promise and the Reality of Distance Education*, 8(3) NEA Higher Educ. Research Center Update 1 (Oct. 2002), available at http://www2.nea.org/he/heupdate/images/vol8no3.pdf.

129. Nearly 3.2 million students were taking at least one online course during the fall 2005 term, representing more than 800,000 more students than in the previous year, for an increase of more than twice that of any previous year. Further, more than ninety-six percent of the largest institutions have some online offerings. I. Elaine Allan & Jeff Seaman, *Making the Grade: Online Education in the United States 2006* 1–2 (Sloan-C, 2006), available at http://www.sloan-c.org/publications/survey/pdf/making_the_grade.pdf.

130. *Id.* at 5.

131. Stephen R. Ruth, *E-Learning at a Crossroads: What Price Quality?* 30(2) Educause Q. 34–35 (2007).

132. *Global Executive MBA Program at Duke's Fuqua School of Business*, available at http://www.fuqua.duke.edu/mba/executive/global/ (last accessed 27 Oct. 2008).

133. Many states now allow all or part of their required Continuing Legal Education credits to be obtained through online courses. *See DigiLearn Online CLE*, available at http://www.digilearnonline.com/stateReqs.asp (last accessed 24 Nov. 2008). *See also California Bar Association Sanctions Legal Training in the Virtual World*, Chron. Higher Educ.: The Wired Campus, available at http://chronicle.com/wiredcampus/article/3175/california-bar-association-sanctions-legal-training-in-virtual-world?utm_source=at&utm_medium=en (18 July 2008).

134. Sam Dillon, *As Costs of Commuting Soar, Students Flood Online Classes*, N.Y. Times A1, A13 (11 July 2008).

135. Bohl, *supra* n. 1, at text accompanying nn. 48–54; Hess, *supra* n. 3, at 947–963.

136. Daniel C. Powell, *Five Recommendations to Law Schools Offering Legal Instruction Over the Internet*, 11 J. Tech. L. & Policy 285–286 (2006) (discussing Supreme Court Justice Ruth Bader Ginsburg's comments about Concord University School of Law's Internet law degree program and the controversy surrounding Harvard Law School Professor Arthur Miller's videotaping of lectures for Concord's students).

137. 2008–2009 *ABA Standards for Approval of Law Schools*, available at http://www.abanet.org/legaled/standards/20082009StandardsWebContent/Chapter%203.pdf (last accessed 1 Dec. 2008).

138. *Id.* Standard 306(e).

139. *Id.* Standard 306(d).

140. *Id.*

141. *Id.* Interpretation 306-3.

142. *Id.* Standard 306(a).

143. *Id.* Interpretation 306-1.

144. *Id.* Interpretation 306-2.

145. *Id.* Interpretations 306-5 and 306-6.

146. *Id.* Standard 306 (c)(1).

147. *Id.* Standard 306 (c)(2).

148. *Id.* Interpretation 306-4.

149. Daniel J. Morrissey, *Saving Legal Education*, 56 J. Leg. Educ. 254, 275–277 (2006); Saba, *supra* n. 127, at 267. Also notable in this regard are the advent of two-year J.D. programs at University of Dayton, Southwestern Law School in Los Angeles, and most recently Northwestern. Katherine Mangan, *Northwestern U. Law School is Latest to Introduce 2-Year Degree*, 54 Chron. Higher Educ. A8 (4 July 2008).

150. Rogelio Lasso, *From the Paper Chase to the Digital Chase: Technology and the Challenge of Teaching 20th Century Law Students*, 43 Santa Clara L. Rev. 1, 58 (2002).

151. Nick Dranias, *Past the Pall of Orthodoxy: Why the First Amendment Virtually Guarantees Online Law School Graduates Will Breach the ABA Accreditation Barrier*, 111 Penn St. L. Rev. 863, 866–867 (2007). Dranias also notes that the ABA has accredited online programs in paralegal studies and health law, and that California allows graduates of online law schools to sit for its bar exam. *Id.* at 867–868.

152. Joni Larson, *The Intersection of Andragogy and Distance Education: Handing Over the Reins of Learning to Better Prepare Students for the Practice of Law*, 9 T.M. Cooley J. Prac. & Clin. L. 117, 138–143 (2007); David I.C. Thomson, *Effective Methods for Teaching Legal Writing Online*, available at http://papers.ssrn.com/sol3/papers.cfm?abstract_id=1159467 (25 July 2008) (last accessed 21 Nov. 2008). Notably, several institutions in the United Kingdom already offer LL.M. degrees via distance learning. Charlene L. Smith, *Distance Education: A Value-Added Model*, 12 Alb. L.J. Sci. & Tech. 177, 180 n. 8 (2001).

153. Lasso, *supra* n. 150, at 22–23.

154. Bohl, *supra* n. 1, at text accompanying nn. 24–25.

155. *Id.* at text accompanying n. 37.

156. Larson, *supra* n. 152, at 135–138; Yi Yang & Linda F. Cornelious, *Ensuring Quality in Online Education Instruction: What Instructors Should Know* (Association for Educational Communications and Technology, Chi., Ill., 19–23 Oct. 2004), available at http://eric.ed.gov/ERICWebPortal/custom/portlets/recordDetails/detailmini.jsp?_nfpb=true&_&ERICExtSearch_SearchValue_0=ED484990&ERICExtSearch_SearchType_0=no&accno=ED484990 (last accessed 21 Nov. 2008).

157. Baggaley, *supra* n. 126, at 42; Zemsky & Massy, *supra* n. 127, at 15.

158. Andrew Booth, *Blogs, Wikis, and Podcasts: The 'Evaluation Bypass' in Action?* 24 Health Info. & Lib. J. 298 (2007).

159. *See* ABA Standard 306, *supra* n. 137.

160. Ellen S. Podgor, Presentation, *Best Practices for Asynchronous Electronic Education (Distance Learning) Classes* (CALI Conference for Law School Computing, 19 June 2008) (available at http://wiki.cali.org/calicon08/index.php?n=Sessions.384 (last accessed 21 Nov. 2008)).

161. Mike Markel, *Distance Education and the Myth of the New Pedagogy*, 13 J. Bus. & Technical Commun. 208, 209 (1999).

162. *See* ABA Interpretation 306–4, *supra* n. 137.

163. Lasso, *supra* n. 150, at 266–268; Lisa O'Quinn & Michael Corry, *Factors that Deter Faculty from Participating in Distance Education*, 5 Online J. of Distance Learning Administration (Winter 2002), available at http://www.westga.edu/~distance/ojdla/winter54/Quinn54.htm.

164. Scollins-Mantha, *supra* n. 100, at 24.

165. Podgor, *supra* n. 160.

166. Kristen Baginski et al., Presentation, *Instructional Technology in Teaching Legal Research: Tricks of the Trade in the Real and Virtual Classroom* (D7) (Am. Assn. of L. Libraries Annual Meeting, July 2007); O'Quinn & Corry, *supra* n. 163.

167. *See supra* text accompanying nn. 82–93.

168. Podgor, *supra* n. 160.

169. *See* Captivate, *supra* n. 9.

170. *See* Camtasia, *supra* n. 8.

171. Traci Sitzmann et al., *The Comparative Effectiveness of Web-Based and Classroom Instruction: A Meta-Analysis*, 59 Personnel Psychol. 623, 625 (2006).

172. A "hybrid" ALR course at University of Maryland School of Law permitted students to choose between classroom attendance with hands-on exercises and completion of online modules that combined CALI Lessons, Captivate presentations, and other modalities, and was very well received by students regardless of their choice of option.

173. Scollins-Mantha, *supra* n. 100, at 24–25.

174. *Id.*; Bohl, *supra* n. 1, at text accompanying n. 52.

175. Podgor, *supra* n. 160.

176. Baginski et al., *supra* n. 166.

177. Eric J. Schmieder, *Communication: The Tool to Interact With and Control Your Online Classroom Environment*, 5 Intl. J. of Instructional Tech. & Distance Learning 39 (Mar. 2008); J. Johnson et al., *Student Satisfaction in the Virtual Classroom*, 3(2) Internet J. Allied Health Sci. & Prac. at text accompanying nn. 5, 6, 8, 10 (2005).

178. Anthony G. Picciano, *Beyond Student Perceptions: Issues of Interaction, Presence, and Performance in an Online Course*, 6 J. Asynchronous Learning Networks 21, 22 (July 2002).

179. Bohl, *supra* n. 1, at text accompanying nn. 43–44.

180. *Id.*; *E-Learning: Successes and Failures*, 53 Chron. Higher Educ.: Info. Tech. B20 (5 Jan. 2007).

181. Gerald F. Hess, *Collaborative Course Design: Not My Course, Not Their Course, But Our Course*, 47 Washburn L.J. 367 (2008); Cobb, *supra* n. 61.

182. Podgor, *supra* n. 160; Dezhi Wu & Starr Roxanne Hiltz, *Predicting Learning from Asynchronous Online Discussions*, 8 J. Asynchronous Learning Networks 139, 147 (Apr. 2004); Schmieder, *supra* n. 177, at 44.

183. Bohl, *supra* n. 1, at text accompanying nn. 52–53.

184. Yang & Cornelious, *supra* n. 156, at 851.

185. Sitzmann et al., *supra* n. 171, at 624.

186. Gabriele Piccoli et al., *Web-Based Virtual Learning Environments: A Research Framework and a Preliminary Assessment of Effectiveness in Basic IT Skills Training*, 25 MIS Q. 401, 421 (Dec. 2001); Robert M. Bernard et al., *How Does Distance Education Compare with Classroom Instruction? A Meta-Analysis of the Empirical Literature*, 74 Rev. Educ. Research 379, 416 (Fall 2004).

187. Byron W. Brown & Carl E. Liedholm, *Can Web Courses Replace the Classroom in Principles of Microeconomics?* 92 Am. Econ. Rev. 444, 447 (May 2002).

188. Dennis Coates et al., *'No Significant Distance' Between Face-to-Face and Online Instruction: Evidence From Principles of Economics*, 23 Economics of Educ. Rev. 533, 545 (Oct. 2004); Yong Zhao et al., *What Makes The Difference? A Practical Analysis of Research on the Effectiveness of Distance Education*, 107 Teachers College Rec. 1836 (2005), available at http://ott.educ.msu.edu/literature/report.pdf (last accessed 21 Nov. 2008).

189. Andrea L. Foster, *Online Colleges to Post Effectiveness of Programs*, Chron. Higher Educ.: The Wired Campus, available at http://chronicle.com/wiredcampus/article/2691/online-colleges-to-post-effectiveness-of-programs (24 Jan. 2008).

190. Allan & Seaman, *supra* n. 129, at 11. *See also* the *No Significant Difference* Web site, available at http://www.nosignificantdifference.org/ (last accessed 14 Nov. 2008).

191. Picciano, *supra* n. 178, at 24.

192. Johnson, *supra* n. 177, at text accompanying n. 7.

193. Barbara Lockee et al., *Measuring Success: Evaluation Strategies for Distance Education*, 25(1) Educause Q. 20, 24 (2002).

194. C. Eugene Walker & Erika Kelly, *Online Instruction: Student Satisfaction, Kudos, and Pet Peeves*, 8 Q. Rev. Distance Educ. 309 (2007).

195. *Id.* at 310.

196. *Id.* at 315–316.

197. Johnson et al., *supra* n. 177, at text accompanying nn. 6, 7, 10.

198. Baginski et al., *supra* n. 166.

199. Podgor, *supra* n. 160.

200. *See* ABA Interpretation 306–4, *supra* n. 137.

201. Yang & Cornelious, *supra* n. 156, at 848.

202. O'Quinn & Corry, *supra* n. 163.

203. Yang & Cornelious, *supra* n. 156, at 849–850.

204. Podgor, *supra* n. 160; Schmieder, *supra* n. 177, at 44.

205. Bohl, *supra* n. 1, at text accompanying nn. 40–42, 100–102.

206. Baginski et al., *supra* n. 166.

Who Gets to Be the Expert?: Legal Research Skills Certification in Legal Education

RICHARD LEITER

Schmid Law Library, University of Nebraska College of Law, Lincoln, Nebraska, USA

This article considers the question of whether there is a need for law schools to offer certification for specialization in legal research skills and discusses various approaches to legal research skills certification. The author argues that it is unnecessary to offer legal research certification as it is presupposed that a basic legal education should include instruction in how to find and read the law. Anything less is a failed legal education.

Exactly how special are legal research skills? Are they special enough to warrant certification? As a matter of fact, the act of legal researching is so intimately connected with the practice of law as to be indistinguishable. After all, is it even possible for a lawyer to practice law without reading it? And is it possible to read the law without *finding it*? And *finding the law* is not only the name of one of the great textbooks on legal research,[1] it's also the very act of research itself. For many years, legal research has been treated as a discipline separate from so-called doctrinal courses in law schools. But this was not always the case. In the early history of legal education, it was impossible to divide the study of law from legal researching. This essay will examine whether there's a need for legal research subject certification in the context of the development of legal research instruction in legal education.

In order to get to an understanding of how we might answer this question, we must first examine what is legal research: Is it knowledge or is it a skill? The corollary is, perhaps, even more problematic: How do we recognize someone with proficiency that warrants certification? Can a skill like this be objectively measured? In my opinion, it is questionable that it can be effectively measured. The thing that can be measured, however, is whether a student has taken the appropriate courses and passed them. In the end, this may be all that we can hope for—that students take all available research and subject specialty courses and pass them.

WHAT IS LEGAL RESEARCH?

The short answer to this question is that legal researching is the ability to find information that answers legal questions. Legal research ability is difficult to judge in part, because in the modern world of legal bibliography, there are often many alternate ways to find needed legal information. As long as the researcher finds the information that s/he needs to form opinions, advise clients, or make legal arguments, who is to say that her method is right or wrong?

In the book, *Educating Lawyers*,[2] a very fine and very detailed examination of the state of American legal education, the discipline of legal research receives no more than a page or two of mention.[3] Even then, it is mentioned only indirectly. It is easy to look at this omission and conclude that legal research was given short shrift or ignored to the detriment of our entire vocation. Librarians, the legal research experts, have often been inclined to feel like the Rodney Dangerfield's of the legal profession: We don't get no respect!

A more careful look at *Educating Lawyers* reveals some important facts about the development of legal education that show how legal research came to be a rather late addition to the law school curriculum. Legal education only became a regular part of the modern university in the late nineteenth century when Langdell is credited with developing what is now considered the standard form of legal education, the so-called "case method." Prior to this, legal education was basically a process of apprenticeship, called "reading the law." This method of studying the law involved working for an established attorney and reading the law under his direction.

As absurd as it sounds, "reading the law" was entirely feasible well into the nineteenth century. James Kent, in his *Commentaries on American Law,* notes that reading the law had, by that time, become very difficult due to the proliferation of serial law reports.[4] A careful look at his footnotes reveals that the total collection of law books extant in his day was only a little more than 800 books. A student in his day would have been required only to read a fraction of these books in preparation for admission to the bar, since s/he would have only had to be familiar with the cases and statutes of their state. By contrast, it was not until the dawn of the industrial revolution and the astounding commercial success of the great legal publishing houses that the bibliography of the law proliferated to an extent that made mastery over the content of primary and secondary legal materials nearly impractical.

It seems obviousthat a lawyer preparing for practice in the nineteenth century would have become intimately acquainted with the majority of sources of the law as s/he studied the law. Even under Langdell's method, as students were reading cases, there were not many options to which to turn to find the cases they were reading. In the early days of legal education, then, is it any wonder that legal research as a skill was not given much attention?

THE LEGAL RESEARCH SKILL

Agents of legal publishers first taught legal research in law schools near the turn of the twentieth century.[5] It is hard to imagine that this was not largely a marketing tool. In those days, as is true in the present day, it was probably the case that these publishers' representatives/instructors tended to favor their own publications over the competition. The good news was, of course, that since the publishers were publishing mostly primary legal materials, it was unlikely that the relative characteristics of the competing materials had much to do with accuracy, and likely that they had more to do with layout, design, and usability.

And so, in the early history of legal education, legal research instruction was largely taken for granted because students studying the law were getting intimate experience with its sources precisely because they were studying the law. The idea that lawyers needed instruction about legal research may have, indeed, seemed as absurd as a school for carpenters teaching students how to use a hammer.[6]

As legal publishing grew to become an industry and commercial publication of legal materials proliferated, legal research as a distinct discipline came into its own. During the Industrial Revolution and the New Deal era, the numbers of primary legal materials increased exponentially. The United States Code and the Code of Federal Regulations only came into existence in the third decade of the twentieth century! With this explosion of statutory and regulatory materials, together with a corresponding boom in case law, came an enormous growth in importance and numbers of secondary materials to explain it all. The need for expertise in collecting, managing, and using legal materials became increasingly necessary during this period. Arguably, before this, studying the law was, essentially, studying the laws themselves, therefore making the study of legal research all but redundant. Prior to this explosion of legal bibliography, expertise in a specific legal subject implied expertise in the bibliography of that area of practice. After all, how could one study bankruptcy and not study the sources of bankruptcy law?

The state of legal bibliography today is quite complex. Not only are there more statutes and regulations (not to mention more cases) with which lawyers must be familiar, but virtually all federal and state agencies have developed numerous official and quasi-official legal documents, such as Private Letter Rulings, policy statements, press releases, as well as operating and procedure manuals that are every bit as important to practice as the statutes, regulations, and cases themselves.[7] Today, expertise in the bibliography of law in a specific subject can no longer be presumed.

Electronic publication and access to legal materials has had an exponential effect on the complexity of legal researching. Where once there were only two or three sources of access to certain statutes or regulations, there may now be a dozen. Even with respect to multiple publications of primary materials, quality and authenticity of the sources cannot be presumed. The proliferation of sources complicates not only the use of materials, but factors, such as physical space, cost, and user licenses, make the process of collecting and managing them as important as using them.

Further complicating the geography of legal bibliography is the advent and importance of blogs, podcasts, and Web sites as vehicles for policy statements and other crucial legal pronouncements and guidance from pundits, scholars, and government officials. Arguably, a lawyer's legal skills today must include much more than simply knowing how to use the materials; a lawyer must also be thoroughly grounded in the bibliographic history of the materials she uses and be able to evaluate their relative merit, usefulness, and value. Of course, lawyers fortunate enough to have a librarian on staff may be able to rely on their special expertise for much of this evaluative and management function.

CERTIFICATION OF LEGAL RESEARCH SKILLS

Turning to the question of whether law students could be, or should be, certified as "legal researchers," it is clear that the skills that would be subject to certification are very complex and, in some ways, very subtle indeed. With myriad sources of legal information available to researchers, would legal research certification measure outcomes or processes? This complexity is reflected in the various approaches to teaching legal research.

There are four general models of legal research instruction, each with its own merit and each receiving considerable attention in the literature. They will only be briefly detailed here. They can be broadly defined as the "bibliographic method," most recently championed by Bob Berring and Kathleen Vanden Heuvel;[8] the "process method" described in detail by Jill and Christopher Wren;[9] the topical method, described by Peter Schanck;[10] and, finally, the "practice or pragmatic method," such as that used at William and Mary School of Law.[11]

The bibliographic method trains lawyers to understand how the bibliography of the law is structured and how it works. The virtue of this method is that students learn the sources of the law independent of their format or publication method and are, therefore, equipped to discover and explore new platforms for delivery of the materials they need in their work. They are also well equipped to evaluate different platforms and assess their relative value depending on the immediate task at hand. By subtle contrast, the Wrens' approach focuses on the way the various platforms and publications work, how they are structured, and their relative pragmatic characteristics. An important aspect of this approach is that it also emphasizes systematic methods for conducting research based on the desired outcome or the specific circumstance for which the research is being conducted. The benefit of this approach is that it equips lawyers with the practical skills for using each kind of research tool covered in the class.

The topical method emphasizes special training in subject specialties. This method is used in many ways. In some schools, short classes are offered on various topics throughout the school year; for example, a course may be offered in securities or tax law. In others, research instruction may be incorporated into the courses themselves. For example, a class in municipal law may bring in a librarian to offer instruction on the use of materials and methods researching municipal law. In these situations, research instruction may be offered in a single class session or it may be introduced at various times throughout the course so that the bibliographic instruction is offered at appropriate times as the material is covered in the course.

The "practice" method teaches law students how to research in the context of writing exercises and forces the student to learn research skills as they are needed to solve real, albeit fictitious, legal problems as they are drafting various legal documents. There is much to value in this approach because it recognizes legal research as a skill that is most easily learned when used and practiced.

As a practical matter, each method can produce fine, intelligent researchers. But in practice, the bulk of research skills are learned by young lawyers and law clerks on the job as they learn to use the resources available to them in their law offices and as they learn the ins and outs of their practice specialties. Given the way that sources of the law are multiplying, and the growing complexities for gaining access to the materials—and particularly given the introduction in the last few decades of so many online resources and their licensing agreements, consortium arrangements, and bulk updating contracts for traditional materials (whew)—it is understandable that few, if any, lawyers can hit the research ground running in law practice or clerking positions. Senior lawyers at law firms understandably perceive a decline in the researching skills of new graduates. After all, when they were young, there may have been only a fraction of the resources available. We should not forget that a little more than thirty[12] years ago, Lexis came into being and during that same time span the law-book publishing landscape would so change that now the two biggest and legal publishers of American primary and secondary law are no longer U.S. corporations.[13]

In this context, the question of whether certification of law graduates' legal research skills is valuable becomes very difficult to answer. What skill can be certified? Should graduates be able to recite lists of sources for the Treasury Department's General Counsel Memos or be able to list the "best" source? And who could possibly determine the "best" source for many primary materials? Try as they might, in the face of an ever-changing legal bibliography, it is doubtful that either *The Bluebook* or Association of Legal Writing Directors citation formats will be able to exert much authority as standards for best resources. Rather, they will simply remain what they really always have been—style books, and not much more.

Law students arguably should be trained in a litany of steps to take when researching certain legal questions. For example, should students be able to list the steps to be taken or resources consulted when researching the protections available to a software engineer who has developed a utility written to mine information from various commercial Web sites? In any scenario, while the learning curve of a new lawyer may be steep, s/he will soon become proficient in the day-to-day access to the materials needed in their practice. Such proficiency will be molded by the materials and resources at her disposal and by the nature of her practice, be it litigation, advisement, or drafting. For example, if the firm owns the Bureau of National Affairs' (BNA) *Labor Relations Reporter*, but not the Commercial Clearing House, Inc. *Labor Law Reports*, it will be understandable that the lawyer will know the BNA materials best. If the firm has an exclusive arrangement with Westlaw, it is natural to assume that the lawyers in the firm will have little skill or familiarity with Lexis.

In the end, legal researching is clearly more than merely knowing how to use the different services. Collecting and managing the materials best suited for practice may be just as important, and if we assume that certification of legal research skills means the certificate warrants a high degree of familiarity and expertise with legal research and bibliography, then there also needs to be some way of measuring familiarity with these skills or this knowledge as well. Quantifying such proficiency or evaluating such knowledge may, in fact, be nearly impossible given the fluidity and growth in legal materials.

It can also be argued that any lawyer studying law should know from where the law comes. That is, if one has taken a course in environmental law, the student should be exposed to the documents that govern the issues of environmental law. In a perfect world, such a student should not need separate instruction on how to research environmental law. It would be redundant and so would certification: if a student were to earn a certificate in environmental law or family law, for instance, it should be presumed that s/he is something of an expert in the bibliography of that field. Perhaps one important contribution that librarians can make to legal education would be to ensure that such certification programs include a research aspect to them.

There is a very subtle conundrum to be considered when discussing the merit of legal research certification. It seems logical that students who receive subject certification in a field such as trial practice, business law, or taxation should have some degree of expertise about research in that field.[14] The presumption is that all law students are experts in basic legal knowledge, which is usually covered in the first three semesters of law school. Certification of a specialized field of legal knowledge, such as business transactions, denotes study of a group of classes beyond those of a typical law graduate. Thus, it seems absurd to offer certification in a first-year subject such as contracts or torts, because all students are presumed to be familiar with these subjects. (Obviously, there is room for in-depth study of these subjects, and students may pursue graduate degrees in such subjects, or may choose to teach them and in the process become experts in contracts or torts.)

If a school were to offer certification in legal research, what skills would be certified? If certification is being proposed for general legal research skills, as contrasted to expertise in a particular subject specialty, then we are talking about broad expertise in legal bibliography. As discussed above, expertise in legal research transcends mere knowledge or skill in how to find materials. Today, true expertise in legal research demands much more than that. Knowing where to look for specific answers will not do much good without *access* to them. Experts in legal research must be able to evaluate resources and make judgments about collecting, organizing, and managing them, as well as simply knowing open Web sites or using indexes and books to find answers. The fact is, virtually all reference librarians, particularly in the academy, have advanced degrees in librarianship or information sciences. Law reference librarians who have law degrees and library degrees are certified (in an informal way) as experts in legal research and bibliography.

All things considered, legal research certification may have practical value for law students in the job market. There is a general perception that new lawyers are graduating with inadequate practice skills (read: research, among others) and law students looking to distinguish themselves from their peers in the job market may find that certification is an important way to do so. Successfully completing an advanced legal research (ALR) class should qualify as evidence of proficiency in legal researching whether taking the class earns the student a certificate or not. Taking specialized law courses or a series of courses, too, should signal to prospective employers that the student has more than a basic understanding of how to perform research in those areas of practice. While one may argue (and some do) that taking a course on, for example, government contracts does not necessarily produce students who are good government contracts researchers, it is obvious that this is a failure of the particular course's pedagogy and should not be an expected outcome of a specialized course; taking a class to become an expert (or at least taking the first step toward becoming one) should surely include attention to the documents and bibliography of the subject, shouldn't it?

Online legal database vendors have occasionally toyed with the idea of offering students the opportunity to earn certificates of proficiency in use of their systems. Both Lexis and Westlaw have offered such training over the years, because, they say, employers are anxious to hire people who can maximize the use of their systems for the least cost, therefore making students with these certificates attractive hires. But there is more than a little subtext to these schemes. For one thing, both companies will, of course, emphasize their own services' value *vis a vis* the competition, turning the certification program into a blatant marketing tool. And students who earn a certificate in only one system may inadvertently limit their marketability to those firms with exclusive contracts to that service. But no matter how you look at it, certification by a publisher in the use of its own products will probably always be looked upon with suspicion because it is, by definition, if not necessity, self-serving.

There are also pedagogical reasons for doubting the value of publisher certification of expertise in the use of their own materials. Legal bibliography and legal researching in any specialized practice is not something that comes from a single source. Even though there are some fields that are dominated by one or more treatise or looseleaf, no practitioner can be a successful researcher if proficient in only one resource. While the great standard works of the law are, indeed, valuable and complex and worthy of special attention in order to master, it is difficult to imagine that a law student would benefit from certification as an expert in the use of *Collier's Bankruptcy Reporter*, *Wright and Miller*, or the *Restatements*.

A WORD ABOUT CERTIFICATION IN OTHER DISCIPLINES

Some have argued that since other disciplines, such as auto mechanics, electricians, or medical doctors, have certification procedures, so should general law. But there are distinct differences between certification of lawyers in specialties and certification in other professions or crafts. A detailed discussion of the processes of certification in other professions is beyond the scope of this article, and so what follows is a general discussion of how certification of legal specialties, especially certification of legal research skills, may differ from those mentioned above.

Certification in many of these other disciplines is often linked with licensure, or with measuring objective expertise (in the sense that certification means that the person certified has completed certain classes, workshops, or training) that may affect public health or safety and transcends mere marketing value. However, an auto mechanic who is certified by a particular automobile manufacturer may be no better at fixing that brand of car than one who is not, but from the consumers' point of view, certification is a fact that implies expertise and helps build trust and confidence. In this context, it is interesting to ponder whether clients are more apt to hire a lawyer with a certification in Westlaw or Lexis. I think not.

In other professions, such as electricians, licensure may be a legal matter, and someone who attempts to practice as an electrician may violate not only state and local laws, but s/he may also run afoul of union contracts. Since safety is at stake, most consumers will prefer a licensed electrician to one who's not, regardless of the legal consequences.

In the case of the medical profession, board certification of medical specialties is interwoven with marketing, safety, and expertise about procedures or treatments affecting life or death. But in these cases, certification is much more than merely taking a class and passing a test: many medical board certifications require years of residency and training. By comparison, most academic legal certifications are more about a student marketing her special skills to potential employers than certifying her skills to potential clients. What's more, a student who graduates without a certificate in government contracts, for example, is free to take on clients with government contracts legal matters and practice in that area as well as write wills or handle criminal matters. Many lawyers have specialized practices, which usually are the result of successfully handling certain types of cases and establishing a reputation for that expertise. Expertise or specialization in law is usually the result of good law school training combined with experience. For reasons set out above, legal research as a certified legal practice skill does not fit easily into any of the other models for professional certification.[15]

IN CONCLUSION

Instead of lobbying for legal research certification, law librarians should perhaps strive in earnest to make effective legal research skills training an integral part of the law school curriculum. As a device to help law students compete in the job marketplace, certification may be very valuable, and law schools and librarians may want to consider ways to facilitate this purpose by offering a rich variety of exposure to legal bibliography over the course of a law school career: research courses, basic, advanced, and specialized, as stand-alone courses or integrated into doctrinal courses.Whether certificates are granted or offered, their completion and recordation on transcripts or inclusion in students' resumes should serve to let employers know that the student has a certain level of proficiency in legal researching.

As a practical matter, however, the best way to prepare students for practice is by offering quality education, and that must include offering as much attention as is practical to the study of the sources of the law. Legal bibliography should be offered at all phases of legal education and at appropriate times: basic materials in the first year, detailed studying of the bibliography of law in elective ALR courses and focused attention to the sources of the law in all upper division electives, particularly in disciplines governed by specialized sets of legal materials. With care, a law degree can be its own certification of proficiency in legal research skills.

NOTES

1. Morris L. Cohen, Robert Berring & Kent C. Olson, *How to Find the Law* (9th ed., West Publishing 1989).

2. William M. Sullivan, et al., *Educating Lawyers* (Jossey-Bass 2007)

3. Richard Leiter, *The Missing Lawyering Skill,* 12 AALL Spectrum 22 (O. Halsted 2007–2008).

4. James Kent, *Of Reports of Judicial Decisions*, in *Commentaries on American Law* ("*Kent's Commentaries*") vol. 1, 439 (1826).

5. Woxland, ed., *Introduction, Symposium of Law Publishers*, 11:3/4 Leg. Ref. Servs. Q. 1 (1991) *special issue; see also,* Woxland, *Why Can't Johnny Research? or It All Started with Christopher Columbus Langdell*, 81 L. Lib. J. 451 (1989).

6. To satisfy the cynical who may take issue with the analogy, it should be noted that, indeed, there are different types of hammers for different types of jobs and different hammer manufacturers. But presumably a hammer used for roofing would be covered in roofing classes, and finishing hammers would be covered in courses about finishing carpentry. The notion of a whole class on hammer using—"Hold the nail, raise the hammer and pound!"—is the scenario that seems absurd . . .

7. By way of example of the increase in volume of primary legal material, consider the following: Volume one of the Code of Federal Regulations occupied about six linear feet of shelf space in 1970; today it occupies more than twenty feet. The Federal Register, too, has grown to staggering proportions. In 1936, volume one contained a total of 2,411 pages; ten years later, in 1946, it contained 14,736 pages. By 2006, it had grown to its present average size of well over seventy thousand pages, after topping out at 83,294 pages in 2000. Case law, too, has increased in size. In its first year of publication, the Federal Reporter needed volumes one through five to contain all the cases from 1880. By 1980, it took twenty-seven volumes to contain the cases from that year, and by 2000, thirty-eight volumes were needed.

8. Robert Berring and Kathleen Vanden Heuval, *Legal Research: Should Students Learn It or Wing It?* 81 L. Lib. J. 431 (1989).

9. Christopher G. Wren & Jill R. Wren, *The Teaching of Legal Research*, 80 L. Lib. J. 7 (1988).

10. Peter Schanck, *Mandatory Advanced Legal Research: A Viable Program for Law Schools?* 92 L. Lib. J. 295 (2000).

11. The program at William & Mary is an integral part of the legal skills curriculum described in detail in Moliterno, *The Legal Skills Program at the College of William and Mary: An Early Report*, 40 J. Leg. Educ. 535 (1990). The research component was well presented and described by James A. Heller, *Teaching the Teachers: Effective Instruction in Legal Research*, (Austin, Tex., Oct. 18–20, 2007) (see http://tarlton.law.utexas.edu/ttt for a complete description of the program).

12. Some colleagues have pointed out that Lexis was *invented* in the 1960s, and that therefore, this number should be *forty* years ago. All I can say is that Lexis didn't become widely available until the *late* 1970s. So, while it may have been *invented* in the 1960s, it didn't find its way into law firms or law schools until later; so, I will stand on my "thirty years" assertion. Maybe I'm stubborn, or maybe I'm just not ready to concede that anything important that occurred during my adult years could have happened *forty* years ago.

13. West is owned by Thomson-Reuters, a Canadian/Dutch company, and Lexis is owned by Reed Elsevier, a Dutch/British publishing house.

14. I am assuming that a student who takes a specialized course of study in tax law learns more than the simple fact that unique materials, such as Private Letter Rulings exist, but also learn how they are made, where they come from, and how to find them. It is incomprehensible to me that anything else can be the case. I hope that I'm not being naive.

15. That is, because there is no "right" way to find legal materials due to the myriad ways they are published and/or distributed. In fact, even for primary materials, there may be as many as a dozen reliable sources for legal materials. In this situation, who could certify that one way for finding the material is correct and another is not?

Testing for Research Competency on the Bar Exam: The Next Steps

STEVEN M. BARKAN

Professor of Law and Director of Library and Information Services, University of Wisconsin Law School, Madison, Wisconsin, USA

SUSAN M. CASE

Director of Testing, National Conference of Bar Examiners, Madison, Wisconsin, USA

MICHAEL KANE

Director of Research, National Conference of Bar Examiners, Madison, Wisconsin, USA

ERICA MOESER

President, National Conference of Bar Examiners, Madison, Wisconsin, USA

All new lawyers should be competent in the fundamental skills of legal research, which suggests that legal research competency should be covered on the bar exam. The authors discuss the essential attributes of a bar exam and the methods that might be used to test for legal research competency. They recommend a multiple-choice testing method, but argue that before legal research competency can be tested on the bar exam, determinations need to be made about the definition of competency and the subject matter to be tested.

Every so often we encounter an idea whose time has come, and it is quite possible that such an idea and such a time have arrived. The idea is that the lawyer licensing process should expand to include the testing of legal research competency. In recent years, law librarians and teachers of legal research and writing have led the charge for including legal research on the bar exam.[1]

If we look at the tenets of licensing—best practices, if you will—one best practice is to sample as broad an array of the skills and knowledge needed in practice as is practical, given the number of examinees, the expenses of testing and grading, the efficiency of the process, and the objectivity of the exercise. Bar examinations today, though ever improving, do not—and probably cannot—test every aspect we would identify were we to list the elements that contribute to what we would deem is the competent entry-level lawyer. Some skills, negotiation, for example, are certainly worthy of consideration. However, these skills may falter as suitable test material when the logistics of drafting and executing fair and effective measures are assessed. Feasibility and cost doom some such measures, particularly when measurement ramifications, such as the reliability of the end product, are considered.

From the perspective of bar examiners, the notion of adding additional test content is not an easy one with which to grapple. Testing time is precious, and decisions about what might be added to the battery of instruments currently in use necessarily include assessment of what, if any, test content and testing time should be supplanted.

Current bar examinations are consistent in their general pattern with considerable variability in the details of their composition and grading. The typical bar exam includes two or three forms of questioning: essay questions, multiple-choice questions, and performance tasks. Each state constructs its own bar examination, often combining uniform, multistate elements with locally crafted sections. Today's bar exams range from one and a half to three days in length. All states but two (Louisiana and Washington) devote one day to the Multistate Bar Examination, a six-hour, 200-item test covering six subject areas (constitutional law, contracts, criminal law and procedure, evidence, real property, and torts). Other uniform components include the Multistate Performance Test (MPT), a ninety-minute written practice simulation task (or two such tasks) in use by thirty-four jurisdictions, and the Multistate Essay Examination, a three-hour, six-question essay test in use by twenty-two jurisdictions. Into this mix, a majority of states add locally crafted essay questions or, in three instances (New York, Hawaii, and Florida), multiple-choice elements, and in other instances (California and Pennsylvania), locally crafted performance tests. All states but three (Washington, Maryland, and Wisconsin) also require passage of the Multistate Professional Responsibility Exam, a separately-administered sixty-question multiple-choice test to measure the examinee's knowledge and understanding of established standards related to a lawyer's professional conduct.[2]

Against this backdrop, the question arises whether or not testing candidates on their legal research competency is a suitable and necessary element in determining their eligibility for a general law license. We contend that it is.

The rhetoric framing bar examinations has matured over the past decade, and the emergence of clarity in its objectives has led to a refinement of the task at hand. More than ever before, multistate examinations are written with the standard in mind that the material tested should sample knowledge and skills appropriate to an entry-level professional. Questions that delve into the arcane are eschewed. Straightforward questions that demand correct application of law to lifelike fact patterns are encouraged. A broad sampling of content that is deemed to be important to establishing the competence of an entry-level lawyer is viewed as desirable. Broad sampling benefits applicants who are given the opportunity to show what they know and benefits the consumer of legal services who deserves an entry-level practitioner who arrives "factory equipped" with the skills and knowledge to render professional service.

Considering this commitment to sampling a broad array of the skills needed in entry-level practice, it would seem difficult to argue that the entry-level lawyer's arsenal of skills and knowledge should omit the ability to conduct basic research. Indeed, the highly regarded MacCrate Report deemed legal research an essential lawyering skill.[3] In a common law jurisdiction, can competent representation occur without it? And if it is job critical, should it be tested? The answer is affirmative, with several qualifiers.

WHAT IS LEGAL RESEARCH COMPETENCY?

The first qualifier is whether or not it is feasible to test legal research skills; that is, is there an efficient, fair way to evaluate these skills? This in turn raises the question of whether or not the subject lends itself to testing large numbers of candidates (typically in excess of 55,000 for each July administration of the bar examinations). Further, it requires serious consideration of what test content might look like if skills were to be tested.

Such an inquiry leads to a consideration of what is fit and fair to teach and test in the legal research domain. Is it enough to know that in a given circumstance a candidate (or a new lawyer) would know which sources to consult? Does it constitute a reasonable requirement that the candidate be able to apply research skills introduced in law school, or should more be expected?

Therefore, if legal research is to be included on the bar exam, it is critical to determine the substance of legal research. Before we can measure competency, we need to identify what competencies we are attempting to measure. The importance of this cannot be overstated. As a part of defining and conceptualizing legal research competency, assumptions need to be made about the nature of the current research environment. Specifically, do we assume that research is conducted in a mixed paper and electronic environment, so as to require examinees to be competent in using both law books and electronic resources? Alternatively, can we assume that the research paradigm has changed and that we have now moved to an electronic research environment so that bar examiners can be comfortable limiting their testing to electronic research skills? Which resources do we assume are available to the examinee? Clearly, what is assumed about the research environment will significantly affect both the substance and method of testing and the determination of minimal legal research competency. Therefore, the most challenging aspects of including legal research on the bar exam will be defining minimal competency and determining how that competency will be measured.[4]

ATTRIBUTES OF A BAR EXAMINATION

As stated above, bar exams present significant economic, grading, security, and resource challenges. They are costly to develop and administer. They are administered to thousands of examinees simultaneously. Bar exams must be administered in a secure, supervised environment. All examinees need equal access to resources. Because it is a mass test, a bar exam needs to be efficiently gradable, yielding scores that can be measured and compared. It is not practical to draft a multitude of different questions and let examinees complete unique tests on their own time or to release a large number of examinees in a given law library to work on bar exam questions.

There are seven basic attributes that should be considered in developing a test component for the bar examination.

1. **Content Relevant to Newly Licensed Practitioners** - Every question should present a task that a new lawyer could reasonably be expected to perform. This is not to say everyone would answer every question correctly, but that each question is a reasonable one to include on the test. This is an attribute that can be met by all examination formats, even multiple choice, if the questions are structured appropriately.
2. **Broad Content Sampling** - The content should be sampled broadly enough and be comparable enough across forms and test administrations that candidates are not disadvantaged by receiving one form of the test as opposed to an alternate form of the test. Examinees should not feel that they were unlucky in the selection of content included on the test. This is one of the benefits of multiple-choice questions; they are the most efficient in terms of testing time per topic, allowing a broad sample of content. Essay and performance tests are necessarily restricted in the number of tasks that can be included, because of the length of each task. Research in the area of problem solving has shown a surprising amount of content specificity—that is, someone who is good at solving problems in one area may not be as good at solving problems in another area. If, for example, a student had researched a similar problem before, that student would be likely to do better than if the problem were a novel one.

3. **Accurate and Valid Grading** - The scores must reflect the quality of the answers and not be affected by things that are not relevant (such as grader preferences or inconsistency). It must be possible to develop a scoring rule that will ensure that grading is consistent.
4. **Equated Scores to Ensure Fairness Across Time** - The scores should be equated over time so that the scores maintain the same meaning regardless of the proficiency of the particular cohort of examinees and regardless of the difficulty of the questions. As a practical matter, equating can be implemented with multiple-choice questions, but it is generally not feasible for essay and performance tests. It is possible to control for variability in essay and performance test difficulty and for differences in scoring standards by administering these tests with multiple-choice tests and scaling the essay and performance test scores to the multiple-choice test scores.
5. **Reliable Scores to Ensure Fairness Across Exam Forms** - The grades should be reliable enough that if a group of candidates were to be tested again, the rank ordering of those candidates and the pass/fail outcomes would be very similar. This attribute is again most easily accomplished with multiple-choice testing because of the broad content sampling that is possible with multiple-choice tests. If scores from essay and performance tests are combined with a multiple-choice component, the overall total score generally meets this requirement.
6. **Anonymity of Applicant to Avoid Bias** - Answers should be graded without regard to the identity of the applicant. The grader would not be able to determine private information about the applicant, such as name, law school, age, gender, or ethnicity.
7. **Reasonable Costs** - The exam should be relatively inexpensive to create and grade. This does not mean cheap, but a component that is more expensive than existing components would be included only if there was a rationale for incurring that additional expense. Research would have to indicate that the new, more expensive component added something to the measurement process that resulted in passing more people who should pass or failing more people who should fail.

SELECTING THE FORM OF TESTING

As a general proposition, if we want to evaluate how well a person performs a particular kind of task, we would ask the person to perform that kind of task for our evaluation. This suggests that the best way to evaluate legal research skills would be to evaluate an examinee's performance of legal research. However, with examinations used for licensure, other issues can be more salient than the desirability of creating a replica of real-life experiences. For example, standardization across examinees (making sure everyone has an equivalent test) and anonymity of the applicants (making sure that examinees are unknown to the graders) are viewed as critically important, and verisimilitude is typically reduced when standardization and anonymity are required.

In a performance test, examinees are given a set of prepared materials with which to solve a problem. Performance tests in law, such as the MPT developed by the National Conference of Bar Examiners, attempt to test what lawyers actually do. They focus on the skills of analyzing and sorting facts; reading and analyzing cases, statutes, administrative materials, and secondary sources; and writing documents, such as a client letter, a brief, a will, or a contract provision. The MPT is a "closed universe exam;" it provides all the information that examinees need to be able to create the document required. Examinees are given the sources from which relevant information is to be drawn, which means that actual legal research is omitted.

AN ELECTRONIC RESEARCH ENVIRONMENT?

In an electronic research environment, in which every examinee has access to a computer workstation through which all research sources are available, a performance test might be an effective method for measuring research competency. Examinees could be given narrative problems to solve using an electronic library. Through either a single complex question or a series of questions, examinees would need to determine what kinds of information are needed and where that information might be found, and to work with and evaluate the information until adequate answers are determined. The answers might be graded using a predetermined scale to measure the relevance and accuracy of the responses and methodology used. The focus would be on identifying and retrieving relevant information, rather than on using the information after it has been found. Alternatively, if an electronic research environment is employed, the current form of the MPT could be expanded to include legal research. It could test legal research simply by not providing the examinees with the specific legal information needed to complete the task, but rather with an extensive "library" in which the information could be found.

There are, however, several practical problems that arise with a research test involving an electronic research environment. First, the current bar exam requires that everyone be tested on the same day. This allows everyone to receive the same test material without a concern about test security. If examinees were to be tested over multiple days, there would be a need to create multiple problems that would have to be judged to be equivalent enough so each iteration of the test is essentially equivalent. Second, if examinees were tested at different sites, using different machines, there would be a need to determine that the sites and machines, for example, are equivalent to each other in terms of hardware, software, bandwidth, and processing speed, among other things. Third, there would be a need to ensure that the grading was equivalent. Essentially, the challenge is to ensure that those who are tested on a particular day, with a particular problem, at a particular site, graded by a particular grader are not advantaged or disadvantaged relative to other examinees tested with a different problem, on a different day or site and graded by a different grader. Another challenge is to make sure that each examinee who is taking the test is the examinee that is supposed to be taking the test and that the examinee does not make use of outside assistance. This requires careful proctoring.

OTHER FORMATS

The other two formats currently used on the bar exam are the thirty-minute essay questions and multiple-choice questions. To avoid the problems outlined above (access to computers and standardization of computer environments), these alternative methods should be considered as options for testing legal research competency. Short-answer essays require examinees to organize and explain their responses. But because answers to essay questions are extended and highly variable, they are difficult and time-consuming to grade. Multiple-choice questions, on the other hand, can cover more aspects of a subject and are objective and, therefore, more easily gradable. It should be noted that in order for a multiple-choice question to be viable, it must have a single correct answer or at least a single best answer. If questions cannot be written with single correct or best answers, the multiple-choice format is not a viable format. This might be a challenge in drafting questions for legal research because often there are multiple ways to approach a legal research problem.

In this context, however, multiple-choice questions and short-answer essay questions would measure the examinee's knowledge of legal research, rather than the examinee's legal research skills. Can we assume a correlation between an examinee's knowledge of research tools, concepts, and methods and the ability to conduct legal research, just as we might assume that knowledge of the rules of evidence and trial procedure correlates to the ability to conduct a trial? Perhaps this is the best we can do if the test cannot be offered in a fully electronic research environment. Indeed, when a group of academic law librarians gathered in Madison, Wisconsin in June 2006 to discuss the issues and concepts of testing bar applicants on legal research skills, the group arrived fairly quickly at the consensus that legal research skills could and should be tested and tested in an efficient multiple-choice format to allow for a broad sampling of research concepts over a variety of issues and legal contexts.[5]

DRAFTING QUESTIONS

Questions might provide a fact scenario, and then there might be a series of questions about what information the lawyer needs to find and where it might be found. Further questions might tell the examinee to assume that certain types of information or authority were found and then to distinguish between and among what was found. Examinees might be given ambiguous statutory language and asked how the meaning and purpose of the language might be clarified. A tax question might present the examinee with excerpts from the Internal Revenue Code, the tax regulations, and case law from different courts or jurisdictions that need to be interpreted and reconciled.

Regardless of the type of test, the questions would be a challenge to draft. The standard—what a competent entry-level lawyer needs to know—must be clearly stated and understood. The questions cannot be too specialized or trivial, testing things that do not meet the standard, or so general that they do not measure competence. Because of their expertise with using and teaching research sources, law librarians must be included in the question-drafting process. Legal research and writing instructors also should be involved, but the task should not be delegated to these groups alone. Rather, it will be important to involve a broad representation of the legal profession: lawyers from large and small firms (and locales), government lawyers, lawyers from other sectors, and judges. This diversity should ensure that both the model of legal research and the determinations of competency reflect realistic expectations. Writing good test questions is a difficult and time-consuming task; however, if competent lawyers find it impossible to write high-quality test questions to assess legal research competency, legal research cannot be used as one of the topics for the bar examination.

Questions should be as media-neutral as possible, focusing on the category of information rather than the use of specific resources or the medium through which the resources appear. Good questions would refer to resources generically with a high level of generality, for example to "an annotated version of the United States Code," rather than specifically to the United States Code Service. Knowledge of specific resources should be required only when necessary. For example, it might be reasonable to expect a lawyer to know the nature and contents of resources such as the United States Code, the Statutes at Large, the Code of Federal Regulations, and the Federal Register. But the examinee should not be expected to know the detailed differences between the United States Code Annotated and the United States Code Service.

CONCLUSION

We believe that the lawyer licensing process should be expanded to include testing for legal research competency. There are two feasible methods for testing this competency. One assumes an electronic environment, in which examinees are given access to a predetermined library of electronic legal resources and then asked to use that library to answer questions or solve problems. The second is a series of multiple-choice questions about legal research resources, concepts, and methodology. Given the current limitations on providing an electronic environment, a multiple-choice exam probably is the most appropriate option. Regardless of the form of testing, essential groundwork needs to be completed to determine the subject matter to be tested and the goals of testing.

NOTES

1. For a general discussion of the subject of including legal research on the bar exam, see Steven M. Barkan, *Should Legal Research be Included on the Bar Exam? An Exploration of the Question*, 99 L. Lib. J. 403 (2007), reprinted in Richard A. Danner & Frank G. Houdek eds., *Legal Information and the Development of American Law: A Collection of Essays Inspired by the Contributions of Robert C. Berring* (Thomson/West 2008) and in 77 (2) B. Examr. 35 (May 2008). This article incorporates and expands upon one aspect of the discussion in that article.

2. Current information on these tests as well as sample questions are available at www.ncbex.org.

3. ABA, Section of Legal Education and Admissions to the Bar, *Legal Education and Professional Development: An Educational Continuum: Report of the Task Force on Law Schools and the Profession: Narrowing the Gap, Statement of Fundamental Lawyering Skills and Professional Values* 163 (1992) [hereinafter the MacCrate Report].

4. To our knowledge, a statement of the specific assumptions about the legal research environment and the legal research knowledge and competencies that would be evaluated on the bar exam does not yet exist. The MacCrate Report, *supra* n. 3, presented a general statement of legal research that is an excellent starting point. A 1997 report of the Research Instruction Caucus of the American Association of Law Libraries (AALL) attempted to build on the MacCrate Report. The AALL report, however, is dated and incomplete. *See* Research Instruction Caucus, Am. Assn. L. Libr., *Core Legal Research Competencies: A Compendium of Skills and Values as Defined in the ABA's MacCrate Report* (Ellen M. Callinan ed., 1997), available at http://www.aallnet.org/sis/ripssis/PDFs/core.pdf. *See also*, Barkan, *supra* n. 1, at 407–409.

5. At that meeting, the group recognized the importance of and initiated the development of a statement of legal research knowledge and competencies that could serve as the basis for drafting multiple-choice questions about legal research. That initiative, however, has not been pursued.

Great Expectations: New Associates' Research Skills from Law School to Law Firm

JILL L. K. BROOKS
Robinson, Bradshaw & Hinson, P. A., Charlotte, North Carolina, USA

This article is a perspective on what research skills new associates in legal practice need. Knowledge of print and electronic resources and cost-effective search strategies are the main focus of the article. A checklist of research skills is included along with recommendations on what law schools and law firm librarians can do to assist law students and new attorneys in learning these skills.

As the leaves start to change and the air becomes a little colder, a little crisper, law firm librarians begin to prepare for the arrival of the new fall Associates. Law firm librarians expect these new associates to have a firm grasp of legal research skills and an idea of the best resources to use in a given situation. Is this an unreasonable expectation?

Generally, a law firm librarian's work with a new associate begins before he or she is hired. As summer associates, the law students are not expected to have highly refined research skills or an understanding of the best resources to use for a particular research project. Law firm librarians spend extra time showing these "green" recruits the basic legal resources, easing them in slowly and not wanting to overwhelm them with too much information. We show the summer associates which treatises to use in what situation and how to formulate search strategies. By the end of their summer with us, the summer associates should have acquired a basic grasp of law firm research strategies.

When they return as new associates, we librarians go through the same steps, showing them our collection and online resources. But there is now a new expectation for the new hires. We expect that, after their years in law school and time spent as summer associates, they should know how to conduct legal research efficiently and know the appropriate resources to turn to for conducting research. Unfortunately, this premise is not always the case. Not only do new associates not know the best research resources to use, in some cases they do not know how to identify the general subject matter area where resources might be found. These unfocused research skills equate to inefficiencies, which lead to lost time and increased costs that law firms can ill afford.

This paper is my perspective on what research skills new associates need and my recommendations on what law schools and law firm librarians can do to assist new recruits in learning these skills. To gain some perspective on this issue, I enlisted the help of my colleagues, both attorneys and law firm librarians, to answer three to four brief questions on new associate research skills. The attorneys polled came from my law firm.[1] I polled thirty-two first- through fifth-year attorneys and received ten responses. Law firm librarians were polled locally in Charlotte, North Carolina and on a national library Listserv, Law-Lib. I received two replies locally and eight replies nationally.

The questions for the attorneys were:

1. What research skills do you think you needed as a new hire?
2. What search methods should law schools focus on?
3. How could law schools and law firm librarians ease the transition from academic to firm research?

The librarians were also asked the first three questions regarding new associate skills, with the addition of a fourth question:

4. How much do you think new associates should know about legal research, either using electronic or books, when they start at a law firm?

The following sections detail the responses I received to my questions and include suggestions and recommendations for helping law students be better prepared to enter practice.

1. WHAT RESEARCH SKILLS DO YOU THINK YOU NEEDED AS A NEW HIRE?

It was surprising that all of the surveyed attorneys agreed with the law firm librarians regarding the lack of research skills they had as new associates. Overall, attorneys and law firm librarians thought new associates needed skills using secondary and industry-specific resources in conducting cost-effective search strategies. "I think law school focuses mainly on online case law research. I wasn't really aware of how helpful *Corpus Juris Secundum, American Jurisprudence*, and *American Law Reports* were until I started as a summer associate/new associate," stated one attorney. Note an important nuance to that statement: the attorney stated that he had had exposure to *American Jurisprudence-* and *Corpus Juris Secundum-*type materials but was not aware of just how helpful and useful these materials were. This is a big problem with research instruction in law schools, not emphasizing how important encyclopedic treatises are. Sixty percent of the responding attorneys stated limited time was given to secondary sources in their legal research class, and all acknowledged at least some unfamiliarity with industry-specific materials.

Law firm librarians also overwhelmingly stated that their new associates had little to no knowledge of secondary and industry-specific resources. Their respective new associates lacked knowledge of particular Web sites and resources, such as Bureau of National Affairs Tax Management Portfolio Series, Commercial Clearing House (CCH) and Research Institute of America (RIA)materials, Pacer, Securities Mosaic, 10-K Wizard, and SEC Net, to name a few.[2] This lack of knowledge seriously limits new attorneys' ability to find relevant on-point information in a timely manner. New associates also lacked an understanding that print resources can sometimes provide more helpful information than blindly searching online. Unaccustomed to using print materials, new associates are obviously unfamiliar with techniques for searching digests and indexes, as well as the use of pocket parts and supplemental materials. To be more efficient researchers, I recommend that new hires use the print and electronic resources available from the law firm library before starting their research on Westlaw or Lexis.

Another area the surveyed attorneys and law firm librarians agreed upon was the new associates' limited knowledge of cost-effective and efficient research techniques. In a law firm setting, cost-effective and efficient searching go hand in hand.[3] An attorney's billable time is wasted if he or she is not doing either effective or efficient searching. While discussing the survey questions with the Westlaw representative at my firm, the representative agreed with the surveyed participants regarding their deficiencies in research skills. Over the years she has noticed that there has been a switch at most law schools from teaching the query style of terms and connectors to teaching natural language in electronic research. New associates do not know how to search using Boolean operators, connecting terms and phrases, or in the case of Westlaw, using key numbers. Because both query style and natural language search strategies can be useful, students should be familiar with both.

Law firm librarians do not expect new hires to know which words and phrases are the best to use to create a proper search string, but they do expect new hires to know basic operator and connector symbols to create these search strings. Law school programs should emphasize both the natural language and basic Boolean searching, such as how to expand a word, how to look for alternate spellings, and how to use proximity operators. Knowledge of both Boolean and natural language searching will ensure that new attorneys conduct their online research in a cost-effective and efficient manner.

2. WHAT SEARCH METHODS SHOULD LAW SCHOOLS FOCUS ON?

Answers to the second survey question focused on what law schools can do to help new hires become better researchers. Survey participants generally stated that law schools should focus on secondary resources and cost-effective research strategies. These results are not surprising since the respondents agreed that new associates needed better search skills in regard to secondary sources. Surveyed attorneys noted the limited amount of time given to teach legal research skills in law school. One attorney respondent said, "I think law schools do just about all they can by focusing on [electronic] case law searching—these are so fundamental, it's necessary to train lawyers on them and only a limited amount of time exists to teach about legal research. However, it would be nice to see a more thorough treatment of secondary sources, particularly in areas where a lawyer has little expertise (which, for law students, is every area). Because the online searches are free for law students, there is little incentive to get a general background in an area of law before diving right in to Westlaw or Lexis."

One of the most common problems I have experienced with new associates is their treatment of Westlaw and Lexis as if these sophisticated databases were Google. The new associates seem to think that the answer to any legal question should be found on either of these databases and are surprised when it is not there. Law students rely so heavily on these databases to the exclusion of other viable resources that they do not know where else to turn for background knowledge on a subject. Some of these new associates use Westlaw and Lexis as a security blanket. They do not trust themselves enough to rely on free government sites and do not recognize that print resources may contain materials that are organized, digested, analyzed, and more useful than the raw material in Westlaw and Lexis databases.

Law schools generally offer just one legal research class, typically taught in the first year of law school. Some of these courses stand alone while others are part of a legal writing course. One attorney described her school's focus on teaching research skills this way: "In the first year, my law school was very focused on teaching the research skills pertinent to our legal writing class. Aside from the three papers in that class, we did not have many opportunities to practice search strings and our research skills. Unless you took a more upper level 'litigation' course (i.e., appellate practice) or seminar classes, you might not have any other opportunities to practice [research skills]."

My firm's Lexis representative agreed with this statement. The absence of classes requiring substantive research in law students' second and third years leaves their search skills rusty. She added that the law students' limited amount of time combined with a professor's tendency to give assignments where the students are all using the same sources and finding definitive answers does little to develop law students' search skills. Students do not learn what it feels like to search around for an answer nor are they taught when to stop searching because no answer exists.

It would be advisable for law schools, instead of requiring just one legal research class (often combined with a writing class), to require two such courses. One could focus on case law and the entire litigation process. The second course, perhaps offered in the third year to provide a natural bridge to the world of practice, could focus on secondary materials and other legal areas outside of litigation. Both of these courses could synthesize print and electronic resources in the overall research process using similar secondary resources, such as legal encyclopedias, digests, and forms. By using similar materials in both classes, the usefulness of secondary resources would be reinforced without being redundant.

My fellow law firm librarians also thought professors should spend time teaching their law students that answers to legal problems are not always black and white nor are they all found in one place. Sometimes a lawyer must construct answers from bits and pieces found in many resources: online and print. New hires need to know where to find all these pieces and that sometimes no answer exists.

Another key factor essential to cost-effective researching is knowing when to stop. New associates need to be confident enough in their research strategies to know when they have conducted a reasonably thorough search of both print and electronic materials. They should know that there may be an occasion when no answer is to be found and should be able to show the partner or senior associate the steps they took to arrive at this conclusion.

Legal research classes should supplement the fundamental lawyering skills of problem solving, analysis and reasoning, communication, organization, and time management skills as listed in the American Bar Association (ABA) report, *Legal Education and Professional Development: An Educational Continuum*.[4] Law schools should focus on methods that encompass secondary resources in electronic and print formats along with case law searching and the use of Boolean search strategies. New associates would then be aware of how useful secondary materials can be in advocating before a judge or jury, writing an opinion letter, or drafting a contract.

3. HOW COULD LAW SCHOOLS AND LAW FIRM LIBRARIANS EASE THE TRANSITION FROM ACADEMIC TO FIRM RESEARCH?

The responses to question three concentrated on law schools providing an understanding of when to conduct online research and when to use print materials cost-effectively. In order to provide a smooth transition from an academic setting to a law firm setting, this survey question also focused on how law schools and law firms can work together on training new hires.

Respondents indicated that law schools should teach that online research is preferable to print when a lawyer is dealing with unique search terms, emerging areas of law, multistate searching, updating cases and statutes, or verifying resources. As an example of when online searching is best, in May 2008, our firm began working with a client in the area of genetic discrimination. A federal law on this topic was passed in April 2008 and there was very little print material available. The only place to locate information on genetic discrimination was online, as this was an emerging area of law and few print sources had had time to move through the publication process.

Respondents also indicated a need for greater education regarding practice-related publications. Because law firms vary in the areas of law they practice and where they practice, having law schools teach industry-specific or local government resources would not necessarily be feasible. However, schools should introduce some practice-specific secondary resources, like *Current Legal Forms with Tax Anaylsis*,[5] *Moore's Federal Practice*[6] or *Collier on Bankruptcy*.[7]

Attorneys stated that law firm librarians should introduce to new associates the various online databases to which the firm subscribes and provide training sessions on these databases. Again, if law schools were to teach general principles about when to use electronic databases, law firm librarians could focus on introducing new associates to the relevant electronic sources to which the firm subscribes and advising new associates on their use.

Survey respondents stated that new associates also need extra training on when to use hourly or transaction-based electronic resources. A discussion of the firm's policies regarding the use of premium resources (those outside the firm's normal flat-rate contract), and client billing procedures should also be included in these training sessions. Law firm librarians need to make sure new associates understand how fast online pay-for-service charges can pile up during searches without scaring new hires into not using the resources when it is cost-effective to do so. Since each firm has different contracts in place with online vendors, the law firm librarian must explain how these contracts work and the best way to conduct research within their parameters.

Firm librarians should emphasize to new associates that we are still in a mixed-media world and that print and electronic resources each have a place. Only since 1994 has the World Wide Web come into general use, making online information plentiful and easily accessible.[8] Many online sites do not provide historical information; therefore, it is necessary in certain cases to turn to print resources.

Print resources can help provide the big picture in an area of law that is new to an attorney; legal research professors can and should teach this skill. Besides providing general legal knowledge on a subject, print resources help attorneys explore complex concepts and legal theories. Law firm librarians surveyed stated new attorneys need to know that books are the best source to use when relevant search terms are too common, ambiguous, or have too many synonyms. Law school research classes should demonstrate how to start in the print collection and then use online resources to confirm results and fill in details.[9] This method is more cost-effective and more accurate. Because historical coverage in electronic resources is minimal, print resources may be superior to electronic when searching for older information. Westlaw provides access to many law review journals but its historical coverage is limited. The print version or another electronic resource like HeinOnline would be the go-to resource in this instance.

One of the surveyed new associates stated, "So much of the transition [from law school to law firm] is just trial and error and figuring things out for yourself. I think [librarians] just being available and stressing that 'no question is a dumb question' might be the best way." Just knowing there is someone available to assist with questions is a great help to most of my new hires. But without law schools providing background on these basic questions, new associates start at a disadvantage. This is especially true for new attorneys who begin practice without the benefit of a law firm librarian.

4. HOW MUCH DO YOU THINK NEW ASSOCIATES SHOULD KNOW ABOUT LEGAL RESEARCH, EITHER USING ELECTRONIC OR BOOKS, WHEN THEY START AT A LAW FIRM?

The fourth question was directed only to law librarians and asked for their opinion regarding areas where new associates need legal research skills. My colleagues on Law-Lib thought new associates should know more than they do about the structure of law, the various branches of government, and the process of searching primary resources. New associates have shown a limited understanding of the relationship of legislative and regulatory materials and because of this disconnect, they are not using the appropriate resources. According to one librarian, new associates need "an understanding of how the legal system fits together and what print material is used to locate what part of that puzzle. I know this would seem to be a given for folks coming directly from law school; however, I am finding a severe general lack of knowledge in this very basic area." Other law librarians share this concern. Lacking an understanding of the interconnection of administrative law, legislation, and regulations, many new attorneys do not know how federal regulations are promulgated, the difference between a statute and a regulation, and the specific stages involved in how a bill becomes a law.[10]

For example, attorneys need to understand how regulations move through the system from an authorizing statute to a promulgated rule to codification of the regulation. They should have a basic understanding of the agencies to which authority is delegated by specific statutes to promulgate detailed rules and regulations for the implementation of those statutes.

Similarly, in order to research legislative history, new associates must know how the legislative process works—from bill, to session law, to statute—and how material is listed in the *United States Code Congressional and Administrative News*, public laws, House and Senate bills, and committee reports. Many associates come to law firms without this basic knowledge, which is necessary when doing legislative history searches. New associates should also know that state legislative and administrative processes often parallel those of the federal government, and need to know where to turn for state materials.[11]

Law librarians also said that new associates should be aware of bibliographic pathfinders and legal research guides. There are many online encyclopedias for legal researchers that provide basic information and resources for conducting legal research. Zimmerman on Lexis is one of the most popular online encyclopedic guides that provides broad and specific information on a variety of legal topics.[12] Many colleges and law firm librarians provide subject area pathfinders listing available bibliographic electronic and print resources. There are guides to other areas of law outside litigation. Harvard's foreign and international law resources[13] and Georgetown's corporate law research guide are two other popular Web sites.[14] Law schools should make new attorneys aware of these "go-to" resources. Professors may not have enough time to cover all aspects of legal searching in their classes, but introducing these guides to their students can provide much needed assistance and also help with legislative and historical searching.

To quickly review, I proposed new associates should possess the following skills:

- When to start research in print and when to start electronically.
- Boolean searching: use of "and," "or," exclamation points, asterisks, and parentheses.
- Ability to search local information: city, county, and zoning codes.
- Knowledge of state and local bar sites for primary resources, amendments to court rules, and professional development.
- Legislative history searching: statutes, session laws, and committee reports.
- Understanding of administrative law and regulation.
- Secondary resources: corporate, real estate, and other areas of law besides litigation.
- Use of Pacer: district, circuit, and bankruptcy docket searching.
- Cost-effective research: difference between transactional and per-minute searching.
- Knowing where current information and updates are located in print materials, pocket parts and supplements.
- Knowledge of comprehensive free Web sites to find legal information: Thomas.gov, GPOAcess.gov, USCourts.gov, and Zimmerman's Guide.

Attorneys, law schools, and law firm librarians must work together to ensure that new associates have a solid legal research background so that they are prepared to handle the many aspects of law that will come their way. New associates should above all understand that searching is work. There is no magic formula to finding the law. Experienced practitioners make it look easy precisely because they have experience. They have extensive knowledge of relevant cases and they know which search terms and words to use since they have been practicing in that subject area longer.

The best step any cost-effective researcher who is unfamiliar with a topic should take is to visit that subject area in the library. Using subject area-specific books is the fastest and easiest method to formulate the most cost-effective search strategy and determine if the use of Westlaw or Lexis is necessary. These books can provide a general understanding of the subject matter and provide better search terms than what may be available on Westlaw or Lexis. Many new attorneys think they are skilled with searching Westlaw and Lexis but find that moving from using a free service at their law school to a fee-for-service at the law firm adds the pressure of doing a search correctly the first time. Lack of knowledge or general understanding of the subject matter only adds to this pressure, causing new associates to make costly mistakes.

While law schools have focused on the study of case law, they have not necessarily focused on how cases progress through the courts, how regulations are promulgated, the various branches of the government, and secondary research resources. Due to the numerous electronic and print resources available, new associates will not have the knowledge to select the best or correct source without exposure to encyclopedic treatises, administrative law materials, and other secondary and industry-specific materials. This lack of fundamental legal knowledge limits new hires' ability to conduct cost-effective search strategies. Offering (if not requiring) more than one legal research class in law school would help new associates develop stronger search skills. Law schools should provide a better foundation in legal research for their graduates and an understanding of when online research or print research is the preferable and most cost-effective method to use.

Having successful new associates does not just rest on law schools—the responsibility rests on firm librarians as well. Life is all about diving in and getting your hands dirty. Law school prepares attorneys for the law firm experience but not with the knowledge of how a law firm operates.[15] Each firm is unique and deals with different aspects of the law, but across the board, law firms expect new hires to have certain basic skills. As one of my library colleagues stated, "[New associates] can't be expected to know everything, but they should understand the differences between and uses of primary and secondary resources, the basics of the legislative and regulatory processes, and the power they have to impact the cost of the research they do." Working together, law schools and law firm librarians can provide the foundation of legal research skills on which new attorneys build to become successful practitioners.

NOTES

1. Robinson, Bradshaw & Hinson, P. A. (RBH), located in Charlotte, North Carolina is a full-service law firm founded in 1960. RBH serves as counsel to public and closely held corporations operating in domestic and foreign markets, limited liability companies, limited and general partnerships, individuals, municipal, county and state agencies, public utilities, health care institutions, financial institutions, and tax-exempt organizations.

2. CCH has a searchable online database of corporate and tax materials as well as print materials. RIA has a searchable online database of tax materials as well as print materials. Pacer is a federal docket database; Securities Mosaic, 10-K Wizard and SEC Net are all securities databases.

3. Bob Berring et al., *Research Skills for Lawyers and Law Students: Ideas and Solutions on Training Challenges Faced by Law Firm, Academic, and Government Law Librarians* (AALL Annual Meeting in New Orleans, La., Thomson West Town Hall Meeting, 2007), available at http://www.west.thomson.com/librarian.

4. ABA, Section of Legal Education and Admissions to the Bar, *Legal Education and Professional Development: An Educational Continuum: Report of the Task Force on Law Schools and the Profession: Narrowing the Gap, Statement of Fundamental Lawyering Skills and Professional Values* (1992), available at http://www.abanet.org/legaled/publications/onlinepubs/maccrate html.

5. Jacob Rabkin & Mark H. Johnson, *Current Legal Forms with Tax Analysis* (Matthew Bender 1948).

6. James William Moore et al., *Moore's Federal Practice* (3d ed., Matthew Bender 1999).

7. William Miller Collier, *Collier on Bankruptcy* (Lawrence P. King ed., 15th ed., Matthew Bender Rev. 1996).

8. Robert Cailliu, *A Little History of the World Wide Web*, available at http://www.w3.org/History.html (1995).

9. Lisa Smith-Butler, *Cost-Effective Legal Research Redux: How to Avoid Becoming the Accidental Tourist, Lost in Cyberspace*. 9 Fla. Coastal L. Rev. 293 (2008).

10. Bobbi Cross, *Top 10 Things Law Librarians Want New Associates to Know*, Law.com (Apr. 2006), available at http://www.law.com/jsp/article.jsp?id=1145442290538.

11. Michelle I. Mitchell, *Setting the Bar: Legal Research Benchmarks Create More Effective Training in Law Firms*, AALL Spectrum 12, 27 (Dec. 2008).

12. http://www.lexisnexis.com/infopro/zimmerman (last accessed Jun. 2009).

13. http://www.law.harvard.edu/library/research/guides/index.html (last accessed Jun. 2009).

14. http://www.ll.georgetown.edu/research/browse_topic.cfm?62 (last accessed Jun. 2009).

15. Barbara Cornwell Holt, *Law Librarians' Role in Developing Associates: Law Librarians Fulfill a Vital Responsibility in Bolstering the Research Skills of a Firm's Most Expensive and Critical Resources: Its Associates*, Prof. Leg. Mgt. Week Mag. (2008), available at http://www.plmw.org/ala_resources/plmwissue_08/PLMW Magazine2008-AALL.pdf.

The Development of the Skills Curriculum in Law Schools: Lessons for Directors of Academic Law Libraries

DUNCAN ALFORD
Coleman Karesh Law Library, University of South Carolina, Columbia, South Carolina, USA

Recent challenges to the status and tenure of law library directors has questioned their role law as teachers and scholars. This article analyzes the development of the legal research, clinical, and legal writing curriculum in U.S. law schools and identifies strategies that law librarians could choose to employ to bolster their status as the preeminent teachers of legal research in the academy.

Law libraries have had a long-standing educational role in U.S. legal education, as law libraries existed even before law schools became the primary institution educating attorneys. Indeed, "reading the law" was the original legal education experience in the United States. Apprentices would work and study with an established attorney who could provide them with an adequate collection of law books to allow them to prepare for their career. The College of William & Mary organized one of the earliest law collections in the United States.[1] As part of the college library, the law collection was started before George Wythe, America's first law professor,[2] began teaching law at William & Mary in 1790.[3] Similarly, in 1817, the Harvard Law School advertised that its students would have access to a "complete law library."[4] Columbia University likewise focused on locating "suitable quarters to provide a law library"[5] when it started its law school in 1858.

I wish to thank Barbara Bintliff for her perceptive comments and patient editing of this article. Her insights greatly added to this article. Any errors or omissions are of course my own.

Cornell University purchased its law library in 1886 before university trustees agreed to create a department of law there.[6] Although their collections were small, these early law libraries developed through "the personal dedication of professors, deans, alumni, and private practitioners who foresaw that the future of the law school would be dependent on the quality of its library."[7]

Law libraries have been central to legal education and important in the professionalization of legal education offered by law schools since the late nineteenth and early twentieth centuries. The original Articles of the American Association of Law Schools (AALS), organized in 1900, recognized the importance of law libraries to legal education. A primary objective of AALS was to improve legal education in the United States. The sixth article of the Articles of Association outlined the requirements of AALS membership and stated that a school must own or have "convenient access to, during all regular library hours, a library that contained the reports of the state in which the school was located and the reports of the Supreme Court of the United States."[8]

Two decades later, the American Bar Association (ABA) appointed a special committee chaired by Elihu Root[9] to study and recommend "what, if any, action shall be taken by this Section and by the ABA to create conditions which will tend to strengthen the character and improve the efficiency of persons to be admitted to the practice of law."[10] In its report issued in 1921 and considered by some to be a "milestone in the evolution of legal education"[11] in the United States, the committee recommended that every law school "shall provide an adequate library available for the use of the students."[12] In 1921, both the ABA and its Section of Legal Education and Admissions to the Bar adopted this standard, among others, recommended by the Elihu Root committee.[13]

Christopher Columbus Langdell, in his reform of legal education at Harvard in the late nineteenth century, promoted the law library as a "preeminent place" in Harvard's program.[14] It was typical in early academic law libraries for a faculty member (or a committee of faculty members) to select the materials for the law library; then, as now, collection development required intellectual as well as practical knowledge. Book selection and general law library oversight by faculty in the nineteenth century was common.[15] In the early twentieth century, as the Industrial Revolution took hold and the United States began its ascent as a world power, the materials of the law grew in scope and complexity. Day-to-day faculty management over collection development and the law library's administration ended. The explosion of legal information (domestic, foreign, and international), its growing variety of formats, and the widening range of faculty scholarship interests and teaching topics made it all but impossible for a faculty member or committee to continue effective library management and collection development.[16] This change was particularly true at the large research libraries, although somewhat less so, at least initially, at the law schools focused on training the legal practitioner.[17] However, as the law continued to increase in complexity and volume, the model of a faculty member whose primary responsibility was teaching and not library administration generally became unworkable for effective library management in all law schools. The need for a trained librarian to manage the increasingly sophisticated system of legal information became clear.

In addition to bringing expertise in information management and especially in collection development, law librarians assumed a teaching role in the early twentieth century and taught legal bibliography to law students, bringing full circle the tradition of the law professor-librarian. In 1923, Frederick Hicks, associate professor of law and law librarian of Columbia University Law School, published one of the first legal research texts (at the time referred to as "legal bibliography"), titled *Materials and Methods of Legal Research*.[18] Thereafter, legal research courses became common in the first-year law school curriculum.[19] In 1939, twenty-three of forty-two law schools surveyed required a course in legal bibliography during the first year.[20] By this time, law librarians were becoming the acknowledged experts in legal research, a role they now serve in modern legal education.

In 1936, seven percent of academic law library directors held a law degree.[21] However, it was fairly obvious that "law school faculties would not bring themselves to consider a nonlawyer on an equal intellectual level,"[22] and faculty status without a law degree was unthinkable. Training in law and librarianship became highly desirable for the academic law librarian. After World War II, legally trained librarians became more common, as did the dual degreed librarian who held both graduate law and library science degrees. By 1962, twenty-nine percent of law library directors were dual degreed, and in 1974, that percentage was fifty-nine percent.[23] The improved credentials of directors, together with their faculty duties of collection development, teaching, and scholarship, commanded faculty status and tenure.

In 1952, the AALS membership standards recommended faculty status for law library directors.[24] Current ABA accreditation standards and AALS membership standards state that law library directors should hold graduate degrees in law and library science, absent "extraordinary circumstances."[25] ABA Accreditation Standard 603(d) requires faculty status and tenure (or security of employment) for law library directors.

Today, as in the 1880s, law libraries are a central component of legal education. Christopher Columbus Langdell recognized this importance when he famously referred to libraries as the "laboratories" or "workshops" of the law school.[26] The early adoption of standards for law libraries by AALS was recognition by the professoriate of this reality. Currently, law libraries provide a complex, sophisticated mix of information and knowledge (in electronic, print, and microform formats) to support the law schools' curriculum and faculty scholarship. Law librarians are educators and teachers who reflect deeply on the methodology of legal research education, as both classroom teachers and as directors of law's academic "laboratories." In order to protect the academic freedom of the law library director to teach and to develop and maintain a high-quality, unbiased collection of legal information that serves and supports the long-term information needs of legal education, law library directors, like other teaching faculty, need, deserve, and have earned the privilege of faculty status and tenure.[27]

Today, approximately eighty percent of academic law library directors have faculty status and tenure at their schools.[28] The system of faculty direction of the law library that began with the creation of modern law schools has been extraordinarily beneficial to the law school; the American law school library is the envy of legal educators worldwide. Yet the library director's faculty status—a status that was recognized as critical early in the development of law schools and institutionalized in accreditation standards in the mid-twentieth century—is being questioned. This questioning has been brought about by changes in law schools, including especially the growth in skills faculties (notably clinicians and legal writing instructors) and their desire for full faculty status and access to tenure, and the aspiration of some law school administrators to introduce a business model to academia that diminishes employment status and protections for some, if not all, faculty. Despite the integral nature of legal research and the law library to the legal education process, law librarians increasingly find themselves defending themselves as "legitimate faculty." This article explores some of the reasons why this challenge to the faculty status of law library directors has occurred and what law library directors can learn from clinical faculty and legal writing faculty about maintaining or improving their status within the legal academy.

THE EMPHASIS ON SKILLS EDUCATION IN RECENT REPORTS ON LAW SCHOOL CURRICULUM

Even before the founding of the ABA's Section on Legal Education in the 1880s, legal education has been an object of discussion and concern among practitioners and the judiciary.[29] Numerous reports on the state of legal education have been issued over the years; among the most influential have been the 1921 Elihu Root report (discussed above), 1973's Cramton Report,[30] and the MacCrate Report of 1992—all products of the ABA. The most recent major report, coming from the Carnegie Foundation,[31] has generated a great deal of discussion about legal education reform in the United States.[32] The main focus of each has been the preparation of attorneys for the practice of law. Each report has emphasized the importance of skills education.

The 1973 Cramton report was the result of an ABA task force appointed to review lawyer competency. The impetus was a public discussion by then-Chief Justice Warren Burger of the professional competence of practicing lawyers.[33] The task force report called for law schools to focus on fundamental skills to improve lawyer competency.[34] The task force identified seven fundamental skills, including "perform[ance of] legal research."[35] The Cramton Report also stressed that "law schools should provide students with greater opportunities in clinical legal education"[36] and legal writing.[37]

In the early 1990s, the ABA's Section on Legal Education and Admissions to the Bar appointed another blue ribbon commission to study legal education. This task force was charged to determine "what skills, what attitudes, what character traits, and what qualities of mind are required of lawyers?"[38] In 1992, this task force issued a report, entitled *Legal Education and Professional Development: An Educational Continuum*, commonly known as the MacCrate Report.[39] The MacCrate Report emphasized the need, identified by practitioners, for additional skills training in law school and explored the role law schools should play in producing practitioners. The report identified ten "fundamental lawyering skills."[40] Among them were legal research and factual investigation.[41] The report noted that legal research is "in essence a process of problem solving."[42] The MacCrate Report praised the "invaluable contribution" of clinics to legal education[43] and noted favorably the funding provided by the Ford Foundation through the Council on Legal Education for Professional Responsibility (CLEPR) to support clinical legal education.[44] The MacCrate Report also recommended that skills faculty should be permanent, full-time teachers within the legal academy.[45]

Most recently, in 2006, the Carnegie Foundation for the Advancement of Teaching issued a report, entitled *Educating Lawyers: Preparation for the Profession of Law*,[46] widely referred to in legal education as the "Carnegie Report." Unlike the earlier reports, this study was prepared by a group of respected researchers primarily outside of the legal academy and the bar. It is part of the Carnegie Foundation's long-term project to examine broadly professional education in the United States.[47] In the report, the Carnegie Foundation identified three "apprenticeships" provided in legal education: the cognitive apprenticeship, the practical apprenticeship, and the apprenticeship of professional identity and purpose.[48]

Law faculty oversee the cognitive apprenticeship primarily through the Socratic method of teaching in substantive law courses. Students develop skills in a practical apprenticeship through clinics and other skills offerings. The teaching of professional ethics and professional responsibility, in the classroom and other settings, constitutes the apprenticeship of professional identity and purpose. The Carnegie Report concludes that the cognitive apprenticeship is currently overemphasized within legal education,[49] and it recommends an integrated approach to law teaching rather than an additive approach.[50] An integrated approach recognizes that education must be "holistic" instead of "atomistic," and that "each aspect of the legal apprenticeship—the cognitive, the practical, and the ethical-social—takes on part of its character from the kind of relationship it has with the others."[51] The prevailing "additive" methodology marginalizes skills and ethical-social education. With its call for a rebalancing of the apprenticeships within legal education, the Carnegie Report has generated a great deal of discussion about the adequacy of the current curriculum in legal education.

A glaring omission from the Carnegie Report is recognition of the importance of the basic skill of legal research.[52] In fact, legal research is barely mentioned at all. Likely this is a consequence of nonlegal academics being the primary investigators in the project, coupled with the reality that research instruction has, in most law schools, been declared a component of the legal writing curriculum. For many, "legal writing" now means "legal writing and legal research," at least in the curricular context. The reality, however, is that legal writing and legal research are different skills, just as negotiation and oral advocacy are different. Writing experts are infrequently also research experts, and the coupling of these fields is an unfortunate development for law students and practitioners alike. These skills have their own, sometimes overlapping, literatures and pedagogies. Law librarians, and especially those with law degrees, are the legal research experts. Why their teaching role in legal education has been deemphasized—and consequently in the latest major report on improving legal skills instruction—is puzzling, given librarians' long dominance of legal research instruction.

A SHORT HISTORY OF THE DEVELOPMENT OF THE LEGAL RESEARCH CURRICULUM

Law librarians have been present in the legal academy almost as long as law schools have been in existence.[53] When Christopher Langdell returned to the Harvard Law School as Dean in 1870, one of his first tasks was reorganizing the law library and hiring the first full-time law librarian there.[54] The publication of case reporters and digests were pivotal developments in the growth of law library collections and the corresponding need for legal research instruction. West Publishing began producing its now-ubiquitous case reporters in the 1880s, and case digests developed shortly thereafter.[55]

Legal publishers were the first legal research instructors, mostly for marketing purposes but certainly beneficial to students. West Publishing was particularly active in providing this instruction,[56] soon sending traveling salesmen around the country to law schools to sell books and teach their use.[57] West also published the *American Law School Review,* which contained articles on how to conduct legal research.[58]

After this initial push by legal publishers, law schools realized the importance of research and assumed the responsibility for legal research instruction; it was soon incorporated into the permanent curriculum. In 1915, Frederick Hicks, the new law librarian at the Columbia Law School, gave a series of lectures on legal research.[59] These lectures proved so popular that he turned them into a series of seminars for law students.[60] Hicks noted that permanent instructors, unlike publisher representatives, would teach resources in an "unprejudiced way."[61] Other law schools rapidly followed Columbia's and Hicks' lead. In 1918, twenty-nine of the approximately 150 accredited law schools[62] offered courses in legal bibliography.[63] By the mid-1920s, half of the law schools in the AALS offered a course on legal bibliography.[64] As one commentator stated, "Since the bibliography courses dealt with description and use of law books, it was natural that law librarians should teach the courses."[65] These early programs were not uniform and typically were organized based on local expediency, such as the availability of books in the library's collection and the availability of enough instructors and funds to pay them.[66]

In the 1940s, legal education changed dramatically, and with it, legal research instruction. Law school enrollments increased rapidly due to veterans returning from service in World War II.[67] Law schools recognized the need for skills instruction in small classes and often combined research and writing. Combined with climbing enrollments, instructional staff shortages became apparent.[68] The University of Chicago Law School addressed this problem by experimenting with graduate instructors hired for one year to teach legal research and writing to small classes of first-year law students.[69] The "Chicago model" was widely emulated nationally and remained the standard until the 1980s. Librarians frequently became "consultants" and "guest lecturers" under the Chicago model, with diminishing responsibility for the entire course.

SHORT HISTORY OF THE DEVELOPMENT OF THE MODERN LEGAL WRITING CURRICULUM

Legal writing instructors appeared in the academy in the mid-twentieth century. The 1953–1954 AALS Directory of Law Teachers listed 126 faculty under the course subject "Legal Writing."[70] Several decades later, in the 1980s and early 1990s, the position of legal writing instructor became commonplace in the legal academy, notably with the influence of the Chicago model but as a result of other approaches to writing instruction as well. By 1992–1993 there were 916 faculty listed under the heading "Legal Research and Writing" in the AALS Directory of Law Teachers of that year.[71]

A galvanizing event in the growth of legal writing faculty was the creation of the Legal Writing Institute (LWI), a professional association of legal writing instructors, which grew out of a 1984 legal writing conference at the University of Puget Sound (UPS).[72] The institute started on a shoestring budget, funded by the remainder of a National Endowment for the Humanities grant awarded to UPS to develop a program of writing across the law school curriculum.[73] During that 1984 conference, legal writing instructors devised a communication strategy and began a newsletter which was first distributed in January 1985.[74] Conference attendees realized that good communication was very important to alleviate the widespread feeling of isolation reported by legal writing instructors, who were few in number in each law school.[75]

The LWI first formally met on March 23, 1985, in Chicago.[76] Its membership was open to anyone interested in legal writing instruction. The initial activities of the Institute were holding a national conference, distributing a newsletter, and later producing a journal, *Legal Writing*, which first appeared in 1991.[77] The journal was a vehicle for scholarly publication by legal writing faculty; the founders of the LWI realized that, in order to gain respect within the academy, their journal needed substantive content and could not be a vehicle intended only to advance legal writing instructors.[78]

In 1990, the LWI began its annual survey of members to determine the range of class size and course content, responsibilities of writing instructors, and a variety of other matters.[79] The results of the survey, detailing and quantifying the duties and achievements of legal writing instructors, were influential in persuading law faculties to improve the status of legal writing instructors.[80] Notwithstanding the annual survey, the LWI retains its focus on teaching and has stayed focused on legal writing education.[81] Legal writing instructors have become involved in the AALS, raising their visibility in the legal professional's scholarly association. In recent years, more than 200 legal writing instructors have regularly attended AALS meetings.[82]

The Association of Legal Writing Directors (ALWD), founded in 1996,[83] has become an advocacy group. It advocates for improved status for legal writing directors and instructors. ALWD also publishes a scholarly journal, the *Journal of the Association of Legal Writing Directors* (*JALWD*). While there is overlap in the membership of ALWD and the LWI, ALWD membership is open only to directors of legal writing programs.[84]

The LWI's newsletter was a critical component in this developing profession, providing information and support for the dispersed professionals. Their scholarly journal, and the zeal with which writing faculty produced academic scholarship for this journal and others, supported their demands for improved status in the academy. Books by writing instructors on teaching legal writing, including research instruction, proliferate and further solidify their case.[85] Creating two organizations—the LWI to focus on educational goals and ALWD to focus on the status of directors and later the status of all legal writing instructors—appears to have served legal writing instructors well.

Legal writing instructors have made great strides in improving their status within the legal academy in recent years and were well positioned to take advantage of the favorable recommendations of the MacCrate Report. They are organized and have successfully persuaded the ABA to incorporate into its accreditation standard guarantees of employment conditions and protections. Writing instructors now are typically permanent faculty with long-term contracts instead of the one-year "Chicago model" graduate instructors. Some writing program directors and, while fewer, some writing faculty members have access to tenure-track positions. Writing instructors usually have many of the perquisites of "doctrinal faculty," including professional development funds, private offices, clerical assistance, and a voice in law school governance. They attend and present at faculty colloquia and works-in-progress sessions, teach substantive classes, and interact with other faculty as colleagues and, almost, equals.

The rise of the legal writing instructors has brought challenges to law librarians. The long-held subject expertise of the librarians, legal research, has been incorporated into legal writing programs. Librarians are too often excluded from the formal instructional program. The classroom responsibility of writing instructors—their unquestionable teaching role—makes them "look" like other faculty. All these developments have raised questions about the rationale for librarian faculty status.

SHORT HISTORY OF THE DEVELOPMENT OF CLINICAL LEGAL EDUCATION

The development of clinical legal education, while less directly affecting law librarians, has many similarities to the development of legal writing instruction. Legal clinics first developed early in the twentieth century at a small number of law schools, including Duke University, University of Southern California and University of Pennsylvania.[86] In 1958, the Ford Foundation, originally motivated in part by the legal aid movement within the United States,[87] awarded $800,000 to establish the National Council on Legal Clinics (NCLC) and to create legal clinics in U.S. law schools. In the mid-1960s, William Pincus, of the Ford Foundation, shifted the NCLC funding toward an educational focus rather than a legal aid focus; the NCLC changed its name to the Council on Legal Education for Responsibility (CLEPR) to reflect its new educational focus.[88] In 1968, after Bill Pincus became CLEPR's president, the Ford Foundation dramatically increased its funding of CLEPR with a $12 million grant for ten years.[89]

Through a series of CLEPR grants to law schools, the number of clinical legal education programs at U.S. law schools grew dramatically from approximately twenty-five to more than eighty between 1968 and 1970[90] representing more than half of the 145 law schools in the United States.[91] Clinical legal education entered the mainstream in U.S. legal education. CLEPR held a national conference in Key Biscayne, Florida in October 1979[92] to assess the ten years of work funded by the Ford Foundation. When CLEPR President Bill Pincus "looked back over the council's ten-year span of activity, he could accurately state that CLEPR had successfully brought together the separate initiatives in the law schools around the country into an effective movement for clinical legal education."[93] Clinical legal education had become "an integral part of legal education in America."[94]

As the Ford Foundation funding ended, the U.S. Department of Education began funding clinical legal education.[95] Through the Law School Clinical Experience Program,[96] popularly referred to as Title IX, the Department of Education granted approximately $87 million to fund clinical education in law schools.[97] As one commentator noted, "no other external funding programs have been as important to the proliferation of clinical legal education programs as the Ford Foundation and Title IX programs. By the end of the Title IX program in September of 1997, there were real-client in-house law school clinical programs in at least 147 law schools."[98]

At the 1979 Key Biscayne meeting, a coordinating committee was formed to improve the status of clinicians in the legal academy. The committee met again that year in New York City to develop a strategic plan. As part of the plan, the committee agreed to advocate for a clinician as a member of the Council of the ABA's Section on Legal Education and Admissions to the Bar (the Section's "executive board"); to reenergize the AALS Section on Clinical Education; and to promote more clinicians for membership on ABA committees.[99]

To further galvanize their profession, a group of clinical teachers formed the Clinical Legal Education Association (CLEA) in 1992, after several years of discussion. Today, the more than 600 members of CLEA include full-time clinical law teachers in U.S. law schools, adjunct clinical faculty, field supervisors, and others interested in clinical legal education.[100] CLEA publishes a scholarly journal, the *Clinical Law Review,* and clinical faculty frequently write articles for other law reviews in addition to books and instructional materials. Their classroom responsibilities, like those of writing instructors, give them credibility as "faculty" in the law school.

These efforts have yielded results. The profession has grown rapidly, and today virtually all U.S. law schools have multiple clinical offerings. In 1972, the AALS Directory of Law Teachers listed 193 faculty under the course subject "Clinical Teaching." In the 2007–2008 edition of this same directory, that number had increased to 1,363 faculty.[101] Clinical faculty successfully argued for ABA accreditation standards that offer them employment benefits and protections, paving the way for writing faculty to do the same. Clinical faculty are increasingly extended faculty governance privileges in law schools, and tenure-track appointments are more and more common, again, often opening the door for writing faculty. Perhaps most telling of the strides made by clinical faculty is that the 2008–2009 chair of the Council of the ABA's Section on Legal Education and Admissions to the Bar, Randy Hertz, is a clinician.

The paths to improved status of clinicians and writing faculty are similar, as are the outcomes. Clinicians began earlier and, consequently, seem to be more likely to be recognized as "real faculty" than are the legal writing faculty, but writing faculty are moving quickly. Meanwhile, law librarians appear to remain on the periphery or at least in the library. Law librarians can learn much from the successes of the legal writing and clinical faculties.

LESSONS LEARNED: KEYS TO SUCCESS

The following are some common factors that allowed clinicians and writing faculty to improve their status in the law school world. As each factor is identified, a corresponding approach law librarians might take is noted. In many instances, law librarians find themselves in very similar positions as their clinical and writing colleagues and only need to capitalize on existing structures and professional activities to answer the current challenges to their status now posed.

Defining an Academic Discipline

Clinicians developed academic disciplines similar to the doctrinal disciplines of the law faculty, focusing on the methodology of clinical legal education, alternative dispute resolution,[102] and the lawyering process as academic fields of study.[103] One commentator notes, "a rich body of clinical scholarship has developed—on the public role of the lawyer, on professional responsibility, on the theory of lawyering, and on clinical legal education itself."[104] To emphasize clinical legal education's intellectual content, CLEA began publishing its scholarly journal, the *Clinical Law Review*, in 1994.

Similar to clinicians, legal writing faculty in their scholarship have emphasized the methodology of teaching legal writing as well as the concepts of legal analysis and communication. They developed academic journals that focused on scholarship and the pedagogy of legal writing; *Legal Writing* began in 1991 and the *JALWD* was first published in 2002. Legal writing instructors have even highlighted their own scholarship by publishing a lengthy bibliography (373 pages) of law review articles and other publications by legal writing instructors.[105] Interestingly, the bibliography reveals that "approximately seventy-five percent of the law review articles legal writing professors have published are about topics in areas other than legal writing, while only twenty-five percent are about legal writing topics."[106]

Law librarians, who are unquestionably academia's legal research experts, have seen their influence over this subject specialty slip away as more and more legal writing programs include legal research instruction. The growth of advanced legal research courses and specialized legal research offerings has slowed this trend, but the minimal role or absence of librarians in first-year research instruction in some law schools lessens librarians' claim to a subject specialty. In addition, many law librarians have focused on bibliographic scholarship or scholarship dealing with the administration of law libraries. With a few exceptions, they have neither brought these topics within the mainstream of legal education nor focused on scholarship related to their educational expertise of teaching legal research. Similar to clinicians and legal writing instructors, law librarians should develop an academic discipline of their own centering on the organization of legal information or on information use, such as the Freedom of Information Act, confidentiality, privacy, the ownership and licensing of information, and the authentication or authoritativeness of information. The development of a pedagogy for legal research is a natural area for law librarian scholarship;[107] this would complement the many works by clinicians and legal writing faculty on pedagogy in their respective fields.

Further, despite having had a scholarly publishing venue for over a century (the *Law Library Journal* was first published in 1908), academic law librarians generally do not emphasize scholarly responsibilities in setting their job priorities.[108] If they wish to retain their status as members of the academic enterprise, law librarians must rethink their priorities. Like the writing faculties especially, law librarians should publish in journals with a wider scholarly audience than the *Law Library Journal*. Bringing attention to important issues related to legal information to a broad audience is an important tactic in bolstering law librarian status.

Using Professional Organizations to Promote Cohesiveness

The relatively small and focused professional organizations serving clinicians and legal writing instructors greatly bolstered their improvement in status. The members of CLEA (with around 650 members), the LWI (about 2,500 members), and AWLD (approximately 210 members) are almost exclusively employed in law schools. CLEA, LWI, and ALWD members have focused agendas and can tailor their activities to most influence their work environment. Each group has an active liaison program with the ABA Council of the Section on Legal Education and Admissions to the Bar and the AALS. These organizations, with a cohesive membership and clear purpose, significantly contributed to the effective advocacy benefiting their membership.

In contrast, the Association of American Law Libraries (AALL), the professional organization for all law librarians, including those in firms, government, and business, has over 5,000 members. Academic law librarians are in the minority in AALL—making up 37.65% of total AALL membership in 2007.[109] AALL's membership and mission are too broad to allow for a concentrated, much less an exclusive, focus on its academic members. However, the very recently organized Society of American Law Library Directors (SALLD) can become the advocacy group that focuses on maintaining and improving the status of law library directors, similar to ALWD, if its members so choose.

Advocating for Status Changes in a Deliberate Manner

Beginning at the Key Biscayne conference in 1979, clinicians organized themselves and developed a plan to advocate for improvement in their status. Legal writing instructors, especially through ALWD, did likewise in the 1990s. Both groups supported their advocacy with detailed factual arguments, such as those generated from the LWI annual survey. Recently, the ABA Section of Legal Education and Admissions to the Bar appointed a task force to study the security of position provisions for all types of law faculty—doctrinal, clinical, writing, library, and decanal—of the accreditation standards as part of a larger review of the standards. The CLEA, LWI, and ALWD submitted letters and position statements to the task force; the ABA Web site did not indicate that AALL, or any other group of law librarians, took a stand.[110]

By developing a plan of advocacy, and with widespread buy-in from their membership, these legal faculty groups have made their cases and improved their status. They are now working to solidify their progress, as necessary, in the face of challenges. Law librarians, who heretofore have enjoyed faculty status in the legal academy, would be wise to heed this lesson.

LESSONS LEARNED: DIFFERENTIATING FACTORS

Law library directors[111] have a unique role in legal education. There is only one law library director per law school, unlike clinical faculty and writing instructors. Law library directors have teaching, administrative, and scholarly duties and oversee programs for faculty, students, the bar, and the public; clinicians and legal writing instructors tend not to have administrative duties and serve students almost exclusively. Therefore, any lessons learned from clinicians and legal writing faculty must be tempered by these significant differences.

Librarians are Scholars and Teachers With Significant Administrative Duties

Law library directors oversee the largest educational program in the law school, an oversight that requires both intellectual engagement and business acumen. Almost all activities and programs of the law library are geared to supporting and enhancing the scholarly mission of the law school. Effective collection development requires full knowledge of and engagement in the school's teaching and research activities. Library programs and services go unused if not coordinated with the needs of students and faculty. Even the arrangement of the collection, which can emphasize research, practice, or the school's subject specialties, reflects an academic purpose. The intellectual activities of the law library director, including teaching and scholarship, encompass a wide breadth.

At the same time, the operational responsibilities of the law library director, which include personnel management, budgeting, space planning, and strategic planning, are business functions that require an administrator's mind. These time-consuming activities cannot be postponed without serious negative consequences to the school's academic mission. Therefore, the administrative duties of the law library director necessarily allow less time for teaching and scholarship than that available to clinicians and legal writing instructors.

Clinicians and Legal Writing Instructors Resemble Teaching Faculty

Clinical and legal writing faculty look like classroom teachers. They have formal classes that include grades, syllabi, assignments, tests, performance evaluations, and all the other typical features of law courses. Doctrinal faculty have, to a certain degree, been more welcoming to legal writing instructors and clinicians because they resemble more closely teaching faculty than most law librarians, many of whom do not teach in the classroom on a regular basis.

THE IMPACT OF THE MacCRATE AND CARNEGIE REPORTS

The relationship between the development of clinical legal education, legal writing instruction, and the two most recent major reports on legal education—MacCrate and Carnegie—is clear. Both reports criticize the legal academy for its preparation of practitioners, and both recommend improved skills instruction as a remedy. The two groups of faculty that offer the majority of law school skills instruction—clinicians and legal writing faculty—have capitalized on these reports and the educational goals behind them to dramatically improve their positions in law schools. The clinicians, who really began their upward trajectory with the Cramton Report, have become very influential players in law school accreditation and scholarly legal organizations. Legal writing faculty have professionalized and are closing ranks in an attempt to do the same.

Law librarians, on the other hand, have been sidelined to a degree in the skills teaching arena and have not benefitted from the increased emphasis on practical legal education. The Cramton and MacCrate reports emphasized the need to improve legal research skills of law graduates. Law librarians generally have not seized the opportunities presented by these reports, unlike clinicians and legal writing instructors.

CONCLUSION

What, then, do we conclude? What is the course of action for law librarians to maintain, and even improve, their status within the academy? I offer the following strategies:

1. *Law librarians must create and take ownership of an academic discipline*. Clinicians and legal writing faculty took ownership of the pedagogy of their disciplines and also created related academic disciplines. They raised the visibility of their disciplines before a wide audience in the legal academy.
2. *Law librarians must energize their professional organizations, or create new ones, to advocate for academic law librarians*. Because of its broad mission and membership, AALL cannot fill this role, and therefore AALL's internal division for academic librarians, the Academic Law Libraries Special Interest Section, will not be allowed to do so. The SALLD may grow into this role. In any event, whatever advocacy organization fills this role, it must devise a comprehensive, strategic plan for advocacy.
3. *The indispensable services of the law librarian must be communicated widely, including to the ABA and the AALS*. Law is a learned profession that is wholly dependent on its information. Law librarians possess intimate understanding of the development, content, and appropriate use of all facets and formats of legal information. Until the practitioners and professors of law understand fully the importance of law librarians, we will continue to face challenges to our status.

If law librarians can organize to implement these strategies, their position in legal education should be strengthened and challenges to faculty status should be quieted. However, until there is a concerted effort among law librarians, the position we have long enjoyed will continue to be eroded and calls for us to justify our very jobs will continue. We, as a profession, must make a choice.

NOTES

1. James Heller, *America's First Law School Library: A History of the College of William & Mary's Marshall-Wythe Library, 1779–1995,* in *Law Librarianship: Historical Perspectives* 45 (F. B. Rothman 1996).

2. *George Wythe, Dictionary of American Biography* (Charles Scribner's Sons 1926–1938).

3. *Id.* at 45.

4. Christine A. Brock, *Law Libraries and Law Librarians: A Revisionist History; or More than You ever Wanted to Know,* in *Law Librarianship: Historical Perspectives* 614 (quoting Arthur Pulling, The Harvard Law School Library, 43 L. Lib. J. 1 (1950)).

5. *Id.* at 615 (quoting Columbia University, Foundation for Research in Legal History, *A History of the School of Law, Columbia University* 44 (1965)).

6. *Id.* at 615.

7. *Id.*

8. Albert J. Harno, *Legal Education in the United States* 89 (Bancroft-Whitney Co. 1953) (citing 23 Rep. Am. B. Assn. 447, 569–570 (1900)).

9. By 1921, Elihu Root was an *eminence grise* of the American Bar. In addition to his prominent legal practice in New York City, Root had served as Secretary of War under President McKinley, Secretary of State under President Theodore Roosevelt, and a U.S. Senator from New York. *Elihu Root*, *Encyclopedia of World Biography* (2d. ed., Gale Research 1998).

10. Harno, *supra* n. 8, at 103 (quoting 45 Rep. Am. B. Assn. 465–466 (1920).

11. Harno, *supra* n. 8, at 103.

12. *Id.* at 105.

13. Alfred Zantzinger Reed, Present-Day Law Schools in the United States and Canada 547 (Carnegie Foundation for the Advancement of Teaching 1928).

14. Brock, *supra* n. 4, at 616.

15. *Id.* at 616.

16. *Id.* at 617–618.

17. *Id.*

18. Frederick C. Hicks, *Materials and Methods of Legal Research* (The Lawyers Co-operative Publishing Co. 1923). This seminal book was published in two later editions—the second edition in 1933 and a third edition in 1942.

19. Marjorie D. Ogden, *First-Year Legal Research and Writing Then and Now*, 25 J. Leg. Educ. 538, 539 (1972).

20. *Id.* at 539, n. 7.

21. *Id.* at 620.

22. Brock, *supra* n. 4, at 619.

23. *Id.*

24. *Id. See generally id.* at 620–621 for a concise summary of changes in the accreditation standards for law library directors. American Association of Law Schools, Standards, Standard III-2(a), Proceedings of the American Association of Law Schools 228 (1953). This revised standard on law librarian status was adopted at the December 1952 AALS annual meeting. Proceedings of the American Association of Law Schools 49 (1952).

25. ABA Accreditation Standard 603(c), AALS Executive Committee Regulation 6–8.6 Related to Bylaw 6–8, available at http://www.aals.org/about_handbook_requirements.php (last accessed 8 Mar. 2009).

26. Langdell stated: "We have also constantly inculcated the idea that the [law] library is the proper workshop of [law] professors and students alike: that it is to us all that the laboratories of the university are to the chemists and physicists, the museum of natural history to the zoologists, the botanical garden to the botanists." Christopher Columbus Langdell, Address at Harvard University "Quarter-Millennial" Celebration (5 Nov. 1886), in 3 L. Q. Rev. 123, 124 (1887).

27. *See generally* Spencer L. Simons, *What Interests Are Served When Academic Law Library Directors are Tenured Law Faculty? An Analysis and Proposal*, 58 J. Leg. Educ. 245 (2008); James Donovan, *Do Librarians Deserve Tenure? Casting An Anthropological Eye upon Role Definition within the Law School*, 88 L. Lib. J. 382 (1996).

28. Linda Ryan, 2004 Academic Law Library Director Survey (on file with the author). Professor Ryan updated this survey in 2007 and found no significant differences.

29. *See generally* Charles Warren, *A History of the American Bar* (Little, Brown and Company, Inc. 1911). In particular, Chapter XIV, Early Law Professorships and Schools describes the various educational programs in the late eighteenth century and nineteenth century America and the reasons for the varied programs available to education attorneys then. According to Albert Harno, "it appears that legal education and bar admission were subjects of concern to the ABA from the time of its origin." Harno, *supra* n. 8, at 73.

30. ABA, Section of Legal Education and Admissions to the Bar, *Lawyer Competency: The Role of Law Schools*, (1979) [hereinafter the Cramton Report]. The Cramton Report is named after the task force Chairman, Roger C. Cramton, dean of Cornell Law School at the time.

31. William M. Sullivan et al., *Educating Lawyers: Preparation for the Profession of Law* 79 (Jossey-Bass 2007) [hereinafter the Carnegie Report].

32. *See generally* Neil Hamilton, *Professionalism Clearly Defined*, 18 Prof. Law. 4 (Winter 2008); Michael Schill, *Beyond the First Year*, Natl. L.J. (7 July 2008); Thomas Adcock, *Report: Clinical Approach is*

Cure for What Ails Legal Education, N.Y. L.J. (12 Jan. 2007); Nelson P. Miller, *An Apprentice of Professional Identity: A Paradigm for Educating Lawyers*, 87 Mich. B.J. 20 (Jan. 2008); James R. Maxeiner, *Educating Lawyers Now and Then: Two Carnegie Critiques of the Common Law and the Case Method*, 35 Intl. J. Leg. Info. 1 (Spring 2007).

33. Cramton Report, *supra* n. 30, at 1.

34. Cramton Report, *supra* n. 30, at 3 (Recommendation 3).

35. *Id.* at 9.

36. Michael I. Swygert, *The Standardizing and Secularizing of Law Schools*, 38 Val. U. L. Rev. 1002, 1006 (2004).

37. Cramton Report, *supra* n. 30, at 15.

38. Robert MacCrate, *The Last Word on a New Beginning*, in The MacCrate Report: Building the Educational Continuum 145 (West Publishing Co. 1994) (citing Judge Wahl).

39. ABA, Section of Legal Education and Admissions to the Bar, *Legal Education and Professional Development: An Educational Continuum: Report of the Task Force on Law Schools and the Profession: Narrowing the Gap, Statement of Fundamental Lawyering Skills and Professional Values* (1992) [hereinafter "the MacCrate Report"].

40. *Id.* at 135.

41. *Id.* at 138–139 (skills section 3, skills section 4).

42. *Id.* at 163.

43. *Id.* at 238.

44. *Id.* at 242.

45. *Id.* at 245. *See also* Recommendation 24, *Id.* at 333–334.

46. Carnegie Report, *supra* n. 31.

47. Other reports in this project deal with the education of clergy, engineers, and future members of the professoriate. The Carnegie Foundation has a long history of analyzing and influencing the development of higher education in the United States.

48. Carnegie Report, *supra* n. 31, at 79.

49. *Id.* at 191.

50. *Id.* An integrated approach combines the three "apprenticeships" into one educational experience. An additive approach sees skills and ethical-social learning as "merely adjuncts" to cognitive instruction. *Id.*

51. *Id.*

52. Richard Leiter, *The Missing Lawyering* Skill, AALL Spectrum 22, 24 (July 2008).

53. *See generally* Frederick C. Hicks, *The Teaching of Legal Bibliography*, 11 L. Lib. J 1 (1918); Robin K. Mills, *Legal Research Instruction in the Law Schools, The State of the Art or, Why Law School Graduates Do Not Know How to Find the Law*, 70 L. Lib. J. 343 (1977); Thomas A. Woxland, *Why Can't Johnny Research? or It All Started With Christopher Columbus Langdell*, 81 L. Lib. J. 451 (1989); Joyce Manna Janto and Lucinda D. Harrison-Cox, *Teaching Legal Research: Past and Present*, 84 L. Lib. J. 281 (1992).

54. Woxland, *supra* n. 53, at 456.

55. *Id.* Even earlier, the Harvard Law School created a system of student law clubs "that provided instruction in legal research." Janto, *supra* n. 53, at 282 (citing Sidney P. Simpson, *The New Curriculum of the Harvard Law School*, 51 Harv. L. Rev. 965, 982 (1938)).

56. Hicks, *supra* n. 53, at 2.

57. *Id.*

58. *Id.*

59. Janto & Harrison-Cox, *supra* n. 53, at 283.

60. *Id.*

61. Hicks, *supra* n. 53, at 4.

62. *Id.*

63. Walter W. Cook, *The Improvement of Legal Education and of Standards for Admission to the Bar*, in *Annual Report of the American Bar Association* 547, 548 (1917).

64. Mills, *supra* n. 53, at 344.

65. Marjorie Dick Rombauer, *First-Year Legal Research and Writing: Then and Now* 25 J. Leg. Educ. 538, 340 (1973).

66. Woxland, *supra* n. 53, at 453.

67. Mills, *supra* n. 53, at 344.

68. *Id.*

69. *Id.*

70. AALS Directory of Law Teachers 51–52 (1953–1954).

71. AALS Directory of Law Teachers 1125–1130 (1992–1993). This provides an inexact count because many librarians were also listed in this category, but the clear and dramatic growth in the ranks of legal writing instructors is nonetheless evident.

72. Mary S. Lawrence, *The Legal Writing Institute The Beginning: Extraordinary Vision, Extraordinary Accomplishment*, 11 J. Leg. Writing Inst. 213, 214 (2005).

73. *Id.* at 215.

74. *Id.* at 230.

75. *Id.* at 225.

76. *Id.* at 227.

77. *Id.* at 233.

78. *Id.* at 233.

79. *Id.* at 239. The recent surveys are available on the ALWD Web site at http://www.alwd.org/surveys/2004-2008.html. The latest survey, 2007–2008 Survey Report, is available at http://www.alwd.org/surveys/survey_results/2008_Survey_Results.pdf.

80. *Id.* at 241.

81. *Id.*

82. *Id.* at 248. Interestingly, the author notes that law librarians were involved in the Legal Writing Section early on, but as the section focused more on legal writing, law librarians became less involved and created their own AALS section. *Id.*

83. Ruth Singleton, *Writing Directors Link Status and New Manual to Teaching Quality*, Natl. L.J. A11 (6 Sept. 1999).

84. Lawrence, *supra* n. 72, at 243.

85. *See e.g.* Amy Sloan, *Basic Legal Research: Tools and Strategies* (Aspen Publishers 2009); Diana R. Donahoe, *Teachinglaw.com* (e-casebook, Aspen 2008).

86. Robert MacCrate, *Educating a Changing Profession: From Clinic to Continuum*, 64 Tenn. L. Rev. 1099, 1103 (1997). Jerome Frank, Herman Oliphant, and Carl Llewellyn were legal realists who called for education in practical skills for law students in the mid-twentieth century. A number of the early legal clinics in law schools were joint ventures with legal aid clinics. For example, the Edwin F. Mandel Legal Aid Clinic opened in 1957 at the University of Chicago Law School as a joint venture with the Legal Aid Bureau of United Charities. Elizabeth Austin, *Clinics Expanding the Range of Law School Education*, 26 Chi. Law. 16 (Sept. 2003).

87. MacCrate, *supra* n. 86, at 1108.

88. *Id.* at 1109.

89. *Id.* at 1111.

90. *Id.* at 1111.

91. U.S. Dept. of Commerce, *Statistical Abstract of the United States* 188 (2007) (Table 297; First Professional Degrees Earned in Selected Professions: 1970 to 2004).

92. *Id.* at 1113. CLEPR held a national conference at Buck Hill Falls, Pa. in 1973 to assess the first five years of the grant.

93. MacCrate, *supra* n. 86, at 1112.

94. *Id.* at 1114.

95. Margaret M. Barry, Jon C. Dubin & Peter A. Joy, *Clinical Education for this Millennium: The Third Wave*, 7 Clin. L. Rev. 1, 19 (2000).

96. Pub. L. No. 96–374, 94 Stat. 1374 (3 Oct. 1980).

97. Barry, *supra* n. 95, at 20.

98. *Id.* at 19 (citations omitted). The Law School Clinical Experience Program and Title IX refer to the same funding program.

99. Interview with Roy Stuckey, Prof. Emeritus, U. S.C., Sept. 2008 (notes on file with the author).

100. Clinical Legal Education Association, available at http://www.cleaweb.org/about/mission. html (last accessed 22 Dec. 2008).

101. AALS Directory of Law Teachers 670–671 (1972); AALS Directory of Law Teachers 1218–1227 (2007–2008). The course subject was first listed in the AALS Directory in the 1971 edition. AALS Directory of Law Teachers 573 (1971). Another source reports that in 1989 there were approximately 800 clinicians

within the legal academy in the United States. In 1999, there were over 1,300 clinical legal educators. Barry, *supra* n. 95, at 29.

102. Carnegie Report, *supra* n. 31, at 111. *See generally* Peter A. Joy, *Clinical Scholarship: Improving the Practice of Law*, 2 Clin. L. Rev. 385 (1996).

103. Frank S. Bloch, Susan L. Brooks, Alex J. Hurder & Susan L. Kay, *Filling in the 'Larger Puzzle': Clinical Scholarship in the Wake of the Lawyering Process*, 10 Clin. L. Rev. 23 (2003).

104. *Id.* at 240. This article focuses on Gary Bellow's and Bea Moulton's *The Lawyering Process* and how this text inspired a generation of legal scholarship by clinicians.

105. Terrill Pollman & Linda H. Edwards, *Scholarship by Legal Writing Professors: New Voices in the Legal Academy*, 11 Leg. Writing 3 (2005).

106. *Id.* at 10.

107. Paul Callister's article in this collection makes a call for law librarians to contribute to a scholarly dialogue on a common hierarchy of research skills. Paul Callister, *Thinking Like A Research Expert: Schemata for Teaching Complex Problem-Solving Skills*, 28 Leg. Ref. Servs. Q. ___ (2009).

108. Donald Dunn, *The Law Librarian's Obligation to Publish*, 75 L. Lib. J. 225, 227 (1993). The recent creation of the Social Science Research Network Subject Matter Journal, Legal Information and Technology is a welcome exception to this statement.

109. E-mail from Ms. Hannah Phelps, Amer. Assoc. L. Libr. (9 Jan 2009) (on file with the author).

110. ABA, *Reports of the Special Committees and Submitted Comments*, available at http://www.abanet.org/legaled/committees/subcomm.html (last accessed 13 Feb. 2009).

111. While all law schools have a number of librarians, this paper focused on the academic law library director. He/she is the only librarian whose faculty status is mandated by accreditation standards.

Index

For Product Safety Concerns and Information please contact our
EU representative GPSR@taylorandfrancis.com Taylor & Francis
Verlag GmbH, Kaufingerstraße 24, 80331 München, Germany